COMMAND FAILURE IN WAR

COMMAND
FAILURE IN
WAR

Psychology and Leadership

Robert Pois
and
Philip Langer

INDIANA UNIVERSITY PRESS

BLOOMINGTON AND INDIANAPOLIS

This book is a publication of
Indiana University Press
601 North Morton Street
Bloomington, IN 47404-3797 USA

http://iupress.indiana.edu

Telephone orders 800-842-6796
Fax orders 812-855-7931
Orders by e-mail iuporder@indiana.edu

© 2004 by Robert Pois and Philip Langer

The paper used in this publication meets the minimum
requirements of American National Standard for Information
Sciences—Permanence of Paper for Printed Library
Materials, ANSI Z39.48-1984.

Manufactured in the United States of America

Library of Congress Cataloging-in-Publication Data

Pois, Robert A.
Command failure in war : psychology and leadership /
Robert Pois and Philip Langer.
p.   cm.
Includes bibliographical references and index.
ISBN 0-253-34378-X (cloth : alk. paper)
1. Command of troops—Case studies. 2. Military history, Modern—18th century.
3. Military history, Modern—19th century. 4. Military history, Modern—20th century.
I. Langer, Philip. II. Title.
UB210.P555 2004
355.3'3041—dc22

2003020259

1 2 3 4 5 09 08 07 06 05 04

To our families, and Patricia D. Murphy

CONTENTS

PREFACE

The reader will observe that these essays provide a forum for exploring the contributions of a broad spectrum of psychological models to selected military events and individuals. We wish to emphasize, however, that none of these psychological perspectives was ever intended to represent a complete and exhaustive analysis of events and participants. Rather, our objective was to provide a sketch of critical factors, both psychological and historical, which we believed were significant contributors to failure in military operations. Paradoxically, the theme of the book lies in a convergence of seemingly disparate psychological models converging on a single theme: military failure due to dysfunctional personal rigidity.

The individuals and events selected for these essays represent the authors' personal interests and knowledge. There was no attempt to provide any balance, although the essays begin with the career of Frederick the Great, and culminate in the snows of Stalingrad. The events described range from a single day's conflict to protracted campaigns, and even entire wars. Indeed, from the outset, we wanted to demonstrate that the explanatory power of our models could extend over significant periods of time.

The use of multiple models represents several ideas in our thinking. While all of us in our passage through life accumulate a significant amount of psychological baggage, we also believe that these factors do not exert equal saliency in all situations. While one might argue that Napoleon suffered from feelings of inferiority as a result of his Corsican birth, it is difficult to imagine how this could be incorporated into his frame of mind at Austerlitz, or much less use the same explanatory derivatives to equate his thinking at Austerlitz with Borodino and the Russian campaign in general. We shall expand on these points later, but clearly our intent is to show that psychology has an ex-

planatory role to play in historical analysis rather than to serve simply as a ve-
hicle for extraordinary generalizations on the nature of man.

Lack of success, as we noted, is the outcome of the interaction of specific
factors within a given set of circumstances, culminating in a failure that might
not otherwise be predicted. In this context, the individual's capacity to deal
appropriately with the military task(s) at hand becomes severely constrained.
As we shall point out repeatedly in these essays, however, although a lack of flexibility does not always spell defeat, under inappropriate circumstances it can
be a major contributor.

The problems associated with rigidity have had a long and interesting existence within the field of psychology. The concept has been studied repeatedly
within the framework of problem solving, which lends itself nicely as analogous to the demands made on military leadership in conflict. We recognize in
these essays that those factors contributing to personal rigidity can and have
been described within a number of conceptual models. Hence, rather than
use a single model as the sole explanation, we have employed a number of diverse approaches in which our selection of the conceptual framework was
based on its appropriateness to the particular situation and the individual(s)
involved.

To expand on a point made earlier, as has been so often the case, cause will
not be universally considered in terms of long-standing, deep-seated personality variables. It must be recognized, however, that depth psychology, a favorite
among psychohistorical explanatory models, has certainly attempted to cast
such blanket causality, even beyond the limits of reasonable doubt. This approach usually contributes little concerning success or failure in a given situation, especially in light of the fact that these individuals, with this particular
psychological baggage, have mixed histories of success and failure. While we
use this model ourselves to explain what happened at Kunersdorf, at no time
do we argue that the model provides a rationale for Leuthen and Rossbach as
well. Putting it in more primitive terms, we firmly believe that one cannot use
the same road map to go everywhere in the world; either there could be some
serious navigational problems, or one must suspend one's beliefs about the realities of the world.

Rather, our intent is to consider the deleterious effects as emerging within
the context of a given situation. Moreover, rigidity, as we shall argue, is not a
synonym for consistency. Rigidity is treated as an outcome of forces that constrain an individual's freedom of thought beyond acceptable limitations. In
military operations, to adhere to a plan of operations is one thing, but to cling
to a plan which appears totally inadequate is another.

As we shall show, rigidity and its consequences come in many guises. Perhaps most pertinent to our analyses is the concept of *einstellung*, or mental set.
Luchins and his famous water jar experiments demonstrated quite convinc-

ingly that individuals would cling to a previously successful solution rather than adapt a newer, more efficient transformation of the available data. From a military perspective, consider the development of the tank in World War I. The tank was, after all, a solution to the machine gun and barbed wire, yet Cambrai was a wasted opportunity. The generals cast the solution not in terms of what this new device implied in the way of revised tactics, but as an addendum to what they had done in the past.

Therefore, it is not surprising to find that in several attempted breakthroughs during that conflict, cavalry was made ready to exploit the penetration, regardless of how absurd the idea in light of massed firepower. Essentially, the psychological flexibility required to evaluate each new situation was sacrificed on the altar of well-learned tactics that worked in the past under different circumstances. However, expected outcomes in the military are all too often truly situational, a fact that is crucial for military leaders to understand if they are to be successful.

Our selection of military events was deliberate. Regardless of the advancing levels of development in military strategies and tactics that have been achieved over the centuries, war is still a human endeavor. Wars are fought between groups of humans led by individuals who have been assigned the responsibility of determining the course of action their group will follow. Unfortunately, as technology has advanced, so has the human price for egregious errors. If the Civil War demonstrated the awful cost of massed frontal assaults against entrenched foes using muzzleloaders, how much more ghastly was the price for employing similar tactics in World War I against high explosives, machine guns, and repeating rifles? Even worse, European military leaders, most of whom considered the Civil War to have been a fight between armed mobs, ignored the lessons learned in that conflict. However, to dismiss all generals as intellectually incompetent is absurd, as foolish perhaps as to explain away all individual efforts with a single psychological explanation.

The *personae* in the historical events reported in this volume were not bumbling incompetents whose careers consisted of an unrelieved series of disasters. Each individual, in the true sense of the word, had—at the time selected for our analysis—a history of leadership that included previous successes. However, we believe that the psychological factors that determined their actions at a time of failure for various reasons did not exert a negative influence at other times. Lee had a McClellan to deal with during the Seven Days, but there were Meades, Warrens, and Hancocks at Gettysburg. Lee simply could not perceive, as Longstreet did, that they were not facing the Army of the Potomac of a year ago, or that Meade was not a military carbon copy of McClellan.

These essays initially grew out of extended conversations between a historian interested in psychology and a psychologist interested in history. We believed that by combining our efforts we might be able to overcome the problems of the historian or psychologist acting alone—and those problems are rather awesome. Indeed, it would be quite accurate to say that the contributions of psychology to historical analysis have not been generally kindly received. The reasons are numerous and complex, but include at least the following.

First of all, most historians do not have adequate preparation in psychology. They are usually not in a position to judge the applicability of the psychological model employed to describe and interpret the historical issues under consideration. This leads to two related problems. One is that more traditional historians may rightfully believe their turf is being invaded by members of another discipline who have no understanding or real commitment to historical analysis. The second problem is equally insidious: When conventionally trained historians do utilize some psychology, their comments may well reflect a "chicken soup" or superficial representation of the psychological model being employed. In a perverse sense, they are engaging in the same kind of academic misrepresentation of which they accuse the psychologists.

On the other hand, few psychologists have been adequately trained as historians and often the historical evidence they cite to support their proposed psychological perspective is inadequate by accepted historical standards. Research in both history and psychology have long-accepted methodologies, but there is bound to be friction between conclusions drawn from laboratory data reflecting raw empiricism and the basically interpretive modes of analysis drawn from documented sources. To a historian, generalizations drawn from laboratory studies may seem woefully inadequate as evidence presented to support hypotheses about complex human behavior. To a psychologist, the historian's inferential reasoning may represent nothing more than a case of selective perception. Indeed, there is reasonable ground for the suspicion that on those occasions when the psychologist turns historian, the choice of psychological rationale seems to be generated by a self-serving selection process. Indeed, a historian's psychological speculations might drive a psychologist up a tree—about as far up the same tree as when historians try to deal with the somewhat interesting belief held by some psychologists that bar presses by a rodent in a Skinner box are clues to universal human existence. Yet, as we shall try to demonstrate, qualitatively differing suppositions about human existence need not be mutually exclusive.

Too often when a psychological model is used, history is made captive to theorizing. Thus, the interpretation of selected evidence is shaped more by a need to maintain the internal consistency of the proposed psychological rationale than to answer the historical questions. The problem really emerges when the intent is clearly to explain or characterize all of a given individual's life experiences with a single monolithic theory. Hence, while one might conclude that the behavior of some general in a given situation reflects unfortunate parental toilet training procedures, realistically it is rather difficult to defend the idea that all of the military operations Napoleon Bonaparte conducted after the age of three had a common origin.

It should be clearly understood that we are not trying to make the argument that humans are inconsistent. In fact, some consistency is a virtue, necessary for extended social interactions. However, psychological explanations can and must be changed, since a theoretical perspective utilized at age twenty in the life of Bonaparte might not be as useful as another approach at age forty. Indeed, to maintain consistency in rationale can be a trap that both psychologists and psychohistorians frequently climb into of their own accord.

The essays in this book are diametrically opposed to these concepts of academic universality and consistency. We have not sought, willy-nilly, a single explanation or model. Instead, we have employed the most parsimonious explanations in the light of the historical evidence available to us. Psychology is an interpretive tool and must be sensitive to the evidence available. Therefore, the appropriate question is not what rationale is correct, but rather which rationale in the light of the kinds of evidence available. Certainly psychological assumptions cannot purport to explain behavior beyond the limits of scientific prudence (except perhaps in the minds of True Believers).

Basically, what we have done in each instance is to spell out both the critical evidence and the underlying psychological model. In the case of the events chosen, we have generally selected our sources on the basis of comprehensiveness and reputation. We believe that, at least in terms of historical evidence, the complete record is now available. It is unlikely, for example, that Douglas Southall Freeman left out much history in his four-volume biography of Lee. That is not the same, however, as arguing that other writers, drawing on the same evidence, would not come to other conclusions regarding Lee's actions. Therefore, a portion of the criticism of our work might be directed toward the inadequacy of the evidence presented in light of the needs of the psychological model proposed.

Additionally, critics might argue that we have exceeded the limits of the explanatory model proposed. This represents another problem, since it can be argued that any speculation regarding an individual's motives represents some form of psychohistory. These speculations, however, are usually not accompanied by any explanation of underlying psychological rationale. Thus, while two historians may disagree on the causes of an individual's behaviors, you cannot be sure why they disagree, even while reviewing the same evidence. To argue that it is a difference in interpretation is essentially begging the question. What was the rationale, usually implicit, for differing conclusions? Freeman might consider Gettysburg, at least in part, a matter of overconfidence on Lee's part, but Dowdey found in the same evidence an overwhelming compulsion to create a conspiracy theory.

As another example of trying to determine the rationale for judgment, consider the assignment of causes for the Japanese failure developed in *Miracle at Midway*.[1] Among the contributing factors was the rampant overconfidence that existed in Yamamoto's staff, including the admiral himself, which led to a lack of security, arbitrary decisions in the war gaming prior to the attack, and a general inclination to believe they could not lose. A behaviorist could follow clearly the unfolding discussion, even though behaviorism was never mentioned. On the other hand, it is not quite clear what the underlying rationale was from the authors' description of Admiral Nagumo's mistakes in command.

Hence, when we compare differing interpretations among historians regarding a common event, the conclusions may pass each other like ships in the night. True, the same evidence is there for both, but the reader can only speculate as to the reasons for a differential in the weighting of events. In this book we have sought to give readers an idea of why we thought as we did.

Observing our choice of what constitutes an appropriate psychological theory or appropriate supporting historical evidence is, as noted, open to question. But it is equally true that intellectual rigidity is no solution, either. While one would like to believe one's interpretation of events is definitive, it is more likely that what has been achieved is additional evidence that can be added to the existing knowledge base and used to generate new ideas. And that, after all, is the basis for scholarship in the world of human behavior.

ACKNOWLEDGMENTS

We wish to express our gratitude to our colleagues who have lent us support over the years. We are grateful to Robert Sloan, our editor at Indiana University Press, for his encouragement, and to Prof. Dale Wilson of American Military University for his superb job of copyediting. Patricia D. Murphy of the Department of History, University of Colorado at Boulder, was of invaluable assistance in the eventual emergence of a rather long-term project. It never would have been completed without her computer and analytical skills. Above all, we are grateful to our families, who put up with rather long absences — maybe not spatial, but certainly spiritual.

ROBERT POIS AND PHILIP LANGER
University of Colorado at Boulder

I was born in Washington, D.C., in 1940. From the time I was aware that a war was taking place, I enjoyed it thoroughly. My father and some relatives were involved in the war and, even at an early age, I knew that war implied risk. Yet, it was a time of great excitement, especially for an otherwise thoroughly repressed child. Later, while in grammar school in Chicago, I was exposed to a ceremony that took place at 11 A.M. on November 11. The class would stand up and turn to the east, facing France. I was baffled by what it all meant, but the First World War became an object of intense interest. Recognizing at least some of the pathologies involved in war, I am still fascinated by it, particularly World War I. Hopefully this work, done in collaboration with my respected colleague, Philip Langer, will demonstrate where fascination ought best to yield to criticism.

ROBERT POIS
September 2003

COMMAND FAILURE IN WAR

INTRODUCTION

L ONG AFTER IMMANUEL KANT wrote *Concerning Eternal Peace* (1795), an essay seemingly rendered pathetic by courses of events since that time, war remains a subject of intense interest, at times bordering on morbid fascination. Even as we recognize its role as a dangerous anachronism in an age of potential universal destruction, people of all nations and political persuasions are drawn to it. Even as we, consciously or not, nourish atavisms that can border on the pathological, we find ourselves enthralled by war, its immense drawing power attested to by more pacific (and probably more rational) souls who declare that, in striving for peace, we must find its "moral equivalent."

Probably one of the most persistently engaging aspects of that subject gilded over by the term "military science" is that of great blunders or disasters. Often, such can be explained by recourse to more or less conventional forms of explanation. A general was defeated or a campaign lost because of simple errors of judgment, enemy technological superiority, lack of numbers or resources, and the like. Sometimes, however, these explanations either are not quite enough or they simply fall down altogether. Sometimes, the story of persistent errors and/or persistently high losses or mystifying failure in the course of a generally successful career calls for a variety of explanations not found within the confines of "traditional" historiography.

In recent years, the "psychohistorical" method has been employed with varying degrees of success in dealing with historical figures or problems that, past a certain point, seem to be opaque to more conventional forms of historical explanation. Military failure or incompetence has turned out to be an area of considerable interest, much as it has been for historians of a more conventional turn of mind. Probably the best-known example of this is Norman Dixon's *On The Psychology of Military Incompetence.*[1] In a well-written, imaginative, and often analytically astute work, the author has applied crucial elements of psychoanalysis to the actions (or at times, lack of them) of various British military leaders from the Crimean War up to, and including, World War II. Aside from the fact that Dr. Dixon has confined himself to considering the British military (although, God knows, he has more than enough material with which to work), there are problems with utilizing one approach, however sophisticated it might be in content and application, to a panoply of military leaders and problems. First of all, there is the obvious one of "reductionism," something that can result if one attempts to bring together historically and temporally disparate figures and circumstances under such covering terms as "repressed aggression," "anality," and "authoritarian personality." There can then arise yet another, perhaps more serious problem, when one attempts to separate out "good" from "bad" generalship along the obvious lines of anality/non-anality, authoritarianism/lack of authoritarianism, and so forth. For individuals such as Bernard Montgomery, one of the "good" generals, this has raised somewhat perplexing problems.[2]

In a broader sense, Dr. Dixon's often valuable work is flawed by a crucial problem: namely, he is concerned with individuals who generally can be marked down as "failures." Thus, consideration of failure on the part of a usually successful general, such as Montgomery, raises questions concerning the relationships established between certain personality "types" and the childhoods which nurtured them and respective patterns of success or failure.

In this volume we will consider eight problems in military leadership and/or planning. In so doing, we will draw upon a variety of psychological approaches in attempting to provide at least provisional explanations for situations that appear to elude more conventional forms. There will be no overarching psychological explanation, for example, psychoanalytical. Rather, we will utilize specific explanations to "cover" specific problems. In a word, to the greatest extent possible, we have allowed particular historical problems to determine the forms of psychological explanation appropriate to dealing with them, rather than attempting to adjust historical circumstances to suit a given explanatory form. There is always a danger when one attempts to apply a single hypothesis or approach to varieties of individuals or circumstances, even if these were "products" of a given society. Through seeking out psychological explanations best suited to given circumstances or conditions, we believe it possible to provide answers to problems posed not only by individual battles, but by extended campaigns as well.

Again, we will be focusing not only upon individuals usually judged to be failures, or at least mediocre, but upon apparent lapses in the careers of individuals usually viewed in a more positive light at least in military terms, or even as so-called military geniuses. In a word, while we will consider problems posed by George McClellan and Douglas Haig, we will also examine "lapses" in the careers of Frederick the Great and Napoleon, among others. Again, varieties of psychological explanations will be used in the process.

If there is no overarching method in this work, is there at least a *theme* that holds together this panoply of individuals and problems? We believe there is, and that it can be discerned without doing violence to historical evidence. This can be described as the persistence of habit, fixed systems of belief, or given attitudes or mental predisposition, and the inability of even the most imaginative military leader, as well as established dullards, to adjust to new or changing circumstances. Differences in ability and supporting psychological makeups are extremely complex and not amenable to analysis using a single analytical theme. Applying not one but a variety of psychological approaches will allow us to deal with the problem of inflexibility as it articulated itself in different forms and in different times.

As we will see, what can be described as inflexibility can be rooted in and reinforced by success. Yet, such successes can lay the foundation for disaster. In this regard, the careers of Frederick the Great, Napoleon, Robert E. Lee, and Adolf Hitler come to mind. Inflexibility also can paralyze someone to the point that success is never obtained at all. George McClellan's peninsular campaign will illustrate this to no small degree. Inflexibility rooted in predispositions or attitudes of some sort can exist side by side with openness to new ideas, serving to hobble their application. Such seemed to occur with Winston Churchill, particularly with regard to his view of airpower. On the other hand, in considering the British approach to war in World War I, we will confront a situation in which the attritional nature of modern military campaigns, particularly those conducted on the western front, allowed that gross inflexibility, rooted in a basic acceptance of a long outdated system, was perhaps *responsible* for ultimate victory, even though at a hideous cost. Inflexible Allied bombing strategies concerning Germany, also intensely attritional, possibly were successful *because* of the protracted nature of a campaign in which what ultimately mattered was overwhelming material supremacy. John B. Hood's Franklin disaster will be considered as a rather singular example of how continued frustration could lead to exaggerated emphasis upon persistent tendencies that had rarely led to any success whatsoever.

In applying various psychological approaches to these individuals and problems attaching to their military adventures, the authors will not be attempting to draw lines between them and "just plain folks" like us. The various forms of psychological dysfunctionalism that afflicted them in one circumstance or the other afflict all people in one form or another, or on one occasion or another. Rarely, though, are most of us in the position—and here, we are paraphrasing Robert G. L. Waite—to transform private psychological lapses or imbalances into public disaster.[3] How this relates to the role(s) of military decision making in an age of potential total annihilation—with or without a cold war—must, at the very least, be viewed as a vexed question.

CHAPTER ONE

FREDERICK THE GREAT AT KUNERSDORF, AUGUST 12, 1759

Will not some accursed bullet strike me?

E VEN AFTER TWENTIETH-CENTURY events have demonstrated for all to see the follics and horrors attendant upon modern war, Frederick II of Prussia (1740–1786) remains a fascinating individual for many people, mostly because of his military adventures. The thought of a possibly epicene lover of French language and culture leading a collection of rough-hewn—and, for the most part, ferociously Protestant—peasants, journeymen and, increasingly, mercenaries, from victory to victory against enormous odds is indeed a tantalizing one. That such victories—and, in the usual masochistic fashion, heroic defeats—contributed to the substructure that later would support German nationalism strikes one as deliciously ironic. This is most particularly the case in view of Frederick's detestation of Germans and the German language. It is certain that Frederick endured rather than enjoyed hearing his ragamuffin representatives of north German Lutheranism sing "Now thank we all our God" after the slaughter of Leuthen on December 5, 1757.[1] And when a soldier, after being praised by the king himself for his courage at the battle of Liegnitz (August 15, 1760), replied, "We fight for religion, for you, for the fatherland," it must have made a strong appeal to his intensely cynical sense of humor.[2]

Yet, if one ignores the fact that the overall effects of Frederick's wars and the social ossification that allowed him to conduct them helped to pave the way for the disasters Napoleon would visit upon Prussia at Jena and Auerstädt, his accomplishments must seem extraordinary indeed. When Frederick II came to power in 1740, he inherited a country with a population of 2.5 million, that is, in sum, slightly less than that of the city of San Diego, California. The army totaled 83,000 men and was in part supported by revenues of 7 million thalers. Utilizing this rather slim resource base, Frederick fought the War of the Austrian Succession, *winning every major engagement*, the most famous of these being the Battle of Hohenfriedberg on June 4, 1745, where 58,000 Prussians demolished an 85,000-man Austro-Saxon army.[3] Due to territorial gains, the most prominent of them being, of course, Silesia, Frederick succeeded in almost doubling Prussia's population. Yet, this country was still rather undersized to take on—even with British monetary support and increasing numbers of mercenaries—the powerful combination of France, Austria, Russia, and Sweden that confronted it in the Seven Years' War. Somehow, however, Frederick and Prussia endured and, by the year of his death, 1786, his country's population totaled 5 million, while the army consisted of 200,000 men supported by annual revenues of 19 million thalers.[4] Of greater importance, though, was the power of the Frederican legend, something that would greatly influence, among others, Adolf Hitler.

Nevertheless, the power of this legend must not be allowed to obscure the fact that once opposing generals became somewhat more accustomed to the Frederican style of warfare, he frequently found it tough going. During the Seven Years' War, Frederick lost almost as many battles as he won and, insofar as such supposed innovations as the oblique battle order are concerned, close scrutiny of his campaigns would suggest that their roles were relatively minor. For example, it is probable that between 1756 and 1762 the oblique battle order was utilized with any marked degree of success only once: at the Battle of Leuthen (December 5, 1757).[5] The really important tools of victory—the iron ramrod and the Prussian infantryman's ability to get off three shots to his enemy's one—as well as the rigid discipline that was responsible for the Prussian ranks' ability to switch fronts with remarkable speed, an especially crucial talent in an age of linear warfare, had been provided gratis by Frederick William I, Frederick's enduringly unlovable father. Outside of his mostly hypothetical utilization of the oblique battle order and his emphasis upon the development of horse artillery and improvements in the state of the Prussian cavalry, it is obvious that Frederick relied primarily upon four factors to provide him with victory: (1) the above-mentioned mobility and superb fire control of his soldiers; (2) the element of surprise; (3) an extraordinary degree of aggressiveness in the face of all odds—"The Prussian army always attacks," he once stated; and (4) the toughness that necessarily characterized a peasantry thoroughly brutalized by an antediluvian system surpassed in barbarity only by Russia's.[6]

In a word, Frederick's successes were due to that frequent mixture of applied common sense, utter callousness, sheer luck, and the occasional lack of a decent opponent that constitutes the essence of so-called military genius. Much of the commonsense aspect of this can be found in his various writings on what—at least until relatively recently—has been referred to as the "art of war." However, before we place the Battle of Kunersdorf in context and consider the battle itself and the problems for Frederick revealed in it, we will first consider, in general terms, the psychological axiom that will inform our approach to these phenomena.

If anything resembles a truism in psychology, it is that all human behavior has both cognitive and affective components.[7] Psychiatrists have long been aware of an ego mechanism that isolates the cognitive and affective components of a given behavior, expressing either only under appropriate circumstances. The mechanism is called intellectualization and it appears to be an adolescent phenomenon.[8] A typical situation involves a psychology course in which a student may discuss very personal problems in a most dispassionate manner, retaining the emotional release for other situations. This tendency toward "splitting" between cognitive and affective personality aspects is an important one with regard to our consideration of Frederick, and we will be considering it again later. For now, we must look at his concepts of warfare insofar as they had developed up to 1758.

As has been pointed out, Frederick's earlier writings on military matters were often highly hypothetical in nature and often reflected a lack of concern for such matters as natural defensive obstacles, terrain, and so on.[9] Apparently, though, he had learned some important lessons from the two Silesian campaigns that constituted Prussia's participation in the War of the Austrian Succession (1740–48). This can be seen in his *Pensées et regles generales pour la guerre* of 1753, a work that, as one can see by its date of publication, appeared three years before the outbreak of the Seven Years' War. Here, Frederick placed a great deal of emphasis upon the importance of terrain, *most particularly with regard to the use of cavalry*.[10] The "nature of the ground must always dictate our dispositions," he said.[11] Indeed, choice of ground was always the first concern. Whether or not an oblique order of battle could be utilized was dependent upon the terrain.[12] In a work published in 1755, Frederick adamantly emphasized the importance of respecting naturally strong defensive positions. "When attacking a strong, natural position," he stated, "do not rush forward." Rather, one should reconnoiter to the greatest degree possible and "never seize the bull by the horns."[13]

Once what later became known as the Seven Years' War began, it would appear that Frederick indeed learned by experience. After being frustrated at Prague and defeated at Kolin, he made excellent use of terrain to rout the French general Benjamin de Rohan Soubise at the Battle of Rossbach on November 5, 1757.[14] Exactly one month later, he chanced upon a set of natural dispositions—in fact, the old *training ground* of the Prussian army—that allowed him to utilize the oblique battle order with immense effectiveness at Leuthen. His experiences, positive and negative, were reflected in a work published in 1758, *Reflexions sur la tactique et sur quelques partres de la guerre*. In this work, he expressed admiration for the Austrian use of terrain. Although he did not mention this specifically, he no doubt had in mind the Battle of Kolin (June 18, 1757), where repeated Prussian attacks were frustrated by bodies of Croatian light infantry artfully concealed in copses of trees.[15] As in his earlier writings, Frederick placed a great deal of emphasis upon the proper use of cavalry. "Do not expose the mounted arm to the fire of either small arms or artillery," he declared. This "robs it of its best order. Reserve the cavalry for the time when it can perform its greatest service—to save the battle or to pursue the enemy."[16] Throughout the 1758 work, Frederick expressed considerable respect for the Austrians, both as soldiers and innovators. "As for the Russians," he saw them as being "as savage as they are inept," and declared "they are not worthy of mention."[17] In virtually all of Frederick's writings on the "art of war" we can discern an emphasis upon the importance of concentrating one's forces, especially *on a field of one's choosing*. The first maxim of generalship, the Prussian king declared, was to "never . . . let yourself be forced to fight against your will."[18] In general, we can say that this work reflected the "cognitive" aspects of Frederick's personality—with perhaps one exception, to which we will return later.

In all events, Frederick's writings on war tended to place primary emphasis upon (1) use of terrain; (2) caution in attacking fortified or naturally defensible positions; and (3) the concentration of one's forces upon ground of one's own choosing. As mentioned previously, Frederick was convinced the Prussian army always had to assume the offensive even if circumstances, especially questions of logistics and terrain, required temporary caution.[19]

In 1759, Frederick stepped away from the powder smoke and chaos of the battlefield in order to philosophize a bit. After all, before a quarrel marred their friendship, Voltaire had virtually endowed Frederick with the title of honorary *philosophe* and seemingly profound musings were *de rigueur* for those whom historians would later brand "enlightened despots." During the course of his reflections, Frederick focused upon the character of Charles XII of Sweden, whose death in 1718 marked the end of Sweden as a military power of any significance: "In all the books about Charles XII, I find high-sounding praises bestowed on his frugality and continence; but twenty French cooks in his kitchen, 4,000 courtesans in his train, and ten companies of players in his army would not have caused his kingdom a hundredth part of the evils brought on it by his ardent thirst for glory and desire for vengeance."[20] As we will see, Frederick had his own "desire for vengeance" from which his country would suffer to no small degree.

Before we place the Battle of Kunersdorf within the context of Seven Years' War developments in particular, we must consider the general nature of eighteenth-century warfare, focusing particularly upon those elements which prevented both Frederick and his opponents from exploiting victory to the utmost and which, particularly during an age when much depended upon the commanding officer's personality makeup, contributed from time to time to disaster for just about everybody. First of all, the highly professional, intensely drilled armies of the time were expensive to maintain, especially for a state like Prussia, whose bureaucracy might well have become adept at trampling upon a cooperatively supine peasantry, but nonetheless had a very frail resource base. Thus, a really decisive battle, which might well have resulted in staggering losses for both the victor and the vanquished, was a truly risky undertaking. Indeed, a commentator upon Frederick the Great has referred to the eighteenth century as being characterized by "limited liability."[21] Let us say, however, that a really smashing defeat—a Rossbach or a Leuthen, for example—has been inflicted upon an enemy. How about a nice, ruthless pursuit? *Occasionally*, as at Rossbach, this did occur to some degree. Usually, however, pursuit and total annihilation of the enemy *à la* Napoleon was precluded by two factors: (1) the difficulty of transforming linear ranks into lines organized for pursuit and destruction of the enemy; and (2) the very real possibility that a substantial portion of one's army, particularly the mercenary element in it, might choose to utilize the relative freedom of a pursuit situation to desert.[22] Thus, Frederick was never able to win the decisive victory that his emphasis upon concentrating his forces and fighting on a field of his own choosing seemed to suggest was possible. A Leopold Daun might well be defeated, and rather badly, on one occasion, only to turn up again in the near future because mercenary practices possibly assured him of a new army. Of course, as we shall see when we consider the Battle of Kunersdorf, the limitations upon pursuit and destruction that flowed from eighteenth-century technological and tactical realities could serve Frederick's interests.

As has already been suggested, Frederick was not as innovative as some hagiographers—Thomas Carlyle, for example—have supposed and, like many eighteenth-century generals, he often found it hard to adjust to circumstances that did not fit into preconceived plans or were disruptive to the rules of linear warfare. The use of light infantry in the form of Pandur or Croatian skirmishers—in such instances, it was the Austrians and not Frederick who anticipated Napoleon—was something to which Frederick could never adjust.[23] Although Gen. Friedrich von Bernhardi, perpetually awash in tidal waves of nationalistic enthusiasm, declared that Frederick had indeed anticipated Napoleonic usages,[24] it is obvious that the above-mentioned eighteenth-century realities had to have obviated the possibility of the Prussian king's anticipating such things as Napoleon's use of skirmishers or a battle of annihilation such as Austerlitz, though, to be sure, Frederick gained a considerable appreciation for massed artillery. In fine, a critical observer would have to agree with the more sober evaluation of Hans Delbrück, who thought a great deal of Frederick, but who, nonetheless, viewed him as being a typical, albeit far more intelligent than the average, eighteenth-century general.[25] As we shall see, Frederick's rather singular eccentricities would create problems for him. At the same time, though, we must appreciate that he was acting and reacting within a given historical context, something that even a person possessed of genius, military or otherwise, could not transcend.

By 1757, the Russians, under the leadership of Gen. Peter Saltykov, had become a decisive factor in the Seven Years' War. On August 30 of that year, a Russian force under the command of Gen. Fedor Matveeich Apraksin defeated Marshal Hans von Lehwaldt at Gross-Jaegersdorf. This disaster, coming on top of Frederick's own defeat at Kolin and the invasion of Pomerania by seventeen thousand Swedes, seemed to presage the overrunning of Prussia. Frederick, however, managed to retrieve the situation through his victories at Rossbach and Leuthen and, as we have seen, became confident enough to ridicule the Russians in his 1758 essay on military affairs. This points to an interesting aspect of Frederick's personality: a petulant unwillingness to see things as they were. The Battle of Zorndorf, which took place on August 25, 1758, should have been an eye-opener with regard to a dangerous opponent. Although Frederick benefited somewhat by his knowledge of the area, Russian stubbornness extracted thousands of casualties from his army. Thus, although victorious in the end, his losses were staggering. Frederick won the battle by throwing his men against the Russian lines in very diluted forms of the oblique battle order. Zorndorf was a close call; his generalship was uninspired and he seemed unwilling to take the Russians seriously as opponents.

In October 1758, Frederick, desperately concerned about the presence of a large Austrian army in Saxony—something that was preventing him from returning to Silesia, where he thought he ought to be—attempted to surprise the Austrians with a numerically inferior force. Instead, his own army was surprised in its camp at Hochkirch on the night of October 13–14. An extremely costly battle ensued, in the course of which Frederick displayed a characteristic that he had shown at Zorndorf: an unwillingness to remain on the defensive. In the face of all odds—and in this case, rationality—Frederick tried to organize counterattacks. They all failed, however, and the king himself came very close to being killed or captured. From what we know of Hochkirch, Frederick's men admired his courage even as they silently deprecated his tactical stupidity.[26]

After the Hochkirch disaster, Frederick was understandably depressed. In a self-pitying tirade to his reader, H. A. Catt, he railed against the fates that had condemned him to sacrifice so many men. He concluded by showing his companion opium tablets that he had concealed on his person. If matters became too desperate, he could and would kill himself.[27]

When all is said and done, in some sort of morbidly paternalistic cosmic sense, Providence perhaps played a role in both Frederick's bare victory at Zorndorf and his outright defeat at Hochkirch. For the mundanely agnostic observer (something that Frederick was most of the time), however, it is obvious that the loss of almost thirteen thousand men in a very narrow victory and over nine thousand in a very real defeat was due to the increasing proficiency of his enemies and certain problems that Frederick had as a general. For Frederick, the Prussian army "always attacks." To be sure, there were times when even he recognized that this could not be done. Nevertheless, he would order it to attack in circumstances that were, at best, extremely doubtful, if not downright dangerous. Furthermore, despite occasional bouquets tossed in the direction of the Austrians, he always tended to underestimate them. He also despised the Russians. As a result, his careless dispositions around Hochkirch and later assumption that all could be put in order if only the Prussian army counterattacked immediately point to, as British envoy A. Mitchell suggested, the "very great contempt he had of the enemy, and the unwillingness I have long observed in him to give any degree of credit to intelligence that is not agreeable to his own imaginations."[28]

Frederick's unwillingness to accept information that ran contrary to preconceived plans brings to mind the work of the psychologist of cognitive dissonance, Leon Festinger, a man very much concerned with how people managed to avoid mental conflict (or "dissonance") by blotting out or ignoring disquieting information. There can be no doubt that Frederick, from time to time, stood out as a remarkable case study for Dr. Festinger. Indeed, the military profession as a whole is one that has to encourage dissonance—avoiding actions or patterns of thought. We will indeed devote a later chapter to military leaders whose actions can best be explained by the approach used by Festinger and colleagues. Frederick's career, however, despite Mitchell's perspicacious remarks, cannot be seen as being *consistently* characterized by efforts to avoid dissonant information. There were simply too many successes, and these—Leuthen, for example—could only have been attained by realistic appraisals of given situations. Another, perhaps more deep-seated, source of Frederick's failures must be sought out, one for which a good deal of supportive information is available. It is in this context that the "affective" aspect of his personality must be considered.

LIKE FATHER, LIKE SON?

Frederick William I, father of Frederick the Great, has long been viewed as a shrewd, hard-working ruler whose bureaucratic and, above all, military reforms served to make Prussia into the military powerhouse that would, in due course, unify Germany. This is a valid description of the man and there is little that can be said against it. He has also been characterized as a coarse, rigid, often cruel martinet who thoroughly brutalized his son. This, too, is an accurate description of the man.

The sad story of Frederick William's relationship with his son is well known. As a small child, Frederick was extremely sensitive. He showed early interest in art and music and these, combined with his sensitivity, made him appear effeminate to his gruffly patriarchal father, who believed that anyone who hoped to rule a relatively small and resource-poor state greatly dependent upon military prowess for its survival ought to have the interests and bearing of a soldier. Since nature seemed to have provided Frederick with neither, his father would assure that he would acquire them. To this end, the ruler-to-be was put on a rigorous schedule of persistent moral and practical instruction. As time went on, however, it became plain to Frederick William that this would not in itself suffice to break the spirit, however epicene it might have been in his eyes, of a son determined to preserve his own interests. Thus it was that his father took a morbidly personal role in the process. Frederick was subjected to constant criticism and ridicule and, at times, was soundly thrashed, mealtimes especially being utilized for this purpose.

Frederick could not respond to such assaults in a direct, physical fashion. In this regard, a gently applied psychodynamic model will reveal several elements that show explanatory promise. It is instructive to note that Frederick responded to his father's aggression with outbursts of his own.[29] Instead of responding by adopting a behavioral posture emphasizing passiveness or learned helplessness, he turned his anger outward.[30] He dreaded being the helpless target of his father's rage, and, until a terrible event that occurred during his eighteenth year, he resisted being broken by Frederick William's brutal assaults. With regard to reactions against helplessness, there is another episode that is at least worthy of consideration even if no firm conclusions can be drawn, inasmuch as it was (and is) shrouded in mystery.

In 1728, Frederick accompanied his father on a visit to the Saxon court of Augustus the Strong. This singularly incompetent military leader seems to have derived his sobriquet from one, or both, of the following: (1) he was capable of bending a horseshoe straight, a difficult thing to do in the best of times, and (2) he sired anywhere from 350 to 360 bastard children. In any case, the Saxon court, either in emulation of him, or quite on its own, had established a well-deserved reputation of moral lassitude. Apparently, Frederick, with or without the knowledge of his pious father (who, nonetheless, might have drawn upon casuistic resources in the name of *raison d'état*), was paired off with a young woman. Sometime after the visit, Frederick became ill and *possibly* had to undergo an operation on his private parts, presumably to deal with an unexpected souvenir of the illicit liaison. As can be imagined, great secrecy surrounded this supposed operation, and its results which, according to some, might well have left him incapable of sexual intercourse.[31] Whether or not this operation, if it indeed took place, was partially responsible for his well-known misogyny (something which was not extended to cover his beloved sister Wilhelmina), a barren sex life that reinforced the suspicion of homosexuality, and an increased interest in flute fondling out of masturbatory frustration, will never be determined.[32] In all events, if there be merit to this admittedly attenuated prognosis, such an occurrence most certainly would have increased his anger toward his father, who in effect, had offered him up for more than symbolic Oedipal castration. That this also would have increased Frederick's fear of being placed in a situation of helplessness is obvious. One thing can be said with certainty: his brutal treatment at the hands of his father left him with a fear of helplessness that was perhaps the most important factor in his life. Such would have determined that he would abandon friends before they turned on him, and that the quality that he saw as being of singular importance for a ruler was "to be firm in your decisions!"[33] To appear weak or indecisive was to invite disaster.

Yet, at one crucial point in his life with a man for whom the phrase "father knows best" was of more than general significance, Frederick would be reduced to helplessness. In 1730, when Frederick was eighteen years old, he attempted to run away from home. A young lieutenant named Katte, with whom he may have had a homosexual relationship, assisted him. The attempt was foiled and both Frederick and Lieutenant Katte were arrested. Frederick's loyal companion was sentenced to death and it was part of Frederick's punishment that he was condemned to watch his beheading. Afterward, Frederick was imprisoned, kept in the dark as to his own eventual fate, and allowed few visitors. His father's last extraordinary measures to thrash any outward sign of independence out of his son succeeded. Frederick, broken to his will, became a pliant student of statecraft and things military. Rarely did he offer any resistance to his father's whims, however much they ran against his own tastes and interests. In 1733, for reasons of state, he was compelled to marry a woman he found to be both stupid and physically repulsive. Their probably unconsummated marriage turned out to be a heart-breaking one for his wife, Elizabeth Christina, and a relationship of little positive significance for Frederick. He had known this would be the case before they married, but obedience to his father was of the utmost importance. By the time Frederick William died in 1740—a porcine, bloated ruin—he had a son of whom he was genuinely proud.

Frederick William had succeeded in "breaking" Frederick, who as a "soldier king" would come to embody the Prussian military tradition in ways beyond the old patriarch's imagination. In view of Frederick's childhood interests in the arts, one could say that his father had enforced a "career choice" that represented an enormous break with his past. To be sure, Frederick continued to write in French, and his interest in philosophical matters deepened, in part through his well-known, if at times rocky, friendship with Voltaire. He also continued to play the flute and write musical compositions—indeed, even symphonic music. Yet, Frederick the Second would become known as "Frederick the Great" not for his achievements in philosophy or the arts, but for his genius as a general. It was a role to which he became accustomed and possibly even enjoyed from time to time. Nonetheless, it had been forced upon him, and there was no small measure of resentment attached to this.

In an important essay that appeared in 1959, Erik H. Erikson talks of the problem of "identity diffusion." He suggested that this was of particular significance for young people, and often revolved around "the inability to settle on an occupational identity."[34] This can result in a variety of aggressive traits, including intolerance and stereotyping, particularly of those conceived of as enemies. For someone like Frederick, who in effect had his "occupational identity" determined by his father and, as a result, was forced to repress crucial personality traits (sensitivity among them) and interests, the term "identity diffusion" would seem apposite. In any event, his concern for adherence to Enlightenment principles was more than counterbalanced by a set of violent prejudices. In a society known for being anti-Semitic and misogynist, Frederick stood out as being unusually prejudiced in these areas.[35] Also, over time, he developed another inordinately strong prejudice, one that would be of greater tactical significance than the other two—hatred of and contempt for Russians. Why this particular group was singled out will be considered later. For now, we can consider Frederick as an individual who, having been compelled to abandon or repress important elements of his personality, can be seen as suffering from that lack of self-esteem, or even self-identity, described by Erikson as representing "identity diffusion."

For Rollo May, one of the worst results of parental or any other suppression is a sense of powerlessness. For, if one is powerless or helpless, then healthy self-affirmation cannot take place.[36] Until he was eighteen, Frederick fought against this feeling and, though frightened of his father, often defied him, albeit probably mostly in ways that today would be described as "passive aggressive." After the horrible Katte incident, however, Frederick's capitulation to Frederick William was just about total, at least on the surface. With this, self-affirmation in any meaningful sense was out of the question.

Yet, Frederick came to know that the man who had, through the most sadistic measures imaginable, compelled him to abandon those elements of his personality of greatest importance—in a real sense, to abandon self—had feet of clay. A skilled bureaucrat and excellent organizer of armies, Frederick William was an amazingly inept diplomat. Perhaps it was not surprising that the man who held his family in thrall through physical terror and who enjoyed spending what spare time he had participating in often cruel practical jokes and raucous conversation with his generals was out of place, or at least seemed to be, in the rarified atmosphere of eighteenth-century diplomacy. His clumsy flip-flopping between possible allies made him the laughingstock of Europe. When he finally decided that an alliance with Austria would serve Prussian interests, particularly with regard to his claim on the west German territory of Berg, the emperor, Charles VI, decided that massive Prussian support in the War of the Polish Succession (1733–36) was not needed, if support of Frederick William's claim on Berg was the price he had to pay for it. Furious at being spurned by Austria, Frederick William's last important diplomatic foray was to sign an alliance with France in 1739.[37] By the time he died in 1740, Frederick William had succeeded in creating an efficient, thoroughly militarized state and the bureaucracy needed to support it. At the same time, this coarse and often brutal man had been revealed as having the political sagacity of a country bumpkin. In a word, the feared patriarch who had succeeded in breaking his son to the point where any variety of self-affirmation was impossible had been shown to have been a virtual moron in foreign affairs, one of the very areas in which Frederick was being thoroughly schooled. Frederick William's almost animal cruelty and peasant cunning could, and had to be, feared, but there was little cause to respect him. As will be seen, it is our opinion that this perception of Frederick William was probably crucial in determining how Frederick, whose diffuse sense of identity drove him to—or at least reinforced a tendency toward—stereotyping, was responsible for the contempt of Russians responsible for the disaster of Kunersdorf.

PORTRAIT OF A LEADER

At the time he ascended the throne in 1740, Frederick II presented the following picture. He was a man who, in the cause of simple self-preservation, had had to sacrifice large—and perhaps, to him, the most important—elements of *his self*. After at least offering some resistance to his father's efforts to mold him in his image, he had been put in a position of total helplessness, a pitiful target for the assaults of a cruel "other" that he feared, but could not respect. As is so often the case with individuals who have experienced helplessness and, in the process, been denied what Rollo May has called "self-affirmation," he was determined that he would never again be put in such a position. Now, as king and commander in chief of his father's army, he had both the will and ability to determine that this would never happen to him.

Hence, "The Prussian Army always attacks." This phrase became more than simple verbal posturing on Frederick's part. With few exceptions, Frederick obeyed his maxim. At Hochkirch he retreated only as a last resort, and then not until after conducting repeated and fruitless counterattacks. To Frederick, inflexible commitment to the offensive must have represented the retention of control in a given situation. While it is true that military history has generally never adored the defensive genius, in Frederick's case being placed on the defensive may have psychologically represented a sense of helplessness as the manipulated and passive target of others. Throughout the Seven Years' War he would endeavor to strike first, no matter what the cost. Only then could his sense of control be assured.

There is another critical factor that must be considered, namely that, from 1740 (the first year of the First Silesian War) until the end of the Seven Years' War (1763), the army at Frederick's disposal was really the one his father had created.[38] As we have seen, Frederick might well have added certain crucial innovations—a much improved cavalry, for example—and the oblique battle order, but the finely honed Prussian military machine, including not a few of its senior officers and generals, was, as pointed out earlier, a "gift" from Frederick William. Indeed, the legendary boon companion of the old tyrant, Leopold of Anhalt (the "Old Dessauer"), played a crucial role in the Second Silesian War (1744–45), winning the last major battle, that of Kesselsdorf, on his own.

Frederick, while certainly appreciative of Leopold's successes, rarely treated the boorish boon companion of his at times savage father with much respect. While there was, perhaps, some truth to Frederick's expressed idea that his father's friend at times moved a bit slowly, the abuse showered upon him was rather out of proportion to his presumed offenses. To be sure, after a truly memorable performance, such as the one at Kesselsdorf, Frederick could be magnanimous, even affectionate.[39] Generally, though, Frederick seems to have viewed Leopold as a sort of substitute father who could be battered about with impunity. This, of course, is to say nothing of the army itself. While there were times, indeed, there *had* to have been, when the Prussian army was compelled to assume a defensive posture—for example, during a substantial portion of the Battle of Chotusitz (May 17, 1742)—for the most part, Frederick made certain that the Prussian army "always attacked." His aggressive policy was responsible for a continuous skein of victories, but they were always quite costly. Except for the legendary one of Hohenfriedburg, the Prussian army—in the two Silesian Wars, which constituted Prussia's involvement in the War of the Austrian Succession—always lost more in killed and wounded than its opponents (the greater *total* loss sustained by the Austrians was due to prisoners taken). Sometimes, as after the disastrous Battle of Hochkirch in the Seven Years' War, Frederick seemed to be concerned about these losses. On the whole, though, he seemed to be, if not callous, then at least indifferent to them. In all events, his inflexible adherence to aggressive tactics assured that such would have to be continuously sustained. Of course, it is true that eighteenth-century commanders in all armies were not noted for being tenderly disposed toward their soldiers. Unlike Frederick, however, few of them ever even pretended to be informed by Enlightenment principles. Moreover, in his stringent devotion to tactics that, if applied under virtually all circumstances, *had* to engender heavy losses, Frederick stood alone.

In her beautifully written and perceptive work, *The Making of Frederick the Great*, Edith Simon describes a dream Frederick had from time to time during his campaigns. In this dream, Frederick was about to be arrested and executed "for not loving his father enough." Then the scene shifts and father and son again confront one another, this time during a campaign. "Have I done well?" Frederick asked his father. "Yes," replied the ghost-king. "Then," said Frederick, "I am content. Your approval is worth more to me than that of the whole world." As author Simon wisely puts it, "One could not dream fairer than that."[40]

Simon follows up this psychologically astute observation with another, more extended one:

> Frederick had won. He had got everything his own way. He had squared himself with his father, and had settled accounts with him. The son had cast the father's every reproach back in his teeth, and at the same time treated the father's memory with a forbearance in the heroic style. He had had a proxy in hand—the Old Dessauer—in whom the son was able now to kick, now to pat the father; and an enemy, the House of Habsburg, on whom the son could piously avenge the father yet also show himself the better man.[41]

This brilliant statement needs only to be augmented in the following ways. Frederick, when he wished to "kick" a father proxy, had at his disposal not only the Old Dessauer, but also his father's army, particularly that portion of it under his immediate command. It is true that, during the later Seven Years' War, this army would be composed of increasing numbers of mercenaries, and this war would see more battles in which the killed/wounded ratio vis-à-vis enemy losses was in its favor. Nevertheless, the battering to which it would be subjected would put Silesian War encounters somewhat in the shade. As has been pointed out by not a few commentators, Frederick, for all the devotion he could occasionally inspire on the part of his soldiers, never really identified with them or with the army in general.[42] This army, the only meaningful "gift" given to Frederick by Frederick William, would be battered or "kicked" time and time again. At times, such as after Hochkirch, the soldier-king would be sorrowfully repentant, only to be quite willing to have a go at it again, inflexibly committed to attacking under all circumstances. In all events, it is at least doubtful whether the Silesian Wars sufficed to "settle . . . accounts" with his father, an individual whose approval was important to Frederick, but one whom he could never really respect.

Contemporary observers and historians would be baffled by Frederick's behavior at Kolin, Zorndorf, Hochkirch, Kunersdorf, and Torgau. In each of these battles, either defeats or sloppily won victories, certain lapses on Frederick's part—that is, transgressions against his own "principles of war"—can be seen.[43] Yet, while it is possible that the Battle of Torgau, fought on November 3, 1760 (a barely won victory against the Austrians), was possibly his single most costly battle, it was the Russian foe—one whom, as we have seen, Frederick despised the most—that seemed to bring out his worst generalship. To some extent this had been true at Zorndorf. However, it would be at the Battle of Kunersdorf, on August 12, 1759, that Frederick would demonstrate perhaps the worst generalship of his career. As we consider this we must bear in mind the possible subjective significance of the Prussian army to its king.

By the summer of 1759, Prussia's situation was, at the very least, obscure. Austria's Gen. Gideon von Loudon had succeeded in linking up with General Saltykov's army of forty-five thousand to fifty thousand Russians, and the threat to Brandenburg in general and Berlin in particular was very real. Naturally, Frederick thought himself compelled to confront this threat. From the very beginning, though, defensive tactical dispositions were out of the question, even if a defensive tactical posture could be viewed as part of an *offensive strategy*. The Prussian army "always attacks," and it did so again on August 12, 1759, at Kunersdorf, near Frankfurt-am-Oder. What resulted was a disaster unprecedented in the history of Prussian arms.

FREDERICK THROWS CAUTION TO THE WIND

As we have seen, despite their performance at Zorndorf, Frederick never really respected the Russians as practitioners of the "art of war." To him, they were uncouth savages, and rather inept ones into the bargain.[44] It thus is quite probable that his deeply ingrained prejudices were responsible for him hurling a fifty-three-thousand-man army against a largely Russian—with Loudon's Austrian cavalry in support—force of about seventy thousand. According to Reddaway, "At Leuthen and at Zorndorf, he had profited greatly by his knowledge of the field. But at Kunersdorf he knew neither the difficulties of the ground nor the extent to which in one important particular, those difficulties [had been] surmounted by the enemy."[45] In the latter instance, Reddaway was referring to a causeway that threaded between lakes and marshes, allowing the Austrians and Russians to present Frederick with a united front. Frederick, on a field about which he knew very little, had made only limited efforts to reconnoiter, and his men thus found themselves in a situation that was hardly conducive to use of the oblique battle order. The Russians were in a naturally defensible position and the Prussian king found himself using tactics that, in their clumsiness and stupidity, rivaled those which German military writers have often identified with Slavic foes. Under a broiling sun, and in the face of murderous fire, Frederick's men were eventually able to turn the enemy's left flank. This served little purpose, however, since the terrain allowed the Russo-

Austrian force to form a more compact front shielded by hills and marshes. The Prussian infantry made little headway, and the army's cavalry efforts were, at first, badly coordinated. Furious, Frederick finally ordered Gen. Friedrich Wilhelm von Seydlitz, the hero of Rossbach, to lead the cavalry in an assault against the center of the enemy's resistance, the Kuh-Grund. After initially driving back the Austro-Russian squadrons, the ferocious fire of the Russian infantry completely frustrated the attack. Seydlitz himself was badly wounded. As the increasingly disjointed attacks of the Prussian infantry were beaten back with staggering losses, the cavalry tried again and again to retrieve the situation. An effort by the Prince of Württemberg, whom Frederick would blame for initiating the debacle, miscarried and the prince was wounded in the process. Major General Georg Puttkammer died attempting to press another one, and a final, desperate assault was shattered by a ferocious Austro-Russian cavalry charge led by General Loudon. Frederick, who had two horses shot out from under him during the course of the fighting, grabbed the banner of his brother Henry's regiment and, in despair, tried to organize counterattacks in person. "Will not some accursed bullet strike me?" he was heard to shout. His men, many of whom probably shared the same sentiment at that point, could not be forced into further futile adventures. The battle ended with the virtual disintegration of the Prussian army and nervous collapse of its leader.

Kunersdorf was one of those battles fought with, by our standards, extremely primitive weapons. Nonetheless, it makes many more modern engagements look trivial by comparison. Depending on the source, Frederick lost between 19,000 and 25,000 killed, wounded, and captured. The Russo-Austrian force lost around 15,000. It had not been an easy thing for Saltykov and Loudon either, but they at least had an intact army. What Carl von Clausewitz called "a mere satisfying of the honour of the arms" left Frederick with just about 5,000 men capable of offering any sort of resistance.[46] To his minister Karl Wilhelm von Finckensten he wrote, "I have no more resources, and to tell you the truth, I believe that everything is lost."[47]

If his Russian and Austrian enemies had chosen to pursue him such might have been the case, at least with regards to the troops under Frederick's immediate command. However, as Hans Delbrück pointed out, and what other writers have often forgotten, there were other Prussian troops in the field and, for the Russians in particular—who also, it would appear, had an exaggerated respect for their opponent—the campaigns against Frederick were part of a "cabinet war." This was an exercise in eighteenth-century diplomatic and military formalism, something that, while it did not rule out that Vernichtungskrieg so adored by later practitioners of what is sometimes referred to as "military science," made such a thing highly unlikely. Also Loudon, and his commander Daun, were, at this point, more concerned with securing Silesia than with destroying Frederick's army.[48] The result was that the eighteenth-century realities that had made campaigns of annihilation impossible for Frederick in this case served his interests rather well.

At Kunersdorf, Frederick violated virtually every principle he had espoused in his earlier writings on war. His reconnaissance had been meager. "Seizing the bull by the horns," he had thrown his infantry into the teeth of murderous fire and, violating one of his most important rules, allowed his cavalry to be committed piecemeal (at least initially) and sacrificed in pointless charges. One could argue, of course, that Frederick had simply "lost his head," as he had at Mollwitz, on April 10, 1741, when, wrongly thinking that all was lost, he fled, or allowed himself to be ordered off, the field. Frederick, however, had matured considerably since that time and it would appear that other factors were involved in his sacrificing his army at Kunersdorf. By attacking in virtual piecemeal fashion (this necessitated by the nature of the terrain) on a ground of the *enemy's* choosing—besides violating all the principles mentioned above—he seemed to be saying "*I* have written certain rules. They are important, to be sure; but, because *I* have put them down on paper, *I* can violate them at will." As will be seen, however, there was probably a more crucial underlying reason why the battle against a foe he despised brought out his worst generalship.

After Frederick had recovered his poise, he wrote an almost peevishly self-justifying letter to his companion and reader, Catt. The Prussian king placed emphasis upon his initial success in turning the Russian left. The Prince of Württemberg charged the Russians at "an inconvenient moment." Driven back in disorder, the disaffection of his troops infected the rest of Frederick's army. "The victory was ours when suddenly my wretched infantry lost courage." They had been panicked by thoughts of "Siberia."[49] In other words, no blame attached to Frederick for the disaster of August 12. Furthermore, and here Frederick lied outright: "It is false, you may be assured, that we had as you were foolishly told, 20,000 men killed, wounded and prisoners. My losses amounted to 10,000 men only all told; my enemies lost 24,000 and this must be so, since they acknowledge it."[50]

Although Frederick was rarely this dishonest in his military writings—or, to place the best possible complexion on it, disingenuous—Kunersdorf was something he simply could not assimilate. He had reacted badly to defeat earlier; for example, the suicide threat he made after Hochkirch. Kunersdorf, however, seemed to bring out a panoply of reactions that, on top of his astonishingly bad generalship, gave the battle a peculiar singularity. Perhaps the enormity of the disaster was simply too much for him to bear. Before considering possible underlying reasons, there is an important obvious point to consider: namely, that Kunersdorf revealed Frederick was concerned exclusively

with *his* army, that is, those troops under his immediate command, and, as indicated earlier, not necessarily for the most wholesome reasons. Even after
Kunersdorf, there were other units in the field, something that, as indicated
before, caused the Russians and Austrians to operate with caution. For Frederick, though, even with regard to their misuse, *his* troops were the only ones
that mattered. This perhaps in part explains his exaggerated response to defeat
and his exaggerated defensiveness once he regained control of himself.[51] At the
same time, it must be seen that *throughout* the Seven Years' War—not only at
Kunersdorf—Frederick insisted on violating one of his best-known maxims,
"He who tries to defend everything defends nothing," thus putting his own
army in a position of maximum peril. There had to be, as he saw it, a standard-
sized army (Normalheer) made up of something between thirty thousand and
sixty thousand men. This was "in direct contradiction to the principle of the
highest possible unification of all strengths for the purposes of battle."[52]

TROUBLING QUESTIONS

Any consideration of Frederick's actions at Kunersdorf in particular faces certain troubling questions. As we have seen, he violated several of his own tactical theorems, as was evident in his failure to properly reconnoiter the terrain,
failure to concentrate his forces, and a gross misuse of cavalry. In fact, Frederick contributed to his own defeat as much as his enemies did, if not more. Second, although he acknowledged he had learned from the Austrians, his blind
contempt for the Russians had not changed. Both Gross-Jägersdorf (although
not a personal defeat) and Zorndorf should have convinced him that the Russians would not leave the field solely on the basis of Frederick's reputation or
the appearance of the Prussian banners. Indeed, his rigidly fixed attitude of
contempt conveys a sense of deeply internalized forces, not the product of
some rational analysis of Russian military capabilities. At Kunersdorf, as at
Zorndorf, he appeared to be attacking not a foe to be observed and dispatched
as at Rossbach and Leuthen, but a symbolic focus of irrational psychological
forces emanating from within him. After a forced march during the heat of
summer, he hurled his tired army on an entrenched Russian infantry mass
supported by Austrian and Russian cavalry.[53] Bearing in mind earlier general
psychological considerations, we must again ask why the Russians brought out
the worst generalship in Frederick.

   First of all, in considering this question, it is crucial to point out that one
must not draw too sharp a line between Frederick's behavior at Kunersdorf and
that which he displayed at other engagements. As we have seen, Frederick's
tactics always offered the possibility that his army would be severely battered,
and this had been the case even at smashing victories such as Leuthen. Fred-

erick, while hypothetically committed to good reconnaissance, more often than not was careless about it in practice.[54] Nevertheless, he always found it hard to accept defeat. In any case, relatively bloodless *victories* (from the Prussian point of view), such as Rossbach, were rare.

Most scientific explanations of human behavior tend to follow the Law of Parsimony, which argues for the conceptually simplest explanation of a given phenomenon. William F. Battig pointed out that, in the service of this principle, psychology may opt for explanations that are academically satisfying, but inadequate for the real world.[55] Following Battig, then, it would be a mistake to suggest that any psychologically grounded explanation could allow a historian to establish qualitative differences between Frederick's actions at Kunersdorf and those that could be observed on other fields. Human behavior, to say nothing of those patterns of overdetermination that inform it, is simply too complex. Differences must, therefore, be of degree, rather than kind.

However, there is clearly a disparity between the nature of his offensive tactics generally, and the incredible impulsiveness of his actions at Kunersdorf. In *Personality and Politics*, Fred Greenstein states: *"The greater a political actor's affective involvement in politics, the greater the likelihood that his psychological characteristics* (apart from his sense of political involvement) *will be exhibited in his behavior."*[56] Most assuredly, the emotionally trying conditions of war provided, and continue to provide, far greater opportunities for "affective involvement" than other areas of political activity. Frederick's hysterical behavior suggests an emotional reaction to failure, that is, the emergence of usually repressed "psychological characteristics" that not only have military and political implications, but deeply personal ones. He had lost before, and had reacted badly, but why this singular combination of bad generalship and the amalgam of dysfunctional reactions? The impulsiveness, tactical ineptitude, and untoward behavior argue that the Russians had symbolized something more than a military obstacle to be overcome. The battles with the Russians seemed to arouse in Frederick something akin to the need for deeply held emotional satisfactions, a desire to punish exclusive of all other military concerns. Failure could and would create massive psychological trauma.

There were pathological implications in his behavior, both during the battle (such as abdicating command by seeking his bullet), as well as in the subsequent use of such ego mechanisms as denial (by avoiding the reality of his losses, for example) and rationalization (by ascribing failure to other generals and soldiers). He clearly was seeking to reduce personal stress, which he had in abundance.

The most obvious question is how he could excuse in his own mind the tactical primitiveness he displayed against the Russians as compared to his other enemies. Frederick was paradoxical in many ways. The same individual who could justify war's excesses was simultaneously preoccupied with philosophy and the arts. Moreover, as a general, Frederick could write about war with a sort of cool, "scientific" precision, often objective about the qualities of at least his Austrian opponents and willing to own up, on occasion at least, to his own mistakes. Yet, as we have seen, he was dismissive of the Russians and, after Kunersdorf, unwilling to credit them with any role whatsoever in his defeat or, of greater importance, to assume any blame for the disaster himself. Those "cognitive" factors that, with one crucial exception, had informed his observations on war were almost entirely absent in his reactions to the Russians in general and the Battle of Kunersdorf in particular. We are suggesting that he equated the brutishness and primitive qualities he saw in the Russians, for whom he held no respect, with those of a father he feared but did not respect. In any event, bearing in mind that the emotional element was *always* important to Frederick (indeed, this hopefully has been demonstrated throughout this chapter), it would seem, nevertheless, that with regard to his enemies he was able to maintain more of an intellect-emotion balance for the "Europeans" while yielding more to emotion when confronted by the Russians.

Here, an observation by Giles MacDonogh is most important: "After Katte's death, there was only one other occasion when he lost control: after his troops were routed at Kunersdorf, just up the road from Küstrin [where Frederick had been imprisoned by his father in 1730], in 1759." There is here, as this writer sees it, a very obvious connection between, in Frederick's mind, the savagery of his father, and that of a Russian opponent whose toughness he appreciated but could never respect.[57]

Moreover, this splitting of cognition and affect was further reinforced by his successes in the field, particularly the combination of victories and failures.[58] Against the "Europeans," his intellectual side was aided and abetted by the occasional incompetence of his opponents, which often resulted in victory. Emotional needs could be met as well, of course, but a more *satisfying* way of meeting them would have had to involve a substantial redirection of the "intellectual" components and here the Russians would serve him well. To Frederick, in order for his vendetta against his father figure to continue without undue discomfiture, losing to the Russians was not even a possibility. Indeed, the marvelous opportunity presented by the Russians was twofold. As before, he could batter the father image—that is, the army—but now he could simultaneously inflict punishment upon this image, in the form of the Russians, by using the very instrument his father had left him. In essence, he could attack his father with his father's own weapons, damaging both. Then, the army, *his* army, could be restored again to satisfy Frederick's cognitive self. *Especially* at Kunersdorf, rigid commitment to the attack was a psychological necessity. Unfortunately, as a foe the Russians required more generalship than that which

could be derived from an inflexible tactical posture grounded in fears of helplessness. Almost two centuries later, another central European victim of childhood authoritarian practices would face a situation in which a Russian foe
would bring out inflexible generalship that, aided and abetted by dysfunctional behavior on the part of subordinates, would be responsible for a disaster
compared to which Kunersdorf would pale in comparison.

CHAPTER TWO

NAPOLEON IN RUSSIA, 1812

Whose blood have I shed?

Some years ago, a student in my Western Civilization class posed the following question: "Well, what *happened* to Napoleon in Russia, anyway?" Emphasizing what I perceived to be decisive logistical and tactical considerations, I offered what the instructor thought to be a convincing explanation. Such was accompanied by a patronizing smile. The student smiled sweetly back, and shook her head. Somehow things still did not add up. And, of course, they did not, particularly when one bore in mind Napoleon's guiding principles: concentration of forces, tenacity, and decisiveness (but wedded to flexibility). The campaign seemed to have been almost monumentally flawed. His later defeat at Leipzig was understandable. Napoleon had been outnumbered, and the perfidious Saxons had deserted at a crucial moment. At Waterloo, a man who knew how to utilize British phlegm to overcome French élan had outgeneraled him. In Russia, though, Napoleon was not outnumbered, and neither Barclay de Tolly nor Mikhail Kutuzov, the commanders who opposed him, was a Wellington. Even when one brought in space and the weather, the disaster of 1812 still did not make sense. There was still too much unwonted hesitation on Napoleon's part, too many lost opportunities. I needed psychological counseling. Kurt Lewin's "field theory" seemed to offer possibilities.

Field theory, in its simplest form, is the social version of theoretical developments in physics, which assume that "the properties of any event are determined by its relations to the system of events of which it is a component."[1] Lewin's fundamental construct is the "life space," consisting of both the individual and his environment viewed as interlocking constellations of facts, from which any explanation of behavior must proceed.[2] Thus, to understand behavior one must not only know something of the individual (that is, attitudes, capabilities, memories) but also the immediate situation. Field theory is an approach that deals with the concrete individual in a concrete situation.

Lewin used the terms "environment" and "person" in several ways. For the purposes of this analysis, the environment has both objective as well as psychological elements. An object may have an existence apart from the perception of the viewer, but it may also be regarded in a particular manner dependent upon the selectivity of the viewer's perceptual processes.[3] "Life space" can be construed, in lay terms, as the world of the individual. This can consist of those geographical realities that immediately surround us, as well as more distant aspects of our existence. The latter, of course, while not part of our current perceptions, are located in our thought processes (the "person") and may just as easily influence our decisions.

Thus, field theory deals with our attempts to navigate through the complex and changing physical existence that surrounds us. This existence has both objective and subjective elements. The relationship of this theory to Napoleon's campaign in Russia takes on metaphorical overtones because any Russian campaign must deal with vast spatial elements. These elements, or "regions" as we shall show, can be defined in any number of ways by the individual. In Napoleon's case, the choice of regional definitions ultimately led to his defeat. "Person" refers to the individual within the life space defined by Lewin in psychological rather than physiological terms.[4] Behavior refers to any movement in the life space that can be explained psychologically. Hence, accidents or unintentional events are not considered behavior.[5]

The life space of any individual can be divided into two regions. A region refers to an ongoing or contemplated activity rather than a geographically defined area. For example, attending a class at the university is considered a region, but not simply the geographic location within the university.[6] Field theory is a response-defined psychology, similar in this respect to behaviorism.

Movement from region to region in the life space may be physical or psychological. That is, one may either actually locomote or think about doing something. The region that terminates a sequence of movements is considered to be the goal region. By definition, the goal region would be the goal activity, and other regions (that is, other activities) are organized so that the antecedent behaviors lead eventually to the goal. For example, going to the movies includes such connected activities as phoning the theater (or looking at a paper) to determine the time of the show, getting one's coat, driving to the theater, so forth. The finiteness of detail used to describe regions is a function of the level of explanation needed.

In a very real sense, a life space may be "mapped" as to regions. While this discussion will involve connecting (bordering) regions, one cannot ignore the fact that the regions leading to a specific goal may in fact be separated. Of course, movement may be either toward or away from a region.[7]

Finally, regions have valence. This refers to the attractiveness or aversiveness of a specific region and is a function of tension systems within an individual. Hence, valence is a psychological phenomenon.[8]

Tension exists within an individual when a need is unfulfilled. A region has positive valence if it is perceived that the activity will lead to a reduction of tension, and negative valence if it will increase tension. The negative region is perceived of as a "barrier" with regard to attaining access to a positive one. The interaction between tension (within the individual) and valence (a perceived regional characteristic) generates a set of forces leading to psychological as well as real movement by the individual. Hence, if I am hungry, and eating at a restaurant nearby will satisfy my hunger, the interaction of need and valence will lead my movement toward the restaurant.

There has been much speculation concerning Napoleon's actions, or lack of them, during the Russian campaign. His lagging behind the army while sending the cavalry ahead in vigorous (and exhausting) pursuit of an elusive foe, his extremely botched performances at Smolensk and Borodino, and his apparent regaining tactical finesse on retreat: these and other aspects of the Russian adventure have caused many to wonder what was on Napoleon's mind. Of course, the specific nature of these thoughts may never be determined precisely, but the effects can be analyzed in terms of field theory.

One basic assumption in field theory, for example, is that if the individual has no immediate perceived goal, psychological conflict occurs. This is important to remember with regard to Napoleon's behavior in his 1812 Russian campaign.

NAPOLEON'S APPROACH TO WAR

Probably, the most often quoted of Napoleon's maxims is, "God is on the side of the heaviest battalions." The second most quoted is, "You engage, and then you see." Taken together, these pretty much constituted his approach to war. As Owen Connelly pointed out in *Blundering to Glory*, Napoleon's "military doctrine" was remarkably unsophisticated. He placed emphasis on concentrating his forces so as to be assured of superiority of numbers either on the field in general, or at least on a vital portion of it, and of bringing them quickly to bear. Careful never to commit himself to complex prearranged plans, he counted on his ability to seize upon the advantage of the moment, upon the tenacity of soldiers fiercely loyal to him, upon the competence and self-reliance of his corps commanders, and last, but certainly not least, upon crucial errors committed by his opponents. At the same time, while putting a premium on tactical and even strategic flexibility, he was always certain as to his ultimate goal and planned carefully with regard to it. These concepts were central to his practice of the "art of war."[9]

Napoleon emphasized the destruction of the enemy's army. Frederick the Great no doubt would have liked doing the same, but due to a variety of circumstances attaching to pre-Revolutionary eighteenth-century warfare he could never have succeeded. For Napoleon, the taking of territory was never of great importance, except to the degree that it could bear upon the destruction of enemy forces.[10]

Napoleon is classified as a "military genius," yet, even according to his own comments on the subject, intelligence, in and of itself, was not the most important quality with regard to determining success in battle. Tenacity, "the determination to win at all costs," combined with those qualities and circumstances described earlier, would always be the best guarantee of success.[11]

While others have made the point, Connelly has been particularly successful in demonstrating how Napoleon's overall approach—careful planning with regard to goals combined with that flexibility which allowed him to capitalize upon his ability to grasp favorable circumstances (as well as upon the often egregious blunders of opponents)—had been responsible for a string of victories unprecedented in modern military history. God, with whom Napoleon at times seemed to confuse himself, had been, after all, on the side of the heaviest battalions. Most certainly, engaging, then seeing, had proven to be an effective approach when confronted with opponents who were not particularly effective at doing either.

By 1812, many in Europe knew that Napoleon's fortunes were in decline. In 1809, the valiant Austrian war of liberation saw him almost defeated at Aspern and narrowly winning at Wagram. His marshals had been consistently beaten in Spain and Portugal by Wellington, and his so-called Continental System had proved to be of doubtful efficacy. On a more personal note, in 1809 Napoleon suffered the indignity of having his tentative approaches to the sister of Alexander I of Russia spurned. At the same time, Alexander resented Napoleon's seeming encouragement of Polish national aspirations and, in 1811, formally withdrew Russia from the Continental System. It was under these circumstances that Napoleon planned one of the most audacious and ill-starred campaigns in military history. He began his "paper work" on the campaign in August 1811, and by December was engrossed in studies of the ill-fated efforts of Charles XII.[12]

As he pondered the fate of the Swedish king, Napoleon must have given some thought to his opponents. The Russians presented a somewhat confused picture in this regard. Austerlitz, his "masterpiece" of December 2, 1805, had not left him with much respect for Russian leadership. Yet, as he knew, Tsar Alexander I had taken control over the Austro-Russian (but largely Russian)

army from Mikhail Kutuzov and ignoring the latter's advice, had been responsible for the rash attacks that had led to disaster.[13] Napoleon's next encounters
with Russian forces, in the wake of his immensely successful 1806 campaign
against Prussia, had been somewhat discomfiting. At Pultusk, on December
26, 1806, one of his best corps commanders, Jean Lannes, had barely held the
tactically ungifted Russian commander, Theophil von Bennigsen, to a sanguinary draw.[14] Worse was to come, and this time Napoleon himself would suffer
embarrassment. On February 7, 1807, the Battle of Eylau took place. It was the
worst encounter of Napoleon's career up to that point. French losses probably
exceeded those of the Russians (although, as always, the emperor, in letters
and dispatches, understated them), and Napoleon was shocked as never before.[15] Only Bennigsen's tactical timidity had prevented a French disaster, and
the tenacity of Russian soldiers, to put it mildly, had left a disturbing impression. Yet, just four months later, Napoleon would enjoy one of the greatest victories of his career fighting Russian troops again commanded by Bennigsen,
who—on this occasion compounding timidity with downright stupidity—was
responsible for losing almost thirty thousand men in one day, half of them
dead. The Battle of Friedland, June 14, 1807, compelled Alexander I to come
to terms with Napoleon, thus ensuring that the Prussian king, Frederick William III, would soon have to do so as well.[16]

For Napoleon, then, the Russians must have presented a somewhat mixed,
not to say confusing, picture. He had beaten them decisively at Austerlitz, but
this was perhaps due to the fact that Alexander I had assumed control over an
army that might have performed better under Kutuzov, a general about whom
Napoleon knew very little other than the fact that he had put in a mediocre
performance in a later campaign against the Turks. In any event, the Russian
army was now commanded by Barclay de Tolly. Putulsk and, more importantly, Eylau, had been grim eye-openers as to the fighting qualities of Russian
soldiery. At the same time, higher leadership, in the form of the almost impres-
sively inadequate Bennigsen, had once again been poor enough that costly
stalemates rather than more costly disasters resulted from these encounters.
Friedland, on the other hand, had been a massacre, with Bennigsen's incompetence more than counterbalancing Russian courage. What did the Russians
really amount to, anyway? Nobody knew. What Napoleon did know, however,
was that the Russians, more than any other army, had been primarily responsible for the near defeat of one of his most admired past military heroes, Frederick the Great. Yet, Frederick could never bring himself around to respecting
them very much. Whatever his private thoughts on the matter, Napoleon publicly voiced respect for the Russians only on the battlefield at Borodino and,
some years later, on Saint Helena.

Whatever his opinions on Russian capabilities were in 1811, he certainly was
aware that the simple question of distance posed problems that were unprece-

dented for any modern army, including his own. As a consequence, even while dismissing warning admonitions from subordinates, he planned in an extra-meticulous manner—something that was unusual even for him.[17] An abundance of supply wagons and horses would be needed to sustain the largest single force brought together under one leader up to that time.

To this day, there is debate as to how many soldiers actually participated in the campaign, but the number six hundred thousand is usually agreed upon as accurate, if one includes approximately 150,000 noncombatant personnel.[18] Of this number, less than half were actually French. A large percentage of the horde consisted of Germans, Italians, Poles, and several other nationalities who, either by desire or compulsion, found themselves allied with France. From the beginning, there were those who asked Napoleon questions regarding distance, logistics, and Russian resistance. To Gen. Armand de Caulaincourt's expressed concerns, Napoleon replied that the Russians would offer no serious resistance. Russian nobles "would fear for their palaces" and force Alexander to make peace.[19] Whether or not Gen. Philippe-Paul de Ségur's opinion that Napoleon was beguiled by a "certain drunkenness arising from past victories" was indeed correct—particularly when we bear in mind the events between 1809 and 1812—there can be little doubt that he had become totally immersed in his invasion schemes.[20]

"He put passion into everything," wrote de Ségur. "Hence the enormous advantage he had over his adversaries, for few people are absolutely engrossed by the moment's thought or action."[21] Caulaincourt, apparently not quite as "engrossed by the moment's thought or action," persisted in his questioning of Napoleon's decision to invade Russia. To all his arguments, Napoleon would tell men that *I had turned Russian, and I understood nothing of great affairs.*"[22]

Some authors have commented upon the fact that by 1812, Napoleon had begun to slide into a soft middle age. He had become quite plump, increasingly accustomed to luxury, and had come to believe that the rigors of vigorous campaigning were no longer for him.[23] "I love my bed, my repose, more than anything," he remarked to Caulaincourt in November 1812, in the final stage of the Russian disaster, "but I must finish my work." As Connelly remarked, he probably should have owned up to that somewhat earlier.[24] In any event, he seemed to be inordinately remote from his officers and men during their preparations. Whether or not decreasing physical stamina combined with a spiritual malaise was responsible for it, a rather worrisome problem emerged. Despite the meticulous preparations, Napoleon appeared to be uncertain as to what would be the actual goal of this most monumental of enterprises. First of all, there apparently was some confusion in Napoleon's mind as to whether the campaign was to be a quick one or not.[25] Such confusion was unusual for him. Even at Wagram, which, as mentioned before, he barely won, Napoleon, although tactically sloppy, was not confused as to his goal. Now, however, before undertaking the most significant and reckless military adventure of his career, Napoleon seemed uncertain about the nature of it. He would win, of course, but how, precisely, would this occur? At a conference with "allied" rulers in Dresden in May 1812, he spoke of reaching Smolensk and Minsk and there going into winter quarters while organizing a second campaign, presumably for the spring of 1813.[26] Yet, unlike earlier campaigns—those of 1806 and 1809, for example—there really was no fixed objective. Rather, immediate goals—the crossing of the Niemen River, the seizure of Vilna, the defeat of those Russian forces that offered combat, and vaguely menacing (somehow) both Saint Petersburg and Moscow—seemed to proliferate.[27]

Whatever the confusion in Napoleon's mind, which field theory suggests results from having no fixed goal, there is evidence to suggest that Alexander I was a bit more certain about the events to come. Napoleon's aide-de-camp, Narbonne, had visited the tsar before the campaign began, hoping to arrive at some sort of compromise. The tsar readily admitted the superiority of Napoleonic generalship and of the French army. He made a statement, however, which should have given Napoleon and his generals some pause: "But space is a barrier. If, after several defeats I withdraw, sweeping the inhabitants along with me, if I let time, deserts, and climate defend Russia for me, then perhaps I shall have the last word on the most formidable army of the modern world."[28] As time would tell, Alexander rather underestimated the virtues of his own army. The general strategic picture, however, would prove to be accurate, this despite Napoleon's realization that, whatever the uncertainty of the final goals, special preparations regarding supplies were certainly necessary.[29]

THE CAMPAIGN

In any case, the invasion of Russia commenced on June 24, 1812 (interestingly, Hitler's was launched on June 22), and the magnificent host of six hundred thousand passed over the Niemen River—and encountered almost no opposition whatsoever. Cossacks occasionally exchanged billingsgate with French cavalrymen, but generally observed the army with a sort of perplexed ennui, and there was no sign of the regular Russian army. Vilna, the capital of Lithuania, was taken without a fight on July 26. Napoleon then spent three weeks there dealing with administrative issues while the army went on ahead to catch the Russians.

This army won several minor clashes, but always the main van of the Russian army eluded capture or destruction. Probably every student of history knows something about the terrible winter that played a crucial role in destroying Napoleon's army during the retreat from Moscow. In at least general texts, however, the toll exerted by the terrible heat of the June and July days of 1812 is not usually mentioned. Nonetheless, the suffering of men and horses was immense.[30] Furthermore, it soon became obvious that, despite Napoleon's special preparations regarding supplies, the vast distances that had to be covered by the emperor's army in its seemingly hopeless attempts to bring an elusive foe to battle would render such insufficient. In due course, hunger augmented the debilitating effects of heat. Napoleon, as well fed on the advance as he would be on the retreat, displayed a noticeable insensitivity to both.[31] All the while, the cavalry, led by Joachim Murat, Napoleon's brother-in-law and "King of Naples," was driven ahead, setting the pace for an increasingly exhausted army.

The army was to be driven forward at all costs. But where? At Dresden, in May, Napoleon had spoken of establishing an arched sort of line anchored on Smolensk and Minsk. At the same time, however, he was desperately eager to bring the Russian army, or at least a major part of it, to bay. Yet, on July 7, when Jean-Baptiste Eblé, his general of engineers, warned him of the serious loss of horses sustained by the army, Napoleon responded by declaring, "We shall find fine horse coaches in Moscow." As one author has pointed out, this was the first time that the emperor had mentioned Russia's spiritual capital as the Grand Armée's ultimate destination.[32]

Even up to this point, however, Napoleon's behavior had been such as to justify a suspicion that, contrary to his usual approach, territorial gains of some sort had been on his mind from the beginning. While it is true that he seemed eager for Murat to make contact with the Russians, he appeared to hold himself back, the delay at Vilna being an example of this. As the army was driven onward, presumably to find a frustratingly elusive enemy, Napoleon immersed himself in minutiae. Throughout this period, Napoleon showed an inflexibility that appeared to render him indifferent to the toll this advance was taking. At the same time, however, if battle were to be joined at this point, it was obvious that Murat would be his surrogate. His concern with the bureaucratic details regarding conquered territory at the very least *suggests* that territorial gains, rather than combat, were on his mind.

As time went on, his generals became increasingly uneasy. Murat begged him to turn back or assume a defensive posture. Napoleon, now seemingly obsessed with taking Moscow, refused while at the same time evidencing emotional distress.[33] His failure to overtake the Russian army seemed to have a double effect on him. On one hand, he would make public displays of bravado, ridiculing his opponents. On the other, he would evidence increasing indecisiveness. As an example of the first, we can consider his response to discovering the abandoned Russian position at Drissa: "You see, the Russians don't know how to make war or peace. They are a degenerate nation. They give up their 'palladium' without firing a shot! Come along! One more real effort on our part, and my brother [the tsar] will repent of having taken the advice of my enemies."[34]

Napoleon's inordinately prolonged delay at Vilna was not indicative of a "real effort," but it certainly was suggestive of the confusion described by field theory when negative and positive valences clash. After arriving at Vitebsk on July 29, he spent fifteen days there on administrative issues. Sometime before he left, he ordered the van of his army ahead. As always, Murat was told to set the pace, while Napoleon, as before, held himself back, catching up with rather than leading his army. During the attack on Smolensk, however, Napoleon made an extraordinary display of bravado. Due to a French artillery bombardment and the Russians' "scorched earth" policy, Smolensk was in flames. Napoleon and his staff were watching the spectacle from a distance when somebody commented that it was a horrible sight. "Bah!" retorted the emperor. "Gentlemen, remember the words of a Roman Emperor: 'The corpse of an enemy always smells sweet.'" Caulaincourt recorded that all present "were shocked at this remark."[35]

At the Battle of Valuntina, which took place on August 18, the day Smolensk was occupied, Napoleon allowed his generals Ney, Junot, and Gudin to operate almost independently of each other. He himself was "not on hand" to lend cohesion to the effort.[36] No real reason was provided for this occurrence, although speculation has ranged from preoccupation with relatively minor concerns to his inability to anticipate a battle at that time. Whatever the immediate reason, one thing seems plain: Napoleon, while often displaying an obnoxious bravado, seems to have been almost hesitant to directly confront the Russian army. Due in part to Napoleon's preoccupations or indecisiveness, the wheeling maneuvers designed to cut the road to Moscow failed. To be sure, there were six thousand Russian casualties, but the French had sustained seven thousand and the Russian army had been able to retire in good order. The battle for *Smolensk proper* had cost the French at least another seven thousand men. In a dispatch to his foreign minister, Maret, Napoleon declared: "*We have captured Smolensk . . . without the loss of a man . . . the Russian Army is marching on to Moscow in a very discouraged and discontented state.*"[37]

It is difficult to imagine how Napoleon could have justified such a description. Perhaps he meant that, in actually *entering* Smolensk, no lives had been lost. At the very best, this missive could be described as a singular exercise in semantic casuistry. We must also note something else, namely, Napoleon's apparent assumption that the Russian army was undergoing some sort of spiritual decline. Most observers agree, however, that it was Napoleon's army that was at this point being swept by pangs of doubt. After the battle of August 18, Napoleon made an interesting remark in this regard: "This army cannot now stop . . . motion alone keeps it together. One may go forward at the head of it, but neither halt nor go back."[38] What this points to is the fact that perhaps in part due to his slipshod performance in battle, in part to persistent and growing uncertainties, the emperor, at least to some extent, had become aware of the parlous state of the army's morale. At the same time, however, he had formed a definite goal in mind, and that was Moscow.

By the time the Valuntina engagement had been concluded, Napoleon's striking force had been reduced, depending on the source, to between 160,000 and 182,000 men.[39] Disease, exhaustion, desertion, battle casualties—all had taken their toll. At the same time, the necessity of breaking off individual detachments to secure routes and supply lines—necessarily more of an eighteenth-century emphasis on a war of position—had proven to be quite costly.[40]

By mid-August, then, the Grande Armée was in a sad state. In a very real sense, we can say that it reflected the mental condition of its leader. What had happened? Here we are able to bring some conjectures grounded in field theory. The reader will recall that this approach posited the existence of "life regions," that is, spheres of activity, contemplated and/or actualized. Depending on whether a given "region" has positive or aversive qualities for an individual, it is described as possessing "positive" or "negative valence," respectively. An individual can choose a particular region as a source of primary activity. Moreover, a primary region can have attaching to it preliminary activities that have to be undertaken in order to achieve, in due course, those more crucial tasks associated with the primary life region. If, however, the subject under consideration is unable to determine which region is of overriding importance, confusion, sometimes of an almost paralyzing nature, can supervene.

By 1811, Napoleon knew that a campaign against Russia would be necessary for what were, for him, very palpable political, military, and perhaps even economic purposes. As we have seen, he undertook systematic preparations for it. Yet, as we have also noted, unlike previous undertakings, he was seemingly very uncertain as to its overriding *goal*. Flexibility always had been an important source of strength for him. However, concerning his inability to determine whether the campaign would be a short or a prolonged one (even geographic objectives were uncertain), other factors appear to have been operative. It is difficult to determine what they were, but several possibilities offer themselves. First of all, there was the simple problem of space. Despite his seemingly overweening self-confidence at the time, he was most assuredly aware of this problem, and his elaborate preparations can be seen as evidence of this. Then there was the problem of the Russian army itself. As we have seen, past experience with this army had given him a very mixed picture of it. It always seemed to have been badly led. Yet, in the fighting of early 1807 it had come close to defeating one of his best generals and, at Eylau, nearly defeated Napoleon himself. Napoleon immersed himself in studying the Russian campaign of Charles XII, an individual whose feral genius rivaled his own. The unhappy fate of Charles's army, the finest in Europe at that time, had to have made an impression on Napoleon. Finally, there was his increasing awareness of the fact that he had grown soft with regard to vigorous campaigning; that he perhaps had reached his zenith at Austerlitz. Whether any or all of these considerations were responsible for his fear of *failure* in Russia is unclear. Nevertheless, despite periodic displays of bravado, he seemed unenthused about a campaign he viewed as being absolutely necessary.

While not intensively concerned about depth psychology, that is, approaches such as psychoanalysis, field theory places a great deal of emphasis on the mental state of an individual faced with critical choices among life regions. Napoleon's state would seem to have rendered him incapable of making such choices. Thus, when the strongest army that Europe had ever seen crossed the Niemen River, there apparently was no clear-cut objective. It is true that the emperor ordered Murat to advance at a rapid—and for the rest of his army destructive—pace in order to make contact with the rapidly retiring Russians. Yet, Napoleon himself appears to have held back. While it is true that he did not speak of Moscow as his ultimate goal until July 7, he seemed to have been hesitant almost from the beginning about *personally* confronting the Russian army in battle. Moreover, as suggested earlier, one is entitled to speculate about the possibility of Napoleon's preoccupation with territorial conquest even before his July 7 pronouncement about Moscow. While he delayed at Vilna and Vitebsk, Murat seemed to function as a sort of alter ego for him. At the same time, as we have seen, the exhausting pace he set—at one point, Davout was constrained to vigorously protest about this to Napoleon—had to have had, and did, an extremely negative effect upon the army as a whole. This was so much the case that by the time Napoleon reached Vitebsk on July 29, 1812, over a third of it had been lost to exhaustion, heat prostration, or disease—and this before a single major engagement had taken place.[41]

As a fighting force, then, the Grand Armée had been almost crippled. Whether or not Napoleon was aware of the immense damage he had done to his army is unclear. What is clear is that he did not seem eager to confront the Russian army in person. Instead, unlike in his earlier campaigns, a fixed geographical target seemed to be his goal. Despite occasional posturing to the contrary, *fighting*—at least on *his* part—seems to have been given a lower priority on this occasion. Thus, when he actually did catch the Russian army at Smolensk and nearby Valuntina, his efforts were confused and hesitant. Several uncoordinated detachments of what was left of the army were to deal with the Russians, and hence, they were able to retire in good order.

This uncertainty in battle was due to his concern for a goal that had now become fixed in his mind: Moscow. When he actually arrived at this goal is debatable, but having done so, he was committed to it in a most inflexible manner. The Russian army, in field theory terms, had become a region charged with negative valence. It was a barrier to be removed as quickly as possible. Napoleon's actions at Smolensk and Valuntina, however, are more indicative of a concern to sort of "defuse" this army rather than meet it head-on and decisively defeat it. At this point, the Russian military leadership, through its concern for avoiding head-on battle, was able to assist him in this project.

On August 30, 1812, Mikhail Kutuzov became commander in chief of the Russian army. Although he had been soundly beaten at Austerlitz in December 1805 and tended to be stodgy and self-indulgent, he was, in many respects, the most formidable foe Napoleon could have faced. He knew that he could never defeat Napoleon in a war of movement and sophisticated maneuver. What he had on his side was Napoleon's already attenuated supply lines and the unchallengeable phlegm of the Russian soldier. He also had, from the beginning it would seem, a rather fixed goal in mind: the protection of Russia from a foe whose military sagacity he respected—and nothing more (or less) than that. This was responsible for what some authors have seen as timidity and lack of resolve on his part, characteristics that would have decidedly negative consequences during Napoleon's retreat.[42] Cate, a partisan of Barclay de Tolly, consistently compares the "sybaritic" Kutuzov negatively to his hero.[43] Certainly during the war of movement that took place from the retreat from Moscow up to and including the Berezina River crossing, Russian tactical sloppiness, informed, it would seem, by the overall timidity of the commander in chief, was extraordinary. Yet, throughout, one must bear in mind Kutuzov's overall goal: the protection of Russia. Having cut his military teeth while losing an eye against the Turks, and sharing a generally held suspicion of *all* things Western (not only the French), it is hardly surprising that Kutuzov would have cared very little about any sort of putative "unified cause" against Napoleon. Seen through Western liberal eyes, this is indicative of that narrow, spiritually stultifying orthodoxy that one correctly associates with the most backward and autocratic major power in the world. Yet, if one bears in mind Kutuzov's perception of things, plus the resources with which the general had to work, there would appear to have been a very definite and consistent underlying logic to his conduct.

Kutuzov inherited an army that numbered approximately 120,000 men. Napoleon had 130,000 troops immediately available. General Bennigsen, whom Napoleon had decisively defeated at Friedland in June 1807, had presumably gained an appreciation for natural defensive positions during the intervening years. It was this otherwise not particularly distinguished general who selected Borodino as the ground for Kutuzov's minions after several perhaps more favorable positions had been abandoned.[44] Kutuzov had mixed feelings about the Borodino site, but it was the last possible one before Moscow. The French would have to attack and he could be counted on to defend with determination.

Napoleon's advantage in numbers was slight, but on earlier occasions this had not mattered much. To be sure, the Russians had about the same number of artillery pieces, but Napoleon's guns presumably were better served. Furthermore, again depending on the source, the Russian army contained between ten thousand and fifteen thousand very poorly trained irregulars. As Ségur put it, "The French had the same number of men, but more soldiers."[45]

The action at Borodino began inauspiciously enough on September 5, 1812, when Napoleonic legions stormed a redoubt near the village of Servardino. This single action, revolving about one forlorn position, cost the emperor two thousand casualties. The Russian casualties were even heavier and Napoleon was astounded by the fanaticism of the Russian defense.[46] The French then paused for a day before launching the *general* assault on Kutuzov's positions.

It was not widely known that Napoleon was in poor physical health. He suffered from dysuria, a condition that made it both painful and difficult for him to urinate. His condition was especially painful at Borodino, and he also had a high fever and a "burning thirst."[47] As his army prepared to go into battle, Napoleon nevertheless declared, "It's the Austerlitz enthusiasm again."[48] As one observer put it, however, he was not the "energetic man of Marengo, Austerlitz, etc. . . . We did not know that Napoleon was unwell and that this type of illness made it impossible for him, as the great events . . . were unfolding before his eyes, to act solely in the interests of his glory."[49]

Still, we have to ask ourselves if physical illness, while clearly a contributing factor, was *solely* responsible for Napoleon's strange inability to make decisions at Borodino. We have already seen indications of something else at Smolensk and, as we shall see, that strange combination of arrogance, bravado, and indecisiveness that appeared there will appear once again at Borodino. In any event, even if one accepts the justifiable notion that battles are won by subordinates — and, as Connelly has pointed out, Napoleon was unusually well served in this regard — the emperor's role at Borodino was oddly limited.

On September 6, Napoleon issued a series of orders calling for Davout, Ney, Junot, and Murat to undertake somewhat uncoordinated attacks against Gen. Peter Ivanovitch Bagration's defenses. General Jozef Antoni Poniatowski was to go off by himself to attack the southern end of the Russian line. In violation of his maxim that concentrating one's forces is crucial, Napoleon apparently did not commit himself fully to any one of these attacks which, under the circumstances, amounted to gigantic probing thrusts involving tens of thousands rather than hundreds of soldiers. On the morning of September 7 there began a terrific exchange of artillery fire involving over a thousand guns. The Russians suffered terribly and huge gaps were torn in their ranks. Yet, after losing Borodino proper, they fought with a tenacity that elicited praise from their opponents. A group of fortifications more or less in the center of the line, the "Bagration fleche," exchanged hands several times with staggering losses on both sides. Furious fighting also raged about and within the Raevsky Redoubt. Almost none of the Russians surrendered, which greatly concerned Napoleon. To General Caulaincourt he said: "We shall win the battle. The Russians will be crushed, but it will not be conclusive if I do not take prisoners."[50] A chance for a rout appeared to offer itself after a successful assault on the Russian village of Semonovsk at the extreme left of the Russian center. Ney and Murat demanded reinforcements. At this juncture, however, Napoleon, according to Ségur, "gave his first sign of indecision."[51] Orders and counterorders were issued and the emperor finally decided not to commit any more troops to that particular action. This, of course, ensured the continuation of the battle—and in large part on Russian terms.

Napoleon did have an excellent view of the Russian center, which, after much battering, appeared to be the possible area of breakthrough. Pacing back and forth with his chief of staff Marshal Louis Alexandre Berthier at his side, he seemed unaware that he was letting victory slip away. When he was not pacing, he sat on a stool in his tent looking disconsolate. At one point, Gen. Jean Rapp suggested that the Old Guard be committed. "I shall take care not to," Napoleon replied. "I do not want it destroyed. I am certain to win the battle without the guard becoming involved."[52] Finally, he consented to sending the Young Guard. After several of his subordinates questioned him about this, however, he ordered the maneuver halted, saying, "I want to see more clearly . . . My battle hasn't begun yet . . . The day will be long . . . Nothing is clear yet."[53] To one query, he responded with a "sorrowful gesture of resignation." He appeared to be "sluggish, apathetic, inactive."[54]

Contrary to von Clausewitz's rather astonishing assertion, the Russian army fought better on the defensive than on the attack.[55] As the day wore on, however, the Russians began launching counterattacks. When Marshal Jean-Baptiste Bessières reported this situation to Napoleon, though, the latter replied: "Nothing is clear as yet. Before I send in my reserve, *I want to see my chess board more clearly.*"[56] General Augustin Daniel Belliard, in commenting that it was impossible to get the emperor to commit his reserves, stated that he found him "looking sick and depressed, his face sagging, his eyes dead, giving orders languidly in the midst of the horrible din of war which he doesn't even seem to hear."[57] When Prince Eugene's troops found themselves in a critical situation, the emperor shrugged and said: "I can do nothing. It is up to him to win. He has only to make a greater effort! The battle is on!"[58] The only truly memorable statement to emerge from Napoleon during the course of the fighting was one involving an evaluation of the opposing soldiers: "The Russians let themselves be killed like automatons; they are not taken alive. This does not help us at all. These citadels should be demolished with cannon."[59] It is not certain that, as one commentator put it, Napoleon had entered into a sort of "fugue state" during the battle.[60] It is obvious, though, that he really played no decisive role in it. He acted as if he were a witness to an awesome event in which he was no doubt very interested, but in which he had little real part to play. It was as if his soldiers were participating in something resembling a natural disaster, utterly beyond the power of even the emperor of France to influence.[61] Perhaps one can argue that, on September 7 at least, physical discomfort alone played a decisive role. Nevertheless, his actions (or lack of them) fit into a pattern we have seen before—and will see again.

At the end of the day, Napoleon's army had won its territorial objectives, but almost no prisoners had been taken, and the Russian army was unbroken. "If the survivors were able to retreat in such good order, proud and undaunted, what did the winning of one field matter?"[62] Casualty estimates vary wildly. French commentator Georges Blond, accepting official casualty figures, gives French losses as 6,547 dead and 21,253 wounded, but this seems a bit low.[63] Most commentators agree that the Russians lost between 40,000 and 50,000 men; the French between 30,000 and 40,000. In any case, all observers knew that, of the tens of thousands of Russian casualties, there were only seven hundred prisoners. Thus, as we can see, between 65,000 and 80,000 dead and wounded—depending on the source—lay in mangled heaps in an area not much larger than a few square miles. As surgeons commenced to saw off limbs—often stuffing rags into the mouths of their "patients" in order to prevent their screams from demoralizing still ambulatory comrades—Napoleon, accompanied by some of his staff, rode his horse over the ghastly field. He seemed unusually depressed and upset and "relieved his feelings by cries of indignation and an exaggerated solicitude for the poor soldier."[64] Once again, it appears the emperor was acting as if, somehow, forces beyond his control had brought on this slaughter. In a strange sort of way, his own apparent withdrawal from decision making could have served to have reinforced this self-serving belief.

Soon, however, his arrogance reasserted itself. As he steered his horse between the sad piles of ruined humanity, he remarked brightly, "There are five dead Russians for every Frenchman." Even Palmer, who had endeavored to be as sympathetic as possible to Napoleon, said that Napoleon had made this remark with "horrible satisfaction."[65] An accompanying French colonel was not impressed and, in a letter written some days later, remarked, "I suppose he took Germans for Russians."[66] Later, in a letter to his wife, Marie Louise, Napoleon lied outright, not that this was unprecedented. "I took several thousand prisoners and sixty cannon." He did underestimate Russian casualties, which he put at thirty thousand. "I lost many killed and wounded," he confessed. "My health is good and the weather is a little fresh."[67] In a letter to one of his several imperial "brothers," Francis I, emperor of Austria, Napoleon presented a more accurate estimate of enemy losses, but, on the whole, was even more disingenuous. "I estimate the loss of the enemy at between 40,000–50,000 men; he had between 120,000 and 130,000. I have lost between 8 and 10,000 killed and wounded. I have taken 60 pieces of artillery and a great number of prisoners."[68] Of course, one could argue that Napoleon always "underestimated" his own losses, and, in view of the possibility of an Austrian rising against him, this was perhaps especially necessary at this time. However, this bravado and self-congratulatory arrogance after a period of confusion and indecision were characteristic of the Russian campaign. He most *assuredly knew* that, as a fraction of the casualties sustained by the Russians, seven hundred prisoners did not amount to a "great number." Even in an age of slow communication, sooner or later the approximate nature of what had happened at Borodino in particular and Russia in general had to come out and, most assuredly, Napoleon was intelligent enough to realize this. A remark of Ségur is of importance here. After the battle of Borodino, Napoleon insisted on seeing the Russian prisoners and captured cannon again and again. In this "the Emperor vainly sought to recapture a shred of illusion by having the handful of prisoners counted again, and collecting a few disabled guns."[69] Napoleon's officers thought themselves compelled to assist the emperor in preparing illusions, which were all that were left to him at that point.

Napoleon had always emphasized that the destruction of the enemy's army was of crucial importance. Yet, after Borodino he did not choose to pursue Kutuzov. Perhaps his knowledge of the fearful losses he had sustained held him back. Our earlier considerations, however, suggest that, while this might have been a factor, destruction of this army was not all that important to him. At least since July 7, but quite possibly earlier, Moscow had been the goal, and the Russian army had served as an irritating barrier to his attaining it. His concern for taking Russia's spiritual capital had been responsible for uncertainty and confusion in battle, even in the massive one just completed. To be sure, once the battle had begun, he certainly wanted to win it decisively. Thus, despite that indecisiveness he had shown throughout—indicative of a *confusion* of goals in his own mind—he wanted to be certain, once it was over, that he had taken a respectable number of prisoners. In the end, though, the inflexible concern with Moscow proper prevailed, and there would be no pursuit of an army that, from the beginning, had been a cause of mental confusion for Napoleon—something that he had tried to compensate for by periodic displays of bravado.

He entered Moscow on September 14, 1812. Within a day, the city was in flames. When messages dispatched to Alexander I went unanswered, it was only because the cabinet in Saint Petersburg thought he might demand too much.[70] Because it was sunny in Moscow, Napoleon convinced himself that Caulaincourt's warnings about the severe Russian winter were ludicrous.[71] In keeping with its best traditions, the army tried to maintain an appearance of fit and proper trim. "The Emperor willingly lent himself to this deception by snatching at every straw to keep his hope alive."[72] Napoleon spent inordinate amounts of time at meals or in an armchair, where he read novels.[73]

At first Napoleon declared that he desired to stay in Moscow until the spring. The winter would not be too severe. "Nowhere should I be better off than in Moscow."[74] There was, as Caulaincourt so delicately put it, a certain "glibness" about all of this, a glibness that delayed the army's withdrawal for several fatal weeks. Not surprisingly, Napoleon's memoirs present a different view of the situation.

"The Emperor had to remain in Moscow to prepare the army for a retreat."[75] To put it mildly, this viewpoint is open to some questioning. It is evident that for some time, Napoleon had no idea at all of retreating. Rather, he expected, as we have seen, that the Russian government would eventually come to terms with him in spite of overwhelming evidence to the contrary. Vain attempts at "parleys" pointed to the fact. Furthermore, he seemed unaffected by arguments that his men lacked the materials, even boots, needed to survive the Russian winter, whether inside or outside of Moscow. The aforementioned phrase, "Nowhere should I be better off than in Moscow," was his standard reply to Caulaincourt's repeated urging that a retreat be commenced as soon as possible. Napoleon at times ridiculed Caulaincourt's warnings about the weather and then would maintain that even if the weather should turn foul, his army was capable of dealing with it.

"He flattered himself that the superior intelligence of our troops would enable them somehow to safeguard against the cold—that they would take the same precautions as the Russians, or even improve on them."[76]

"Alas," Caulaincourt exclaimed, "the Emperor deluded himself, and our ruin followed on his misfortune."[77]

That Napoleon had deluded himself is certain. His army would not be able to deal with a severe winter in a fashion superior to that of their opponents. There was no reason to assume that Alexander would be eager to come to terms, especially with an enemy that was badly weakened. A gutted city could not sustain an army under any circumstances, but particularly not during the winter season. Yet, bearing in mind our considerations up to this point, it is obvious that there was a very crucial, underlying reason why Napoleon was reluctant to leave Moscow, one that had little to do with tactical, much less strategic, realities. For more than two months, Moscow had been his fixed goal. In a campaign that had, from the beginning, been infused with disquieting uncertainties, it had emerged as the one *positive* goal of which Napoleon was certain. Now, in a sea of uncertainty—with strained supply lines and a still intact Russian army lurking out there somewhere, conditions for which he, of course, bore sole responsibility—the city had become an island of certainty. Napoleon had attained, after all, that goal toward which he had driven his army with inflexible and destructive vigor. In the back of his mind, he probably knew that he would have to leave it in the not-too-distant future. For now, however, he could enjoy this triumph, however hollow, and occupy himself by reading novels.

Just how much Napoleon reflected on the events of a flawed campaign is uncertain. Yet, while bearing in mind that psychologically informed interpretation, if applied with too much enthusiasm, can add support to Voltaire's assertion that "history is a bag of tricks played on the dead," we can offer some at least provisional explanations. First of all, as we have seen, Napoleon had good reason to be uncertain about the nature of his opponent. Past experience had served to provide a mixed picture, at best. In all events, he was not overly enthusiastic about embarking on a campaign dictated by what he saw as political necessity. Certainly, if he had a mixed opinion of the Russian army, he was appreciative of the demands posed by space, and, as seen at the beginning of this chapter, he devoted much time to the questions of logistics. He did this with his usual single-mindedness. Yet, in the back of his mind there lingered a persistent awareness of Charles XII.

There was, at the beginning, apparently no clear-cut goal. To be sure, as has been pointed out, Napoleon was a master at improvisation—as one historian has put it, he liked to "play it by ear."[78] Yet, even for one who reveled in the ad hoc, his uncertainties about the goal were unusual and probably quite disconcerting, especially for himself. Despite the lack of a clearly defined goal, the campaign began with a rapid, almost frenetic, advance that exhausted his army. While somewhere in his own mind he might have been keeping various options open—that is, "playing it by ear"—he was absolutely inflexible with regard to the pace of the advance, one with which he paradoxically had little enough to do. That had been Murat's task, while Napoleon devoted vast amounts of time at Vilna and Vitebsk to dealing with administrative issues. Although it may have appeared that he wanted someone to catch up with and engage the Russian army, that someone was not himself. Rather, he was concerned with tasks associated with governing conquered territory. With regard to the "life regions" posited by field theory, we can say that the Russian army was charged with negative valence. Whether Moscow was his ultimate goal before July 7 is uncertain. In any event, he did not give evidence of that purposeless roaming—psychologically and/or with regard to locomotion—ascribed by practitioners of field theory to individuals caught between two regions negatively charged, or two deemed to be of equal attraction.[79] His administrative concerns and obvious and inflexible commitment to a rapid advance are suggestive of an individual concerned with conquering territory as rapidly as possible while on the way toward some fixed target.

Of course, Napoleon's delays allowed him to avoid dealing with the Russian army as long as possible, at least on a personal basis. Whether or not he was consciously aware of this is impossible to determine. All we can say is what has been said before: namely, that this army certainly presented him with a very mixed picture. It was, in a word, unpredictable. Moreover, especially for one whose tendency to improvise made him dependent upon his opponent's making predictable mistakes, this had to have been especially disquieting. After July 7, Moscow was his *stated* goal and, while it was obvious that the Russians would not let him have the city without a fight, he had come to view them as a negatively charged barrier rather than as a force to be eagerly engaged and cheerily annihilated.

Encountering the Russians at Valuntina, Napoleon's botched performance suggests that fighting was definitely a region of negative valence. Penetrating or removing the barrier (that is, the Russian army) was an aversive event for Napoleon, something distasteful to be done as quickly as possible. Since seizing Smolensk was an activity directly in line with the Moscow goal, the Russian army could not be ignored. However, by allowing the Russians to escape, the distance placed between them and Napoleon reduced their negative valence. The forces corresponding to a negative valence tend to decrease more rapidly as a function of distance (psychological as well as objective) than for a positive valence. This means that if a person approaches a highly positive goal that also has negative valent elements, he will paradoxically show a strong fear or avoidance tendency. That is, the forces relating to a positive goal tend to increase more rapidly as the person approaches, and hence the equilibrium point is reached when the individual is close enough to maximally react to the negative influences.[80] In real terms, the closer Napoleon got to Moscow, the more hesitancy he would demonstrate in fighting the Russians. The territory regions (Smolensk and Moscow) and Russian army activities were contiguous psychologically as well as geographically, and thus psychologically fused.

Napoleon's dispatches regarding Smolensk were probably an unconscious reflection of his true feelings. Territory, not fighting, was his goal. His tactics suggest that he was, in a military sense, trying simply to defuse the Russians. His comments about the dispirited Russian army can be construed as a classic incidence of projecting one's own mental state onto someone else. However, this psychological self-deception served to continue his march toward Moscow since it maintained the integrity of the territorial goal.

Borodino came as a shock to Napoleon. The fighting has been described in detail, but what is critical in explaining his indecision is the fact that he had once more encountered the barrier he thought he had previously removed (at least in his own mind). At Borodino, some of his behavior suggests that, having finally confronted the entire Russian army at one place and head-on, he once again might have been struggling with the possibilities of abandoning the territory goal in favor of destroying the Russian army. His remark about Austerlitz is suggestive in this regard. At least at Borodino both goals were in considerable strength, and the conflict between them helps to explain his lack of desire to participate in the battle.[81]

There is further evidence of growing concerns about whether the Russian army was his legitimate goal. His concerns over the number of Russian prisoners taken as well as his self-promptings concerning Austerlitz do not reflect territorial aspirations. Napoleon was hardly inspired tactically, although strategically he removed the Russian military barrier before Moscow. Kutuzov could not have psychologically done Napoleon a worse turn: by simply interposing a fixed mass of men he reminded Napoleon that the barrier he thought he had removed at Smolensk was still viable. During the battle the opposing constellations of tensions within Napoleon created a paralysis of will; his physical illness merely magnified the psychological dilemma.

In another sense, though, Borodino served to fortify Napoleon's commitment to the territory goal, which would be *announced* by taking Moscow. Given the distances he had traveled, and his own botched performance, to have reversed or abandoned his territorial goal would have been too much. Indeed, it would have meant that both the geographic as well as military activities would have become negatively charged. After Borodino, Napoleon ignored geographic distances that might have given another commander pause. At that point the tsar had won: Napoleon had fully assigned positive valences to Moscow and pursuing Kutuzov was out of the question.[82] The acquisition of territory meant that space itself could not be considered a barrier. At Vilna and Vitebsk, he paused; after Borodino, he denied the problem.

At last, of course, Napoleon had to leave Moscow. He rationalized the humiliating—and late—withdrawal in his twenty-sixth "Bulletin of the Army" on October 26, 1812. After first attacking the dastardly conduct of the Russians—the iron men of Borodino were now cowards who violated truces—he talked of the necessity of abandoning Moscow. "Moscow today is a true cloaca, diseased and impure. A population of 200,000 souls is wandering in the neighboring forests, dying of hunger."[83] Once again, we can detect something we saw at Borodino: a tendency to observe a truly hideous situation with the attitude of one who really had little if anything to do with it. The Russians, to frustrate the French invaders, had indeed burned Moscow. Without Napoleon, however, it is obvious that suffering on so massive a scale would never have taken place.

Much has been said about Kutuzov's presumed timidity at Borodino and later in harrying Napoleon out of Russia.[84] Perhaps these criticisms have some merit. In any event, one fact remains: although Kutuzov's army sustained heavy losses, *he succeeded in keeping it intact up to the disastrous withdrawal of the Grand Army over the Berezina.*[85] If strategy implies, as it must, not merely tactical finesse, but rather the utilization of armies, weather conditions, terrain, and space in an integrated fashion, then perhaps we can say that the superior tactician, Napoleon, was in the end defeated by the superior strategist, Kutuzov. Nevertheless, his own strategic abilities had been blunted by precampaign uncertainties and a later inflexible commitment to territorial gain that was to compensate for them.

Throughout the course of the retreat, during which he fought off Kutuzov's somewhat cautious pursuers, Napoleon was well served, enjoying his favorite foods and, apparently, worried more about Gen. Claude François de Malet's frustrated conspiracy in Paris than about the suffering of his men. It must be admitted, however, that the illusion of Napoleonic grandeur seemed to have affected his soldiers to no small degree. When the emperor passed through groups of freezing, starving soldiers, he encountered no reproach from them. "They cursed the elements, but had not a single word of reproach for *La Gloire*."[86] It is interesting to note that even observers critical to Napoleon — Ségur and Caulaincourt, for example — saw nothing perverse or, at the very least, odd about this apparent unwillingness to recognize the role their leader played in a truly ghastly fate. At the same time, however, it is entirely possible that *Napoleon's sangfroid* (an appropriate phrase when considering retreat in a Russian winter) was due to his virtual blotting out of what was happening all around him. When the emperor reached Smolensk on November 9, 1812, it had been snowing heavily for four days, and it was bitter cold. According to Ségur, the "disorder was at its height." Napoleon's response to this was to "shut himself up in one of the houses on the new square, not leaving until the fourteenth, when he continued his retreat."[87]

In Napoleon's *Memoirs*, as recorded by his private secretary, we have a curious disjuncture. On one hand, the hideous retreat of Napoleon's army was almost a good thing in that it allowed the French soldier — other nationalities are not mentioned — to display all of those sterling qualities that emerge under adversity. On the other hand, however, "It was no longer possible to preserve even the shadow of discipline, and each man left to himself tried to reach Vilna as best he could."[88] Some years after the fact, the balance of cheeky defiance and unhappy inward recognition of reality that produced indecisiveness was still operative.

On November 28, the main body of Napoleon's army passed over the Berezina River. Desperate rear-guard actions succeeded in keeping the Russian army from destroying this pitiful remnant altogether. Nevertheless, Russian artillery fire was intense and thousands, including women and children who had accompanied the army, were slaughtered. There was, of course, bitter cold, and virtually no food. General Eblé, the Swiss officer who had accomplished engineering miracles in constructing bridges across the river, said he attempted to persuade the emperor to show more celerity in getting his army to the relative safety west of the Berezina. Napoleon, who had been complaining about various matters up to that point, snapped, "'That will do.' He looked at the ground. A few moments later he began complaining again and seemed to have forgotten what the general had said."[89]

Napoleon's success in bringing most of his army over the Berezina was due in no small degree to the timidity and, at times, incompetence of the Russian generals. They were overawed to some extent by Napoleon's reputation, while at other times they were raw and overconfident.[90] In any case, it cannot be maintained that the Russian army "won" a battle at the Berezina. It is perhaps a measure of the cheekiness inspired by the Napoleonic legend (or perhaps of simple French nationalism) that contemporary commentators have referred to the Berezina episode as constituting a *French* "victory."[91]

Yet, it is true that Napoleon had succeeded in saving at least a crucial remnant of the Grand Armée from annihilation. Part of this, as suggested above, was no doubt due to the incompetence of his pursuers. There is another factor that was certainly of crucial importance, however. Paris was now his goal and it was charged with a valence even more positive than Moscow had been. Malet's conspiracy had to be dealt with, where the emperor could act with the certainty characteristic of one who finds himself back in a familiar setting. The Russian army, of course, was still a negatively charged barrier, but in a pursuit characterized by a mixture of timidity and tactical sloppiness, it was, paradoxically, less of a threat—at least to Napoleon personally—than it had been when he first led his six-hundred-thousand-man host into Russia in the first place.

As inflexible as he had once been during the advance, he now was frantic in his effort to return to Paris. Just as during the advance, this necessitated that he occasionally not allow himself to see fully what was going on around him. Napoleon also was assailed by doubts, and patterns of avoidance could not continuously prevent him from knowing of the suffering of his remaining troops. Ahead, however, were Paris, safety, and the possibility of raising a new army. Behind him was a gutted city, the taking of which had at one point been the inflexibly held goal that had compensated for original uncertainties about a campaign undertaken with reluctance. More immediately behind him was an army whose badly coordinated pursuit allowed Napoleon to avoid it or, on occasion, to defeat it in detail. His men might still die by the thousands, but the life region of Paris, even more positively charged than Moscow had been, had become a second "sun of Austerlitz" for a man to whom negative valence was no longer of paralyzing significance.

After crossing the Berezina, a river now choked with the debris, human and otherwise, left behind by a disaster unparalleled in military history up to that time, Napoleon dashed off his famous Grand Armée Bulletin Number 29. Dated December 3, 1812, it contained an admission that things were not well. Napoleon blamed everything on the weather, the "cruel season" as he called it, and dwelled lovingly upon the military incompetence of the Russians and the cowardice of the Cossacks. The latter, he declared, attacked only wagons and supplies and were miserable as cavalry. A group of Cossacks, he said, "makes only noise and is not capable of beating a company of *voltigeurs*." Only the peculiar circumstances surrounding recent events allowed them to succeed.[92] After further self-serving ramblings, Napoleon ended his message with the well-known phrase, "His majesty's health has never been better."[93] Napoleon's apologists have maintained that the last sentence was necessary, at least in his own mind, because he was still worried about Malet's conspiracy. At the very least, however, one can bring up the question of taste.

Napoleon raced ahead to Paris believing, and he was unfortunately correct in this regard, that his presence would set things aright. "Our disasters will make a great sensation in France," he told Caulaincourt, "but my arrival will counterbalance their bad effects."[94] To his assembled marshals he said, "I am leaving you, but this is in order to look for 300,000 soldiers. It is necessary to undertake such measures in order to sustain a second campaign since, for the first time, one campaign has not ended the war."[95] This statement is very important, especially from the point of view of our considerations. It points to the fact that Napoleon's confidence would return as soon as he was back on familiar soil. There would, of course, be a second campaign, and this time he would be meeting an enemy whose pursuit would lead it into territory that he knew well. He would be eager to meet it now. No longer would it, along with allied troops, be a negatively charged barrier to a territorial goal. Defeating it would be a life region of positive valence because he would be protecting France itself from invasion. Until the Battle of Leipzig in October 1813, and even afterward, he would perform wonders in holding off the Austrian, Prussian, and Russian armies.[96] At no time did Napoleon recognize the magnitude of the disaster he had brought upon his country and, until the day he died, he accepted no responsibility for the defeat and never acknowledged that the Russians had beaten him. In a letter to the king of Denmark and Norway in January 1813, he remarked, "My losses are real, but the enemy can take no credit for them."[97] Such a remark, which reveals a total disdain for reality, is understandable when one bears in mind that there simply could *be* no defeat in the eyes of a man who perceived himself as coextensive with the purpose of history. There is, however, another, perhaps from a psychological perspective more crucial, reason why Napoleon found it almost impossible to own up to defeat by the Russians: He had been beaten by an enemy he had never wished to meet in the first place, despite his lack of respect for it. In a sense, we can say that we see in this obviously self-serving (in a very literal sense) statement a final, crowning act of denial and avoidance.

During truce negotiations in 1813, Napoleon made the following statement to Prince Klemens von Metternich: "A man such as I am is not concerned over the lives of a million men."[98] This came from a sense of grandeur, the counterpoint of which was his almost self-pitying musing in Saint Helena, "Whose blood have I shed?" We can dismiss the latter query as a plea for forgiveness from an individual who found gardening on Saint Helena a poor substitute for a career of conquest. We must see, however, that a sense of grandeur—arrogance, perhaps, combined with a perhaps warped view of political necessity—was necessary if a campaign such as the one of 1812 was to be undertaken in the first place. In this regard, it would be pleasant to be able to blame what occurred as the almost natural result of hubris. While this certainly played a role, the argument has been made that Napoleon's downfall in Russia can be explained by recourse to field theory.

CONCLUSION

Originally uncertain as to his goal(s), Napoleon—perhaps out of fear of, if not necessarily respect for, the unpredictable Russian army—decided rather early on that he would conquer space, this achievement to be crowned by the taking of Moscow. The taking of territory in general and Moscow in particular thus became a life region charged with positive valence. The Russian army, on the other hand, became a barrier which, even if it had to be dealt with in order to attain the positive goal, was a region charged with negative valence and thus aroused intense anxiety in the emperor. He was not eager to confront it personally, and his delays along the way and his sloppy performance in battle can be explained by this uncertainty. Yet, having decided on taking territory, he drove his army forward with inflexible determination, just about ruining it in the process. This inflexibility masked a variety of uncertainties about the campaign, as did periodic exhibitions of noxious bravado. A statement Napoleon made while in retirement on Saint Helena revealed this uncertainty: "The most terrible of all my battles was the one before Moscow. The French showed themselves worthy of victory, and the Russians worthy of being invincible."[99] In a word, Napoleon's army had defeated a foe that had not lost. Even on Saint Helena, albeit only for a moment, the conqueror of Moscow revealed himself to be the individual who, as the campaign was about to begin, had no goal— a condition for which an unwonted rigidity would have to compensate. Concern over possible defeat at the hands of a foe that was in so many ways a mystery to him would be overcome through territorial conquest. What in fact would function, much as Alexander had supposed it would, as a lifesaving barrier for him and his army, Napoleon was able to turn into something of positive value.

Of course, those geographic distances—which were not a conscious psychological barrier during the advance (indeed confirming that more territory had been conquered)—haunted Napoleon throughout the retreat, aided and abetted by the weather. Yet, wanting only to get "home" as quickly as possible, there was no longer any spiritual confusion and, except for delays at Smolensk and at the Berezina River—which for obvious reasons must have had strong symbolic significance—he was able to fight off an army whose pursuit was less than wholehearted. With clarity and purpose restored, and all ambivalences and hesitations a memory (if that), the emperor could go about his task of raising a new army with cold-blooded energy.

Napoleon's Russian adventure perhaps can best be explained by recognizing that since he had no clear goals originally, he had allowed his opponent to delude him into accepting the one that would most benefit his foe. The tsar was right when he remarked while riding into Paris, "and they thought I was the fool."[100]

CHAPTER THREE

McCLELLAN'S FLAWED CAMPAIGN: THE WOUNDED EGO

If I save this army now, I tell you plainly that I owe no thanks to you or any other person in Washington. You have done your best to sacrifice the army.

THIS WAS TO BE THE culmination of all of Lee's efforts over the past week. On July 1, 1862, Gen. Robert E. Lee watched as his laurel-laden Army of Northern Virginia advanced straight uphill at the Army of the Potomac, a supposedly beaten force commanded by Maj. Gen. George Brinton McClellan. McClellan's troops were burdened with the memories of six days of constant conflict and retreat. Forced back from Richmond, the Union troops now positioned on Malvern Hill, with their backs to the James River, were the lost souls of a failed campaign. Through a combination of Lee's aggressiveness and McClellan's anxieties, they were, for all intents and purposes, awaiting the inevitable and final disaster.

While Lee's planning this day left much to be desired, he had no reason to doubt that this was to be the final and crushing defeat for a foe adroitly prized away from Richmond six days before. Incredibly, determined Union troops arose from the ashes of a shattered campaign to repulse Lee's army. Shaken and stunned Confederate infantrymen fell back, wondering what had gone wrong.

In some respects, Malvern Hill portended Maj. Gen. George Pickett's disaster a year later, when a driven Lee failed to fully comprehend the nature of events leading to a fatal decision at Gettysburg.[1] However, even after the Union victory at Malvern Hill, critical issues remained unresolved: How and why did McClellan find himself fighting for his very survival at the James, when the initial prospects for the Richmond campaign had been so bright?

Interestingly enough, in trying to unravel the mystery that was McClellan, a starting point might be found in his behavior *after* Lee's defeat. Basically, all he did was to continue to complain to Washington about being outnumbered—and little else. There was no continuance of the campaign, although the opportunity was certainly there. McClellan the general, if not his army, was a beaten man. He had, in fact, lost the campaign before ever setting foot on Virginia soil. To understand Malvern Hill, one has to understand what led up to it.

The war began splendidly for McClellan when a victorious campaign in western Virginia made him a media hero. After the Union defeat at Bull Run, McClellan was called to Washington in July 1861 to reorganize the broken regiments and train the incoming recruits. It was a task he accomplished well. Indeed, it may have been his greatest contribution to the Union war effort.[2]

Unfortunately for McClellan, his successes in West Virginia and Washington ultimately betrayed him, exposing personal weaknesses that would forever deny him the fame he so desperately needed and sought. It was inevitable: While McClellan paraded and pouted, glorying in his new endeavors and prominence, the threats to his self-esteem began to loom like a storm mass on the horizon. Once Lincoln satisfied himself he had a trained army, the administration began to have thoughts that would prove to be most unsettling to McClellan.

Not without cause, Lincoln decided it was time to use that army to fight the Confederates. Unfortunately, this was a concept McClellan never enthusiastically embraced. The process of procrastination began immediately. He dragged his heels every time the government tried to prod him into action. Drilling and posturing seemed much safer, and certainly more rewarding. In fact, McClellan subsequently showed more of a commitment to talking than he ever did for combat, but the political realities would not let him continue his excuses. Unfortunately for Lincoln, he had a general who was always almost but never quite ready to act.[3]

Pressure continued to mount for some kind of movement. What was he going to do about Richmond? What about the Confederates waiting across the river? The war was costing a bundle and there was nothing to show for the accumulating men and materials. From the very beginning McClellan never understood that the military was an arm of Washington policy, and not the other way around.[4]

Finally, running out of time and excuses, McClellan devised a Richmond strategy based on a decisive flanking maneuver.[5] He would land at Urbanna on the Rappahannock River and move swiftly overland against the Confederate capital.[6] Richmond would then find itself under siege. Once trapped, the Southern forces could and would be systematically destroyed. Yet, it never happened—at least not under McClellan. It is important to note, in terms of what followed regarding reinforcements, that Lincoln agreed to the Urbanna move only after being assured that sufficient forces would remain in Washington to guard against a Confederate move on the Union capital.[7]

McCLELLAN THE PARADOX

McClellan still remains an enigma to many Civil War historians. Strangely, Lee considered him to be by far the best Union general he encountered.[8] A cynic might argue that since McClellan probably contributed as much or more to Lee's career and subsequent legendary status than any other Union general, Lee was simply ex*pressing his gratitude. The point remains, however, that McClellan's Richmond campaign plan was, at least on paper, a sound one. Properly carried out, it might have shortened the war considerably. In reality, McClellan lost this early opportunity of his own devising and the carnage went on for three more years. We shall see that, once committed to action, his military options forever froze in the face of his fears.

The Confederates were always wary of McClellan. Still, even at the beginning of the war some of his contemporaries doubted his military capabilities, especially his capacity to act decisively. He was in some respects a known quantity, having served in the war with Mexico. In a conversation with Confederate president Jefferson Davis at the outset of hostilities, James Longstreet, who later became a corps commander and perhaps Lee's closest associate, dared to suggest that McClellan would be extremely cautious in his movements. Davis, a West Pointer himself, was quite put off by this hint of a defect in McClellan's skills. After all, in spite of the war, McClellan still was one of "the Brethren."[9]

One could, of course, inquire into the validity of Davis's estimates of military capabilities, especially in light of some of his subsequent choices for commanders. At that point in time, though, West Point graduates were generally highly regarded on both sides. Indeed, writing on the failures of the Maryland campaign, Longstreet criticized the Southern command for underestimating McClellan's strategic capabilities.[10] Longstreet probably addressed the issue more directly when he asserted that McClellan simply was not a combat leader. He brought well-trained troops to the field, then failed to employ them properly.[11]

Warren Hassler, one of McClellan's biographers, described him as brilliant but a victim of political pressures.[12] McClellan's brilliance, however, resided more in his verbal behavior than actions on the field. Strategy and tactics to McClellan were the unfolding of a scripted sequence of events in which everything had been planned for and anticipated.[13] Abrupt changes in the script raised doubts in his mind with which he could not cope. His view of military operations was orchestrated to his perceptions of how events should occur. Basically, he created his own world and expected everyone else to live in it.[14] He became obsessed with precise planning, seeing it as a means of avoiding unexpected changes that would constrain his options. The problem was getting others to follow that script.

While careful preparation is no sin, McClellan's military career was dominated by an attitude based on the invariant premise that he must expect and be prepared for the worst of all scenarios. His anxieties persisted longer than those of any other major commander in the war, paralyzing his efforts.[15] McClellan seems to have been convinced that the unexpected invariably was followed by the worst of all possible outcomes. It thus is easy to see why he hesitated so often when snap decisions had to be made. Things can go bad if you act quickly, but staying put until you are absolutely certain is a way of reducing danger. McClellan contributed more to his woes than anyone else, friend or foe.

In another explanation for McClellan's problems, William Myers offers the premise that McClellan's religious sensibilities were incompatible with military demands.[16] While the Duke of Wellington's remarks about men of principle and military success were direct and to the point, it is true that McClellan never fully accepted the fact that battle meant human sacrifice.[17] Yet, it seems a bit overdone to suggest that this religiosity of spirit accounted for much of McClellan's failures, just as it is to assume that Grant's successes were attributable in any significant manner to his enervation in conflict.[18]

McClellan's sensitivity toward his troops was perhaps more a reflection of concerns about himself. Still, it is ironic that he was the Union commander at Antietam, which resulted in the single bloodiest day in the Civil War. On the other hand, from his West Point days on he showed himself a personally ambitious and hard-driving individual. As Myers suggests, he was the worst of subordinates and the best of superiors.[19] Paradoxically, the key to McClellan's failures lay in his very need to succeed—and without exposing his fragile ego to any significant danger of assuming personal failure.

Yet, in assessing McClellan's weaknesses, any explanation must go beyond the simple assumption that he was so afraid of failure that he risked nothing.[20] As a matter of fact, he undertook a number of operations that carried a very high risk. It is this paradoxical behavior that provides a clue to the source of McClellan's failures. Before proceeding further, however, it would be well to consider for a moment how supporters viewed his problems. Oddly enough, his supporters often came to the same conclusion McClellan did; that is, they saw him as a victim.[21] In his defense of McClellan, Thomas Rowland argues he was a victim of Unionist historians such as Stephen Sears.[22] Rowland includes those historians who sought to criticize McClellan in order to elevate the status of other Union commanders. While this begins to approach the idea of historical revisionism, Rowland further pursues his case by criticizing writers who concluded that McClellan labored under crippling pathological defects. He cites any number of historians who attributed serious disorders bordering on the psychotic as contributors to McClellan's difficulties. In fact, he argues with some support that applying modern-day diagnostic classifications to other periods is not without significant danger.[23]

Yet, if one were to eschew the assignment of such modern clinical classifications as manic-depressive, delusional, paranoidal, and so on, the fact remains that McClellan did have some crippling psychological problems that precluded battlefield success, especially where he was solely responsible. The historical evidence is there: Despite all his advantages, McClellan failed in both the Seven Days' and Antietam campaigns, where success in either instance could have ended the war much earlier.

The work of Henry A. Murray and his colleagues at Harvard is most instructive in this respect. As early as 1938, Murray created and enlarged upon the concept of a specific need for achievement.[24] To Murray, achievement meant: "To overcome obstacles, to exercise power, to strive to do something as well and as quickly as possible. This is an elementary Ego need which may also prompt any action or be fused with any other need."[25] Murray categorized needs as either social or biological in origin. Achievement was considered a social need (that is, psychogenic) that differed in origin from organically derived needs such as hunger and thirst.[26] The pervasive influence of the achievement need in human behavior is clearly evident in his definition.

A need is a force, driving behaviors induced by a given situation. This drive (or need) both propels and guides the actions necessary to restore psychological equilibrium and insure survival. Hence a need serves to both organize the requisite behaviors and energize them.[27] In Murray's lexicon, a need is characterized as a push based on the individual's perception of the environment as hostile, friendly, nurturing, and so forth.[28]

What is also pertinent is whether the individual perceives the accompanying environmental factors as under personal control or "autonomous" (to use Murray's term). In the latter instance, events are perceived as being beyond the ability of the individual to manipulate them.[29] Readers familiar with McClellan's posturing before and during the Peninsular campaign will immediately recognize the relevance of this psychological construct. When events went against him, he always firmly convinced himself he had been thrust into that particular fix by forces beyond his control and was therefore not to be blamed.[30] While this may have protected his ego, it severely limited him as a commander. It also precluded the possibility of continued friendly relations with Washington.

After Murray's initial research efforts, other psychologists, including David McClelland and John Atkinson, began to explore the achievement need more closely. Research findings generally supported the notion that levels of performance under a variety of circumstances were highly correlated with the strength of the achievement need.[31]

Besides their experimental work, researchers uncovered social and cultural correlates of achievement. Richard De Charms and George Moeller, for example, found a high positive relationship between the amount of achievement imagery in children's readers and the number of patents issued in the United States.[32] While correlation is not directly translatable into causality, this association (among others) is intriguing. McClellan himself came from a long line of Scottish high achievers. His father was a graduate of Yale University and the University of Pennsylvania Medical School.[33] There is no evidence to indicate that his parents did anything but encourage their son to succeed, and his subsequent career would tend to support this assumption. After all, he did eventually run for the presidency, even after a blighted military career.

It could be argued, of course, that if higher levels of achievement motivation are associated with increased performance, then McClellan should and would have been a vastly different general before Richmond, or at Antietam for that matter. The problem is that the relationship between achievement and performance is actually not all that simple and direct. As work progressed on the achievement motive, researchers began to distinguish between the need to succeed and the need to avoid failure. Both tendencies exist within an individual, but one is dominant.[34]

The individual who is motivated to succeed tends to select activities at an intermediate level of difficulty. The moderate risk situation represents a challenge, which in turn serves as an incentive. The perceived level of risk is, of course, subjective. On the other hand, the same moderate risk level becomes a major problem for an individual whose desire for success is overwhelmed by greater fears of failure. Such individuals are likely to select activities they perceive as having either a very high or very low probability for success, and avoid those in the intermediate range.[35]

It is immediately apparent that one can reduce the likelihood of failure by always selecting easy tasks. What is not easily inferred is the choice of a very difficult task. Actually, by choosing an extremely difficult task, failure can be ascribed to events beyond individual control (that is, "I never really had a chance"). In this instance there is less of a personal sense of failure.[36] The result is that people motivated to avoid failure will select tasks at the extremes of risk because they tend to reduce the possibility of personal loss either by practically guaranteeing success or assigning the cause of failure elsewhere.

The worst scenario for McClellan, therefore, was the moderate risk situation, or more precisely, one he perceived as having moderate risk. An individual fearing failure turns this situation upside down. While the success-oriented commander would act, accepting this level of risk as offering at least equal chances for success, a general beset with strong and chronic fears of failure simply would not seize the initiative. Moreover, given the right circumstances, he might persist in actions that are doomed to fail. That is, he would hope to avoid defeat by doing nothing or by simply persisting in what he was already doing, believing it to be the safest course. Conversely, he would accept defeat because he believed at that point in time that he was a victim of forces beyond his control. Both are critical to an understanding of McClellan.

The evidence was there early on. For example, during the West Virginia campaign, which brought him the fame he so desperately sought, and eventual command of the Army of the Potomac, McClellan failed to promptly support a flanking movement at Rich Mountain by Brig. Gen. William S. Rosecrans, one of his commanders. John Beatty, a colonel in the 3rd Ohio Infantry, characterized McClellan at the moment he was to launch the supporting assault as "indecisive." It is a pity no one ever debriefed Beatty after the battle. The Army of the Potomac might well have been spared much of its subsequent agony.

McClellan did not send his remaining forces forward at the critical moment because he could not be absolutely certain that Rosecrans's movement was coming off as planned. On the other hand, he could not be absolutely certain Rosecrans *had not* attacked as ordered. His fear was that by engaging in a move that might lead to a repulse if Rosecrans had misfired, he would be liable for all the blame. Still, Rosecrans was out there somewhere on the Confederate flank—and on McClellan's orders. Torn between fears of Rosecrans's possible failure and the promise to support him, he hesitated and wound up doing nothing. Fortunately for McClellan, Rosecrans, being a less tormented soul, had turned the flank by himself.[37]

As he would do again in the Richmond campaign and especially at Antietam, he imagined the worst that could happen and behaved in terms of those exaggerated fears.[38] Especially at Antietam. When one more assault might have routed the Confederate left flank, he chose to believe a demoralized Maj. Gen. Edwin Sumner, one of his corps commanders, that failure could result in defeat. Equally revealing, when Maj. Gen. Israel Richardson, a division commander, broke the Confederate center at the Bloody Lane, McClellan did not pursue the breakthrough.[39] He had ten thousand men in reserve and nothing between him and Lee. But ten times that number might not have been enough. McClellan never discovered that he was his own worst nightmare.

Although caution is not necessarily considered a defect in combat, at some point it becomes a pathological indecisiveness, an unwillingness to do something. After all, he did move to Rich Mountain in the western Virginia campaign, he did land on the Yorktown Peninsula in his efforts to take Richmond, and he eventually did attack at Antietam. In each instance, however, there arose at a critical point that moment of truth when McClellan's fragile ego betrayed him. It was not military caution in any normal sense of the word, but an overwhelming fear of failure that could be directly attributed to him, without any mitigating circumstances.[40]

When McClellan proposed his original Urbanna move to the Rappahannock, he had planned to avoid a prolonged land campaign against supposedly overwhelming Confederate numbers posted at Manassas.[41] He correctly assumed that by flanking Gen. Joseph Johnston, he would bring him back on the run, forcing him to fight at a disadvantage.[42] But McClellan could not convince McClellan to go out and fight.

One chronic, but easily understood excuse for delay was his belief regarding the relative strengths of the two forces. He continually overestimated both the manpower requirements of his own forces as well as the probable strength of the Confederate armies. Allan Pinkerton, who gained fame as a private detective, was simply out of his league in the military intelligence domain. He was supplying McClellan with vastly overinflated Confederate numbers. Calculating enemy troop strength was clearly not one of Pinkerton's strengths, but his reports only fueled McClellan's despair.[43] McClellan would have preferred to go on drilling, but pressure was mounting for him to use his army. He procrastinated and postured but still did not move. Ominously, some of the behaviors he had exhibited in the West Virginia campaign were coming to the fore.[44]

There is no need to trace all of the ensuing dialogue between Lincoln, the Joint Committee on the Conduct of the War, and McClellan. However, two outcomes of the deliberations were growing concerns over his secretiveness and questions regarding his ability to command.[45]

Adding to his personal uncertainties, McClellan had created a mutual love affair between himself and the Army of the Potomac. The troops had become, in a manner of speaking, his Praetorian Guard.[46] From the start, the Army of the Potomac was primarily a volunteer force. For that matter, neither side was really prepared for the tactics, strategies, or even logistics needed for the size of the armies placed in the field.[47] In the process of shaping these raw recruits into soldiers, McClellan began to view them as a father might view his sons. It is interesting to note that commanders on both sides often referred to the troops as their "boys," but probably never in the sense that McClellan felt.[48] McClellan never completely and openly reconciled himself to the fact that the army, like himself, inherently faced risks.[49] Hence, he might well identify his own personal fears with legitimized concerns for the welfare of his troops. Unfortunately, the administration (read: civilians) was a constant irritant to his ways of thinking. Indeed, these problems began early in his career and persisted.

Starting with the Mexican-American War, McClellan had nothing but contempt for civilian interference in military matters.[50] This attitude undoubtedly contributed further to his anxieties, since he could always rationalize his difficulties as a product of the machinations of political hacks who were militarily incompetent.

All too soon he made enemies of men who earlier had been his friends, and some indeed became implacable foes. Secretary of War Edwin Stanton, for example, was among the first McClellan loyalists. But Stanton wanted war and this led to an inevitable split with a very hesitant McClellan.[51] To be fair, once in the field McClellan encountered significant intervention from Washington, which never did contribute to his peace of mind.[52] Nor did he have the skills necessary for compromise and adjustment. Above all, he never realized that if he started fighting and winning he probably would have reduced Washington's influence to an absolute minimum. Yet that is exactly what he did not do.

He precipitated much, if not most of his problems. He saw enemies (real or imagined) everywhere and was coming to view himself in the role of a glorious martyr, the penultimate victim.[53] While the tenor of his complaints certainly suggests a paranoid frame of reference, it is possible that cause and effect might well have been reversed here. By convincing himself that the actions of others were deliberately meant to destroy him, McClellan created a belief system in which the urgings of others could only be countered, and justified, by a need to act with extreme caution. On the other hand, he might well have deliberately persisted in actions that would place him in a dangerous situation, which he could and would justify as a creation not of his own doing. In the latter instance, since his problems were created by the actions of others, he was free of blame.[51] At some perverse and unconscious level he was encouraging others to do their worst to him. McClellan raised self-abuse to an art form.

His hesitancy in moving against Johnston further contributed to his woes. Not appreciating McClellan's genius, the Confederate forces undertook a unilateral action before the wavering McClellan moved. Johnston retreated from Manassas, taking a position on the Rappahannock near McClellan's proposed landing site at Urbanna. By withdrawing so precipitously, the Confederates had rendered the Urbanna movement useless. McClellan quickly revised his plans, probably fuming inwardly at Johnston's lack of cooperation. McClellan next decided on an alternative strategy, based on a landing at Fort Monroe, located at the tip of the Yorktown Peninsula. This subsequently proved to be the plan he would follow. On April 1, 1862, he finally embarked.[55] A troubled and uncertain McClellan had taken a first giant step, physically if not spiritually.

ON TO RICHMOND?

His next campaign moves became an ominous portent of things to come. After landing at Yorktown, McClellan quickly demonstrated he was not committed to an aggressive campaign, although his army's operations on the James Peninsula had been predicated on rapid movements.[56] What he did instead was to sit down in front of Yorktown and pout. Of course, he had to have reasons, and these were wonderfully beyond McClellan's power to rectify. First, the Warwick River was in the wrong place. Knowledge of terrain was never one of McClellan's strong points, and the misplacement of the Warwick on his maps became a heaven-sent basis for adopting the safer course of action, which translated immediately into a siege. In addition to a treacherous river, Maj. Gen. John Magruder had inexplicably erected defensive works across the entire Peninsula.[57] First Johnston had retreated, then the Warwick had moved, and now Magruder had built fortifications where McClellan expected none. Neither God nor man was willing to help him.

His strategic script had been undermined. Whatever one's loyalties, the defensive works were certainly not a tactical stroke of genius upon the part of the Confederates. Since the original script did not call for these complications, McClellan bowed to the fates and sat down in front of Yorktown. At least he did not retreat back to Washington, as the army had in the first Manassas fiasco.

Soon, however, other problems arose. The political infighting that had begun in Washington now haunted a despairing McClellan watching his options change almost daily at Yorktown. Washington began to fill the action void created by McClellan's procrastination. The withdrawal of Maj. Gen. Irvin McDowell's I Corps came as a shock as McDowell had originally been slated to reinforce him with some thirty-five thousand men.

The problem was that McClellan had never made it clear to President Lincoln just how Washington would be protected when McDowell left. Putting it even more bluntly, McClellan never did deal fairly with Washington as to the number of troops actually available to defend the city. He had tried to convey the idea that he had left more than seventy thousand troops to guard the capital, but the actual count was less than thirty thousand.[58] When Lincoln became aware of this discrepancy in numbers he was understandably upset. This contributed to further erosion of the administration's confidence in McClellan.[59]

Another source of conflict with Washington was the magnitude of the forces committed to the Peninsula. Where Washington counted 108,000 as sent or *en route*, McClellan came up with eighty-five thousand. Unlike Washington, McClellan was only counting those who were present for duty. Though his counting procedure was legitimate, McClellan's failure to explain to Washington the basis for the difference cost him even more in terms of what little credibility he had left.[60]

It can be argued that while McClellan may have devoutly accepted Allan Pinkerton's estimates of overwhelming numbers of Confederates, playing the numbers game with his own administration was an act of incredible arro-

gance, duplicity, or both. In the course of his attempts to clarify matters, Mc-
Clellan failed to convince the administration that McDowell's corps was
needed more urgently at Richmond. Unfortunately, Brig. Gen. James Wads-
worth and others were also contributing to panic in the capital.[61] The result
was that McDowell stayed put and, since the size of McClellan's army did not
increase, his uncertainties blossomed.

On the other hand, once McClellan began laying siege to Yorktown, he
could convince himself that he was not only taking action, it was the appropriate action. After all, not only were the tactics for siege warfare well established, he also thought he could regain control of the situation. Tempo and
movement would be at his direction, for the besieger generally called the
shots. At least, that was what he hoped would happen. But was laying siege the
only option he had?

In McClellan's mind there was never any doubt. The best evidence, in fact,
is that news about the withholding of McDowell's corps actually followed *after*
the announcement of his decision to lay siege.[62] The news about McDowell
simply solidified his strategy. All subsequent complaints about what a difference McDowell would have made were basically an exercise in self-justifying
nonsense. McClellan even made use of a letter in his memoirs from Maj.
Gen. Erasmus Keyes to Sen. Ira Harris supporting his plan to lay siege to Yorktown. The content of the letter, as one might suspect, pretty much described
his own thinking.[63] In truth, the Confederates under Magruder were outnumbered at least three to one and hoping that McClellan would not force the issue.[64] Even Hassler, who is sympathetic to McClellan, concedes that had he
attacked Yorktown directly he would have taken the position.[65]

Hassler further argues that if McDowell had been used as scheduled, the resulting sequence of events would have changed. Specifically, Yorktown would
have been evacuated, the battle at Williamsburg never fought, and the Confederates would not have had forty-five days to concentrate.[66] However, it is
equally true that if McClellan had attacked immediately without McDowell,
the general outcome would have been the same—which probably would have
been as much of a shock to McClellan as to the Confederates. For that matter,
in addition to the loss of McDowell, the navy was being difficult, further ham-
pering possibilities for maneuvering.[67]

One might also wonder how much of McClellan's hesitation was due to a
personal sense of pique. Although McDowell himself never came, troops from
his command were eventually sent.[68] However, McClellan's continuing lam-
entations over the loss of McDowell in an effort to justify the siege of Yorktown were in part pure fantasy. Even if McDowell's corps had been sent on
schedule, the first contingents were not due for ten days to two weeks at best.
Furthermore, Lincoln insisted that McDowell had to cover Washington.[69]

If McDowell had arrived on time, he might well have had to contend with the rather considerable remaining Confederate forces not facing McClellan at Yorktown. He could well have been beaten on the other side of the York, which would have been a military disaster.[70] There is absolutely no evidence that McClellan would have attacked Yorktown to relieve pressure on Mc-Dowell, or transferred his base of operations to allow McDowell to form on him. If McDowell had bypassed Gloucester Point and joined McClellan directly at Yorktown, he most likely would have remained dormant with the rest of McClellan's army.

Meanwhile as siege operations continued, McClellan saw himself more and more as a victim of circumstances, a "pawn" to use Richard De Charms's term.[71] In fact, there was never a time that he believed the Peninsula campaign was entirely up to him. He expressed this overwhelming fatalism in a conversation with Maj. Gen. Ambrose Burnside.[72] Unfortunately for McClellan, Burnside's military capabilities were few, making him a less-than-desirable confidant. McClellan by this time had convinced himself that he was either losing or had lost control of the campaign and could only react as best he could to externally driven events. Looking to the future, uncertainties would increase as he moved toward Richmond.

As the siege dragged on, McClellan's never-ending cries for reinforcements became the most aggressive part of his campaign. Pinkerton continued to supply mythical Confederate numbers and McClellan continued to embrace them with all the fervor of a true believer.[73] The Confederate defensive posture at Yorktown was hardly consonant with supposed numerical superiority, but this never-doubted belief of being badly outnumbered supported McClellan's hesitation about attacking Yorktown.[74] On the other hand, Magruder, by adopting a defensive posture, fit in nicely with McClellan's strategy for coping with his fantasies and fears.

But if McClellan was prepared to sit and wait, Lincoln early on saw something else. In a letter to McClellan dated April 6, he concluded with the ominous and prophetic statement: "I think you had better break the enemy's line from Yorktown to Warwick River at once. They will probably use time as advantageously as you can."[75] As a matter of fact, Lincoln was becoming very impatient. In a subsequent letter dated April 9, he complained that he could not fathom McClellan's reports on his own forces, which he suggested were underestimated. More to the point, he told McClellan in rather simple and direct terms that he would find enemy and entrenchments everywhere. He was down there to fight.

In fairness to McClellan, the army arrayed in front of the Confederate entrenchments at Yorktown in no way resembled the armed mob that had fought at Bull Run. The organization and training of the Army of the Potomac may well have been his greatest contribution to the Union effort, but Lincoln was telling him that it was time to use that army.[76] What could not be subsequently ignored was that while McClellan sat and whined, Robert E. Lee turned Maj. Gen. Thomas "Stonewall" Jackson loose in the Shenandoah Valley with consequences that McClellan, writing twenty years later, still could not comprehend. McClellan acknowledged it as a distraction but never acted upon it.[77]

One of the greatest ironies of the Yorktown siege is that Brig. Gen. William "Baldy" Smith, an aggressive division commander under Maj. Gen. Erasmus Keyes, launched a local assault on his own authority that managed to develop a lodgment in the Confederate lines.[78] Smith's success might have suggested something else to McClellan, but McClellan was now and forever committed to his policy of siege. He would sit before Yorktown till hell froze over.

In his memoirs, McClellan continued to rationalize his decision, arguing that no one "at that time" thought a siege could be avoided. Yet, nowhere in his own writings or reports does he ever convey the idea that he gave serious consideration to anything else.[79] Lincoln had put his finger precisely on the problem. Delay was McClellan's undoing and, ironically, the more he delayed, the more directives from Washington changed his plans. As night follows day, this in turn led to a further fueling of McClellan's fears and suspicions.

The Confederates, meanwhile, did not hesitate to give McClellan additional opportunities to display his talents for indecision. Following General Johnston's orders, the badly outnumbered Magruder abandoned Yorktown on May 4 and retreated up the Peninsula to Williamsburg. The startled McClellan was not even organized for a pursuit. With Magruder gone, McClellan had no choice but to move.[80]

Even with Magruder's unexpected departure, McClellan was in a relatively good position. With his base of operations at White House, McClellan could eventually use the railroad to bring heavy siege guns down and pound the Confederacy into submission at Richmond. The outcome, in spite of McClellan, would be certain. He would simply move forward until he ran into Richmond and the Confederate army. Better yet, the Confederate commander, Gen. Joseph Johnston, was preparing to accommodate him.[81] This was the same Johnston who would later execute his famous *pas de deux* with Maj. Gen. William Tecumseh Sherman, which probably had its origins around Richmond.

And yet, by withdrawing, Johnston was creating a very perplexing psychological dilemma for McClellan. With Magruder's departure, McClellan was simultaneously presented both risks and opportunities. It would be nice if he could follow Johnston at a safe distance and lay siege to Richmond. But if the Confederates sought not merely to fall back but to contest the withdrawal every step of the way, his chances for defeat would be increased. Be that as it may, with Johnston retreating, McClellan could not stand still.

As expected, he initially chose the safest course. By following the retreating Johnston with his main force, McClellan was, at least in his own mind, minimizing the risks. A fight at Williamsburg came to nothing.[82] After this minor skirmish, McClellan helped the Confederates get across the Chickahominy by following them at a conveniently safe distance.

As McClellan launched his pursuit (to use the term loosely), he began to consider other alternatives. He could probably depend on Johnston to fall back without contesting the issue, but what if he decided to make a stand? Direct pursuit would have involved going north of the Chickahominy around White Oak Swamp. However, another plan began boiling up in McClellan's mind. It consisted of crossing south of the Chickahominy and using the James River as a supply base.[83] Unlike the first plan, which would have kept pressure on Johnston, the latter did anything but that.

McClellan offers some revealing insights in trying to explain the James plan, which meant giving up the line of the York River and the railroad. Keeping in mind that the move to the James most appealed to him, his subsequent actions (and inertia) become more meaningful. According to McClellan, it would give him complete control of the movement of both armies. He would lead and the Confederates would have to follow.[84] It appears that he had learned nothing during the campaign to date.

How he could believe that Johnston, who was seeking the sanctuary of Richmond, would immediately turn to follow a foe moving away from him is an example of mind over matter. Actually, McClellan pursued neither option completely for a while, pushing only part of his army south across the Chickahominy River at Bottom's Bridge.[85] Still, at some primitive level of consciousness, he was beginning that shift to the south.

A RISKY PROPOSITION

McClellan acknowledged from the beginning that crossing the Chickahominy and using the James to move supplies would be very risky because it would have to be accomplished in the face of an enemy supposedly double his numbers.[86] Given his own belief that the plan was inherently dangerous, it still had one overwhelming and marvelously redeeming virtue: He could (and would) assign the blame for failure elsewhere. It simply was against his nature to employ such a high-risk option unless he could prove to himself with all certainty that he had been driven to it by the actions of others. The trick would be to arrange events in his own mind so that it appeared he was being forced to adopt the movement to the James River—which is precisely what he did.

As he would at Antietam, McClellan avoided the direct onset of uncertain conflict as long as possible. While Johnston, now and later, never offered evidence of a singularly combative nature, a McClellan embedded in his own psychological timidity would never see his foe as possessing this same trait. McClellan, however, had one minor problem to overcome: In light of the Confederate retreat, he could not easily justify completing the James option, which meant breaking off direct pursuit.

On May 18, Secretary Stanton further upset McClellan's world by ordering McDowell's forces to move south by land.[87] McDowell would now supposedly reach McClellan within a week. With McDowell on the move, the high- (or low-)risk move to the James had to be put aside at least for the moment since McClellan could not very well explain even to himself how he could move away from the very reinforcements for which he had been screaming. He was, however, leaving himself in a vulnerable position: Part of his forces were south of the river, while those still north of it had to remain there awaiting McDowell. By maintaining his position astride the Chickahominy he clearly recognized he was adopting a position of increasing risk, for which he, of course, was not responsible. As he put it so revealingly in his own words: "I was not responsible for the fact I was obliged to select a faulty and dangerous plan as the least objectionable of those from which I would chose."[88]

McCLELLAN AND THE ONSET OF UNCERTAINTIES

To make things even better for McClellan's sense of martyrdom, McDowell's move south was stopped short on May 24 by Jackson's raid down the Shenandoah Valley.[89] Lee, though, had seen enough of McClellan.[90]

The Chickahominy position was a strategic monstrosity that in principle committed McClellan to two mutually incompatible objectives. Sitting there astride the Chickahominy, his right flank was extended to meet McDowell's forces, while his left now supposedly represented the major threat to Richmond. The forces north of the river had to remain in place to receive the expected reinforcements; those to the south were committed, at least in theory, to offensive operations. He did, meanwhile, manage to fight successfully north of the Chickahominy at Hanover Court House on May 27.[91] The attack cleared away an immediate threat to his right flank and also severed direct connections between Lee and Jackson. McClellan later spent a lot of time musing over what would have happened if McDowell had advanced earlier, but he was always willing to see faults in others if not himself.[92]

By adopting a policy of continuous withdrawal, Johnston would have seemed to be more than willing to accommodate McClellan's inane tactical stance by laying the groundwork for a siege. But Johnston was also coming under tremendous pressure to do something. The one bright spot in the campaign, Jackson's move north, had been ordered by Lee. A goaded Johnston finally struck at the Union forces south of the Chickahominy on May 31, and was thrown back. Actually, it was a confused, mismanaged affair on both sides. Edwin Sumner, the one active force in Union generalship, saved the day. He may not have been the most intellectually astute of commanders, but he could be counted on to fight. Called variously the Battle of Seven Pines or Fair Oaks, the tactical blunderings resulted in the loss of six thousand Confederate and five thousand Union soldiers.[93]

Worse yet, from the Union's viewpoint, Johnston went down and Lee took over. If Johnston had not been wounded at Fair Oaks, the Confederates might have forced McClellan to go on in spite of himself. Through sheer inertia and Johnston, McClellan eventually might have arrived at Richmond. Unfortunately for McClellan, Lee had no intention of withdrawing. Instead, he began gathering for a strike at McClellan's weakened right flank. At the beginning of the Seven Days, McClellan had about 105,000 men facing Richmond, to Lee's barely eighty thousand, including Jackson's force.[94]

The battle had one ominous outcome, however; it brought McClellan to a halt. Upset because the peaceful withdrawal had ended, he could no longer assume Richmond would cooperate. But he could explain why he did not follow up the Confederate repulse. Writing later, he put forth the preposterous idea that since he could not have united his wings and overtaken the retreating Confederates before they reached Richmond, he did not attempt to actively pursue them.[95] The fact that the Confederates had to cope with the same weather conditions seems to have escaped the hesitant McClellan.

The Confederates were in general retreat, but nothing could force McClellan to change his plans. The rebels would have had to cooperate right up to the gates of Richmond before rendering the James move meaningless. The battle further demonstrated that McClellan would react first to his own fears rather than the necessities of the situation. He could not adjust the script to include mauling the Confederates outside of Richmond or arriving on their heels.[96]

McClellan, it might be added, was well aware of the risks inherent in his position. For one, a dispatch from Stanton apprised McClellan that Jackson was probably returning south on his right flank.[97] As June progressed, he slowly began to shift troops south of the river, creating a greater potential for the move to the James. The process began in spite of the fact that he would never get McDowell's corps in its entirety. Jackson's move had seen to that. Nevertheless, he had received reinforcements that more than exceeded the number of troops withheld.[98]

Always sensitive about his lines of communication, McClellan was dealt a rude blow earlier when, acting on Lee's orders, Stuart began his famous ride around the Union army on June 12.[99] Not only did Lee gain a good idea of the Army of the Potomac's dispositions, the ride also unnerved McClellan, who up until then had been exuding at least verbal optimism over his prospects. Stuart's foray made the Union commander quite apprehensive and, true to form, McClellan shuddered and sat still.

McClellan finally twitched his military nerves on June 25 and prepared once more to start some kind of movement toward Richmond.[100] Now, however, he received further word from Stanton reaffirming that Jackson was still a potentially serious threat to his right flank.[101] The news made him angry. With his right flank already weakened by withdrawals, those damn Washington bureaucrats were not only warning him about Jackson, they still wanted him to advance on Richmond. Mounting psychological pressures began their final destruction of McClellan as a general in this campaign.

Responding to his inner turmoil, he began by announcing his anticipated crucifixion. Firing off a letter to Stanton later in the evening on the Twenty-fifth, he fixed the blame for any forthcoming disaster to the Army of the Potomac on everyone but himself. McClellan was as prepared as any martyr ever was: "I will do all that a general can do with the splendid army I have the honor to command, and, if it is destroyed by overwhelming numbers, can at least die with it and share its fate."[102]

There is always the interesting speculation of what might have happened if McClellan had gone down with Johnston at Fair Oaks. However, no charitable Confederate supplied the necessary ordnance. A more aggressive and reasonably competent Union general might have ended Lee's career quite early, or at least tarnished the forthcoming aura of invincibility. There were a few capable of that in the Army of the Potomac.

At no time during the Peninsular campaign did McClellan reveal more accurately his state of mind. Incredibly, the letter was written *before* Lee had even begun his major assault on McClellan's right flank. His fate was Washington's doing, and the underlying fears emerged full-blown. He was preparing for a disaster that had not yet occurred and for which he was not to blame when it finally did. McClellan was setting the record straight before any record was established. Still, there was a way out. He might be able to kill two birds with one stone: by heading south, he could avoid defeat and execute the movement dearest to his heart.

In fact, as early as June 18, he had begun significant and obvious preparations for the James contingency; for one, he had provisions sent up the James.[103] However, by abandoning the York Railroad he was actually giving up much of his siege artillery, which could not be moved on the regular roads.[104]

He would endure in the face of impossible odds created by others, including some who were not Confederates. What he still lacked was the obvious excuse to begin the move. Lee would provide it to him the next day, but McClellan's fall from grace began on the evening of June 25, the day he sent the letter to Stanton.

TWO DIVERGENT STRATEGIES

Earlier that day he had opened up with his artillery all along the line and sent Maj. Gen. Samuel Heintzelman out on the Williamsburg Road south of the Chickahominy, essentially to straighten his lines. A battle ensued with Maj. Gen. Benjamin Huger and the Confederates at Oak Grove, resulting in more casualties but little else. Johnston, under pressure, had precipitated the battle.[105] This clash, considered the beginning of the Seven Days' battles, still did not provide a perfect excuse for the James move, except in McClellan's mind. Better news came the next day.

On June 26, Lee struck McClellan's right flank with two-thirds of his army at Mechanicsville, north of the Chickahominy. Lee basically was assaulting thirty thousand Union troops while seventy-five thousand remained south of the Chickahominy.[106] But things did not go all that well for Lee. Adding to McClellan's miseries, while Brig. Gen. Fitz-John Porter's advance guard was driven out of Mechanicsville, his main force was strongly posted farther east along a tributary of the Chickahominy called Beaver Creek. Porter repulsed the initial Confederate attacks with heavy losses. Major General A. P. Hill had moved too soon and Jackson had not moved at all.[107]

In one sense, Lee was adopting McClellan's original plan for McDowell by using Jackson to play the role of the hammer on Hill's anvil. Simultaneously, Magruder began a reenactment of his Yorktown theater for the benefit of the Union forces south of the Chickahominy.[108] Lee expected a tough fight, not knowing McClellan had long since committed himself to a shift to the James. Ironically, what Lee really did was give McClellan the final excuse he needed. He now could evacuate the line of the Chickahominy and, in the face of those overwhelming odds, shed Lee.[109]

Even if the southward move resulted in defeat, McClellan was blameless. He would lose where he was, that was for sure. He was in no frame of mind to slug it out with Lee on this battlefield. But nothing in life is ever all that simple. To a McClellan intent on withdrawing there was a major problem. How could he run while Porter was holding firm?

In fact, here was a golden opportunity for anyone *but* McClellan. Sending additional reinforcements to Porter and launching a general assault south of the Chickahominy would have put Lee in a quandary: McClellan was actually closer to Richmond, and with many more troops. Lee, on the other hand, was fighting with his army divided and thus was vulnerable to anyone willing to knock heads.[110]

Yet, such a response at this point was not in McClellan—and perhaps never would have been. In support of the Union commander's hesitation to act, Hassler argues that even if McClellan had moved south of the river, Magruder's field works would have held him up. He also correctly points out that Magruder's playacting fooled other Union generals.[111] This, however, is a classic example of begging the question. A forward movement south of the river would have forced Lee to reconsider his strategy. Had McClellan moved quickly enough, Lee would have found himself cut off from Richmond. Fortunately for McClellan's anxieties, he had support among some of his own staff.

It was Yorktown redux: McClellan once again sought and found timidity on the part of others to justify his own. All McClellan wanted now was for Porter to buy him some time for the James move.[112] Even after Lee's initial attack had been stopped, Porter, acting on McClellan's orders, retreated eastward to Gaines's Mill—or more precisely, Boatswain's Swamp, which is east of Gaines's Mill.[113] For all McClellan knew, Porter might stop Lee—or even worse, take the offensive, which would really undo his plan.

Porter dug in on a hill fronted by a boggy stream. It was a natural fortress. Moreover, his units were still intact and full of fight, which the Confederates soon discovered to their sorrow and horror. Boatswain's Swamp was a death trap awaiting Lee's army. However, Porter's withdrawal was another Union strategic mistake: it uncovered Mechanicsville Bridge, which meant Lee's wings were no longer isolated.[114] McClellan, never considering any other options, continued to prepare for his move south.[115]

Yet, there still had to be some hesitation on McClellan's part. Porter's situation did not provide the immediate and complete justification required for the proposed shift. That damn fool was providing a lot of evidence that fighting Lee did not necessarily lead to only one outcome. Twisting in his own psychological wind, McClellan continued to mutter intermittently about reinforcing Porter, telling his commanders he would take advantage of Lee's turning movement. Had he been psychologically able, one obvious move would have been to refuse (bend) Porter's flank and strike south of the Chickahominy. He could have fed reinforcements to Porter in sufficient numbers to maintain a defensive stance, but eventually all he did was send Brig. Gen. Henry Slocum's division in piecemeal, along with two brigades from Sumner's corps. The reinforcements were inadequate, really only a sop to Porter, who was fighting for his life.[116] Like Rich Mountain and later at Antietam, others had to deal with the decisions of a McClellan concerned only with McClellan.

Worse yet, those perverse fates were still tormenting him. As June 27 wore on, Jackson had still not arrived and Porter was inflicting terrible losses. Lee kept sending units to take Porter, and just as regularly they came streaming back, considerably reduced in numbers. Confederate casualties mounted significantly as the day wore on, but Jackson eventually came up and a final desperate charge by the Confederates won the day. Nevertheless, it had been a near thing for Lee.[117]

Throughout that time, McClellan did nothing but wait for Porter to collapse. However, with Porter finally defeated, McClellan could continue with his plans. Continuing the fight along the Chickahominy might have provided someone else with a more reasonable alternative to the high-risk operation McClellan was contemplating.[118] Not "Little Mac," though; all that mattered to him was avoiding the responsibility for a defeat not of his own contriving. The James River thus became the Promised Land.

His panicked state of mind is clearly shown by the fact he had moved most of his heavy guns and wagons south across the river during the night of the Twenty-sixth.[119] He was not going to leave Porter much of an opportunity the next day.[120] It all could have ended differently, but as Porter finally retreated across the river, McClellan prepared to play the role of victim.[121] What followed is the best available evidence of McClellan's complete demoralization.[122]

THE BEGINNING OF THE END

The strain of the three days had swelled McClellan's anxieties to a level where he engaged in behavior that was dangerously close to treason. The letter of June 25 had been bad enough, but shortly after midnight, on the morning of June 28, McClellan lost his head completely. He sent an incredible message to Stanton blaming him and the president for his predicament.[123] While it was true that the right flank was gone courtesy of his own vacillation, McClellan was no hairsplitter. He simply dissociated himself from any blame in his own mind and adopted a high-risk move that would make him a winner if it succeeded, and others losers if it failed. Fortunately for McClellan, the offending lines were removed before Stanton saw them. Lee could not take sole credit for defeating the Army of the Potomac in this campaign; McClellan had ably assisted him. In the end, McClellan chose not to fight Lee but to instead save his ego.

Having abandoned the north side of the Chickahominy, McClellan headed determinedly south toward the James. After a day's hesitation trying to find a McClellan who was actually retreating in a direction quite different from that which a sane general might take, Lee set out to destroy him somewhere between the Chickahominy and White Oak Swamp.[124] On June 29, Lee attempted to pin the Union army and McClellan against White Oak Swamp. There was a fight at Savage Station, but Jackson again did not cooperate and McClellan escaped.[125] Jackson proved to be a trying man for Lee during the Seven Days, but Chancellorsville would more than repay the trust the rebel commander had in him. The next day, June 30, Lee struck again at Glendale.

This was to have been Lee's decisive stroke during the retreat—a three-pronged attack designed to smash McClellan—but it failed. The battle demonstrated that from the very beginning of the Seven Days it was McClellan and not his army that was whipped. In spite of (or because of) the fact McClellan was not even on the field, the Union forces held.[126] Savage Station and, even more likely, Glendale were the major opportunities Lee had to make good on to achieve his goal of destroying the Army of the Potomac.

Ironically, Maj. Edward Porter Alexander, the Confederate gunner of Gettysburg fame, thought that Confederate mistakes at Glendale could and would have cost them dearly if the Union forces had taken advantage of them.[127] He was right; McClellan was a beaten man, but his army was giving as good as it got. At this point, McClellan was single-mindedly trying to carry out his retreat to the James as quickly as possible. He probably never forgave Lee for bothering him.

In a perverse sense, he not only gloried in an undertaking that aided his psychological needs, but also in his own mind enhanced his military reputation. It is an open question, though, how much his military abilities would have availed him during the retreat if the Army of the Potomac had not been a cohesive force ready to engage in combat. As matters stood, however, McClellan arrived at Malvern Hill with a relatively intact army and trains, elated over the success of his plan.[128]

Still, McClellan had exhibited some rather curious behaviors during this move. During the early part of the retreat he spent most of his time at the rear of the army organizing traffic. Then, at Glendale, which was the most critical of Lee's attacks, he rode off to the James and boarded the gunboat *Galena*. He literally left no one in charge. At Malvern Hill he did not appear on the field until dark. Not without cause, Stephen Sears raises the question of fear for his own personal safety.[129]

This leads to another interesting interpretation of events. In support of Sears's argument, the gunboat *Galena* and the James indeed represent personal safety. However, the more likely explanation is that they represented psychological closure, the culmination of his James strategy. Going aboard the gunboat meant he had arrived. At a rather primitive and deep level of thought, perhaps having identified himself with the army, he equated his safe arrival with theirs. In his own mind he had succeeded; in a somewhat distorted sense he had.

Given the willingness of his army to fight and the combativeness of other commanders in that army, McClellan, by his flight to the gunboat, may very well have also been seeking to remove any possibilities of having to take the offensive. Counterattacks, especially successful ones, would have necessarily threatened the psychological structure upon which his whole James strategy rested.

Meanwhile, a rather frustrated Lee came up with his army to face those same Union forces now arrayed on Malvern Hill. From his perspective, total victory had been just beyond reach ever since he had launched his campaign. Short of temper and fatigued, he decided that this was his last chance to crush McClellan, who after all had done nothing but retreat when attacked.[130] Unfortunately for Lee, Malvern Hill was a situation in which neither he nor McClellan had any maneuverability. All McClellan had to do was let Lee come straight at him. To help the Union cause, Fitz-John Porter was in tactical command.[131] Porter would and could fight; the Army of Northern Virginia would and could attest to that.

The Confederate attack was a classic example of selective perception, mismanagement, and plain incompetence. The Union artillery was lined up hub to hub on the 150-foot-high undulating plateau with four divisions of infantry waiting in line.[132] The solidity of the Union position was obvious to everyone, but Lee might well have presumed McClellan would accommodate him one more time. Unfortunately, there was no other place for McClellan to go. His back was to a river, and he was finally where he had wanted to go in the first place. Malvern Hill had to be held, by Porter if not by him.

The original Confederate plan was to first soften up the Union forces with artillery. The attempt was a disaster. The Confederate batteries were brought up piecemeal and systematically demolished by the Union guns.[133] This scenario was in many ways a portent of things to come: the dominance of Union artillery was never seriously challenged throughout the war.

However, Lee earlier had ordered that if the shelling appeared to be successful, Brig. Gen. Lewis Armistead's men on the right flank would begin the infantry assault, signaling a general attack all along the line. Seeing his artillery tactics thwarted, Lee told Longstreet he was prepared to give up the fight. Unfortunately for the rebels, no notice was sent to the other generals, particularly Magruder.[134] The disaster began unfolding when a late-arriving Magruder found Armistead driving back some Union sharpshooters who had been pestering his troops. After a hurried and somewhat intemperate set of observations, Magruder decided that an advance could be made. The rest of the Confederate forces followed the assault, beginning on the Confederate right flank. After all, a previous chit from Lee to Magruder, never canceled, had urged this action. A second message had confirmed it.[135]

From the beginning of the campaign Lee had given his field commanders considerable latitude. While mistakes had been made, McClellan's failings had more than compensated for any errors in Lee's command. This time it was different: all McClellan (or rather Porter) had to do was sit still and shoot. Southern valor would not make good on Lee's orders this day. The Confederate assault was sheer folly; Maj. Gen. Daniel Harvey Hill, another of Lee's division commanders, called it mass murder, not war.[136] The Confederates proved their courage with fifty-five hundred casualties in a fight that basically resembled a shooting gallery. Freeman, perhaps fretting over the possibility that the Union infantry could be a formidable foe when well led, suggested that the artillery almost exclusively caused the casualties.[137] Charge after charge only increased the casualties until dusk ended the carnage. The Seven Days' campaign was over, with twenty thousand Confederate and sixteen thousand Union casualties, including the missing.[138]

A VICTORY THROWN AWAY

As one might expect, McClellan withdrew his army from the field, falling back to Harrison's Landing. It is true that both military organizations had been battered, but the grim irony of Malvern Hill was that McClellan had reached the line of the James and seen the Confederate army badly hurt in the bargain. He could have delivered the obvious counterstroke and renewed the fighting on his terms.[139] Yet, he refused to strike when his own commanders urged him to attack.[140]

It is easy to see why McClellan balked: for all his posturing, there never really was any idea of renewing the offensive once he reached the James. From start to finish the withdrawal was not the start of a new campaign. If it was, he should have counterattacked Lee after the repulse at Malvern Hill. In a revealing letter to Lincoln dated July 4, he argued and worried about the *defensive* weaknesses of his position. There was no talk of rest and resuming the offensive. He was more concerned about saving what he could of his army if the Confederates attacked him.[141] McClellan was incapable of creating any further fantasies about an offensive campaign against Richmond. Having gotten to the river, he conveniently forgot why he wanted to get there in the first place.

McClellan never did see the Army of the Potomac as beaten, which was a self-serving statement in many ways. Critical to his psychological stability was the argument that the move to the James was basically his decision; the army's retrograde motion was self-determined. He was not driven; rather, he went.[142] He was absolutely correct in this respect. He was always in the position of warding off Lee's attempts to stop him from achieving the line of the James. In addition, he was accurate in his argument that a Union presence on the James would force the Confederates to commit to that front.[143] It is equally true that he was more concerned about his enemies and possible threats to himself. Lee eventually masked his lines and moved elsewhere.

McClellan had his chances, and he would have more of them at Antietam. But he invariably threw away every chance for success because his fragile ego paralyzed him with the threat of failure. At some point in each campaign or battle there came that moment when a critical decision was needed. And when the moment arose—that time for a promising yet risky decision-making action—McClellan would blink. It might have turned out differently had he been able to fight the war alone. But there were always enemies—real and imagined, on both the Union and Confederate sides—and he would be damned if he would allow them to see him lose. Paradoxically, he always contributed much less to gaining a victory than he did to avoiding defeat.

CHAPTER FOUR

LEE AT GETTYSBURG: THE FAILURE OF SUCCESS

Too bad. *Too bad.* O too bad.

P ROBABLY NO SINGLE ACTION during the Civil War has received more attention than Pickett's Charge, the culmination of the three days of vicious conflict at Gettysburg. On July 3, 1863, Gen. Robert E. Lee, commanding the Army of Northern Virginia, delivered what was to be his coup de main, a massive and decisive stroke at the center of what he presumed to be a battered and stunned Union army atop Cemetery Ridge. The Army of Northern Virginia would demonstrate once more to hesitant foreign powers, and inevitably to the Army of the Potomac, that its aura of invincibility was still intact.

Incredibly, less than an hour later, after having been preceded by a fierce artillery barrage, the massed infantry assault collapsed in the face of rifle and cannon fire from determined Union troops. The shattered remnants came flooding back past a stunned and anguished Lee. The once inconceivable had become a reality: Lee's vaunted infantry had been stopped dead in their tracks.

The scene could have been taken from a Greek tragedy: How could the Fates have so conspired against Lee? It was more than a defeat. Indeed, considered in any number of political and military dimensions, this repulse should have conveyed an inescapable conclusion to both Confederate leaders and survivors: The South could not win the war on its own, although the North conceivably might still lose it.[1] Still, the killing would go on for almost two more years.

To many historians, Gettysburg represents perhaps the single most critical passage of arms in which a Confederate victory might possibly have meant an

73

end to Northern hopes for a successful resolution of the conflict. The unknown advancing Confederate lieutenant who cried out, "Home, home, boys! Remember home is over beyond those hills,"[2] may figuratively have been speaking the truth. What if shattered Union forces were forced to retreat from the scene of yet another military debacle, with Maj. Gen. George G. Meade, the third commander in as many campaigns, reporting heavy losses and another failure? First there had been Fredericksburg, then Chancellorsville, and now some small town in Pennsylvania. When would it end? Perhaps more importantly, *how* would it end? Unfortunately for the South, as the Confederate forces fell back from Ziegler's Grove atop Cemetery Ridge, the last opportunity for a Southern-dictated political or military settlement probably vanished.

Since that tragic moment, many military historians have tried to explain away the possibility that the successful and saintly Lee had erred, sacrificing his army in a suicidal and ill-fated attack. Yet, how does one justify a frontal assault against a waiting and veteran foe? It is hard to believe that this was the decision of a general who had suffered fifty-five hundred casualties a year earlier in a similar ill-advised move against Federal troops dug in on Malvern Hill below Richmond. For that matter, six months later he shot to pieces a Union army that lost almost thirteen thousand men when Maj. Gen. Ambrose Burnside returned the favor at Fredericksburg. The tactics were the same in both instances, although the strategic reasons differed.

After two years of experience with massed firepower, both sides were fully aware of the enormous risks attendant upon a headlong charge against troops holding established positions. Malvern Hill and Fredericksburg might well have given Lee pause, but the warnings went unheeded. Indeed, it is possible to conjecture that these battles actually contributed to Lee's disastrous choice of tactics on the third day at Gettysburg. Therefore the question becomes: How could two bloody repulses contribute to a third?

Malvern Hill, as we have seen, was the last battle in Lee's campaign to drive Maj. Gen. George Brinton McClellan's Army of the Potomac away from Richmond. Relentlessly attacking a retreating Union army, Lee came up to find it holding Malvern Hill, a plateau overlooking the James River. He recognized from the outset that he was facing dug-in Union troops with heavy artillery support. However, he also believed that the enemy had been sufficiently demoralized that one more attack would finish the job.

As he would demonstrate repeatedly during the war, especially during the first two years, Lee did not back away from visions of total victory. But the Union troops fought well at Malvern Hill, and the Confederates were forced to retire after suffering ghastly losses in the span of a few hours. Confederate planning and tactics were flawed from the start, but in the end Lee's campaign objectives were not hindered one whit. He was sorry about the casualties, but McClellan was still pinned against the James and not going anywhere.[3]

PRELUDE TO A DISASTER

Unfortunately for the Union armies, especially the Army of the Potomac, Lincoln was using a trial-and-error procedure in his search for aggressive commanders. The early results were a sequence of bad choices for command that thoroughly tried the fortitude of a more deserving Army of the Potomac. General Burnside's selection was another such egregious error. Burnside managed to exceed the magnitude of Lee's fiasco at Malvern Hill by ordering his forces to cross a river and attack Lee's entrenched infantry, posted behind a stone wall along the base of Marye's Heights. In a series of near-suicidal assaults, the Army of the Potomac shattered itself without any gain whatsoever.[4] It was probably the only time during the war that Burnside managed to accomplish anything of significance, good or bad.

Given Lee's presence at those two monumental blunders, an objective observer would surely have concluded that he would not order his men to execute a battle plan which prior experiences must have shown him would have very little or, even more likely, no chance of success. Rather than accept this dissonant evaluation of Lee's military acumen, a number of pro-Southern historians have since argued that Lee would have succeeded but for the failure of several subordinates, most particularly two of his corps commanders, Lt. Gen. James Longstreet commanding I Corps, and Lt. Gen. Richard Ewell commanding II Corps.[5] It thus was not an inept Union army that defeated Lee, but the very men he trusted.

Lee's problems actually emerged long before Gettysburg. One critical element was the lack of staff planning, most easily observed in the tactical decisions organizing Pickett's Charge. While the specific details will be presented later, it is not always appreciated that after Stonewall Jackson's death at Chancellorsville, Lee completely reorganized his army. He created a third corps, keeping Longstreet in command of I Corps, and assigning the other two to Ewell and A. P. Hill respectively. Neither was to distinguish himself at Gettysburg. There were similar significant command changes at the brigade and regimental levels. He essentially had a new command structure, with the exception of Longstreet.[6]

The result was that during the first two days at Gettysburg the Army of Northern Virginia had done little more than engage in a series of disjointed attacks. The command structure, to use the term loosely, was at times practically nonexistent. In fact, nearly all of Lee's trusted subordinates could have been charged with some leadership failure. Subsequently, however, blame came to rest specifically on Longstreet and Ewell. But if these officers were to be criticized for the problems of the first two days, the Confederate attack on the third day was clearly Lee's own doing. Whatever blame might be leveled on Confederate leadership for actions taken that day belongs primarily to Lee.

The ensuing criticism really amounted to maintaining the almost mystical belief in Lee's invincibility, at the cost of excoriating Longstreet and Ewell. To accomplish this, revisionists have had to argue that the final assault might not have been necessary if Lee's subordinates had acted properly. That is, if Ewell had kept on going the evening of the first day there would not have been any Yankees left dug in on Culp's Hill or Cemetery Ridge. Ewell wavered, however, and the Yankees dug in, dashing any hopes Lee had for a quick victory. Longstreet, meanwhile, was damned for dragging his feet on the second day, delaying the Confederate assault on the Union lines. Still, the general consensus among historians is that Lee's planning on the third day did not seem to be based on any personal sense of desperation stemming from earlier command failures.[7]

Indeed, a better argument could be made that Lee acted on the basic belief that he could not lose, which was obviously a very erroneous assumption in light of what followed. Nevertheless, the postwar attacks on Longstreet and Ewell have made life a lot easier for "Leephiles" trying to explain away the disaster at Gettysburg. The unacceptable alternative, of course, was to ascribe fallibility to the godhead of the Confederacy.

Longstreet was the first to face the fire. The charges, the most serious of which could be characterized as tantamount to treason, were first offered up after Lee's death by generals Jubal Early, a division commander in II Corps under Ewell, and William Pendleton, Lee's chief of artillery, to use a title rather loosely.[8] However, the performances of those two during the battle offer substantial evidence that neither was in a position to cast aspersions on anyone else's military abilities. Then again, the Civil War was never entirely a logical conflict. Unfortunately for Longstreet's reputation, historians such as Freeman and Dowdey subsequently supported these criticisms.[9]

Longstreet struck back in his memoirs, but Lee had been canonized by then.[10] It is not unfair, though, to expect that the same critics who were quick to give Lee full credit for his victories might also assign him equal responsibility for his failures. Testifying to his sense of honor, Lee recognized this equality of praise and blame when he told the blasted survivors returning from the assault, "It was all my fault this time."[11] Lee was not simply being magnanimous. He was presenting the unvarnished truth to his numbed formations, and probably to himself.

LEE PROVES HE IS HUMAN

There are a number of explanations for Lee's behavior during the three days, especially his order for that last futile assault on the Union lines. Pickett's Charge is probably the single most critiqued engagement of this campaign, as well as any other, drawing forth elements of fantasy. What if Lee had succeeded? Would the war have ended? Would the fall of Vicksburg have offset a victory in the eastern theater?

There was some speculation that England and France were awaiting the outcome of Lee's campaign, possibly giving them the final excuse to support the Confederacy. Gettysburg thus was a big roll of the dice in many ways. Surely Lee must have had good and impelling reasons for launching that final, catastrophically unsuccessful assault. What drove Lee to order Pickett into the killing ground before Cemetery Ridge? To answer that question, there has been no end of explanations ranging from the mystical to the mundane.

Toward the mystical end, a few writers have traveled into relatively uncharted psychohistorical realms espousing the concept of national character. For example, Grady McWhiney and Perry Jamieson argued, "Southerners lost the Civil War because they were too Celtic and their opponents too English."[12] Continuing this rather intriguing argument, they claimed that the Southerners' Celtic heritage led them to glorify war, seek combat, and fight with reckless bravery. Acting with independence and carelessness, the Southern army is seen as basically a mob of fighting men who followed bold and daring leaders.

Pursuing this line of reasoning, the argument follows that the Confederates, like all Celtic forces, relied almost exclusively on the charge. Southerners utilized the assault because they could not or would not dream of any other form of military tactics. Unfortunately, while the Celts won battles, the English won wars.[13] Lee thus moved forward because the clans and their chieftains had only one military solution.

As is the case with most generalizations of national character, one is tempted to inquire just how universally this Celtic virus was distributed throughout the Confederate forces. A much better point was made earlier by these same authors when they observed that most of the Civil War commanders had also served in the Mexican-American War, where the tactical offensive had been generally successful.[14] Interestingly enough, they had adopted a behaviorist position, which is theoretically poles apart from the concept of national character.

Moreover, the issue here is to explain Lee's behavior. Somehow, a cause-and-effect relationship derived from a portrayal of the patrician Lee as a wild-eyed clan chieftain leading his equally frenzied men into battle does not quite ring true. Indeed, on that third day, most of the Southern troops preparing to assault Cemetery Ridge did not display any marked eagerness to hurl themselves at the enemy. Yet Lee sent them, and they did go, so just how did prior successes contribute?

The most common and perhaps mundane explanation for Lee's behavior revolves around the accusation of overconfidence. Douglas Southall Freeman, Lee's major biographer, raises this as a significant issue in his analysis of the defeat.[15] Yet that causal explanation must ultimately fall back on the assump-

tion that what Lee did or thought he could do at Gettysburg had to be an outcome of what had occurred in prior battles such as the Seven Days, Second
Bull Run, Fredericksburg, Chancellorsville, and Antietam. How could these
conflicts contribute to his undoing at Gettysburg?

We suggest that the generalized outcome of these engagements was that
Lee basically believed he would succeed regardless of the odds. This was
surely the case at Antietam, where he reunited his army, bloodied McClellan,
and led a successful retreat when McClellan froze in indecision. Overconfidence thus may well have led to failure. Yet the question remains: What
happened at Gettysburg, especially on the third day, to make hubris such a
critical element in Lee's thinking? Was Lee driven, or was he pushed?

In much of traditional psychology, human behavior is often "explained" in
terms of internalized motives and personal characteristics that are frequently
given causal (that is, explanatory) properties. But there really is no need for an
in-depth analysis of Lee the man, or to develop a protracted study of his childhood history, to assign causality for those decisions made on the Gettysburg
battlefield. For that matter, he left no memoirs. A psychological analysis derived from the consequences of Lee's earlier encounters with the Union army
provides a more easily understood explanation for his behavior. This view of
human actions is to be found in the behaviorist school of psychology.

The behavioral viewpoint suggests that learning is an outcome of functional
associations experientially developed between responses and outcomes.[16]
Within the framework of behaviorism, inferences about internal or covert activities are kept to a minimum. Behavioral scientists deal with the observable,
the data immediately available to the senses. In terms of judging Lee's actions,
we can assume that he had only to look across the fields. What he saw was the
Army of the Potomac, which had been unable to cope in the past, the present,
and, by extrapolation, the future.

Behaviorists accept as a basic postulate that both the initiation and maintenance of voluntarily directed behaviors are the result of environmental events,
called consequences, which follow the behavior.[17] That is, the result or outcome of what an individual has experienced in the past as a consequence
comes to control that person's subsequent actions. Indeed, whether or not we
act is a function of those outcomes.

Michael Palmer makes the same arguments within a nonpsychological context. Lee tended to operate consistently without formal plans. Putting it another way, he acted upon the consequences of his actions, with the overriding
objectives of engaging, repelling, and possibly destroying the enemy. At Antietam, and possibly at Gettysburg, he did not have these objectives clearly tied
together in mind, and both were defeats.[18]

The element of personal control clearly distinguishes these behaviors from
the reflexive, involuntary feelings and actions that provide the foundations of

classical conditioning. For example, one may have to drive on a snowy day to meet an important appointment, but dread of the roads and weather is not easily controlled by a simple exercise of will. Whether to go or not is likely to be a function of what has happened in the past under those particular conditions. Similarly, Lee saw a Union army and a general of a type he had beaten before and spent three days convincing himself it was just like old times.

These critical, controlling consequences can be categorized as follows:

(1) *Positive reinforcement:* A response is followed by a satisfying state of affairs (a reward of some kind), and thus the probability is that the particular behavior in question is likely to be repeated. Or, more simply put, we persist in what pays off.

(2) *Negative reinforcement:* Our behavior terminates some aversive or unpleasant condition in the environment or ourselves and as a result the behavior is *also* sustained. Turning off a loud television set or going for a walk to relieve personal stress are instances of negative reinforcement. That is, because we can eliminate or reduce an unpleasant situation, we persist in doing the same thing in a similar situation. Escape and avoidance behaviors are examples of negative reinforcement.

(3) *Punishment:* Some unpleasant consequence or loss of a reward follows a behavior. Subsequently, the likelihood of that particular behavior being repeated is either decreased or suppressed, depending upon the severity of the consequences.[19]

From a behavioral perspective, therefore, the paradox is that Lee's successes prior to the Gettysburg campaign contributed substantially to his eventual undoing. Lee may not have been sure about a lot of things in this world, but overcoming the Army of the Potomac was not one of them. There is significant historical evidence to support the idea that Lee moved north brimming with confidence, perhaps even overconfidence, knowing that the same group of failures, generals and army, were once more on the field opposing him.

Major General Isaac Trimble, later wounded and captured in Pickett's Charge, recounted a most telling conversation with Lee on June 27, 1863. Lee told Trimble in no uncertain terms how he planned to end the war in this campaign.[20] There was no element of doubt in his remarks; the tone reflected Lee's certainty of what would happen to the Union forces when he struck. In rather prosaic terms, Lee was spoiling for a fight, an attitude he conveyed to his staff as well.[21]

CONFIDENCE WORKS BOTH WAYS

Not only did Lee have this sublime confidence in himself, he was equally confident in his army. After his defeat at Gettysburg, Lee wrote to Jefferson

Davis, "I alone am to blame, in perhaps expecting too much of its prowess and valor."[22] Even earlier, in a perhaps even more telling letter to Maj. Gen. John Bell Hood, Lee wrote: "I agree with you in believing that our army would be invincible if it could be properly organized and officered. There were never such men in an army before. They will go anywhere and do anything if properly led. But there is the difficulty—proper commanders. Where can they be obtained?"[23]

While it is true there is a critical caveat in Lee's statement, there could not have been much doubt in his mind as to his ability to lead his army to victory. Given his habit of making plans and allowing his subordinates a free hand in executing them, it seems clear Lee was perhaps more concerned with the skills of his commanders, as compared to the caliber of his troops. This is perhaps the strength as well as the weakness of a decentralized command. While it was true that Jackson was dead and Longstreet was his only tested corps commander, in the end, if all else failed, Lee believed his troops would succeed. Indeed, the Army of Northern Virginia had consistently made good on Lee's orders. However, accommodating Union commanders all too often contributed to his success.

Still, the war was two years old, and Lee was no closer to Washington or the final destruction of the Army of the Potomac then when he took over. All this might have given him pause with regard to what he had actually accomplished, but it did not. The result was that Lee contained within himself the seeds for disaster. Critical studies of the battle on both sides agree that his sublime confidence would be a major contributor to his fall from grace. George Stewart went so far as to call it a "cancer."[24]

Overconfidence is a pernicious contributor to a common human malaise that might be called psychological rigidity. There is the confidence born from an accurate and thorough appraisal of one's current situation, and another based on the recall of previous events. Confusing the two can be disastrous. A fixed conviction as to the ultimate success of one's undertakings may sharply decrease the possibility of seriously considering options dissonant from those envisaged by one's fond hopes. In short, "overconfidence" in and of itself is really too broad a term to use in Lee's case. The key to understanding Lee's behavior is ascertaining what factors at Gettysburg significantly contributed to his overconfidence, and ultimately to defeat.

The line between confidence and overconfidence is a fine one, but crossing it can be fatal to one's perception of reality. The ultimate tragedy lies in the fact that the individual usually does not know the line has been crossed until after the fact. Lee could assure himself that all would be well until that awful moment when the remnants of Pickett's command stumbled past him in retreat. Until then, he had no reason to believe he would not succeed as he had done in the past. He could not and would not admit to himself at any time

during the three days that the battle would not in the end be successfully resolved by his personal touch. Although the Union forces stood their ground
and gave as good as they got, he had never doubted that the outcome would
be a Southern victory.

Thus, from a behavioral perspective, Lee's overgeneralized perceptions and
responses to unfolding events derived from outcomes resulting from *both* his
previous generalship and mistakes made by Union commanders. It might well
be argued that George McClellan's greatest contributions to the Union cause
at Gettysburg may well have been his failures against Lee in the Seven Days'
and Antietam campaigns. For that matter, the successive appearances and dis-
appearances of other flawed Union officers had to have consistently sustained
Lee's self-confidence. John Pope, Ambrose Burnside, and Joseph Hooker all
displayed a singular ineptitude for general command.

In short, the Army of the Potomac had paid for Lee's command confidence
in blood, and it was, after all, the same army up on those hills. He could well
afford risks that might have caused others to pause. Yet Lee failed to recognize
that the performance of the Union forces during the previous two years was
not due to any singular lack of courage or skills. The Army of the Potomac was
not, *a priori*, an inferior force. As Freeman correctly noted, the missing and
key element was that of adequate leadership, particularly at the higher levels.[25]

Moreover, the Army of the Potomac was quietly developing competence at
the middle and lower levels of command, which simply required adequate top
leadership for success. Meade could supply that, at least in this fight. The
Army of the Potomac's performance at Gettysburg only reaffirmed what Chancellorsville and Fredericksburg should have warned Lee: The troops could and
would fight well, if not eventually crippled by the incompetence of their commanders. They had held together in spite of monumental blunders and had
returned to fight again and again.

The psychological as well as military ramifications of the Gettysburg campaign are even more astounding if one remembers that as the Confederates
moved toward Gettysburg, the Army of the Potomac was losing seasoned veterans as their enlistments ran out.[26] Furthermore, the Union forces had suffered two major defeats within a short period of time. Fredericksburg should
never have been fought, and Chancellorsville was a missed opportunity for
Hooker. In fairness to Lee, he would have been less than human if he had
moved north in any state of mind other than high optimism. Yet the recovery
and performance of the Union troops and commanders at Gettysburg has in
general only grudgingly been recognized by historians sympathetic to the
South, as contributing to Lee's undoing.[27]

Introspection, however, was not one of Lee's strong points. If so, the results
of the first two days might well have given him pause. Both sides literally blundered into each other at Gettysburg.[28] Neither Lee nor Meade, who assumed

command of the Army of the Potomac after Lincoln removed Hooker, was looking for a fight at those crossroads, but events on the battlefield quickly took over. The fighting on July 1 saw Brig. Gen. John Buford's cavalry division, armed with repeating carbines, providing Maj. Gen. Harry Heth's division a very rough welcome to Gettysburg. Subsequently, the Union I Corps, first under Maj. Gen. John Reynolds, killed later that morning, and then under Maj. Gen. Abner Doubleday, found itself fighting stubbornly and skillfully alongside Buford's cavalrymen to hold their positions west of Gettysburg. However, the Confederate columns were closer, and as the day went on the Union troops found themselves fighting increasing numbers of rebels moving in from the east and north. Major General Oliver O. Howard and the XI Corps swung into line north of town, but broke as the result of late afternoon Confederate assaults. With the rout of Howard's XI Corps, damned forever by the rest of the Army of the Potomac, Union forces abandoned positions north and west of Gettysburg to take up new positions along the high ground east and south of the city.[29]

One might speculate as to whether the rout of the XI Corps, Chancellorsville redux, may not have found a place in Lee's perceptions as perhaps the equivalent of the sun at Austerlitz. There is no real evidence, but the sight of retreating Union troops must have spurred Lee's confidence.

While its retreat through the town itself was not well coordinated, the Union force that took up defensive positions on the hills east of Gettysburg was still a determined one. Much has been made of Ewell's failure to continue the advance and assault on Cemetery Hill. But what many historians subsequently ignored—and may well have been by Lee at that time—was the fierceness of the Union resistance during the day, coupled with the Confederates' exhaustion and disorganization.[30] Lee's orders had been discretionary, and Ewell, probably unlike Jackson, felt he had had enough.

Still, it was a battered but not necessarily broken Union force that began digging in atop Cemetery Hill.[31] Lee was unaware that the retreat had not been a complete rout. The sight of Union troops digging in should have removed any idea that they simply wanted out once more from the embrace of the Army of Northern Virginia.

As the remainder of the Army of the Potomac came up that night and the next day, its final position came to resemble a fishhook. At the north end the lines ran west from Culp's Hill to Cemetery Hill, then turned south along Cemetery Ridge and ended at the Round Tops. Meade would be fighting on interior lines and was quite capable of making use of his excellent tactical position.[32] Moreover, unlike previous conflicts, Lee would be fighting a set-piece battle against a general who, if not capable of grand strategy, was at least capable of staying and slugging it out.

LEE SEES WHAT HE WANTS TO SEE

The second day should have been equally instructive to Lee. Of critical importance to both commanders was the fighting along the Union center and left flank. Major General Daniel Sickles compromised the entire Union position when he moved his III Corps away from the southern end of Cemetery Ridge to form an exposed salient resting on the Emmitsburg Road. After Sickles's monumental blunder, Lee's original plan to sweep northward along the Emmitsburg Road actually bore prospects for a major Confederate victory.[33]

Longstreet attacked both sides of the salient, eventually pushing the Union forces back. However, in spite of repeated Confederate attempts to destroy it, the Army of the Potomac counterattacked in the gathering dusk, forcing the rebels back from their advanced positions. Major Generals Andrew Humphreys and David Birney, two of Sickles's division commanders, worked miracles to preserve the Union position atop Cemetery Hill, but it had been a long and bloody afternoon for both sides.[34] The 20th Maine held Little Round Top in an iron grip, while the 1st Minnesota had kept Cemetery Ridge out of Confederate hands with a show of valor that rivaled anything the Confederates had seen in their army. At the end of the day the Yankees still clung to their main lines of defense, and the Confederates had suffered enough casualties to suggest there was not much, if any, weakening of the Union forces' resolve.[35] The Army of the Potomac had held in the face of those deadly, previously invincible, Confederate assaults. The Union lines had bent but not broken. There were no easy Confederate gains.

Yet Southern fantasies abounded, even then. For example, Brig. Gen. "Rans" Wright, a brigade commander in Maj. Gen. Richard Anderson's III Corps division, contended that he actually broke through the Union center and made it to the top of Cemetery Ridge. However, he was not nearly the threat he thought he had been.[36]

At the northern end, Ewell's belated attack on the Union's weakened right flank was also repulsed by veteran troops under competent field commanders.[37] Southern claims that inexplicable command errors cost them victory ignore the realities of a skilled and courageous foe that had thwarted the rebels and was ready to fight again.[38] What would cost the Confederates dearly the next day was that the troops had seen and felt the carnage while Lee, the commanding general, was off in his own realm.

Regardless of what actually happened, it is apparent that Lee viewed the results of the second day's fighting within a positive frame of reference.[39] Sickle's command had been shattered and some ground had been taken; all that was needed was a final thrust against a reeling foe. In reality, both sides had battered themselves into exhaustion.[40]

3rd day

Lee's plan for the third day was to continue the offensive. Unfortunately for the Army of Northern Virginia, he was responding more to what he had done to the Union army yesterday and yesterdays before, than what would inevitably follow on the morrow. Lee did not acknowledge even to himself what actually had been done or could be done to his own forces. In short, he perceived all damage assessments as pertaining to the weakening of Meade's forces, and not his own.[41] Andre Trudeau estimated Union casualties at about 19,000 after two days of fighting, with Confederate losses at about 14,000. On the other hand, Jeffry Wert estimated the combined casualties for both sides at about 14,000 for the first day and 16,500 for the second.[42] If nothing else, reliable casualty estimates were hard to come by.

As noted before, overconfidence may diminish tactical and strategic considerations. Flexibility, in terms of options, becomes an even more rare commodity. It was probably inconceivable to Lee that he had seriously underestimated Meade and the Army of the Potomac or, more importantly, overestimated his own troops' invincibility. However, as Freeman pointed out, historians sympathetic to the South's cause generally ignore these misguided beliefs.[43]

Freeman

look up!

In the flood of historical analyses of the Gettysburg campaign, the most common theme has been *what if*, especially *what if* Maj. Gen. George Pickett had succeeded in breaking the Union center? But a better question might be made: *what if* Lee had broken off the fight after the second day? The ultimate tragedy of Lee's overconfidence was that the battle continued on the third day. This does not mean that Meade and his army should have been routed on the second day, or that Lee should have felt cheated of victory. Both sides had made enough mistakes to satisfy any critic.

Even so, Union losses at the end of the second day equaled if not exceeded Confederate casualties.[44] More important, despite Longstreet's and Ewell's failure to push the Yankees off Cemetery Ridge and Culp's Hill, Lee had accomplished his initially stated objectives for the campaign as the sun set on the second day. In a letter sent to Confederate adjutant and inspector general Samuel Cooper before beginning his move North, Lee had envisioned his movements in terms of a raid rather than a penetration.[45] Militarily, a raid is characterized by temporary possession of enemy territory, whereas penetration involves more permanent occupation. Tactically, a raid is structured in terms of a fast-moving campaign designed to accomplish specific objectives at minimum cost.[46]

Lee's objective partially accomplished

It could be argued that the first two days at Gettysburg were in keeping with a raid concept, but the third day involved much more. Indeed, the most common assumption at the beginning of the campaign was that Lee had two objectives in mind: The first was to disrupt the Union's summer campaign strategy and the second was to relieve the lower Shenandoah Valley from the task of supplying his army. He was also well aware of the political consequences of an-

2 obj.

other decisive Southern victory. He might well foster a political climate in the North leading directly to a negotiated peace.[47]

However, it is not really all that clear just what Lee had in mind. Indeed, critical to understanding Lee's operations is that he was not given to making very specific promises, and perhaps more significantly, outlining his intentions in detail. Lee was essentially an opportunist. When encountering Union forces he would react as the battlefield situation dictated. Yet he also had made it clear from the outset of this campaign that his goal was to destroy the Army of the Potomac, which he failed to do at Chancellorsville.[48] Lee's determination to destroy Meade's army would have serious consequences.[49]

Michael Palmer also suggests that Lee himself was not all that certain about his ultimate objectives. The Confederate commander was undoubtedly telling different things to different people at different times. Still, there were several other factors involved in Lee's decision. Among other things, he wanted to remove the constant threat of having his forces supply troops to other theaters, and by producing a major victory he could possibly redress the balance in the western theater.[50]

Lee was quite cognizant of the fact before he started northward that he was in no position to match resources with the North in any protracted conflict.[51] From the beginning, it was an accepted fact of military logic that the South could never occupy the North and force the Yankees to sue for peace. On the other hand, the North's military policy was dictated by the need both to defeat the Confederates and to occupy the South. Therefore, the only realistic strategy available to Southern leaders was to stand on the defensive, utilizing offensive-defensive tactics wherever possible, and compel a war-weary and exhausted North to give up. Lee's obvious contribution would be to keep his army intact.[52]

He had accomplished miracles with limited assets from the day he took command, but after two days at Gettysburg a more objective and perceptive Lee might have recognized that the Yankees were dealing out more punishment than the Confederacy could afford. Unfortunately, for Lee in particular and the South in general, there never had been a grand strategy. Lee had shown himself to be offensively minded from the beginning, and as long as he was winning no one asked what effect the loss of men and materiel would have on the South in the long run.[53]

On the other hand, if Lee fell back on his own accord, Northerners would have had a hard time claiming they had thrown him back. As at Antietam, the war would go on and any glow from Northern victory claims would be short-lived. Moreover, by 1863 the thought of continuing a losing conflict, if not a lost cause, might have been more than the Lincoln government could sustain. Indeed, Lincoln would face that problem in the 1864 presidential campaign. Fortunately for him, Atlanta and Winchester would prove to be crucial justifications for carrying the war to a by then clearly perceived end.

It is not difficult to believe that with Lee retiring after the second day and Meade staying put and reorganizing his battered army, the South might well have claimed the raid a success. In fact, shortly after Gettysburg Lee did argue that his campaign was "a general success, though . . . not . . . a victory."[54] Lee may have proclaimed that after the first two days, but after the third day he was living in a fool's paradise. The third day represented a dramatic shift from any objectives related to a raiding strategy.

In fact, it is not unreasonable to conjecture that somewhere between the second and third day Lee crossed over the line between confidence and overconfidence. Yet, the tactical consequences were not what Lee could have envisioned from those two years of successful campaigning. Besides the irreplaceable loss of men and materiel, it would give the North a much-needed victory and an accompanying boost in morale. Perhaps most important of all, Robert E. Lee and the Army of Northern Virginia would once again become human.

Lee had only himself to blame. His tactics during the first two days were those of a confident general still possibly adhering to a raiding philosophy. When he dropped the concept of a raid, however, he committed himself completely to a strategy in which defeating Meade's army would clear the way to Washington and perhaps result in a negotiated peace.

This final blow could and would be achieved at what Lee firmly believed was an acceptable level of risk. What is interesting is that if Lee had stopped to think about it, after Chancellorsville and Fredericksburg, a voluntary withdrawal could only be interpreted as a deliberate Confederate decision. It would mean that he was not driven, but that he had pulled back freely of his own accord. Lee attacked, though, and the South lost control of the war.

According to Nolan, Col. Porter Alexander said much the same thing. He argued that Lee held a wonderful defensive position after the second day and could have forced Meade to attack. Instead, Lee went forward. To Alexander, the third day was a "desperate venture."[55]

Early on the morning of the third day Lee met with Longstreet and found, much to his chagrin, a trusted subordinate contemplating a move around the Union flank. Longstreet's idea was to get Meade off the hills and beat him on a level playing field. Irritated by such opposition to his proposed plan, Lee forcefully ordered Longstreet to renew I Corps's attack on the Union left along the Emmitsburg Road.[56] Lee was looking for an immediate and decisive result, not extending the engagement or awaiting an attack by Meade. He could not have made his point clearer to Longstreet. Lee pointed toward Cemetery Ridge and told Longstreet that was where he was going to hit the Union troops.[57] The destruction of the Army of the Potomac had taken precedence over any other consideration, strategic or tactical.

Longstreet, who was neither a coward nor a fool, demurred, fearing a flanking counterattack by the Union forces presently aligned along Cemetery

Ridge and the Round Tops. He had been at the front the previous day, directly experiencing the defenders' fierce resistance.[58] It is not too difficult to understand why he had no desire to make another attempt at breaking the Union line. From a behavioral perspective, Longstreet's contemplated flanking maneuver is a classic example of avoidance behavior: He wanted out of those frontal assaults.

Also, from Longstreet's point of view, the Army of Northern Virginia had previously managed to confuse and neutralize superior enemy numbers by movement. There was no reason for him to believe Gettysburg would not be amenable to such a practical and well-tested tactical solution. Fredericksburg and Malvern Hill must have provided Longstreet, if not Lee, additional knowledge regarding the folly of ordering an uphill assault against a determined foe supported by artillery. These beliefs were undoubtedly uppermost in Longstreet's mind, and for good reason.

Longstreet had seen the Union forces retreat during the second day but then go over to counterattacks later that evening. This was hardly in keeping with the notion of a dispirited and beaten foe. Lee's planning would not carry the day, and Longstreet would subsequently be vilified for proving he was right all along.

Lee did change his plan of attack to a more northerly axis, but the change did not alter his tactical stance. He would strike, organizing the attack around Pickett's division. Basically, Lee was going to hit the center of the Union line on Cemetery Ridge.[59]

A now distraught Longstreet was to follow with the remainder of the I Corps, exploiting the never-doubted success of Pickett's command. However, Longstreet was convinced from prior experience that Pickett was going to suffer badly before he reached the Union lines.[60] Early on in the planning, Longstreet pointed out to Lee that Maj. Gen. Lafayette McLaws's and Maj. Gen. John Bell Hood's divisions had been badly hurt the day before. Lee might have initially believed the I Corps could renew the attack, but Longstreet was now giving him some bad news.[61] Subsequently, the decision to use General Pickett's fresh division was a military necessity born out of the fighting on the first day. Just how realistic Lee's appraisal was of what Pickett could accomplish, even if he reached the Union lines reasonably intact, is a matter of conjecture. It has been argued that even if the assault had succeeded in routing the Union forces on Cemetery Ridge, they would not necessarily have been destroyed as a military entity.[62] However, these thoughts probably never crossed Lee's mind.

The "fog of war," to use Clausewitz's term, had enveloped Lee. Certainly the fragmented and conflicting reports that reached him on the second day contributed to his impression that the Army of the Potomac was very close to defeat. His previous successes may have led him to believe that it perhaps would always be close to defeat, at least when he was leading the Army of Northern Virginia. As Lee later wrote: "The result of this day's operations induced the belief that, with proper concert of action, and with increased support that the positions gained on the right would enable the artillery to render the assaulting columns, we should ultimately succeed, and it was accordingly determined to continue the attack."[63]

His intention was to pursue the attack on the Union left, coupled with simultaneous pressure on the Union right. The plan reaffirms the earlier argument that Lee appears to have had no clear grasp of the significant losses his own forces had taken. Still, at least some of the ground taken from III Corps had been held, and this knowledge encouraged a very confident Lee to see this territory as a springboard for the renewal of the Confederate offensive.[64] However there was precious little in the way of other gains to support his lofty objectives.

The Army of the Potomac was still intact. Indeed, Ewell's failure that evening to seize Cemetery Hill was further evidence that this was not at all going quite as Lee believed it should. The Yankees were making a fight of it everywhere. Meade, in contrast, was a little more realistic about what had happened. He had been in closer contact with his subordinates. In fact, his assessment of what Lee would do the next day proved rather accurate.[65]

As has been argued, Lee's confidence had always been coupled with an offensive frame of mind. By the war's end, he would have suffered proportionally heavier casualties than any other Confederate or Union army commander.[66] It is obvious that any considerations in a military decision must lead to the weighing of possible losses against the significance of results to be achieved. In Lee's case, the only outcome he would now accept was the rout of the Army of the Potomac. He had told Trimble what he wanted to do; now he would achieve it. Lee was not a butcher (nor was Grant), but like Grant, Lee always saw fighting as a means to an end. Longstreet believed that a frontal assault on the Union center would end with unacceptable losses and no victory. Lee, on the other hand, believed he would have his victory, making his losses acceptable, no matter the toll.

The tactics Lee employed on the third day have been subjected to close scrutiny. The spectacle of Confederate regiments in tight linear formations, flags flying, has attracted the attention of writers of all persuasions. However, the specific military details share equal importance with an understanding of Lee's frame of mind. He had made mistakes before, but he had gotten away with them. Whatever he lacked, Union commanders would supply. Lee's detractors, on the other hand, still affirm that the attack really never had a chance.

The problem for Lee is that the Union commanders had "seen the elephant" enough times to begin to anticipate what Lee might do next. Major T. J. Goree, a member of Longstreet's staff, put it bluntly when he said in effect, based on a conversation with Lee, that Lee had no reason to believe that the Union army would not know where he would attack.[67]

A better conjecture is whether that made any difference to Lee. The fierceness and tenacity of the Union resistance on this battlefield might have cautioned a more observant Lee that this might be a different tactical situation. But he gave no hint of any doubts. The Army of the Potomac, which he was now regarding in rather cavalier fashion, had for two years been given some rather painful and costly lessons by an eminent tutor. Unfortunately for Lee, at this point in time and on this very ground these lessons would bear a bitter fruit beyond anything he could have ever contemplated.

The evidence is found in his own words. A month later, after his retreat into Virginia, he still clung to the idea that his perceptions of the first two days were accurate. In his July 31 report to Adjutant General Cooper concerning the fighting on the second day, Lee stated: "These partial successes determined me to continue the assault the next day."[68] As has been shown previously, those "partial" successes were, in reality, small and dearly bought.

Lee's sublime confidence, if not arrogance, showed itself not only in his choice of tactics, but also in his ill-conceived organization of the attacking forces. As usual, his orders granted his field commanders wide latitude. The selection of Maj. Gen. George Pickett's division of Longstreet's I Corps represented the use of elite fresh troops. However, his decision to use Harry Heth's division from Hill's III Corps was, on the other hand, a very poor choice. The unit had been mauled badly during the first day's fighting and was in no condition to do much of anything.[69]

The choice of two III Corps divisions also represented some very bad staff work. Both units were fighting under new commanders, although the nature of the assault itself precluded the likelihood of the need for major tactical changes as the advance proceeded. Heth had been wounded and Brig. Gen. James Johnston Pettigrew was in command of his troops, and Maj. Gen. Isaac Trimble assumed command of Maj. Gen. Dorsey Pender's division after Pender was mortally wounded on the second day.[70] Yet, after all else was said and done, this was the Army of Northern Virginia. Troops fighting under desperate circumstances and under new leaders might represent a problem to other commanding generals, but not to Lee. In summary, from Lee's perspective, success meant crossing the valley with minimal loss while maintaining cohesiveness. In addition, he had to assign sufficient troops for the initial assault and provide support to exploit a break in the Union lines. Much of that support would come from Maj. Gen. Richard Anderson's troops, who also came from Lt. Gen. A. P. Hill's III Corps.[71]

Besides some rather bad decisions regarding the forces to be used, there is other evidence that Lee definitely was seeing only what he wanted to see, and hearing only what he wanted to hear. At this point he was accepting only perceptions consonant with his plans. On the morning of the third day, Lee encountered Brig. Gen. William Wofford, a very pugnacious Georgian in Longstreet's I Corps. When Lee suggested that they were about to take the heights, Wofford replied, "No General, I think not."[72] The unexpected remark gave Lee no pause at all.

In fact, fighting earlier that day should have considerably sobered his expectations. Lee had ordered Ewell to coordinate with Pickett's assault by attacking the Union right flank on Culp's Hill, which was held by XII Corps. Ewell found himself fighting for his life, and losing, long before Pickett started. The performance of the Union forces on Culp's Hill should have warned Lee that they were far from the beaten foe he so desperately wanted to believe them to be.[73] Unfortunately, like Admiral Yamamoto sailing to his fate at Midway, Lee remained firmly convinced of his ability to control the destiny of the conflict. However, achieving his military objectives required the execution of specific tactics. Regardless of Lee's confidence, a wave of the hand alone would not drive the Union troops from those hills, especially Maj. Gen. Winfield Scott Hancock's II Corps.

To prepare the way for his advancing forces, Lee ordered a massive artillery bombardment concentrated on Cemetery Ridge, particularly II Corps. The primary target was the Union artillery batteries, although he also hoped to break up the Union infantry formations.[74] Above all, the Union guns had to be silenced. At that point in the war, every general knew what artillery could do to advancing troops, and every general on both sides knew that veteran troops would not vanish merely at the sight of the advancing foe.

All morning long, Col. Porter Alexander, Longstreet's I Corps artillery commander, rolled the Confederate guns into a line facing Cemetery Ridge. When the firing began at one o'clock, the Confederates probably had more guns concentrated on that front than the Union army did.[75] Alexander figured he had enough ammunition for about an hour's firing.[76] After about thirty minutes, Alexander sent a note to Pickett suggesting that if he was going to advance he must do so at once. Alexander had also been in contact with Longstreet, and it is evident from their exchanges that Longstreet was still hesitant. Indeed, Longstreet seemed to be asking Alexander to make the final decision.[77]

After a time, some damaged Union batteries along Cemetery Ridge were observed to be pulling out and their gunfire generally began slackening, except along the II Corps front. In all, about thirty-four Union guns had been disabled.[78] Since the Union artillery had been the primary target, Alexander hopefully assumed that the Confederate bombardment had done its work. The Union infantry and guns were still there, but if they had been sufficiently knocked about, well, the assault just might work.

Given the volume of smoke along Cemetery Ridge, Alexander really had no other means of estimating the effectiveness of his cannonade, except through changes in the intensity of the Union gunnery. Ultimately, the Confederate infantry would have to provide a bloody indicator as to the validity of his conjectures. Equally important, the Confederates were now running low on ammunition; unfortunately, the trains had been withdrawn to the rear.[79]

Unbeknownst to Alexander, Brig. Gen. Henry Hunt, the Union artillery chief, had ordered the guns to stop firing in order to conserve ammunition. Hancock countermanded this order on the II Corps front and the guns there continued to return fire.[80] Meanwhile, a second message from Alexander to Pickett urged even more strongly that he begin his advance. Then, to his horror, Alexander discovered that he could not provide adequate artillery support for Pickett's men. With ammunition almost gone and the ammunition trains in the rear refilling the gun chests, it would mean a delay of an hour. This would definitely give the Union troops time to recover. Additionally, Major Gen. William Pendleton had removed guns intended to directly support the advancing troops. It was a very trying time for Alexander.[81]

To compound Pickett's problems, the Confederate gunners' aim had been uniformly high, although they had done enough damage. During the barrage, firing into the increasing smoke on Cemetery Ridge had caused the Confederate gunners to overshoot the crest itself. Worse yet, the Bormann fuse that the Confederates used on their ordnance had a very high failure rate.[82] Finally, the remaining Union batteries, particularly those on Cemetery Hill and the Round Tops, remained undamaged and potent deterrents. Some guns had been silenced, but not nearly enough, to the eventual sorrow of the advancing Confederates. The odds had been shortened, but not sufficiently.[83]

Moreover, the waiting lines of Union infantry remained relatively unscathed.[84] The bombardment had been much less effective than Lee had hoped for in his planning, but it might be enough. After all, he had broken the Union lines at Gaines's Mill and Boatswain's Swamp during the Seven Days' battles. Of course, George McClellan, whose strategy centered on retreat, had been in command then. But was Meade so different?

There was nothing subtle about the attack. The men would be going straight ahead and up the hill into the heart of the waiting Union forces. Pickett's division would attack on the right in two lines. Heth's division, under Pettigrew, was formed on Pickett's left, also advancing in two lines. Brigadier General Cadmus Wilcox, with two I Corps brigades, was placed to the extreme right and rear of Pickett's division to prevent a flanking attack. Wilcox would not participate in the initial advance. When finally formed, the Confederate front extended for at least a mile.[85]

The advancing forces would have to cover about a mile before reaching Cemetery Ridge. This was the tactical nightmare Longstreet dreaded. Although history generally records the charge as involving 15,000 men, Stewart suggests the total was only about 10,500. On the other hand, Trudeau suggests an attacking force of about 11,800, while Wert believes Longstreet had about 13,500 in the main assault force.[86] The Union forces at the point of the attack,

Ziegler's Grove, totaled less than 6,000. These were General Gibbon's and Brig. Gen. Alexander Hays's II Corps divisions, covering a two-thousand-foot front.[87] The Confederates would outnumber the Union forces when they finally met—assuming the attackers could get across the valley without sustaining crippling losses and in good order. Unfortunately for Lee and his men, that was not to be the case.

Given the possibility of a heavier concentration of Confederate forces at the point of attack, the question still remained as to whether they could cross the valley in sufficient numbers and order to have any chance of success. Longstreet argued that no fifteen thousand men (or perhaps more) ever arrayed for battle could take those heights.[88] Not that the hill was steep or the position heavily fortified. On the contrary, the ascent was gradual and the Union forces had done little in the way of preparing fortifications.[89] The key difference between Lee and Longstreet at that moment was that Longstreet believed the Army of Northern Virginia was mortal.

ARTILLERY VS. RIFLES

From the outset, Lee had known he was facing a tactical problem of no small magnitude. The key to success lay in overcoming the initially unequal contest between Union artillery and Confederate rifles. This was the discrepancy Lee had hoped to reduce with the intense preliminary bombardment. To the advancing Confederate infantry and waiting Union troops, the weapon at hand was a muzzle-loading rifled musket. The two best models were the British Enfields carried by the rebels and the Yankees' Springfields, manufactured in Massachusetts. Firing a lead slug measuring about two-thirds of an inch in diameter and weighing almost an ounce, the weapon was dangerous at up to half a mile.[90]

Tactically, however, the rifles were generally used at ranges of less than three hundred yards. Most veterans could get off two or three shots in a minute, although the weapon had to be fired from a standing position. Unfortunately for the Confederates, they would have to cover almost the entire mile between their lines before coming close enough for an accurate exchange of musketry —and do it within range of the Union artillery.

Indeed, the artillery presented a real and immediate problem for the Confederates. About half of the Union guns (as indeed was the case for the Confederates) were smoothbore Napoleons with an effective range of twelve hundred yards with twelve-pound shot. The rate of fire was about two shots per minute with explosive shell or solid ball, and four shots a minute with canister. The latter was most feared by advancing infantry. It consisted of iron or lead balls embedded in sawdust and enclosed in a tin can. When the propellant exploded, the can shattered and the balls spread out in a pattern not unlike that of a shotgun blast.[91] Canister, however, was used only at close range, with murderous effect on massed troops.

The remaining guns were rifles, including the three-inch Ordnance gun and ten-pound Parrots. These had a range of over two miles. Firing a smaller projectile, they were primarily used to destroy enemy batteries, although in this instance they would be used on the advancing Confederates. To complete the recipe for disaster, throughout the war the Union artillery consistently had more reliable weapons and ammunition, and outgunned their Confederate artillery counterparts.[92]

Thanks to Hunt's prudence the Union guns would be able to subject the Confederates to a murderous pounding all the way, while Alexander could provide no compensating support. The Union artillery could focus single-mindedly on the advancing Confederate infantry and not worry about diverting guns to silencing Confederate cannons. Lee implied in his subsequent report that if he had known about his ammunition problem he would have postponed the assault.[93] This is debatable: If Lee really believed his troops would succeed where other mortals might fail, why hesitate?

As we have noted before, massed formations moving against waiting artillery and infantry were regarded as less than a satisfactory tactical solution at this point in the war. The troops might succeed, but victory required overwhelming strength at the point of attack, which would not be true in this case. Ultimately, Lee's personal beliefs dominated military considerations. Lee had decided on an offensive gamble that he believed just might end the war.[94]

Paradoxically, the rifled musket had now placed artillery on the tactical defensive. The range of the infantry weapon made it impossible to continue the offensive artillery tactics of the Mexican War. The earlier scenario of longer-ranged artillery pieces destroying infantry formations using inaccurate and short-range smoothbore muskets no longer existed. Artillery could be engaged with rifle fire at several hundred yards.[95]

Yet, with artillery relegated to the defensive, it was equally true that both the musket and artillery had reached the point where their combined defensive firepower could prove devastating to offensive forces. Unless the enemy artillery could be neutralized, advancing infantry losses might be reduced through the use of such tactics as the two-line advance, or even columns. Lee believed, though, that with the protected flanks, and above all his superb infantry, he would carry the day.[96] Still, the offensive forces faced at best difficult odds. Still, Alexander's guns fired as the massed Confederate infantry in the woods behind them awaited their turn.

After the bombardment ceased, it took a while to organize the waiting Confederate units. Troop formations of that size take time to establish their positions in the lines of advance. At about 3 P.M., the Confederates moved out in tight linear formations. Starting at the bottom of a swale, it took several min-

utes for the Confederates to come into view of the waiting Union forces. Brigadier General Joseph Davis's small brigade, which had been inexcusably
placed on the left of Heth's division, was already shaky. Pettigrew may have
realized from the start that his left flank was suspect.[97] To make matters worse,
they were going up against II Corps and Maj. Gen. Winfield Hancock, troops
and commander as good as any on either side.

Once the Confederate lines came into sight, the Union artillery opened up.
The artillery tactics were not based on any notion of an ambush; the preva-
lence and effectiveness of the Union guns were evident from the onset. The
Union guns continued firing on the infantry from front and flank, with no
compensating Confederate gunnery. At first, it was the rifled pieces doing the
damage, in particular Maj. Thomas Osborn's guns on Cemetery Hill and Lt.
Col. Freeman McGilvery and Lt. Benjamin Rittenhouse's battery on Little
Round Top.[98]

An ever-growing trail of dead and wounded marked the Confederates' passage, but they kept closing ranks as casualties mounted. The carnage was unbelievable as the Union gunners had an open field against massed formations.[99] The advance continued in spite of the obvious fact that the Union
forces were standing firm. The Confederate infantry undoubtedly believed
and hoped—based on past experiences—that once they got close enough
their foes would break and run. Considering it was II Corps they were being
thrown against, that was less than a forlorn hope.

One should keep in mind the fact that the advancing Confederates were not
raw recruits. After two years they had been bloodied more than enough. In behavioral terms, the advancing Confederate troops had psychological support
based on the outcomes of previous battles. On the other hand, the Yankees
were buoyed by their own fighting prowess during the last two days. The
Union troops recognized that they were in a good tactical position. Now let
those rebels come up the hill. Fredericksburg was a more pleasant situation if
you were behind the wall. In fact, some of the Union troops were reminding
the Confederates of that fact.[100]

In spite of the continuous and deadly shelling, the Confederates kept moving across the valley. At no point during the advance did Lee ever give the order recalling his troops, even though the volume of Union fire portended very
heavy and perhaps critical losses. From a behaviorist position, Lee's most pre-
potent response was to persist in the attack, regardless what might emerge later
from retrospection.[101] Moreover, to turn the advancing troops around might
have caused such mass confusion as to prove just as bad as a direct repulse.
There is an old military maxim that argues that order and counterorder bring
disorder, so Lee probably felt he had no choice. Even if the volume of Union
artillery fire was an evil omen and the Union infantry was staying put, the un-
spoken hope was that the troops would make good any command errors.

Union defensive tactics did not simply consist of letting the artillery fire eviscerate the Confederate ranks as much as possible and then allow the waiting infantry to administer the coup de grace. The Confederate left flank, already a weak point, began to waver under enfilading artillery fire coming from Cemetery Hill and then disintegrated. But it was not artillery alone.

Compounding the destruction of the artillery fire, the 160 troops of the 8th Ohio, which had been posted near the Emmitsburg Road, flanked Pettigrew on his left and began contributing a not insubstantial amount of ordnance of their own. After breaking up Brig. Gen. John Brockenbrough's brigade, the Ohioans turned their attention to the next flanked units. Lacking needed resolve from the start, the survivors simply turned and ran; staying alive took precedence over any hopes of victory. The limitations of flesh and blood against iron had been reached. The units next in line now received their share of flanking as well as frontal fire.[102]

The fences along the Emmitsburg Road broke up the Confederate lines. Too stout to knock down, as the Confederates climbed over the top they were slaughtered.[103] To increase casualties, the Yankee gunners now began to fire canister. Huge gaps were torn out of the massed infantry formations and functional organization began to disappear. By this time tactical cohesion had been lost and units were hopelessly intermingled. Indeed, there is even conflicting evidence on whether separate lines existed.[104] When the range had closed to about a hundred yards, the Union infantry opened fire.[105] Confederate troops on the right flank had earlier begun "drifting" toward the center to avoid enfilading artillery fire, and this movement was now accelerated. The advance had utilized Ziegler's Grove as a landmark, which guided the main axis of attack, and units began to collapse on that axis.[106] Then, as the Confederates reached the Union lines, Hays sent the 108th and 126th New York and a detachment of 1st Massachusetts' sharpshooters along the Bryan farm lane on the Confederate left.[107]

South of the advancing Confederates, Brig. Gen. George Stannard swung his big Vermont regiments out to flank Pickett's right.[108] The tactical situation was now a classic representation of the Battle of Cannae, the double envelopment. Smote both front and flank, what Confederate forces reached the Union lines consisted of shattered and essentially leaderless units.[109] Brigadier General Lewis Armistead, a brigade commander under Pickett, became a symbol of Southern courage, but he was not functioning as commander. He led men into the inferno, but that was the extent of his control. He died within a few minutes at the head of his troops, engaged in trying to make good what from the beginning had been a flawed plan.

After some moments of desperate hand-to-hand fighting, Union troops from surrounding units crushed the Confederate spearhead that had reached "the Angle." Union field officers took command at the point of attack, acting promptly and courageously. Confederate survivors fled toward their own lines, but many surrendered.[110] It was probably the bravest who undertook the trek back across the valley, because it meant retreating under a steady hail of artillery and rifle fire.

Of the approximately 10,500 Confederates who advanced, one estimate is that 5,674 were killed or wounded and 792 were taken prisoner. Union losses came to about fifteen hundred dead and wounded.[111] The result, however, was more than a military defeat. The myth of Lee's infantry was forever shattered; the aura of invincibility was gone. To be sure, the Army of the Potomac would always recognize the Army of Northern Virginia as a deadly foe, but now it was at least vulnerable.

Lee's personal torment is a matter of record. A stunned Pickett reported that his command no longer existed, but Lee told him that it had been his fight, and upon his shoulders rested the blame. As Lee moved forward to steady the survivors streaming back past him, he kept repeating that it was all his fault.[112] He, not they, had endured defeat, although at least some of the survivors might have respectfully disagreed.

Perhaps the ultimate expression of Lee's agony occurred that evening when, in evident anguish, Lee said to Brig. Gen. John Imboden, one of his cavalry commanders, "Too bad. *Too bad.* O, too bad."[113] There is no other record of Lee displaying such personal anguish over a defeat except perhaps after the surrender at Appomattox. Even after the repulse at Malvern Hill his confidence had not been shaken.

WHAT HAPPENED?

In analyzing the causes for the defeat, Douglas Southall Freeman grudgingly begins to acknowledge the growing competency of the Union army and its commanders.[114] What was emerging from Union defeats was a veteran army that had begun to create a sense of pride and competency in itself, which might well overcome serious defects in leadership, particularly at the top. Any analysis of the battle must conclude that leadership and rank had together thwarted Lee.

Among Confederate mistakes, Freeman does list Lee's overconfidence as one of the several contributing factors. However, in keeping with the basic need to maintain Lee's halo, to which he contributed so much, Freeman finds it necessary to place most of the blame on Lee's subordinates.[115] Freeman not only shared Lee's exalted view of the Confederate infantry; he also seemed to believe that Union mistakes should be considered Lee's due. These had contributed so much to Lee's success in the past that some writers assumed he factored them into his planning. In contrast, Confederate errors in command are treated as crimes against "The Cause." A consistent belief among those sympathetic to the Confederate cause was that Southern valor and Union incompetence were inexorably related.

And yet, if Lee had Longstreet and Ewell, Meade had Howard and Sickles. Still, it all comes down to the fact that Lee was ultimately responsible (as was Meade), and it was Lee's mistakes that primarily contributed to his undoing. The argument that Lee would have won but for subordinate errors is not a proven fact. The tragedy for Lee and the Confederacy is that at no time during the first two days did he ever allow a breath of fresh air to enter into his planning. He was reacting to a past that in the end betrayed him. "What was" was simply equated with "what is."

Clifford Dowdey, on the other hand, is so preoccupied with his betrayal hypothesis that nothing makes sense to him other than the failures of Longstreet and Ewell. Starting with the assumption that Lee was completely right (which even Freeman admits was not true), Dowdey can only assume that evil overcame good on this occasion. He unwaveringly pursues the idea that it was these Confederate generals and not Meade and the Army of the Potomac that were Lee's foes. For that matter, it took a while for even Lee to admit publicly that he had been defeated tactically and strategically.[116]

The magnitude of the losses on both sides during the three days was unbelievable. Lee had attacked with 75,000 men to Meade's 85,000 at Gettysburg. It is now generally accepted that Lee's casualties amounted to 28,000 killed, wounded, and missing; Meade's about 23,000.[117] Noah Andre Trudeau insists on more precise figures: 22,813 Union, and 22,874 Confederate.[118] However, while admirable in intent, complete casualty counts, especially Confederate, were notoriously inaccurate throughout the war. In some cases the data is simply missing. However, Lee's army was still a potent fighting force. Indeed, any army he commanded was dangerous, as Meade and Grant both discovered.

Still, it was now up to the Army of the Potomac to force a final resolution. Lee had been hurt so badly that, given the ever-diminishing resources of the South, he could no longer carry the war to the North again. The Confederacy had suffered irreplaceable losses, but, like their foes, the Army of Northern Virginia would rise from the ashes to fight again. At Gettysburg a surfeit of confidence distilled from past successes led to Lee's defeat. After Gettysburg it would be a sobered but still able Lee who would continue to lead until the end of the war.

Gone, however, were any fantasies his army could roam unchecked over the eastern landscape. For the Army of the Potomac, times had also changed. Given the adequate leadership that a Meade and ultimately a Grant could provide, the Union forces would endure staggering losses before finally laying siege to the Confederate capital. The end was inevitable after Gettysburg, even if it would be delayed another two years. And finally, gone were any remote Southern dreams for recognition by either France or England.

However, no discussion would be complete without an acknowledgment of the argument that Lee's illness and anxiety contributed to his defeat.[119] It is true that there are some hints at Gettysburg of the heart ailment that was to kill him a few years later, but there is nothing in his actions during the three days that can be directly attributed to his illness. There are many instances of Lee's usual care in directing the attack. His reconnoitering of the Union flank on the second day, and the artillery bombardment on the third are hardly illustrative of a sick man ignoring adequate preparations. No matter what detractors of Longstreet and Ewell might want to believe, there could be no doubt Lee was in full control of the final assault.[120]

Lee chose the offensive at Gettysburg because he never doubted the eventual outcome. Shortcomings in tactics and subordinates' mistakes had been present in previous campaigns, but there were some rather unique problems at Gettysburg. First, Lincoln had failed to provide him with a Hooker, Burnside, Pope, or McClellan. Second, the Army of the Potomac finally had been given an opportunity to demonstrate what had been true for some time: It was a competent fighting force if properly led. In the end, it was Lee, an overconfident general, and an increasingly competent and confident Army of the Potomac that contributed to the Confederate defeat.

CHAPTER FIVE

FRANKLIN, TENNESSEE: THE WRONG ENEMY

In my utmost heart I questioned whether or not
I could ever succeed in eradicating this evil.

—Gen. John Bell Hood

T HE CONFEDERATE ARMY OF Tennessee had known both triumph and failure. However, on November 30, 1864, an incongruously warm, late autumn afternoon, its destiny was writ in the blood of an incredibly ill-advised attack on entrenched Union forces. The battle fought at Franklin, Tennessee, has often been characterized as the Gettysburg of the West. Like its more famous predecessor, a massive frontal assault resulted in the strategic demise of a campaign and a badly shattered army.[1] General John Bell Hood's Tennessee campaign foundered on a battle so poorly conceived (to use a term in its loosest sense) as to destroy Hood's military career and ultimately cast a long and dark shadow over the rest of his life.

Unlike its namesake, given the late stages of the war it is debatable whether success by Hood in this battle, or even the campaign itself, could have approached the strategic and political gains that might have resulted from a victory by Robert E. Lee a year earlier. Nevertheless, if Hood had even simply flanked the Union forces at Franklin, he would have given Washington a sizable headache. At a minimum, Hood would have been able to lay siege to Nashville with something resembling an intact army. In addition, if he had also chosen to bypass Nashville, which might have been an even wiser move, a Confederate army raging along the Ohio River was not the sort of scenario Union strategists wished to contemplate that late in 1864.

Instead, in the gathering dusk a frustrated and angry Hood hurled eighteen brigades of veteran Confederate infantry, close to twenty thousand men, against Death in the guise of equal numbers of Union infantry commanded by Maj. Gen. John M. Schofield.[2] Hood's subordinates tried to argue him out of the attack, but the thesis is made that the assault satisfied Hood's psychological as well as military goals. Bereft of maneuver and artillery support, the Army of Tennessee was immolated in a battle lasting five hours. Repeated charges were met with such a volume of fire that Confederates trapped before the Union lines implored the defenders: "Don't shoot, Yanks; for God Almighty's sake, don't shoot!"[3]

Union guns only grew silent when the Confederate attacks ceased, leaving an army that had only a few more weeks to live in any guise of a military entity. Shadow would persist, but substance was gone. The Union troops began falling back toward Nashville around midnight, leaving behind their dead and nonambulatory wounded.[4] The Confederates were in possession of the field, but to describe Franklin as even a draw, as Stanley Horn does, is to add new dimensions to the concept. As chronicler of the Army of Tennessee, Horn's infatuation with that organization at times exceeded Freeman's love affair with the Army of Northern Virginia. He figured that since Schofield did not hold Hood for the three days Maj. Gen. George Thomas asked for, Hood had gained some measure of success. The reality is that there was nothing left to hold and Hood was no longer a threat. Strategically, of course, Franklin was an absolute disaster for Hood.[5]

Every relatively impartial historian recognizes Hood's state of mind at the time of the conflict. However, the relationship between Hood's evident anger and his decision to strike directly and immediately at Schofield is a lot more complex than simply labeling Franklin the consequences of a temper tantrum. Hood has never been characterized as a military genius, but even he knew how to use the options available in the limited two-dimensional tactics employed by Civil War commanders. Hood was no novice; he had seen it all from the beginning. Starting at the rank of lieutenant in Virginia in 1861, he rose to brigadier general and command of the Texas Brigade by 1862. Early on, his bravery was never in question. The Texas Brigade became one of Lee's elite units, and it is hardly likely that the Texans would have followed someone whose valor did not match their own. Hood never disappointed them.

A man of unquestionable personal courage, he lost the use of his left arm at Gettysburg and later had his right leg amputated at Chickamauga. He was by nature a fighter, and he expected no less of the troops under his command, whether the Texas Brigade or others. At Franklin, his men certainly gave him no cause to doubt their courage. In those five desperate hours Hood lost seven thousand men, including 1,750 killed. By comparison, Maj. Gen. George McClellan, commanding the Union Army of the Potomac in the spring of 1862, suffered fewer killed during the entire Seven Days' campaign around Richmond. In addition, the Army of Tennessee lost twelve generals, six of whom were killed, five wounded, and one captured.[6]

Until fairly recently, historians have usually accepted the argument that Franklin was Hood's inevitable response to the earlier fiasco at Spring Hill, where Hood believed he had been deprived of a tremendous strategic opportunity. Through command inaction and mistakes, the Union army had escaped certain disaster. Acting on that knowledge, he impulsively sent his troops headlong at the Union forces dug in at Franklin. Historically, Hood is labeled at fault for failing to act at Spring Hill, and at Franklin for overreacting. However, more recent historical analyses have begun to question assumptions about Hood's actual chances at Spring Hill, or the ultimate consequences, even if his plans had succeeded.

For example, in a revisionist mood, Stanley Horn now argues that the Union forces could have avoided the trap at Spring Hill, a view which others have also proposed.[7] In effect, the newer argument is that there never was any real chance for a major success at Spring Hill, so why did Hood become angry? From an academic perspective a century or more later, the claim might be true, but it also denies Hood's perceptions in real time. In short, it is a classic example of begging the question.

Hood firmly believed to the end of his life that his plans could have succeeded, resulting in much personal glory. To say that there was no reason for Hood to have lost his temper is at the same time avoiding the issue of why he did lose it, and why he subsequently attempted that reckless and futile attack at Franklin. From a psychohistorical viewpoint, an individual's actions must be studied in the world of the participant. The argument to be made is that Hood was a ruined general *before* he ever reached Franklin.

HOOD TAKES COMMAND

Basically, the tragedy of Franklin began much earlier. While Hood was capable of inspiring and leading troops into action in the grand manner of the cavalier, he lacked those capacities necessary for independent command. Early on in his Tennessee campaign, Hood showed little skill in directing, maintaining, and supplying an army committed to a protracted campaign.[8] In fact, Franklin is generally treated as confirming the notion that Hood was a man of limited intellectual capabilities, fit perhaps to command part of an army, but not the whole.

Hood's tactics on that battlefield provide firm support for these beliefs, but the most perplexing part of Franklin is that his performance there was atypical of Hood in a number of ways. Hood may not have been the most astute of generals, but the tragedy at Franklin was that it brought to the fore all of Hood's weaknesses. At Franklin, Hood was a man driven by basic psychological forces from which he could not and would not depart. He was the wrong man in the wrong place, and his men would pay an awful price in bloodshed for his personal problems.

The key to understanding Hood's actions at Spring Hill is to recognize that, from his perspective, the failure there was clearly due to a lack of military ardor at all levels of the Army of Tennessee. This belief led inexorably to the orders he issued at Franklin. While anger may have been present throughout the entire Tennessee campaign, emotion and belief joined in after Spring Hill. Simply put, Hood became a man driven by an overwhelming belief system fueled by very strong emotions.

Indeed, at breakfast the morning following the Army of the Ohio's escape from the supposed trap at Spring Hill, the quarreling almost came to a matter of pistols.[9] To an army proud of its courage, such questions struck raw nerves. It would be a grim army and a distraught general that caught up with Schofield and the Union forces that very afternoon.

Traditionally, therefore, it has been easy to simply assert that Hood's anger got the best of him after Spring Hill and that this loss of self-control led directly to orders for an immediate, all-out attack. Indeed, there was no planning, reconnoitering, or artillery support. And yet, it is sometimes overlooked that Spring Hill was not the only military failure Hood had endured since assuming command of the Army of Tennessee from Gen. Joseph E. Johnston.

True, he had retreated with Johnston, but Johnston had been in command. However, when Hood took command it became his army and his responsibility. Strategically, Johnston had left him in a precarious position. Major General William Tecumseh Sherman was closing in on Atlanta, a direct result of the failure of Johnston's Fabian strategy.[10] Even the rawest recruit in Johnston's army had to admit that Sherman had come a long way, and to the politicians in Richmond it was far too long.

In assigning Hood to command Johnston's army, Jefferson Davis was in many respects quite limited in his choice of commanders. He could possibly have selected Gen. Pierre Beauregard, but given the immediacy of the situation someone already in the Army of Tennessee seemed a more logical choice.[11] Unfortunately for the South, Davis saw himself as commander in chief in a very military sense throughout the war.[12] This would cost the South dearly, since Davis held grudges. It is important to observe how Hood acted at this time of crisis. Right from the beginning of his stewardship as commander of the Army of Tennessee, the evidence was that Hood would fight and fight again, regardless of the outcome of any single battle. He planned to strike at Sherman immediately, and if he failed, he would plan and attack once more.

Hood never contemplated a defensive strategy when he took over at Atlanta, then or thereafter. First of all, it was not in the man, and second, Jefferson Davis clearly wanted someone to come out and fight. In choosing Hood, President Davis had the right man if he wanted action. Hood would come out swinging, and the Army of Tennessee, by its casualties, would provide ultimate proof of the sincerity of his efforts. The fact that Hood would fight was a given, but Davis also was clearly taking a risk. In a telegram to Davis, Lee character-ized Hood as a bold fighter who lacked other necessary qualities for com-mand.[13] Politically, though, Davis could not concede Atlanta without a struggle, and Johnston had given little evidence throughout the campaign of any marked willingness to fight. Atlanta and the industrial complex around it could simply not fall into the hands of Sherman like some ripened fruit. Else why replace Johnston?

Probably from the very beginning Johnston never understood that his re-treat had serious political as well as industrial consequences. Johnston had convinced himself that, as he drew nearer to Atlanta, he was causing Sherman significant casualties.[14] The real blow, however, was that Johnston failed to comprehend that when he gave up the line of the Chattahoochee River he was giving up mills, the iron works at Rome, and eventually the rail transpor-tation network that was Atlanta.[15] Quite likely the triggering mechanism was that, when queried by Richmond as to his plans, Johnston simply replied he was waiting for an opportunity to strike Sherman.[16] Johnston simply yanked the rug from underneath himself. What is important, however, is that Hood's offensive thrusts around Atlanta could not be characterized as spontaneous, reckless, or unplanned. In many respects, Hood could legitimately feel he was a victim of preexisting circumstances. Sherman was at the gates, and he had to stop Sherman's threats as quickly as possible.[17] While Johnston might want to believe he had lured Sherman into his embrace, Hood undoubtedly recog-nized that once Sherman dug in it would be all over. His only hope was to hit Sherman on the march. His first decision was to strike hard at Maj. Gen. George Thomas, who was moving his army across Peachtree Creek. In the course of Sherman's maneuverings, Thomas had been separated from the rest of the Union forces. Hood's assault was a reasoned response. It was a near thing, but Thomas personally brought over the reserve artillery and Hood was forced to fall back.[18]

Getting whipped by Thomas was not unique in Confederate annals, but something more revealing about Hood emerged. Furious over the defeat, he lashed into Lt. Gen. William Hardee, one of his division commanders, hold-ing him personally responsible. In fairness to Hood, Connelly does support the contention that Hardee's leadership was open to criticism.[19] Horn, who never really forgave Hood for what he did to the Army of Tennessee, grudg-ingly recognizes that Hood's plan had some merit.[20]

However, Hood's reaction was an ominous portent of a general unwilling or unable to accept final responsibility. Hood had planned the Peachtree attack reasonably well, although he may not have had the overall strength to defeat Thomas and a veteran Union army. Still, placing the blame on Hardee could well tear his army apart. Like Lee, he had given his orders and left his subor-dinates to execute them; unlike Lee, he would not accept full responsibility, and that was the fatal distinction. Of course, it could also be argued that he really did not have a Jackson or Longstreet, either. With all due respect to the Army of Tennessee, it was not the military equivalent of the Army of Northern Virginia. Moreover, Sherman and Thomas represented a lot more command talent than Lee had faced, especially early in the war.

Hood moved against Sherman's left flflank two days later and was repulsed again. Hardee struck hard, but Maj. Gen. Grenville Dodge's XVI Corps was an unexpected obstacle and, after sharp fighting, Hood again fell back into Atlanta.[21] It was a second bloody setback, but Hood managed to find a silver lining: he perceived the casualties as improving morale, although it certainly was a rough way to increase that vital military commodity.[22] Ezra Church, Jonesboro, and the fall of Atlanta followed inexorably, as a battered Army of Tennessee found itself unable to deal with superior Union forces and generalship. Still, in all fairness to Hood, the South never really did find anyone capable of campaigning successfully against Sherman.

THE BEGINNINGS OF A FLAWED CAMPAIGN

After Atlanta's surrender, Hood began a war of maneuver against Sherman's lines of communication. His reasoning was that if Sherman came after him he would eventually fight, but if Sherman turned south Hood would follow and give battle. Georgia would not be abandoned.[23] In fact, Hood himself initially planned to give battle somewhere near the Tennessee line.[24] He changed his mind repeatedly, however, and subsequent planning took him farther and farther away from any direct challenge to Sherman. It was a convoluted campaign of maneuvering, one that did a better job of confusing his own government than it did Sherman.

Perhaps in the back of his mind lay the old Confederate dream of reaching the Ohio River. Jefferson Davis might dream of reaching the Ohio, but it was now 1864 and the reality of the dream was long gone. It is not inconceivable, too, that in Hood's mind maneuvering was infinitely more appealing than directly facing Sherman again. However, the plan that was beginning to develop had him crossing the Tennessee River, essentially abandoning Georgia to Sherman, and undertaking a campaign that was Napoleonic in concept.[25] The consequence for Georgia was that if Sherman would make the state howl, under Hood's plan it would have to howl alone.

After chasing Hood for a time, Sherman finally departed from Atlanta and struck out through Georgia. At the same time, Hood began his move north across the Tennessee border. The two armies had turned their backs on each other in order to accomplish their own independent objectives. The basic difference was that Sherman knew for sure where he was going; Hood's plans were rather vague. He was probably aiming somewhere at Nashville and Thomas, but he had no clear idea of where the Union forces were in Tennessee, or even how many men they had.

In fact, not knowing about Thomas's growing strength at Nashville, he may very well have thought that Maj. Gen. John Schofield's forces, consisting of the XXIII and IV Corps, were the only troops Thomas had available to stop him.[26] Moreover, Schofield and his forces did not represent an overwhelming obstacle. Thus, if Hood could defeat Schofield, he might wind up crippling Thomas at Nashville. After capturing Nashville, Hood then envisioned a campaign in which he would first defeat a frantic Sherman coming north, and then move east across the Alleghenies to join Lee and attack Grant.[27] There was nothing halfhearted about his objectives, even if they were little more than fantasies.

Such a plan might have held faint glimmers of hope early in the war, but it was impossible now. Hood clearly lacked the necessary men and supplies. However, in an ironic twist of fate, Sherman gave Hood at least the semblance of a chance. When Sherman headed out of Atlanta, he took the better part of his troops with him, both quantitatively and qualitatively.[28] Sherman was leaving Thomas widely scattered forces to fight an army already in the field. Sherman, on the other hand, was moving out against minimal resistance.

That left Thomas in a quandary. He would eventually have the forces necessary to defend Nashville, but as of that moment they were scattered and *en route*. What he most needed was time to concentrate for the defense of Nashville, and Schofield would have to buy it for him. Therefore, the delaying strategy meant Schofield's forces would repeatedly interpose themselves between Hood and Nashville, and then fall back.[29] The leadership odds were not all that uneven. Schofield was probably a notch above Hood in competence, but then again, Hood had Maj. Gen. Nathan Bedford Forrest and his cavalry. The opportunity was there for Hood to create a great deal of mischief.

Thomas's delaying strategy probably reflected his belief that it was not likely Hood could be defeated outright before he reached Nashville. On the other hand, Hood's chances would be considerably enhanced if he moved quickly. Time was Hood's ally; the faster he moved, the less time Thomas would have to put in place all of the troops promised to him. The idea of attacking a fully formed-up Thomas behind fortifications was enough to give any Confederate general a lot to consider.

If Hood pushed Schofield fast enough, and Schofield was not by any stretch of the imagination an aggressive commander, he might get to Nashville under the best possible circumstances. But Hood could not take advantage of the situation. He was slowed considerably from the beginning trying to obtain sorely needed supplies.[30] Lee's portrayal of Hood was proving to be accurate: The cavalier general had lost his campaign advantage at the outset, bogged down in a morass of quartermaster reports. Hood, unfortunately, lacked the

skills necessary to expedite solutions. It was also true that the logistical infra-
structure needed to support the Confederate armies was unraveling throughout the South. The net result was that time was slipping away all too quickly.
Perhaps it would have made no difference in the end.

Yet, even with the diminution of that invaluable ally time, when Hood finally
did cross the Tennessee border he found himself advancing on a foe that was
neither really prepared nor even willing to meet him in a decisive battle before
Nashville itself. With thirty thousand infantry—plus eight thousand cavalry
commanded by General Forrest—he outnumbered a very hesitant Schofield
and posed a real threat to Thomas, who was frantically gathering in troops.[31]
Given Schofield's innate caution, Forrest's presence undoubtedly added to concerns for his safety. There still existed some small hope for Hood's forces.

Nevertheless, a month later, Hood was a ruined commander bemoaning a
failed campaign that even some of his foes characterized as well-conceived.[32]
Like McClellan, at a critical moment Hood had defeated himself, a victim of
psychological forces that overwhelmed his military training and experience.
The nagging problem is why Franklin followed Spring Hill, when defeat at
Peachtree Creek was followed by a bold and detailed plan for a strike at Sherman's flank. Moreover, the fall of Atlanta itself was followed not by *guerre à ou-
trance*, but by a campaign of maneuver. Hood was ever the fighter at Atlanta, and
again at Franklin, but in the latter instance, psychological forces that limited his
choice of tactics to a series of suicidal assaults overwhelmed Hood the general.
Gone at Franklin was any sense of maneuvering beyond the days of the phalanx.

HOOD THE MAN BETRAYS HOOD THE GENERAL

Combining behavioral and psychoanalytic models, the work of John Dollard
and his colleagues at Yale offers one possible explanation for Hood's rigid and
irrational behavior at Franklin. While other models have emerged since then,
the underlying rationale has not changed. When they are examined closely,
the major variables underlying the Yale theory remain, including those involving the person (which includes internal states such as affect, cognition, arous-
al), the specific situation, and the possible outcome of the aggression.[33]
Basically they embedded Freud's death instinct (that is, aggression) within a
stimulus-response framework, creating the famous "Frustration-Aggression
Hypothesis." They took the aggressive impulse, which was characterized as an
innate drive in Freud's model, and treated it as a product of learning rather
than as an instinctual and uncontrollable urge. Basically, the Yale model assumes that when some sequence of behaviors is thwarted (that is, frustrated)
from terminating in the acquisition of a goal, the result is *always* aggressive behavior on the part of the denied goal seeker. In fact, frustration is always
defined as a consequence of interference.[34]

Aggression in turn is represented as a set of behaviors in which physiological or psychological injury to the frustrating agent is the major objective.[35] This means that the immediate objective of the ensuing aggressive behavior is not to reach the original goal, but to inflict some form of punishment on the source of frustration. In this sense, the key to Franklin is to recognize who was the real object of Hood's anger, that is, the perceived frustrating agent. Unlike his reactions to previous failures, the argument will be made that Hood saw the Army of Tennessee and its generals as directly and solely responsible for the Spring Hill fiasco. Franklin then becomes the psychologically induced military result.

Furthermore, the Yale model asserts that while aggression against the source of frustration may lead to a reduction in the aggressive drive, per se, there is not a parallel weakening of the original goal-seeking frustrated behaviors.[36] In a sense, whatever happened at Franklin, to Hood's way of thinking the goals of the campaign itself had not been compromised. This is vitally important, because the theory not only explains why Hood acted as he did at Franklin, but why he continued on to Nashville. Regardless of what happened at Franklin, the campaign goals remained intact. Franklin would tap at the source of Hood's frustration, but leave untainted his overall objectives. Since Franklin shared both psychological as well as military elements, Hood had to categorize Franklin as a victory, at least to himself. His troops had attacked boldly, displaying the valor Hood sought from them, and the Yankees had retreated. He could now move on Nashville.

The Yale researchers went on to derive a set of basic theoretical postulates. First, the strongest aggressive action will be taken against the agent perceived as most directly responsible for the frustration, with weaker actions toward those seen as less responsible. Second, the more inhibitions there are to direct acts of aggression, the more likely the individual will engage in indirect acts.[37] Hood initially directed his anger over the military failures around Atlanta to Hardee. He also perceived a lack of offensive spirit in the Army of Tennessee as the consequence of Johnston and his defensive strategy. However, at that point in time, from Hood's perspective the army was more to be pitied than scorned. Unfortunately for Hardee, he was more to be scorned than pitied. By Spring Hill, however, this distinction between general and private was lost.

The failure at Spring Hill changed the focus of Hood's anger. The Army of Tennessee became part of the conspiracy, with Hood as sole victim. With this change in target, Hood was now free to correct the spiritual flaws in his army, that is, a lack of élan which prevented the campaign from being successful. This was the critical problem to which he addressed himself. He could get rid of generals, but he needed his army. He could not dismiss or abandon the army, but a spiritual rebirth was definitely needed.

The tragedy was that the only solution Hood knew or cared about was hard fighting. Worse yet, morale equaled casualties in Hood's lexicon. As noted, the causal relationship between Spring Hill and Franklin was psychological, in the sense that it supplied a rationale for the tactical considerations. It would result in an army signaling its return to an appropriate level of offensive spirit, and Hood's anger would be diminished. He could now restore the army to an appropriate place in his esteem. But did he have to blame his own army?

The target of aggressive impulse is not always external to the individual. On certain occasions, the aggression may be directed at one's self, especially if one is prone to self-blame. Following Saul Rosenzweig's categorization of aggressive modes of behavior, Hood would be described as extrapunitive, that is, tending to place the blame on others.[38] Historians have in fact always recognized this as a pervasive attribute of Hood's personality. In his foreword to Hood's autobiographical *Advance and Retreat*, Richard Current observes that Hood would sacrifice historical accuracy to advance the cause of his position.[39] Hood's perception of reality, fueled by an overriding sense of frustration and anger, led to his tendency to see everyone else as the cause of failure. By so doing, Hood invariably avoided the personally odious process of condemning himself for his failures. This pattern of blaming others started early in his military career and persisted. His ego would be preserved even if his body was shattered.

The basic outline of the frustration model has remained relatively stable for many years, although Leonard Berkowitz's work resulted in a number of modifications. Berkowitz argued that while anger is the driving force behind aggression, whether or not any aggressive behaviors are observed is dependent on a great many situational deterrents.[40] For example, the strength of the aggressive drive is proportional not only to the anger released, but also the presence of cues inviting the expression of hostility. This explains why crowds may get out of hand at sporting events, particularly where there is a lot of violence (for example, football, soccer, and so on). These cues are associated with the frustrating agent, but are not necessarily physical. Thoughts about the frustrating agent, for example, may serve both to release and direct hostility.[41] Thus, if an official in a game is seen as directly causing a team's defeat, then anger is directed toward this poor unfortunate. Coaches often attempt to convince the crowd that this is indeed the case, and direct angry thoughts away from errors made elsewhere. Hood's approach was basically the same, that is, he believed his problems were due to other's mistakes. Indeed, writing years later, Hood could still not control his feelings for those he felt had let him down at Spring Hill. One can understand if not condone his mood the day after Spring Hill. After all, every time he looked at his army, the fires of resentment were kept burning.

The question could be raised as to why Hood never considered the Union forces as the legitimate target for his all-consuming anger. After all, their continued existence posed a threat to Hood's planning. Why not get mad at the

Yankees? A partial explanation for this dilemma is the concept of instrumental aggression. Berkowitz argued that in the case of instrumental aggression the real focus of the aggressive impulse is on the attainment of some goal rather than just basically expressing anger. As a modern military example, observers noted that the crews of planes engaged in bombing raids during World War II did not necessarily have any significant emotional feelings about the target populace.[42] They were not bombing because they were angry with the people; rather it was their assigned duty in a complex military picture. Of course, the German and Japanese civilians probably held a different view.

The issue is perhaps best explained by a Confederate soldier who succinctly observed, "They fit us, we fit them."[43] Similarly, Hood had no cause to become enraged at the Union forces opposing him. After all, they were doing what they were supposed to do by attempting to thwart his plans whenever and wherever they could. At Franklin, the attack represented a classic example of instrumental aggression, but the tactics Hood used were based more on a need to satisfy his emotionally laden responses to frustration. Hood's actions represented a fusion of two motives, attacking the Union army and salvaging the soul of his own command.

Most significantly, Berkowitz suggests that frustration which is perceived as unexpected or arbitrary is more likely to produce stronger aggressive drives.[44] This is critical to any understanding of the effects of Spring Hill and accounts in a large measure for the debacle at Franklin. To say that Hood lost control of his emotions is well understood by traditional historical analyses, but Berkowitz's work explains why the violent outburst after Spring Hill was not necessarily found elsewhere. At Spring Hill, Hood never saw the Union army as really contributing to his failures. The Franklin disaster resulted from Hood's perception that it was his army and his generals who were the chief culprits in his failure. The Yankees did not thwart him; his own army did. Tragically for the Army of Tennessee, there was no Hardee upon whom he could vent his feelings.

Finally, Berkowitz argued that aggression does not necessarily lead to personal catharsis. Rather, an opportunity to express hostility may lessen the initial anger, but it may also evoke or strengthen habitual hostile tendencies.[45] Hood was in a bad mood at Spring Hill, but he always had a reputation for a quick temper. By setting out immediately after Schofield, he would sustain and then unleash his still simmering anger as soon as he caught up with the retreating Yankees. He was not only after Schofield to defeat him, but to do so with the tactics needed to accomplish an equal if not more important set of objectives.

For Hood, the Tennessee campaign and his self-esteem were inescapably tied together. Hood was an ambitious individual, although in Lee's army he had been content to serve. Out West, however, this changed. He had helped get rid of Johnston, and now the glory (if not ultimate responsibility) were to be all his. The magnitude of his temperamental outburst at Spring Hill and the apparent mindlessness of the Franklin attack clearly suggest that frustrated military aims were tied to deep-seated self-concerns.

Tennessee and the Ohio might very well be the last hurrah for a maimed general avidly pursuing Sally Preston, a famed Richmond beauty. Spring Hill meant much more to Hood the general than a single failure in an extended campaign. He had been able to cope with several defeats at Atlanta, but he fell apart after Spring Hill. At Atlanta he could rationalize defeat as the consequence of the situation he had inherited from Johnston, but Spring Hill was a battlefield of his own planning.

A CHANCE FOR RECOGNITION, SUCCESS, AND GLORY

From the beginning, the Nashville campaign was never a smooth operation. There were, as noted earlier, logistical delays, but these were only part of the problem. Hood also probably had little or no information about the Union forces concentrating in Tennessee, especially around Nashville. While intelligence gathering in the Civil War was primitive to say the least, it was close to nonexistent in Hood's army. There is also some question of how Hood proposed to actually take Nashville. Aside from the fact he had no knowledge of the forces Thomas had or would have available, Nashville was a fortified city. Even worse, George Thomas, who had emerged as the one defensive genius on either side, commanded the army there.

It could also be argued that as a consequence of his lack of knowledge and rather vaguely held grand objectives, Hood never had a firm grasp of the necessary campaign strategy. His initial move toward Pulaski and Schofield's forces could hardly be characterized as one of rapid deployment. Nevertheless, he scared Schofield, which was not all that difficult. Realizing his isolation, a nervous Schofield moved rapidly to the Duck River and then across it. Columbia would be a good place to interpose his forces and buy Thomas at least some of the time he needed.[46] There is no compelling evidence, however, that Schofield was prepared to dispute every foot of Hood's passage through Tennessee. The distance between Columbia and Franklin is about thirty miles, with Spring Hill located about halfway between. The Columbia–Franklin Pike—which connected Columbia, Spring Hill, and Franklin—was the only macadamized road available to Hood and Schofield, and served as the thoroughfare for Schofield's line of retreat as well as Hood's advance.

Hood's reaction was not to call for an immediate and direct assault on the Union works. He hesitated, recognizing it could well be a costly venture. Instead, he came up with a reasonable and certainly less bloody alternative: He would execute a grand flanking maneuver, like his idols Jackson and Lee, and cut across the Union line of withdrawal at Spring Hill. Hood knew Schofield was a cautious man who might well remain within the confines of his Columbia fortifications. The plan was to leave Lt. Gen. Stephen Lee's corps and the bulk of the artillery to hold Schofield in place while Hood moved across the Duck River with the rest of his forces.[47] Certainly at Columbia, Hood demonstrated he was capable of developing a sensible alternative to forcing a river passage against an entrenched foe.

Although Hood's unopposed flanking maneuver at the Duck is historical fact, his objectives are less certain. Indeed, there is some question as to whether the purpose of his move to Spring Hill was to trap Schofield or to gain the macadam road and interpose himself between Schofield and Thomas. The main basis for believing that Hood might be planning to interpose his forces and then move on Nashville comes from his conversations with his chaplain, Bishop Quintard.[48] If the latter was truly Hood's objective, then Hood's subsequent claim that the Spring Hill move was meant to destroy Schofield is a later rationalization, designed to justify at least to himself his rage and subsequent assault at Franklin.

One could easily argue further that if Hood had indeed wanted to get past Schofield he should have flanked him again at Franklin. In fact, that is precisely what Schofield presumed Hood would do. A better argument can be made, however, that Hood's subsequent tactics at Spring Hill fit more easily into a strategy reflecting the interdiction of Schofield, not getting ahead of him. But whatever Hood's objective, Schofield was not blocked at Spring Hill. Instead, Hood found himself still on the road behind him. In either scenario, Hood had failed.

When he caught up with Schofield at Franklin there was never any doubt in Hood's mind of the necessity for an immediate and direct assault. Whatever he had originally thought, he now chose to believe (or had believed from the beginning) that Spring Hill was a failed trap resulting from his troops' unwillingness and inability to close with the enemy. Moreover, because this had become a fixed idea, an attack on Schofield was completely justified. Hood would hurt Schofield as badly as possible, which his army had failed to do at Spring Hill. Further, if he wanted to take on Thomas at Nashville, it was important that his army develop a significantly better offensive spirit. At Franklin his tactics would meet all these requirements.

This view of Hood's thinking is not entirely speculative or even unique. Horn, in his later analysis, still believes that at some point after crossing the Duck, it became Hood's intention to trap Thomas's army.[49] Horn's reappraisal is not intended to reduce Hood's culpability, but rather to increase it. Nowhere does Horn ever suggest that Hood's problems were compounded by real failures of command, particularly by Lt. Gen. Benjamin Franklin Cheatham.

In fact, Horn still believes that the move to the Ohio was a reality. His theory is that even if Hood had not originally intended to trap Schofield at Spring Hill but get past him instead, sometime during that November evening the idea of trapping Schofield became the newer reality. Failure subsequently drove him to Franklin in a blind rage, unarguably committed to give battle under any circumstances. Hence, Hood's assertion that Spring Hill was a trap may not necessarily be a postwar creation. In fact, as one examines his tactics at Spring Hill, they are more suggestive of interdiction than of a hasty attempt to gain the turnpike ahead of Schofield.

Schofield had held on at Columbia, deceiving himself if no one else, although he now had a note from Maj. Gen. James H. Wilson, his cavalry commander, telling him the Confederate forces had crossed the Duck upstream.[50] Led by Hood, the flanking force represented the major part of the Army of Tennessee. He had General Cheatham's and Lt. Gen. Alexander Stewart's corps, along with Forrest's cavalry. However, Hood gave no specific orders regarding what was to happen when they got to Spring Hill. Nevertheless, he had his head start and would be at Spring Hill with superior forces before Schofield fall back. With Hood across the Duck, Schofield had no sound strategic basis for maintaining his position, but he clung to the river.

In his memoirs, Schofield rationalized his strategy by arguing that by staying put he denied the Confederates the use of the better road and thus delayed them. However, trying to defend a strategy that allowed Hood to place the Confederate army between himself and Thomas is more an exercise in rhetoric rather than reason.[51] On November 29, Hood's strategy, whether based on interdiction or getting ahead of Schofield, was coming very close to fruition, given Schofield's unstinting cooperation. It was a bold move, one Wilson later characterized as "brilliant."[52] Even Schofield subsequently acknowledged Hood's plan was sound enough, which was as close as he ever came to recognizing he had been placed in an awkward position. Interestingly, he also believed that Spring Hill was always intended as a trap.[53]

Arriving near Spring Hill at the head of Cheatham's troops, Hood could taste victory. It was about three in the afternoon, time enough if he acted quickly. Meanwhile, Schofield had sent Maj. Gen. David Stanley north at eight that morning along the Columbia–Franklin Pike, with two divisions from IV Corps. Schofield, however, was not preparing to fall back with the remainder of his forces till dusk.[54] Within the guidelines established by this timetable, Schofield could not have supported Hood's plan any better. Moving rapidly along the turnpike, Stanley arrived at Spring Hill about noon with one division. Having a greater sense of urgency than Schofield, he acted quickly and drove out Forrest's cavalry.[55] Stanley soon recognized that he was facing a superior Confederate force of infantry and cavalry. The fighting ranged unabated between skirmishing and some sharp clashes that finally died down about 7 P.M.

As events were to prove, this was not to be one of Forrest's better days. By the time Hood arrived, Stanley had about fifty-five hundred troops in and around Spring Hill.[56] The turnpike north and south of Spring Hill was still completely vulnerable, if not the town itself.

The problem now facing Hood became one of deploying his forces as they came up. If he was intending to trap Schofield, he had precious little daylight left for maneuver. He was facing a growing late autumn darkness that would settle in about 5:30. Since Cheatham's corps arrived first, Hood instructed one of Cheatham's division commanders, Maj. Gen. Patrick Cleburne, to move west and cut the turnpike south of Spring Hill.

Cleburne was probably the hardest-hitting general in Hood's army; the choice was a good one. If Hood wanted action, Cleburne was the logical choice. However, Hood never ordered an attack on Spring Hill directly, and this created problems that would have far-reaching consequences. Hood had no idea that Stanley was in Spring Hill, and his decisions were clearly based on the assumption that any or all of Schofield's forces he encountered would be moving north along the pike. As he moved forward in response to Hood's orders, Cleburne neglected to make contact with Forrest, whom Stanley had driven out earlier that day. As a result, Cleburne, unaware that Union troops were in and around Spring Hill, led his division into a nasty situation. As he deployed west toward the turnpike, his right came under fire from Stanley's troops to the north in Spring Hill.[57]

Surprised, but ever the fighter, Cleburne realigned his division to face north, toward the town. Incredibly, Hood was never informed of the maneuver. Hood next ordered Maj. Gen. William B. Bate's division, also from Cheatham's corps, to form on Cleburne's left. His instructions were to block the turnpike and sweep south. As Bate came up, Cheatham countermanded this order, telling Bate to move from the turnpike and form on Cleburne's left, which was now facing Spring Hill.[58] What followed was a tragedy caused by command errors. Instead of directly informing Hood that the axis of attack had shifted from east–west to north–south, Cheatham said nothing. His two divisions were now clearly focused on Spring Hill, but he also knew this was not Hood's original intent.

When Maj. Gen. John Brown's division arrived, Cheatham ordered him to form up on the right. Cheatham's corps was now entirely committed to operations on Spring Hill. Brown was to begin the attack, signaling a general assault from right to left. Brown, however, immediately realized that the Union forces at Spring Hill outflanked him. Cheatham told him to go ahead anyway, but Brown insisted he had orders to wait until Lt. Gen. Alexander Stewart came up with his corps. Since Brown did not begin the attack, Cleburne and Bate also waited.[59] Meanwhile, daylight had run out, undoubtedly contributing to the confusion. Hood, hearing no sounds of a general engagement, which he had assumed from the beginning would be along the turnpike, was growing frantic.

When Stewart came up with his corps, Hood—who still believed that Cheatham's corps was positioned along the turnpike, facing west and south—ordered him to halt. Stewart was supposed to cut off the Union forces that should be fleeing along the Rally Hill Road, east of Spring Hill, now that, in theory at least, the turnpike had been cut. When Hood learned that Brown was outflanked, he ordered Stewart to move past Cleburne's right and seize the pike north of town. This was a logical move if the army had been where Hood had intended it to be.

The tragicomedy played on. First, Stewart got himself lost.[60] Hood then sent Stewart new orders to align on Brown's right, but this placed him farther south and east, not north and west of Spring Hill. Instead, Stewart bivouacked for the night.[61] Hood had, of course, assumed that the move would place Stewart's right flank on the pike north of Spring Hill, his left protecting Brown, and everyone still facing the turnpike. Whether or not Hood could have taken Spring Hill and cut the pike is problematical, but it is clear that what he thought was happening differed unbelievably from the actual state of affairs: Cheatham was conducting one battle and Hood was directing another. The crux of the problem, of course, was Stanley's presence in Spring Hill, of which Hood apparently was unaware at that moment.

O'Connor suggests that Hood might have gone forward then, taken direct command, and personally led the attack.[62] However, a general who had lost a leg at Chickamauga and carried a shattered arm from Gettysburg might very well believe he had left enough of his body on various battlefields. Given his physical condition, it is quite conceivable that he was exhausted by late afternoon. Moreover, emulating Lee, he left his commanders free to execute his orders as they saw fit.

Another but somewhat more speculative possibility is that once having arrived at Spring Hill, he may have felt, in part at least, that he had accomplished or eventually could accomplish what he wanted. With Schofield still at Columbia, or at the most moving along the pike, perhaps he had enough time. Pausing would be consonant with a plan based on cutting the pike rather than getting ahead of Schofield. Whatever Hood's reasons, darkness had come and Union forces still held Spring Hill. More importantly, the turnpike was still open. At this critical point in the campaign, Hood's command had become a travesty of the concept. His objectives, whatever they might have been, were thwarted not by Schofield, but by his own staff.

With the road still open, tired and anxious Union troops from Schofield's command stumbled along through the gathering dusk and later that night, with Confederate campfires blazing only a short distance from their columns. Even at this close proximity, no major fighting broke out. It was, however, a situation that definitely had the potential to turn into a disaster for Schofield. In fact, about midnight, a private in Hood's army visited his headquarters and informed the rebel commander that Union troops were still moving along the pike. Hood immediately ordered Cheatham to cut off the escape.[63] According to Hood's aide, the message was not sent. Incredibly, Cheatham states that he did get the note, but his officers found no troops on the pike. Someone's memory or grasp on reality had slipped.[64] Hood went back to sleep. Ever scornful, Horn raises the old canard that Hood may have been drunk.[65] Nevertheless, the Union forces were incredibly lucky that night. The Army of Tennessee, on the other hand, deserved a better fate.

Descriptions of the situation are mixed, but a hurried night march would seem to belie any argument that there was never any real danger.[66] No Union report conveys anything but a sense of urgency and concern. Colonel Emerson Opdycke, commanding the 1st Brigade in Maj. Gen. George Wagner's division, reported sharp fighting as the last of the Union forces left Spring Hill at four in the morning on the Thirtieth.[67] Schofield would escape to enjoy Hood's disaster at Franklin.

Some critics of the trap theory argue that Hood would not have succeeded even if Cheatham had initially carried out Hood's orders to the letter. Basically, the argument is that the Union forces had available alternate routes to Franklin. In fact, James McDonough suggests that at least some of Schofield's forces actually may have used a road west of the turnpike while moving up.[68] What Schofield feared most was that Hood would cut the pike *north* of Spring Hill, bypassing Stanley. Horn agrees with this, noting that by cutting the pike south of town Hood would have placed himself between Stanley at Spring Hill and Schofield coming north.[69] It is difficult, though, to accept the simple premise that if Hood had indeed cut the pike south of Spring Hill, Schofield would have been able and willing in the darkness to call for Stanley's assistance or veer off and avoid Hood. A more likely scenario is that if Hood had struck south of Spring Hill he might well have been able to mask Stanley and defeat Schofield in detail, inflicting heavy losses.

Cutting north of Spring Hill would leave Schofield with several options, including trying to bypass Hood or forming on Stanley's forces in Spring Hill. The Franklin fight thus might well have been made in and around Spring Hill on the Thirtieth. Obviously, there were no absolutely safe choices for either Hood or Schofield. However, one of Thomas's officers who was with Schofield believed that placing a Confederate brigade across the pike could have resulted in the destruction of Schofield's army.[70] Given this exaggeration from one of the enemy, Hood's loss of temper is not an entirely unreasonable reaction. His generals and his army had let him down, resulting in a clearly unexpected failure.[71]

At Spring Hill, Hood felt his "golden opportunity" had been destroyed, not by actions of the Union army but by mistakes that were entirely the responsibility of his own army. The psychological pressures of a leadership lacking victories, beginning in Atlanta, climaxed at Spring Hill. Months earlier, Hood had been able to handle personal frustration by blaming Johnston and getting rid of Hardee. With those emotional outlets, command still meant planning. But now there were Hardees everywhere, and no Johnston. His tolerance for failure collapsed at Spring Hill, exceeded by the unexpectedness of his army's lack of aggressiveness. He had flanked Schofield, arriving at Spring Hill in time either to get ahead of him or cut off his forces. Neither option had been realized. Hood, the general, was now both the military and spiritual leader of his army. One might note that Gen. Henri Philippe Pétain faced similar military-psychological problems upon taking over the French army at Verdun, but he admittedly was a lot more cautious and realistic in his solutions.

HOOD AS PRIEST AND GENERAL

Sometime after Spring Hill and before Franklin, Hood—after months of brooding—had completely convinced himself that the Army of Tennessee needed an immediate refurbishing of its collective soul. He was not to blame; his army's failure was the result of his subordinates' lack of military ardor.[72] Hay, however, sees the issues as more complicated, in that Hood's orders may not have been as precise as given in his memoirs. Brown, for example, who was supposed to initiate the attack, insisted he received no orders to begin. Nevertheless, regardless of their clarity, Hood failed to accept ultimate responsibility.

The topic of morale comes up constantly in Hood's memoirs. The very frequency of his concerns suggests Hood might well have also been asking himself if he still possessed the necessary will to fight on in the ever-growing atmosphere of a losing conflict. He was a physical wreck, but even maimed generals could still receive accolades and honor for victories.[73] The triumph he sought at Spring Hill would almost certainly have bolstered his self-esteem, but an inept and hesitant army and generals had snatched it all away from him. Spring Hill would have been his moment of truth, his claim to leadership qualities that would confound critics who perceived him as a militarily limited field commander.

Again, the failure at Atlanta could arguably be attributed to Johnston, but the Tennessee campaign was all his. Hood's fury clearly suggests he truly believed Spring Hill could and would have been a major coup, and his army's failure to spring the trap undoubtedly sustained his anger throughout the next day and throughout his life.

His army would suffer because he felt that as general, he had the power to do so.[74] Never in his memoirs does Hood acknowledge that the Union forces had the capacity to thwart his attack. Forrest and Cheatham might have disagreed, but there is no record he ever asked for their opinions. Hood assigned failure at Spring Hill to his army alone. This was the unexpected frustrating element that contributed to his psychological undoing. In spite of all his planning, he had been betrayed by his own forces. Thus, when Hood came upon the entrenched Union forces at Franklin the next day, aside from necessary military outcomes, the attack had to be designed to correct those flaws in morale existing in the Army of Tennessee and its leaders. Franklin would serve Hood in a dual psychological-military role.

The basis for this belief is found in Hood's memoirs:

> The best move in my career as a soldier, I was thus destined to behold to come to naught. The discovery that the Army, after a forward march of one hundred and eighty miles, was still, seemingly unwilling to accept battle unless under the protection of breastworks, caused me to experience grave concern. In my inmost heart I questioned whether or not I could ever succeed in eradicating this evil. It seemed to me I had exhausted every means in the power of one man to remove this stumbling block to the Army of Tennessee.[75]

While the first sentence is extensively cited, it is the third sentence that is particularly germane. Hood refers to an "evil" in his army. After Spring Hill and before Franklin he convinced himself that he must once and for all purge the army of its spiritual shortcomings while maintaining, of course, his military objectives. While Hood would certainly protest that he was seeking solely to defeat Thomas's army, it is hard to understand why he chose a tactical stance that placed his troops in great jeopardy. In truth, the tactics actually chosen served an equally compelling nonmilitary purpose. Up to this point the campaign had been one of maneuver, but this vanished in the face of Hood's righteous rage. Given the constraints imposed by Hood's tactics, his men had no recourse but to succeed by coming straight at the Union troops. The rites of exorcism would be brutal; the manner of attack admirably suited all purposes. It would be to the Army of Tennessee's everlasting sorrow that he did not use the less sanguinary and more traditional bell, book, and candle.

Hood's generals would be given no opportunity to hesitate or maneuver out of harm's way, thus failing to carry out the spiritual refurbishing proposed by Hood. The resulting bloodshed would cleanse the army of its sins, and at the same time he would defeat Schofield. He would win and, to his way of thinking, the price paid in blood would more than be compensated by the accompanying boost in morale. Hood's rigidity would be a personal tragedy not only for himself, but also for the Army of Tennessee. He was not to be dissuaded.

Indeed, when his generals first saw the Union lines, they realistically demurred. The Union forces were entrenched in a long, concave line south of the Harpeth River. Forrest, whose aggressiveness could never be questioned, suggested a flanking maneuver. Such a move had a high probability of success against Union cavalry still not up to the task of defeating Forrest. Cheatham also hesitated, knowing enough about the risks involved in hitting entrenchments head-on.[76] Furthermore, to even reach the Union lines, Hood's army would have to cross a level plain for almost two miles, directly into entrenched Union troops supported by artillery.[77]

To compound the tactical disaster, the Confederates would have no artillery support. Hood later claimed he was fearful of firing into the village and hitting civilians, but the truth was that most of the artillery was still with Lee at the Duck River and thus not available.[78] Never mind, he would crush Schofield. Betrayed by his anger, Hood had irrevocably convinced himself that his army's psychological needs and military objectives could be fused to achieve the triumph that had eluded him at Spring Hill.

And yet, if Pétain succeeded, why did Hood fail? Hood's attack at Franklin represented a very rigid and unfortunate solution to both sets of objectives. Hood clung to the principle of the offensive throughout his career; at Franklin his tactics were fueled and driven by raw emotions. One could argue that a flanking move at Franklin would also have satisfied the requirements for an offensive thrust; Hood had used this same maneuver before, at Columbia. Now, though, Hood was marching to the sound of another drummer. The inflexibility of his thinking was never more obvious than when he ordered his army to move forward, bereft of artillery and observation.

In Hood's lexicon, ardor was necessarily accompanied by casualties. A frontal assault would mean greater losses, but the nature of the attack would secure victory for the Army of Tennessee while cleansing its collective soul. The army could fight and win on Hood's terms. It had to be done here and now. To delay purification would mean an army ill-prepared to carry out the rest of the campaign.

Incredibly, the Army of Tennessee almost succeeded. Stanley had posted two brigades under Maj. Gen. George Wagner some distance in front of the Union lines. Wagner insisted that he had orders to develop the enemy attack, but the suddenness of the Confederate onslaught threw his forces back in confusion.[79] He may also have been dreaming of his successes at Spring Hill. Whatever the case, he stayed in his exposed position too long and Schofield almost came to grief. In rebuttal to Wagner, Maj. Gen. Jacob Cox later insisted that Wagner had been placed there to observe the advancing rebels, not fight them.[80] Regardless of whose fault it was, Wagner's men started running rearward with the Confederates right behind them. Thus it was that the pursuing Confederates reached the outer works of the Union lines at the same time as Wagner's men.

The presence of Wagner's fleeing men prevented Union troops from immediately firing on the advancing Confederates. A XXIII Corps brigade holding that part of the line was swept aside and for a moment the Confederates actually succeeded in penetrating the Union position.[81] Fortunately for the Union forces, Col. Emerson Opdycke, commanding the 1st Brigade of Wagner's division, and Col. John White, commanding the 16th Kentucky of Cox's division, acting on their own initiative, promptly counterattacked. The Confederate forces were thrown back to the outer lines where they grimly hung on.[82] Hood or no Hood, this was a veteran Confederate army with its own history.

Although Brown and Cleburne had been responsible for the initial breach of the Union center, flanking forces were repulsed and there were no reserves to follow up their temporary successes.[83] What followed was a slaughter. Particularly hard hit were Brown's men just west of the pike. Thrust back to the outer defenses, they were caught in an angle formed by the Union defenses. With most of their commanding officers down, they were torn apart in a cross fire from which they could not extricate themselves. They could not retreat, nor could they advance. Within a relatively short period of time there were no commanding officers left to reorganize them in any semblance of military organization. Cleburne's men were in a similarly impossible position, since the angle in the Union defenses actually began east of the pike.[84]

Meanwhile, the Confederate commanding generals sat in a state of ignorance as dark as the night. Neither Hood nor Cheatham exercised any real field leadership. At some distance from the front lines and separated from each other they sat and waited. When Lt. Gen. Stephen Lee finally came up from Columbia, Hood, utterly ignorant of the tactical situation, ordered Lee to send Johnson's brigades forward.[85] From Hood's perspective he probably felt he had accomplished what he wanted anyway. It is hard to believe, though, especially from his behavior afterward, that he realized the magnitude of the growing losses.

Yet Hood's men still persisted. At least five separate charges were recorded, although toward the end they probably were uncoordinated attempts. These were veteran troops who were well aware of their deadly situation. Hay suggests that the commanding officers and men, stung by Hood's censure after Spring Hill, were prepared to "conquer or die."[86] There indeed appeared to be a certain element of utter madness.[87] To a Private Watkins, in the ranks, the analogy was to Hell itself.[88] The grim humor that had sustained men like Watkins throughout the war appears nowhere in his narrative of Franklin. Operant psychologists might describe it as an example of pain aggression. Two animals placed in proximity on an electric grid will fight each other when a charge is passed through the wire. The closeness and ferocity of the conflict is not an unreasonable parallel. At about 9 P.M. the killing stopped and Schofield withdrew later that night.

The Army of Tennessee was in shambles, having suffered casualties that could not be borne by any command, certainly not in terms of meeting Hood's grandiose visions. Nonetheless, at least one of Hood's objectives had been met:

His commanders and troops had paid in blood for whatever sins of commission or omission had occurred the previous day. They had been suitably shriven for the work ahead. To any objective observer, however, it was obvious Hood's campaign plans had foundered before the barricades at Franklin. Hood's views, though, were based on far more subjective perceptions of reality. The next morning he found himself with essentially three alternatives: retreat, advance on Nashville, or bypass it and move north.[89]

In fact, what Hood did first was issue a general field order calling Franklin a victory, a display of the army's invincibility.[90] He did indeed hold the field, which was a tactical victory from his point of view. Moreover, the Army of Tennessee had displayed all the intestinal fortitude one could have desired. From Hood's perspective, therefore, the campaign could and would go on. In fact, it was not until January 1865 that he would inform the Confederate government as to the full extent of his losses.[91] To admit to himself that morning that his army was so shattered that he could not go on would have been psychologically impossible. At Franklin, there was no one else to whom he could assign the blame, if such an irresponsible failure was to be acknowledged. The Army of Tennessee had done exactly as ordered. He could not allow himself that moment of objectivity, wherein he would acknowledge that he had let personal feelings get in the way of sound military planning.

Hence, the retreat option was psychologically out of the question. He had no recourse but to believe that Franklin was a tactical victory. And that is exactly what Hood did in his proclamation. The second option, to slip past Nashville, was also not a good one. Logistics were an ever-present albatross around his neck. He needed Nashville as a supply base.[92] He also probably had little or no idea even at that time how heavily Nashville was defended. Subsequent statements about knowing Thomas's strength are probably a product of later knowledge.[93] The sad part of the whole campaign, Franklin in particular, was that even if he had come to Nashville intact, the end result, albeit bloodier, would likely have been the same.

In addition to all his other troubles, the Union cavalry was beginning to create problems for Forrest. Wilson was finally putting together an effective cavalry force. Hood would no longer have the freedom of maneuver he had once enjoyed. At Franklin, Wilson had beaten Forrest back, denying him a rather limited flanking movement across the river.[94] It was not much of a victory, but then again, he had not lost. Finally, maneuverability had also been compromised by the wholesale slaughter of high-ranking officers. An army does not easily absorb the loss of a dozen generals in addition to dozens more lower-ranking field officers.

Hood at last acted on his third option, which was to continue on to Nashville. This represents the only viable decision he had left, if the frustration model is to explain his behavior. The immediate goals of his anger had been met, at least to his satisfaction. But the aggressive drives that had always characterized Hood remained undiminished. He could now concentrate his fury on the Union army. At Franklin he had dealt with the internal problems of his army, but the overall military objectives of the campaign were yet to be satisfied. Schofield had retreated to Nashville and Hood now had troops whose martial spirit had been reborn. Southern valor would overcome Yankee steel. Unfortunately for Hood, it was George Thomas, a very tough and capable Virginian, who was waiting for him in heavily fortified Nashville.

Horn puts it differently: Hood was presenting himself to Thomas.[95] Hood hardly had the forces even if he had arrived intact to beat Thomas and capture Nashville. With Schofield back in Nashville, Thomas's Army of the Cumberland was finally concentrated. Most historians now agree that Hood never really knew at that time just how badly he was outnumbered at Nashville.[96]

Hood subsequently explained his strategy as one of awaiting reinforcements, receiving Thomas's attack, defeating him, and then carrying out the remainder of his campaign across the Ohio.[97] Napoleon once characterized the passive defensive as a form of deferred suicide. In this case, he was absolutely right. Two weeks later Thomas would hammer Hood into final disgrace and the Army of Tennessee into oblivion. Spring Hill, the "best move of his career," was forever lost, along with command and career.

Hood would never live down the awful outcome of the Tennessee campaign. Nevertheless, he clung firmly to his beliefs. For the rest of his life he believed his failure was the result of the fiasco at Spring Hill, the short duration of daylight at Franklin (!), and the failure to send reinforcements to him at Nashville (which he had no reason at all to believe could be made available). Hood believed to the day he died that he was the victim of fates not of his making.[98]

The disaster at Franklin did indeed have its origins at Spring Hill, as many historians have argued. However, it is not the failure, per se, at Spring Hill, but the unexpected source of the failure. Hood reacted on the premise that the Army of Tennessee and his generals had to be rid of all spiritual weaknesses before he could succeed. At Franklin, the Union forces became a means to that end. In a ghastly sense, the tactics employed at Franklin were in keeping with Hood's fusion of military and psychological necessities regarding the needs of the Army of Tennessee. Worse, even after Franklin, he could still move on Nashville without admitting that Franklin had destroyed his campaign. Franklin, perhaps like Stalingrad, is a classic example of how a leader, for personal reasons, not only sought to punish an army and its commanders through battle, but also believed it could be done without relinquishing objectives. That is why neither Hood nor Hitler could ever retreat, or even admit to the fallacies in their thinking.

CHAPTER SIX

BEYOND CONVENTIONAL HISTORICAL EXPLANATIONS: THE BRITISH MILITARY IN WORLD WAR ONE

(WITH PARTICULAR EMPHASIS ON DOUGLAS HAIG)

The machine gun is a much overrated weapon,
and two per battalion is more than sufficient.
— Gen. Sir Douglas Haig

LEON FESTINGER, in his work *A Theory of Cognitive Dissonance*, has declared that "dissonance" results when an individual's choice of action or belief is challenged by new situations and information. In such a case, the individual attempts to preserve consistency—or "consonance," as he calls it—by "actively avoid[ing] situations and information which would likely increase the dissonance."[1] In any choice between alternative courses of action there are "cognitive elements" corresponding to favorable aspects of the rejected choice and elements corresponding to the unfavorable ones of the selected choice. Once a choice has been made, dissonance "can be materially reduced by eliminating some of these elements or by adding new ones that are consonant with the knowledge of the action taken." Dissonance-increasing information can be nullified "by various means such as misperception, denying its validity, and the like."[2] Even if a choice is made in a putatively rational manner—and Festinger and his colleagues seem to think most choices are made in this fashion—postdecision thought and behavior (if dissonance is present) thus tend to be one-sided and biased.[3] The degree to which an individual will seek to suppress dissonant information, as well as the speed with which this process is commenced, are in large measure determined by two crucial factors: (1) the degree to which a choice has been decided upon after an examination of alternatives (this does not, however, rule out the possibility that impulse might have something to do with the decision-making process itself), and (2) the degree of commitment to the choice eventually made.[4]

In nineteenth-century England, there lived a noble lover of the rustic life who did not want to admit that railways existed. He made certain that, during the course of his daily peregrinations, he never ventured into areas in which, according to rumor, trains could be observed. This individual presumably died convinced that stories of unnatural, cinder-spouting machines were the products of diseased imaginations.

In several World War I histories there is a famous photograph of the British royal family and other notables about to review a parade of British troops held in celebration of victory in November 1918. There on the reviewing stand is George V, his somewhat more sturdy-appearing wife ("the other four-fifths," as she was referred to by irreverent American soldiers), and assorted family members and ministers. Below the stand one can contemplate the members of the Imperial General Staff. Study these figures closely. Any one of them could have been related to the previously mentioned nobleman. With a few notable exceptions, the British war effort between 1914 and 1918 was characterized by a seemingly perverse commitment to stale, unimaginative tactics that were responsible for slaughters that would be equaled only by those on the eastern front in World War II.[5]

Military minds of all countries are often not noted for breadth of imagination or subtlety. In the case of England, however, one is struck by certain persistent problems that plagued the military establishment during the First World War. This chapter examines what we think are the most prominent ones, problems that, in our opinion, cannot be explained in traditional historical terms. After considering various personalities and events, focusing in the end upon Sir Douglas Haig as representative of the basic problems involved, we will apply the cognitive dissonance hypothesis to these problems and, in the course of such, reach an overall conclusion that will be somewhat disquieting.

A LONG, BLOODY ROAD

At the beginning of World War I, there were some—such as Lord Horatio Kitchener, the secretary of state for war, and Douglas Haig—who realistically expected the conflict to be a long one. As for the British army of 1914, it was relatively small. However, despite overall problems with training, it had assimilated certain painful lessons learned during the Boer War and was probably the best in the world with regards to marksmanship.[6] Committed to battle in August 1914, this army (the "Old Contemptibles") was, along with the armies of France and Belgium, steadily pressed back by its German opponents. In numerous engagements, however—in the course of which Field Marshal Sir John French provided several examples of tactical incompetence—it demonstrated what accurate rifle fire could do against packed masses of advancing troops. Moreover, in the actions at Ypres and along the Yser River that marked

the end of a war of movement and helped to initiate one of trenches, it inflicted staggering casualties upon the Germans. The German general staff also
learned much from these engagements. The Imperial General Staff, itself in
large measure responsible for the superb marksmanship training that made
the British army so dangerous a foe, seemingly learned nothing from the successes of its own soldiers.

Beginning in March 1915, and in part because of pleas from their French allies, the British Expeditionary Force (BEF), at the time under the command
of Sir John French, launched a series of offensives at several points along the
line. General Douglas Haig, commander of the BEF's I Corps, had shown
considerable skill in the first defensive battles at Ypres. Now, as commander
of the First Army, he was to play a crucial role in them. On March 10, 1915,
the army struck at Neuve-Chapelle. After initially breaking through the German defenses, it was brought to a halt by German artillery and machine-gun
fire from nests located eight hundred to a thousand yards behind the first line
of defense. This, plus the difficulties of moving up reserves fast enough to exploit initial successes, served to frustrate the heroic British effort. In the final
analysis, Neuve-Chapelle turned out to be a costly stalemate. Further offensives, in conjunction with those planned by the French, were contemplated.[7]
As new approaches were being considered, Haig, who before the war had demonstrated considerable interest in the machine gun, made the following statement in a minute submitted to the War Council on April 14, 1915: "The machine gun is a much overrated weapon, and two per battalion is more than
sufficient."[8] What the *overall* commander of the BEF had to say about machine guns has not been recorded. It would appear, however, that despite his
differences with the at that time subordinate Haig on other matters, he agreed
with his opinion on this issue. A reason why Haig changed his view on the matter will be offered later.

The British army struck again, this time at Aubers Ridge, on May 9, 1915,
and once again "massed man-power was to be asked to overrun a thin firing
line." At day's end, almost no gain at all had been recorded and the British
army had lost 458 officers and 11,161 men. "It had been a disastrous fifteen
hours of squandered heroism, unredeemed by the faintest glimmer of success."[9] Obviously, still more adequate preparations had to be made.

Both Haig and his commander, French, had become convinced that the complexity of the German defenses ruled out the possibility that any form of "surprise attack" could be successful. The sudden, brief artillery bombardment used
at Neuve-Chapelle and Aubers Ridge was now ruled out as well. The emphasis
would now be placed on methodical preparations and methodical artillery
bombardment.[10]

Even with the somewhat inadequate preparations, there had been initial
success at Neuve-Chapelle. Surely with more adequate measures, plus the
emphasis upon sustained weight of shell, complete success would be assured.[11]

What both Haig and his chief did not take into consideration—or at least to the degree appropriate in such situations—was that the German defenders would also make changes and that, as the *defenders*, they were in the position (literally) to make more substantive ones more rapidly. Beginning with the 1915 battles, we can observe a response to rebuff or stalemate that will prevail at the higher levels of the British command structure until rather late in the war—some relatively minor tactical adjustments, even, as we shall see, when involving the use of new weapons, plus an emphasis upon increasing weight of shell. In such an approach, the trump card would always be the attacking mass. Unfortunately for the British, there was not yet an ample enough supply of shells to provide for sustained support of this mass. Thus, gas, which the Germans had first introduced in April 1915, would be used as a sort of substitute in operations conducted in the near future. Such was done in the attack on Loos, launched on September 25, 1915. To be perfectly fair about it, one must point out that the ill-fated battle was undertaken by a general staff that lacked confidence in its ability to achieve victory. Moreover, it was ordered by the government, which was fearful that if the British did not play an even greater part in the war effort, her allies might be tempted to make peace with Germany.[12] After August 1915, the British government was in fact committed to a vigorous policy of warfare which necessitated the use of millions of men. Thus, one could say, a desire for total victory on the part of the civilian leadership was firmly in place, and a synergy between this desire and the perhaps "natural" inclinations of military men cleared the way for the mass slaughter that followed. Important civilian leaders, especially David Lloyd George, who became prime minister in 1916, and Douglas Haig might well have loathed each other. Nevertheless, they shared a commitment to total victory. This is a theme that we will consider again later in this chapter.

In some regards, Haig, who as before was in charge of the assault, showed caution, particularly when it came to using poison gas. He also was, initially at least, somewhat skeptical as to the possibility of a rapid advance. On the first day, some success was obtained when a portion of the 47th Division broke through the German line. As in previous battles, at least partially successful efforts to breach the first German line were responsible for raising false hopes as to the possibility of a general breakthrough. Reinforcements were needed to exploit the meager gains of September 25. Unfortunately, those available, XI Corps's 21st and 24th Divisions, had been kept well to the rear by Field Marshal French, despite the fact that his subordinate, Haig, had indicated that he wanted them close by in order to exploit any breach in the enemy lines.[13] After an exhausting forced march on the night of September 25–26 and much trouble finding their way into line, the troops were tired, hungry, and hardly in any condition to attack. Haig was not unaware of this, but he threw them into the Loos battle on the morning of September 26 just the same.

The Germans reinforced the threatened areas, especially the area where XI

Corps was to attack, with scores of machine guns. Meanwhile, the far-from-battle-ready troops of the 21st and 24th Divisions attacked as if they were not there. "One of the German battalion commanders spoke later of the revolting and nauseating impressions made on them as they watched the slaughter; so much so that after the retreat began they ceased fire."[14] In German military circles, the second day of fighting at Loos would be remembered as the "Leichenfeld von Loos" ("corpse-field of Loos"). The British lost 385 officers and 7,861 men. The German army, as all armies, had officers with a statistical bent who liked to determine ratios of losses between their own troops and the enemy's. On this occasion, though, they must have been mildly frustrated since the German army at Loos suffered no casualties at all on September 26, 1915.

After the battle, Haig maintained that the terrible events of the second day were due to his commander's withholding of the reserve forces. XI Corps was too far back, so the troops, after making exhausting marches, were too "played out" to play an effective role in the battle. Most military historians agree with this, although there is some question as to whether the reinforcements could have achieved a breakthrough even if they had been available earlier and *not* been in a depleted state.[15] The German defenses were just too strong. Yet, blame for the slaughter at Loos must be equally distributed. French may very well have been responsible for holding back the reserves Haig anticipated needing. Haig, though—and this would point to future problems—was unwilling to call off an attack he knew would involve troops ill-prepared to participate in it. Even more important, he persisted in attacking even after the pointless nature of it became apparent.[16] At this point, however, the overall impression Haig made on people was one of competence, at least in comparison to his commander in chief.

In rationalizing the slaughter, which would become common, the future commander of the British Fifth Army, Gen. Sir Hubert Gough, declared that Generals Haig and French had not really been in favor of attacking at Loos, but had done so in response to French demands (Gough did not implicate the British government). There is a strong possibility that this was the case. Besides, and this was of crucial importance (and somewhat more debatable), the German troops were being worn down by such attacks and the morale of the German people was being severely affected.[17] How the loss ratios—or, as we have seen, at times, lack of one—between two opposing armies fit into this analysis was something not explored by Gough. Yet, this argument is an important one, and in due course we will be returning to it.

In all events, even after the terrible losses of September 26, British attacks in the Loos area continued until October 15. This was due in large measure to French pressure, but there is little doubt that the British leadership was confident that, sooner or later, a breakthrough would take place. Once the battle was over, and the meager results of it obvious to all, a curious sort of optimism prevailed.

The British leaders were not shaken by the results of the battle, even though they had lost 50,000 men and were no closer to victory than they had been before. If anything, their confidence had increased. They had seen, or knew, that the German front line had been captured, that British infantry had penetrated over two miles in some places, and that localities fortified at leisure with all the skill and experience of the most accomplished German engineers had fallen before them. This surely proved that the German front was not impregnable and that the BEF, given luck, proper leadership and sufficient ammunition, was capable of achieving a decisive victory. Next time it would be different.[18]

In fact, General Haig contemplated a renewed offensive in the Loos area in November. Increasingly bad weather conditions forced him to call it off, although even these would come to be discounted in the future. What had become obvious by December 1915 was that the commanders of the BEF had developed an extraordinary faith in a "system." Individual commanders might be deficient with regard to its application, and Field Marshal French was increasingly being regarded as such, but if one were steady and persistent and the appropriate amounts of men and munitions were available, the "system" would, in the end, prevail. What *was* the system? Grounded in a pre–World War I emphasis upon simply grabbing enemy-occupied land and holding on to it—something which we will consider further later in this chapter—it was, in its essentials, mass infantry assault supported by increasing weight of shell.

GENERAL HAIG ASSUMES COMMAND OF THE BEF

In December 1915, French was replaced as commander in chief by Haig, who had at the very least acquiesced in a vicious, if understandable, behind-the-scenes campaign against French. Born in 1861 into the Lowland Scottish family of the whiskey-making Haigs, the new BEF commander showed much interest in military affairs, but little in the way of ability. Indeed, according to one historian, he was generally viewed as the "dunce" of an otherwise successful family.[19] He had been able to avoid taking the entrance examination to Sandhurst, failed the staff college entrance examination, and, from all accounts, was dependent upon contacts and the "pull" generated by them to finally gain admission to the college, an obvious prerequisite to advancing a military career of any consequence.[20] In the Boer War, Haig was chief of staff to John French, whom Haig succeeded as commander of the BEF in 1915. French's unspectacular performance in the Boer War was equaled by that of Haig, who throughout showed a stodginess and adherence to predetermined plans that drew unfavorable comment at the time.[21] Douglas Haig has been described as a man whose sense of ambition and purpose was grounded in fear of failure. His rigidity, conservatism, and insensitivity to the losses his army sustained have been seen as symptomatic of the sort of "authoritarianism" engendered by rigid upbringing in a home shot through with Victorian values, not the least of which was the belief that success was an indication of providential favor.[22]

Thus, Haig was driven by a powerful ambition. Seemingly oblivious of both his obvious deficiencies and of his colleagues' awareness of them, he cultivated the favor of those above him, including that of King George V. In this regard, his marriage to one of Queen Alexandra's maids of honor was of no small importance.[23] His performance in the 1912 military exercises was abysmal to the point of embarrassment. Nonetheless, his contacts continued to stand him in good stead.

Haig showed an interesting tendency in his rise to the top. While virtually inarticulate in conversation, he was quite expressive in his journal and in letters and, very often, his expressions took the form of snide, at times sarcastic, attacks upon colleagues above, below, and on the same level as himself.[24] At the same time, Haig—admittedly not unlike many of his fellow officers— showed an extreme conservatism with regard to matters of military science. While it is not true that he was contemptuous of, or uninterested in, all innovation—he was, for example, interested in the uses of the machine gun, at least for a while—Haig continued to believe in the value, if not supremacy, of the cavalry. Indeed, he envisaged ever-increasing uses for the mounted arm in future wars.[25] He did not think that artillery fire would have a devastating impact upon any but "raw" troops and, all in all, seemed perfectly content not to question the previously mentioned assumption, widely held in British military circles, that the army's primary task was to assault enemy-held territory and seize and hold on to it. His conservatism, of course, was no doubt rather appealing to that significant portion of those in the British establishment who wanted nothing better than to be confirmed in that in which they so strongly believed.[26] By the standards of the time, he also seemed to be one born to command. "His excellent horsemanship, his good looks and his pleasant, if reserved, manner, made him a popular figure in the circle in which he moved." He was also admired for his "rock-like quality, that imperturbable calm with which he met disaster and triumph alike."[27]

By the time war broke out, we can see the following picture of Haig. A man of not notable intelligence, but of immense ambition, he had to rely on influence-peddling and good fortune to advance in his military career. He had aroused no small degree of enmity in the process. Slow and inarticulate verbally, he was sarcastic and vindictive to his comrades in arms in writing. Yet, while seemingly holding much of the military establishment in contempt, he was himself extremely conservative, in his own eyes standing foursquare for traditions that he saw as central to the time-honored heritage of the British army.

As mentioned earlier, Haig, under Sir John French, commanded I Corps and, during engagements around Ypres in November 1914, showed some skill in defensive operations. As we have seen, the 1915 battles revealed certain problematic qualities in his leadership, but whatever deficiencies he had were overshadowed by the miserable performance of his chief. From the time he assumed command, Haig saw that the British army had to assume a more prominent role on the western front, going so far in a January 14, 1916, letter to Lt. Gen. Herbert Plumer of the Second Army as to declare that the war had to be "won by the forces of the British Empire." While perhaps a bit hyperbolic, this view was in keeping with the overriding concern of British civilian leaders that British forces had to play a prominent role in attaining a total victory. Haig thought victory could be achieved in one of three ways: 1. "Winter Sports"—the continuation of raids and various local actions; 2. "Wearing out fights"—similar to but on a larger scale than the first approach, with attacks along the entire front, the eventual aim being the drawing in of the German reserves; and 3. "Decisive attacks at several points, with the object to break through."[28]

Haig contemplated an attack in Flanders, with the aim of driving the Germans out of Belgium and thus regaining the coast. General Joseph Joffre, however, put pressure on him to shift his attack to the area of the Somme. At first hesitant, Haig became increasingly enthusiastic about such an operation, so long as it received appropriate artillery support. Haig, like others in the British military establishment, had convinced himself that the costly failures of 1915 had been due to inadequate artillery support, and there was evidence that the British government *as a whole*, as well as the commanders of the BEF, had been slow to adjust to the demands of modern mass warfare.[29]

Here, however, we must once again point out that Haig shared a general confidence in a given approach to war, or "system." As described earlier, this was faith in the very basic infantry assault properly supported, of course, by artillery. Earlier failures had been due to improper applications of this system. "Next time it would be different." Next time it would be on the Somme, and this would be Haig's first large-scale independent action. At his disposal, in every sense of the word, were the levy of Lord Kitchener's new mass army.

ATTACK ON THE SOMME: A NECESSARY EVIL

Haig and his later defenders subsequently declared that the attack on the Somme was necessary to save the French army from defeat at Verdun—and there is no doubt that once that battle had begun the French wanted the attack on the Somme to be expedited to help ease the pressure. As we saw earlier, though, Haig had planned a major British operation for some time before the German attack. Haig's January 14 letter to General Plumer established that, and while, as pointed out earlier, he would have preferred to attack in Flanders, once preparations for the Somme campaign began (well before the Verdun battle), he, along with the entire British high command, exuded opti-

mism. Haig differed from some of his colleagues in one respect: perhaps because he thought himself to be divinely inspired, he expected a rapid
breakthrough.[30] Should a breakthrough occur, Haig's beloved cavalry would
serve to turn the German retreat into a rout. Moreover, even if a breakthrough
did not occur, the battle could be turned into a "wearing-out one" in which
the Germans would suffer far heavier losses than the British attackers.

In part because the British generals had little faith in the combat abilities of
Kitchener's new mass armies, preparations for the Somme battle were both
enormous and detailed. It can scarcely be said that the generals, Haig included, took the anticipated battle lightly. Yet, when all was said and done, the
attack scheme that finally emerged bore an astonishing resemblance to earlier
ones simply writ large. Outside of a feint by the Third Army slightly to the
north of the anticipated main area of attack, this was to be a straightforward
bludgeoning assault preceded by a massive artillery bombardment. The soldiers of the Fourth and Fifth Armies who were to participate in the main attack—
like those of the Third, for that matter—were provided with the simplest tasks
imaginable. Being mass levy, it was assumed that any order beyond that of
marching straight up, with sixty pounds of equipment on their backs, would
be too much for their semi-civilian minds to assimilate. At first, Haig had been
opposed to the men attacking in waves, but subordinate commanders, having
even less faith in surprise than he had, persuaded him that the old tried-and-
true way was best.[31] Haig, wishing to be certain of the availability of mountains
of shells, had wanted to put off the attack until August; but, under French
pressure, agreed that July 1 would do. Sustained by his faith in being a (perhaps
the) God-ordained purveyor of victory, he knew that such, either in breakthrough or "wearing down" form, would be his. As an author sympathetic to
him has pointed out, however, German soldiers, whose belt buckles were
stamped "GOTT MIT UNS," could also choose a similar source of spiritual
sustenance.[32]

As the day of battle approached, Haig paid visits to various corps commanders. He was himself quite optimistic and expected a rapid advance. The corps
commanders shared his optimism. Everything was going according to plan.
The men were well prepared and in excellent spirits and, as Haig recorded in
his diary, "The wire has never been so well cut, nor the artillery preparations
so thorough."[33] John Terraine has offered an articulate, if controversial, defense of Haig. Although this writer believes he has gone rather too far in this
effort, Terraine raised a point that certainly must be taken into consideration:
As the day of assault approached, the entire British army was awash in a sea of
delusion.

> The gap between reality and the words which were being used in order to
> convey it is so astounding that it almost defeats comment. Nothing could

have reduced the gap except a constant stream of urgently expressed misgivings from the line itself. They did not come. From top to bottom there was a tendency to "look on the bright side," a valuable British characteristic which can, at times, be perilous; this was such a time. Where reports conflicted, it was the optimistic ones that filtered upwards.[34]

We will comment upon the significance and the at least World War I–period source of this "British characteristic" later in the chapter. The crucial role of Brig. John Charteris, Haig's eternally optimistic (at least publicly) intelligence officer, will be singled out in particular. For now, it will suffice to note that all signs that there were problems ahead were treated as if they were illusory or nonexistent. Whether or not a singularly authoritarian figure was finding amplification for his own problems, dissonance-producing data was being filtered out at all levels.

On July 1, 1916, after an unprecedented artillery bombardment, one that, contrary to Haig's perception, did *not* do extensive damage to the enemy wire, much less his artillery or machine guns, the British infantry went over the top. Soldiers dribbling a soccer ball led one group. Basil Liddell Hart offered this description of the advance: "Battalions attacked in four or eight waves, not more than a hundred yards apart, the men in each almost shoulder to shoulder, in a symmetrical well-dressed alignment, and taught to advance steadily upright at a slow walk with their rifles held aslant of them, bayonets upward — so as to catch the eye of the observant enemy."[35]

Everything seemed to be going splendidly as far as the commander in chief of the BEF could tell. A visit to an aid station, rare for him, convinced Haig that "The wounded men were in wonderful spirits." His July 2 diary entry was cheery indeed. Total casualties for July 1 and 2 had been forty thousand (a gross underestimate, as we will see), and this toll "cannot be considered severe in view of the numbers engaged and the length of front attacked."[36] Matters were, in fact, quite different.

On the first day, Haig's army suffered almost sixty thousand casualties, twenty-one thousand of them dead. By the end of July, British casualties totaled 165,000. Haig, however, was "not perturbed" by them. Taking into account what the British army liked to call "normal wastage" — that is, those killed or wounded in the course of routine shellings, gas attacks, raids, and the like — he came to the conclusion that the BEF's July losses "were only about one hundred and twenty thousand more than they would have been had we not attacked." In his view these were not "sufficient to justify any anxiety as to our ability to continue the offensive."[37] In any case, even though there obviously would be no breakthrough of consequence, this battle, now officially a "wearing down" one, was costing the enemy even more dearly in lives and morale.[38]

Haig and his generals were certainly correct in stating that the Somme attacks were costing the enemy dearly. General Erich Ludendorff himself testified to this end and, as has been pointed out, the Germans certainly became aware, if they had not been already, of the immense reserves of manpower and materiel that were at the Allies' disposal.[39] The enemy's morale had been affected and his losses had been high—in the later stages of the battle, probably higher than those of the British because of desperate counterattacks to regain lost ground. The British offensive, however, had not, as Haig thought it had, used up 30 percent of the enemy divisions by the end of July. How successful Haig was in tying down the Germans is also open to debate, inasmuch as they had been able to move nine divisions from the western front to the eastern front—this to meet Gen. Aleksey Brusilov's initially far more successful offensive against admittedly somewhat inferior Austro-Hungarian troops—in June and October. By the end of July, Haig was also predicting that, after six more weeks of offensive pressure, "the enemy should be hard put to find men."[40] By the time six weeks had passed, the fighting raged as furiously as ever. A September 13 pronouncement from British GHQ, however, described an enemy staggering on last legs, demoralized and disorganized. Thus,

> Under such conditions risks may be taken with advantage which would be unwise if circumstances were less favourable to us.
>
> *The assault must be pushed home with the greatest vigour, boldness, and resolution, and success must be followed up without hesitation or delay to the utmost limits of the power of endurance of the troops.*[41]

Astonishingly enough, British, and, for that matter, French troops attacking on the Somme almost always did so with "the greatest vigour" and the meager gains thus obtained were defended tenaciously. Yet, there was no breakthrough and, however demoralized the enemy might have been, he certainly could not have been perceived to be staggering on stumpy last legs.

Nonetheless, as Haig and some of his subordinates saw it, where there were delays or snags in the overall victory march, such were due to a lack of tenacity on the part of one or the other unit. As an example of this, we can consider an entry in Haig's diary concerning the failure of a particular division to attain objectives considered impossible by all commentators:

> Monday, 4. September. I visited Toutencourt and saw General Gough. The failure to hold the position gained on the Ancre is due, he reported, to the 49th Division. The units of that division did not really attack and some men did not follow their officers. The total losses of this Division are under a thousand! . . . I had occasion a fortnight ago to call the attention of the Army and Corps Commanders . . . to the lack of smartness and slackness of one of its Battalions in the matter of saluting when I was motoring through the village where it was billeted. I expressed my opinion that such men were too sleepy to fight well.[42]

Overlooking the fact that the 49th Division's casualties had been grossly underestimated, we can see that Haig, Gough, and no doubt other commanders as well were convinced that failure to attain objectives was due to lack of determination, or slackness, and not to systemic flaws of any significance.[43]

In any event, British generals spoke and acted as if a major victory was in the process of being achieved. Haig was hardly alone in this. As a matter of fact, he had wanted to close down operations after taking Beaumont-Hamel in mid-November, but General Gough urged him to approve another, in this case, totally futile, attack beyond that forlorn hamlet.[44] By this time, the campaign was over. More than six hundred thousand Allied troops, well over two-thirds of them British, had been lost and the maximum gain was seven miles. There had been no breakthrough and, of course, no cavalry action of consequence.

Haig quietly adjusted himself to the situation and, in a December 23, 1916, dispatch to the secretary of state (appropriately entitled "The Opening of the Wearing-Out Battle") declared that in the first five days on a six-mile front, "our troops had swept over the whole of the enemy's first and strongest system of defense, which he had done his utmost to render impregnable. They had driven him back a distance of more than a mile, and had carried four elaborately fortified villages." Furthermore, by July 5, ninety-four officers and 5,724 men had been captured.[45] The battle, in a word, had been a success. To be sure, Haig admitted, "The style of warfare in which we have been engaged offered no scope for cavalry action." However, thirty-eight thousand prisoners had been captured between July 1 and November 18. "Our main objects had been achieved," he enthused. "Verdun had been relieved, the main German forces had been held on the Western front, and the enemy's strength had been very considerably worn down." Of utmost importance, "the enemy's losses in men and materiel have been very considerably higher than those of the Allies, while morally the balance of advantages on our side is still greater."[46] There is no doubt that Haig had convinced himself that the taking of thirty-eight thousand prisoners and the holding of German troops in the Somme battle zone constituted a crushing victory. The earlier goal of a decisive breakthrough had been shelved and the Somme campaign was now seen as a successful "wearing-out battle" in which German losses had been higher (a debatable assumption, in any case) than those of the Allies.

While there probably always will be controversy over the question of who suffered the heaviest losses on the Somme, certain conclusions can be drawn. First of all, even if the battle had been to no small degree "forced" upon Haig and his subordinates by the French, once it was decided that the British would indeed attack, albeit sooner than Haig would have preferred, extreme and totally unwarranted optimism prevailed at all levels within the British command structure. A breakthrough of major proportions was expected. If this did not in fact happen, then the great "wearing down" battle that would follow would thoroughly wreck the German army, leaving it incapable of future sustained operations. In keeping with this assumption it had to follow that British (and French) losses, while admittedly heavy, would, in fact, in the minds of Haig and his subordinates, *could* not be heavy enough as to constitute any sort of strain on their respective military establishments. It also had to be assumed that the German army was being pinned down by the Somme operation, so much so, that it could not siphon off troops for other fronts. Total success was always "just around the corner." Just one more shove, assisted perhaps by some technological innovation or new tactical wrinkle, would do it. This explains Haig's error of committing tanks in relatively ineffective driblets as soon as a small number of them became available in September 1916.

The German army no doubt was shaken by the Somme operation and, as has been noted earlier, could (and did) not perceive its eventual outcome as a victory. Yet, to view it as an *Allied* victory, as it seems most of the British military establishment did, strains credulity.[47] Most important of all, far more important than whether or not one counts a battle as a victory for one side or the other, is the fact that Haig and his associates appear to have learned little, if anything, from it. If there were some disappointments attaching to the Somme operation, these were due to the weather, to inexperience, and to a lack of supplies on various occasions. These were never perceived as having been due to a *system* of warfare pursued by the commanders.[48] The "system" was still intact, much as it had been after Loos. As mentioned earlier, this equaled massive artillery preparations plus masses of men plus an innovation or two, such as the tank. Next time there would be more of everything, the Germans would have significantly *less* of everything (as for tanks, in fact, none at all until 1918), and the long sought-after breakthrough would occur. Maybe this time even the cavalry could get into the act. As for the Germans—shaken, to be sure—they were reconsidering tactical realities and "planning to shorten their line" to meet another offensive that they correctly saw as being mounted in due course by an enemy seemingly incapable of learning either from success or failure.[49] How much anybody really learned anything, or at least anything meaningful, from World War I is open to debate. That Sir Douglas Haig and his subordinates learned almost nothing at all from the Somme experience is not. Dissonance-producing information, and even *experiences*, could not be allowed to challenge an established system. Here, the fatuously unrealistic pronouncement of September 13 and the complaints regarding lack of commitment on the part of one or the other unit can be borne in mind. One point raised in the December 23 dispatch was absolutely correct, however: "the enemy's strength had been very considerably worn down." This is especially crucial for our considerations.

As mentioned earlier, Haig had long thought the critical area of concentration to be Flanders. Many high-placed civilians agreed with him, to say nothing of the Admiralty, which, as the war waxed on, became increasingly concerned with the elimination of German submarine bases on the Belgian coast. After the Somme campaign, the anticipated Flanders operation once more began to take center stage, at least in Haig's mind and that of his colleague and at times cautious supporter, Field Marshal Sir William Robertson, chief of the Imperial General Staff. Haig was perhaps entitled to think that he enjoyed the confidence of the government. After all, had he not been made a field marshal on December 22, 1916, as a reward for his victorious Somme operation? Certainly, he would have its support with regard to an offensive that increasingly enjoyed the support of the Admiralty as well. Unfortunately, the Flanders operation had to be put on the back burner for a while as Haig's troops had been called upon to mount an offensive in the area of Arras. This quite costly, albeit by World War I standards fairly successful (at least initially) offensive, was mounted in support of a French one under the ill-starred direction of Gen. Robert Nivelle, an offensive that enjoyed no success whatsoever (this will be discussed further below). With the failure of the Nivelle offensive, Haig could get back to planning and gaining support for the Flanders operation.

PLANNING OPERATIONS FOR 1917

In considering options for 1917, and with the recent Somme battles in mind, Gen. Sir Henry Wilson declared that the British army could not count on any sort of rapid breakthrough, nor could it "do nothing," that is, remain on the defensive. The only option was another "wearing down" type of operation, such as the Somme offensive had turned out to be. This would have to be, however, "a Somme, with intelligence."[50] The last two words, of course, constituted an obvious judgment upon the Somme operation and thus, of course, upon Haig as well. The new field marshal was not unduly disturbed about it. In any case, he had plans of his own. The Flanders offensive would *not* be a wearing down operation. A breakthrough would be made and, in pursuance of this objective, Haig showed an unusual interest in tactical innovations — from organizing British machine-gun units into platoon sections to envisioning amphibious operations along the Belgian coast in support of the main attack out of the Ypres salient. The latter scheme was eventually shelved due to a lack of men and appropriate landing craft.[51] Nonetheless the expectation of a major breakthrough remained.

Indeed, according to Haig, the operation would end up with British armies ensconced on a battle line running between Ostend and Bruges. Thus, and this was particularly delightful for the Admiralty, a large portion of the Belgian coast would end up in British hands. Such a thrust was particularly attractive to Haig because in the opening operations (involving the capture of the

Passchendaele-Westroosbeke-Staden ridge) "opportunities for the employ-
ment for cavalry in masses are likely to offer."[52] A crucial preliminary operation, the taking of Messines Ridge, had been successfully completed (using
gigantic mines combined with unusual tactical finesse) on June 7, 1917. The
main blow would soon fall.

Before considering the inevitable results of the July 1917 venture, we must
once more examine a most interesting phenomenon, namely Haig's caution
when considering operations carried out by individuals other than himself. As
noted above, Gen. Robert Nivelle, one of the heroes of Verdun, had planned
and carried out a disastrous offensive in the Aisne River sector. This operation,
which was responsible for widespread mutinies in the French army in May
1917, called for Haig's being a subordinate to the French general. He responded by raising serious and well-founded objections to the scheme at staff
conferences. Among the most important of these concerned the weather,
something that was brushed aside by the French general, who at that point was
utterly mesmerized by the thought of his own success.[53] Questions of weather
conditions, and to some extent even logistics, however, did not deter Haig to
any significant degree when it came to his own operations.

The British Tank Corps, for obvious reasons sensitive to questions of terrain
and weather, sent map after map to Gen. Sir Hubert Gough's Fifth Army, the
presumed spearhead of the Flanders offensive. These maps outlined matters
as they would be—operations conducted in a water-logged terrain, made even
more difficult to negotiate by seasonal Flanders rain and by water released by
the artillery smashing dikes and canals. General Gough's headquarters,
buoyed by Haigian offensive optimism, sent a reply to the Tank Corps that included instructions to "Send us no more of these ridiculous maps."[54] The
warnings of Belgian weather experts were similarly ignored. Haig and his supporters had raised serious objections to the operations of others. However,
when his chance for victory—so-called—appeared on the horizon, such caveats were abandoned.

The offensive that was to result in the establishment of an Ostend–Bruges
line began on July 31, 1917. The spearhead of the attack, General Gough's
Fifth Army, advanced into intense fire over a landscape made sodden by days
of intermittent rain. A drizzle began in the early afternoon. As time passed, it
turned into a steady downpour. Some minor gains were registered, but for the
most part, the attack, supported by a covering barrage that, advancing according to a fixed plan, bore no relation to reality, quite literally bogged down. Initially, no one was certain as to losses, although everyone sensed that they had
been heavy—so much so that even Haig, during a visit to Gough's headquarters, had to caution his extremely optimistic "plunger" against headlong assaults without adequate artillery support.[55] This was one of the few cautionary
notes injected by the commander in chief. In various stages, the Flanders of-

fensive would be pressed until an end that only uncomprehending civilians, a few virtually disloyal military subordinates, and most historians would deem "bitter."

Of course, some British (and French) attacks during the Flanders offensive were relatively more successful than others and, as in the case of the Somme operation, German losses were hardly light. Just as many an Allied soldier or general filled the dismal Flanders air with complaints, so did their German counterparts. Yet, unlike the Germans, British commanders seemed unable to separate fact from fiction, reality from wishful thinking. The most qualified of successes gained through the usual bludgeoning methods were celebrated as though they were major victories. An example of this is the response of General Charteris (admittedly even more inclined toward a rosy view of things, at least in public, than most) to the extremely costly "victory" gained at Brood-seinde, on October 4: "Now we have them on the run—Get up the cavalry!" Yet, at a conference three days later that involved Haig and two of his subordinates, Gen. Sir Herbert Plumer (Second Army) and Gen. Sir Hubert Gough (Fifth Army), reality seems to have sunk in, at least with regard to the latter two. Earlier in the campaign, as we have seen, Haig had had to "rein in" the overly enthusiastic Gough. Now, he joined Plumer in urging that their commander call off the offensive. Haig flatly refused. Besides sweeping considerations involving other fronts (his judgments on these were only partially accurate), he remarked upon the miserable position of his troops, ensconced as they were in a dreary, boglike flatland beneath that ridge, the taking of which had been the first objective in the campaign. Obviously, they could not stay there, exposed as they were both to the elements and to well-directed enemy fire.[56] Any sort of withdrawal was completely out of the question, of course. One final blow and at least a significant portion of the Passchendaele-Westroosebeke-Staden ridge would be theirs. This would have a pleasing effect on public opinion, assure the troops of a decent position for the winter, and crown a successful battle of attrition against a vastly weakened enemy.[57]

Haig was certainly right in one respect: His soldiers were in a terrible position and could not remain there for the winter. They had to go forward or go back, and political, perhaps even more than military circumstances, precluded the latter course of action. Yet, it was obvious by then, if one chose to see it, that the Germans were no nearer exhaustion or collapse than they had been after the Somme operation. In fact, they were probably a good deal less so. Russia's collapse had allowed the Germans to shift large numbers of troops to the west to reinforce a line that was even less broken than that they had held in the Somme region a year before. In any case, the last very costly attacks would go on, attacks which in due course would encompass the site of Passchendaele (the village itself had long since vanished), but little else. "What Haig still hoped to achieve on that day of decision in early October, and what he was trying to prove, are perhaps questions more appropriate to a psychiatrist than to the student of military science."[58] Yet, as Haig saw it, as in the Somme operation, all that was required was that continued, unrelenting pressure be applied in inflexible adherence to a prescribed plan, to that "system" whose value had been demonstrated all along. As an example of this, we can ponder the following, contained in a memorandum Haig sent to Robertson on October 8: "I strongly asserted that Germany was nearer the end than they [the War Cabinet] seemed to think, and that *now* was the favorable moment for pressing her and that everything possible should be done to take advantage of it by concentrating on the Western from *all* available resources. I stated that Germany was within six months of total exhaustion of her available manpower, *if the fighting continued at its present intensity*."[59]

An attack on October 9 that gained very little ground at a hideous cost to the units involved was evidence of a very "intensive" effort, indeed. Haig, knowing that the gains were not what they ought to have been, declared in his diary: "The results were very successful."[60] Under the circumstances, except for minor adjustments, Haig saw no reason why the offensive ought not to continue.

The reality was rain, mud, flooded trenches, and an inordinate number of wounded who had drowned miles away from the sea. The offensive finally slogged to a close in November 1917, hundreds of thousands of casualties and an average gain of four miles after its auspicious beginning. Once more, Haig proved himself capable of quietly adjusting expectations. In place of an originally envisaged first-stage advance that was to take the Passchendaele-Westroosebeke-Staden ridge, we are supposed to ponder the immense success of the Fifth Army in carrying "the first system of defense south of Westhoek." This army had advanced "on the whole front for distances varying from 200 to 800 yards."[61] In a dispatch dated December 25, Haig declared the Flanders offensive to have been an overall success. "Our captures in Flanders since the commencement of operations at the end of July amount to 24,056 prisoners, 74 guns, 941 machine guns and 138 trench mortars. It is certain that the enemy's losses considerably exceeded ours."[62] Furthermore, "The addition of strength which the enemy has obtained, or may yet obtain, from events in Russia or Italy has already been largely discounted, and the ultimate destruction of the enemy's field forces had been brought appreciably nearer."[63] Both Haig and Gough insisted—the latter considerably after the fact—that the Flanders offensive was absolutely necessary in order to preserve the French army from destruction, this being particularly the case after the disastrous failure of the Nivelle offensive in April 1917. Here Gough, whose offensive fervor occasionally exceeded his chief's, was even more strident than Haig. If, he declared, Haig had not attacked in July, the Germans might well have assaulted the French army and "moral ascendancy [would have] passed to the enemy and the prospect of Allied victory [would have] been long delayed."[64] It is certainly possible that the British military establishment had believed in the danger of a French collapse unless the British army itself moved to the attack, although Haig, while making note of this in his journal, never chose to emphasize this argument in justifying his plans to Lloyd George or the War Cabinet. Furthermore, it is instructive to note that Haig had wanted to strike in Flanders for a long time. In any case, one thing is obvious: Haig, much as he had done before the Somme campaign, had anticipated a breakthrough. Only when such obviously was not going to occur did he decide that his primary objective had been all along to "wear down" the enemy in a singularly unimaginative slugfest in which not a few advantages were on the side of the defense.

So much for a campaign that was to result in attaining an Ostend–Bruges line and was to have been so fluid as to have allowed for the use of massed cavalry. Yet, there is no doubt that Haig convinced himself that the ghastly battle of attrition that had just taken place was more or less what he had in mind to begin with and that, indeed, enemy casualties were higher than his own. Naturally, he was hardly alone in this outrageous self-delusion. In reporting on one of the last important Flanders battles in October 1917, the *Times* of London declared, "In short, the particular task which Sir Douglas Haig set his armies, has been very nearly accomplished." As Lloyd George pointed out, this referred to the capture of the southern two to three kilometers of the ridge, *all* of which was supposed to have been Haig's first objective.[65] In any event, the results of the Flanders offensive were not satisfying. The seemingly eversanguine Charteris was out before the end of the year, as was Haig's chief of staff, Lt. Gen. Sir Launcelot Kiggell. In February 1918, Gen. Sir William Robertson, who from time to time had offered caveats with regard to Haig's plans but, in the end, had usually come down on his side, was replaced by Henry Wilson as chief of the Imperial General Staff.

As the year turned, Haig, genuinely upset at losing Charteris and Kiggell, returned to an old theme. The French army, he suggested, was unable to withstand a major assault or mount one of its own. Thus, he reasoned, the best way to prevent a French collapse in the west would be for the British army to resume the offensive in Flanders. Even a sympathetic commentator on Haig has been compelled to deem this suggestion "astonishing."[66] Perhaps, in light of what was to occur, Haig's conclusion that the German army was in no position to launch a "breaking through" type of offensive (one assumes that, in view of his opinions of French capabilities, Haig was talking of one mounted against the British), this due to their having "only one million men as reserves for the year's fighting," was even more astonishing. Two and a half months later, Ludendorff launched the most successful offensive seen on the western front since 1914. It was launched against a British army that had been starved of reinforcements in large measure out of fears of what Haig would choose to do with them.

The Haig of 1918 was in many ways somewhat of a different sort than his more recently known variant. First of all, when thrown on the defensive during the battles of March and April 1918, he proved to be a good tactician, rather like the Haig who had served the incompetent Sir John French quite well in 1914. Fighting in what one author, referring to another battle in a later war, called the British army's "spiritual home, the last ditch," Haig's troops, forced ever backward by a German army utilizing (at least at first) totally new tactics of infiltration, never broke. One army, the Fifth, was almost shattered, another, the Third, badly handled, but the line held, the men perhaps (up to a point, of course) inspired by an unusually elegant missive written by Haig. Moreover, Haig offered no resistance at having his army, as well as that of the newly arrived Americans, placed under the overall leadership of Marshal Ferdinand Foch. In fact, he seemed to encourage it. Finally, with American aid, the German offensives were strained and then broken. Then, from August until November, it was the German army that was gradually but inexorably pressed back by weight of numbers and resources.

There can be little question but that sober analysis of the campaign during this time will reveal that, if one had to choose between those armies to determine which was primarily responsible for the eventual victory, the British army played the leading role. Under Haig's leadership it took almost as many prisoners as the French, American, and Belgian armies combined, and some consider its cracking of the Hindenburg Line (Siegfried Stellung) in early October to be the single most crucial event of that period. Historians have argued that the BEF was a much-improved organization by 1918. By that time, in part through its response to Ludendorff's spring offensives, it had gained considerable proficiency in utilizing "combined arms," that is, integrating infantry, artillery, tanks, and aircraft. Douglas Haig obviously played a role in this. The successful Amiens operation, beginning on August 8, 1918, is often seen as indicative of this.[67]

Once the British army, along with those of its allies, undertook sustained offensive operations, its casualties were greater on a day-to-day basis than they had been during the 1917 Flanders campaign. In a word, while the British army was "on the move," attritional "wearing out" considerations were still of guiding importance. Recently, Niall Ferguson has produced a work in which, among other challenges to "traditional" interpretations of the Great War, he has stated that because German soldiers until the very end had superior casualty-producing ratios to those of their opponents, the attritional argument is not valid. Rather, a quite sudden drop in German morale due to an awareness that the military leadership assumed that all was lost was the decisive factor in the Allied victory.[68]

This argument does not hold. In the Wilderness campaign of 1864, Lt. Gen. Ulysses S. Grant's forces suffered substantially more casualties than Lee's. Until early August 1944, Allied forces in western Europe lost more men than the Germans. For the most part, with significant exceptions of course, the armed forces of the Soviet Union sustained higher casualties than their German opponents. In the end, of course, both the Confederacy and Nazi Germany were decisively crushed. In a word, with regard to attrition, raw casualty figures need not mean a great deal. What matters is a country's ability to sustain greater losses of men and materiel than its opponents. The battles of 1915, the Somme in 1916, and Flanders in 1917 were blood-smeared steps along the way to an attritional victory "crowned" by those attained in a now restored "war of movement" (relatively speaking). The British army of 1918 *was* much improved with regard to the utilization of combined arms. But this happy development merely allowed for an increasingly successful "wearing out" of an opponent inferior in human and materiel resources. In the end, by successfully holding out in a kind of personal attritional campaign of his own, Haig had won. So, of course, had the military establishment of which he was its star representative.

In point of fact, as mentioned earlier, this army lost more men on a per diem basis in the last months of the campaign than it did in the ill-starred Flanders offensive. But, prisoners were being taken in large numbers and gains could be measured in miles rather than in yards. In 1918 we see an interesting phenomenon, namely that—while in a subordinate role, in this case acting in concert with Allied armies under the overall command of Marshal Foch— Haig revealed good military qualities, and the superb performance of the British army in the last months of the war was in large part due to them. Perhaps while he was in this subordinate role the "curse" of having to function in keeping with the dictates of an imposed "system" was lifted.

Yet, crucial though the role of the British army certainly was in the Allied victory in 1918, it was still not doing it alone—something that Haig had hoped to achieve in his 1916 and 1917 offensives. In his relentless maintenance of pressure, a characteristic of Haig in all circumstances it would appear, he made his own contribution to the Allied successes. Yet, even if he then assumed—as he and his supporters later did retrospectively—that the great "wearing out" campaigns of 1916 and 1917 had played a crucial role in weakening the German army so that it was ripe for eventual defeat in 1918, the victory would have to be seen as a "shared" one. It is here that we can see again a characteristic that we have observed on earlier occasions, namely a somewhat deprecatory attitude on Haig's part toward armies other than his own and their achievements.

On October 19, 1918, the field marshal attended a meeting of the War Cabinet, one concerned with the terms that were to be offered to an enemy now seen as severely strained. Haig, in suggesting that the terms had best not be too harsh, gave an extraordinarily pessimistic report as to the state of operations on the western front, particularly so in view of his earlier expressed opinion that the war could be ended in 1918. Before examining this report in more detail we must again remind ourselves that Haig, as well as his American counterpart, Gen. John J. Pershing, was under the command of Marshal Foch and had been for some time. Although Haig outwardly offered encouragement to this measure, there can be no doubt that he maintained the grave inner reservations he had always had when placed in a subordinate position to Frenchmen. In any case, among other things, he stated: "The French Army seems greatly worn out. . . . Reports say that many of their men are disinclined to risk their lives. . . . Next year a large proportion of the French Army will probably be Black! *American Army* is disorganized, ill-equipped, ill-trained with very few N.C.O.'s and officers of experience. It has suffered severely through ignorance of modern war and it must take *at least a year* before it becomes a serious fighting force."[69]

Besides these factors, the British army was tired and understrength. The upshot of it, in Haig's opinion, was that the war had to last into 1919. When Haig issued this report, the Germans, fighting courageously against immense odds, were nonetheless being pressed back all along the line. It is probably true that, as we have noted, the British army made the single greatest contribution to victory in 1918. Yet, French troops, while not advancing as rapidly as the British, and in some cases the Americans, were nonetheless making steady progress against the enemy. Moreover, it would not be jingoistic to declare that the American army, while not exclusively responsible for victory in 1918, and displaying a certain degree of organizational confusion, most assuredly had demonstrated that it was, at the very least, a "serious fighting force" and certainly was viewed as such by its opponents.

HAIG: CAUTION OR "SOUR GRAPES"?

Haig's tendency toward caution and deprecation with regard to the actions and decisions of others was a sort of psychic antipode to his lack of realism with regard to himself and challenges that had been made with regard to his abilities. It also, quite simply, can be seen as a case of "sour grapes." More than a lack of realism, this was a further example of self-deception—something which was manifested in his declaration that in 1918, "the attacking British troops were numerically inferior to the German forces they defeated," and, while coming around to admitting the value of machine guns and tanks, his inserting an essay entitled "The Value of Cavalry in Modern War" in the so-called Final Despatch sent on March 21, 1919.[70] Of equal interest, however, and possibly of greater significance, Haig's October 1918 observations revealed something we have seen earlier—a tendency toward caution when serving in one or the other subordinate capacity. In this case, of course, caution was obviously informed by petulance. Nonetheless, Haig's military performance in

1918 underscores the point that, when acting in a subordinate capacity, or involved in operations over which he did not exercise sole command, he was a competent enough commander whose actions were informed by a sense of caution. When left to his own devices, he seems to have been held captive by approaches to war that ensured there would be thousands of casualties in offensives in which gains would be measured in yards. What did this suggest, not only for Haig as a man, but also as a representative of the British military establishment?

In French and in Haig (and others as well), we can see taking place a most interesting psychological process. They had what they perceived to be a well-justified approach to war, a "system." And this system, by virtue of its existence —and because it was an article of faith of those in *overall command* of British military operations—had to succeed. Thus, despite massive and at times publicly recognized evidence to the contrary, success was always attained. In his diary, French recorded his fury at a 1915 debate in the House of Lords: "Lord Milner said in so many words, that the battles of Neuve-Chapelle and Loos instead of victories were in reality defeats. Lord Courtenay adopted the same line of argument."[71]

In his diary entry for November 7, 1914, Douglas Haig mentioned something he found distressful, at least at that time: "Few French generals or staff officers ever seem to go forward to visit their troops in advanced positions. They rely too much on telegrams and written reports from regiments."[72] Naturally, it would have been assumed (had anyone had access to Haig's journal) that measures would be undertaken to make certain that so unfortunate a situation could never arise in the British camp.

At a 1917 GHQ conference, Col. C. D. Baker-Carr, who was familiar with conditions at the front, attempted to explain them to other generals. Afterward, an angry brigadier, John Davidson, took him aside and scolded him for his conduct. The following exchange ensued:

Baker-Carr: You asked me how things really were and I told you frankly.
Davidson: But what you say is impossible.
Baker-Carr: It isn't. Nobody has any idea of the conditions up there.
Davidson: But they can't be as bad as you make out.
Baker-Carr: Have you been there yourself?
Davidson: No.
Baker-Carr: Has anyone at O.A. been there?
Davidson: No.
Baker-Carr: Well then, if you don't believe me, it would be as well to send someone up to find out.[73]

Eventually, Haig's chief of staff, Lt. Gen. Sir Launcelot Kiggell, did pay a visit to the fighting zone. As his car ground slowly through the muddy, shell-pitted fields, he exhibited increasing signs of distress. Finally, it is said, he burst into tears: "Good God, did we really send men to fight in that?"[74]

One is tempted to draw the conclusion that the individuals we have considered were both cruel (or, at the very least insensitive) and stupid. Indeed, a recent biography of Sir John French does suggest that he at least was something of a dimwit and, to make matters worse, rather a disingenuous one.[75] Yet, the overall picture that emerges of these people is that, with the exception of French, they were reasonably intelligent individuals (hardly "geniuses," to be sure) who, while sometimes appearing blandly indifferent to certain matters, were hardly cruel. Even a severe critic of French (he seems to have had no friends after the war ended) has pointed out that he always evidenced a genuine concern for his men, although various tactical blunders he committed did little to assure lives and limbs.[76] General Gough may have been reckless, but he hardly comes across as heartless and, as for the most important figure under consideration in this chapter, Field Marshal Haig, it is now fairly well accepted that Lloyd George's depiction of him as a vain, cold-blooded monster was rather off the mark. Indeed, in Haig's case, vanity, on the conscious level, anyway, seems to have played a relatively minor role in his decision making. In this regard, a rather well-known story bears repeating.

The artist Sir William Orpen was sent to France in April 1917 to depict the war. He did so with a blend of reasonable accuracy and adherence to prewar conceptions of decorum. One of his assignments was to paint a portrait of Haig, which he did after meeting the field marshal in May. As Orpen began his work, Haig suddenly remarked, "Why waste your time painting me? Go and paint the men. They're the fellows who are saving the world, and they're getting killed every day."[77] There can be no question that his comment to Orpen represented Haig's true thoughts on the issue at hand. Unlike someone like Joffre perhaps, Haig was not unimpressed by the fact that his decisions meant agony and death for thousands of those under him, and so was sensitive enough in this regard to make the suggestion he did to the artist. Moreover, several authors have pointed out that as the war was grinding down to its end, Haig became increasingly concerned that the terms of the eventual peace treaty with Germany not be too harsh. Otherwise, he feared, Europe would be facing monumental difficulties in the future.[78] Perhaps, one could argue, his views were at least in part informed by a suspicion of the French that was virtually habitual with him. Whatever the case, his voice was one of the relatively few of reason at that time and more heed should have been paid to it. It would appear that other generally held criticisms of Haig seem to have been exaggerated or off the mark as well.

It is certainly true that Haig demonstrated an attachment to cavalry that suggested he was out of touch with its relatively limited value in conditions such as those that prevailed on the western front. At times he did seem to think that the shock of the cavalry charge retained at least metaphoric significance in the planning and carrying out of operations in which such had been precluded. Yet, as has been pointed out by friend and foe alike, it was the British military in general (or at least some of it), and Haig in particular, who showed an interest in one of the most significant innovations of the war, the tank. Moreover, Haig at least was always interested in new ordnance and in various tactical refinements involving its use. As we have seen, he even envisaged the use of amphibious warfare along the Flanders coast, bearing in mind the fact that special types of landing craft suitable for such an operation would first have to be developed.[79]

Yet, even after certain justifiable qualifications are added, it is still plain that British leadership in World War I in general—and Haig's contribution in particular—revealed an extraordinary inflexibility, a general unwillingness to adjust to changing circumstances, except in relatively minor ways. Machine-gun detachments might be formed, training techniques might be changed in certain ways, tanks utilized, amphibious operations planned—but almost always, it seems, basic fixed plans remained the same. Haig's defenders quite justifiably have quoted German generals who spoke of the immense drain on their resources caused by the Somme and Flanders operations. It is, however, equally appropriate to quote Feldmarschall Paul von Hindenburg who, when asked which of his opponents on the western front was more inept, the English or the French, replied: "The Englishman was undoubtedly a less skillful opponent than his brother in arms. He did not understand how to control rapid changes in the situation. His methods were too rigid."[80] On the other hand, *all* German military leaders were fulsome in their praise of the bravery and extraordinary stubbornness of the English soldiers. They were the opponents Germans at all levels seem to have respected the most, and it is highly doubtful that any other army on the western front would have held together as well in the Somme and Flanders campaigns as the one headed by Field Marshal Haig. As has been pointed out, this was the only major army that, while experiencing occasional episodes of "indiscipline," never broke.[81] This, however, says more about the nature of the British soldier and the social arrangements of British society than it does about the quality of British military leadership. In any case, we will briefly deal with this issue in due course.

Defenders of the British approach to war, but particularly of Haig, have stated that the "wearing down" campaigns of World War I were successful in the end and that the war could, in fact, only have been won in that fashion.[82] At least by war's end, Haig had arrived at the opinion that the whole war had to have been viewed as one continuous battle and, under the circumstances, each of its integral "wearing down" aspects had to be seen as constituting a vital role.[83] Putting the possibility of *a posteriori* reasoning to the side, we must point out that while the campaigns of 1915, 1916, and 1917 were being prepared, and during at least the initial stages of these campaigns, BEF generals and, from time to time, the general staff in London talked and acted as if a major victory was being achieved or was, at the very least, just around the corner. They acted as if adherence to the system described above *had* to lead to victory. Agencies at the highest level of command were woefully slow in introducing new equipment, even helmets. Once items such as the tank *were* introduced, even commanders interested in the new weapons simply integrated them into the established system.[84] A criticism of Haig offered by a not unsympathetic military historian can be applied to the British military establishment in general: Haig could be "open-minded in deciding his plan." However, once he made a decision, he "went far beyond proper resolution and optimism in holding to the set course." Here, Haig was providing an almost textbook example of an archetypal dissonance reducer in action. Even after the Somme experience, something that did result in improvements in training methods, the "general pattern of tactics was the same and most of the attacks were persisted in far beyond the hope of success."[85]

A valid criticism of Haig is that he "was not, as were Marlborough and Wellington, a master of the weapons and tactics of his day."[86] In place of this mastery, Haig, and quite a few of his colleagues as well, substituted determination. Here, we can bear in mind the September 1916 injunction on the need to press attacks even harder, or Haig's decision of October 7, 1917, to press on with the attacks in Flanders. Determination certainly is important for a commander. "But Haig perhaps failed to see that a dead man cannot advance, and that to replace him is only to provide another corpse."[87]

Defenders of the British military commanders, most notably of Haig, have maintained that they were persistently misled by the falsely optimistic intelligence of Brigadier Sir John Charteris. This less-than-wholesome representative of that general British tendency to always try and see things in the best possible light often provided misleading information, particularly on the state of the German army. This information, some say, had particularly deleterious effects during the Flanders campaign. Here, an evaluation by Gough (who, by the way, never really considers his own important role in occasionally pushing matters even further than Haig would have desired) is crucial. Charteris was "a good psychologist—if not a very strong character—and always told Haig something he especially wanted to hear."[88] As has been pointed out, Charteris, Haig, Gough, and, for that matter, everyone in England desperately wanted a victory. Illusions were needed. Charteris was only too pleased to provide them; yet, in his diary (where he was often more soberly realistic than in public pronouncements) he made the following statement: "D.H. has not only accepted *in toto* my report . . . but he has gone much further."[89] Charteris, one might say, came to be trapped in his own misrepresentations, or, simply put, lies. He was also representative of a process that informed British military decision making during the greater part of World War I on the western front, a process that made dissembling necessary, indeed, even virtuous.

As indicated earlier, pre–World War I British military thinking tended to place primary emphasis upon the infantry attack. Artillery would, of course, be used in support of it, but the main purpose of an assault was to seize ground held by the enemy.[90] "Firepower," either in the form of supporting artillery fire — almost always perceived of as "direct" rather than "indirect" — or in the form of infantry weapons, was of secondary importance to the sustained vigor of the assault itself.[91] There were those who warned of the increased firepower of the defense, ridiculed overemphasis upon the supposed shock value of the assault, and went so far as to suggest that, as recently demonstrated in the Russo-Japanese War, the role of rationally directed artillery fire would be crucial in any future war.[92] In the end, however, there was little effort to provide for an integrated approach to the use of infantry and artillery either in the assault or on the defense, and those who persisted in emphasizing the critical role of firepower were ignored.[93] Haig and some of his colleagues did take an interest in the use of machine guns, and the less-than-gloriously won Boer War did lead to an emphasis upon rifle marksmanship. Nevertheless, these seemed to have been viewed in the context of the small-unit tactics of a professional army fighting a limited war; this, despite the recognition that the next war would probably be fought on the continent against the well-trained, well-led, and well-equipped citizens' army of Imperial Germany. The relatively small British professional army, which man for man had probably the best marksmen in the world, could do marvelously well in the *defensive*, relatively "open" battles of 1914. As we have seen, however, prewar British military "doctrine," uncoordinated and badly articulated as it often was, placed emphasis upon the assault. While the leaders of all of the major military powers before World War I had placed emphasis on offensive operations, concessions to harsh realities eventually were made, albeit at bitter cost.[94]

From 1915 through 1917, the British army was always on the attack, its movements planned and led by men who had little appreciation of the increased role of firepower and the more rational integration of infantry and artillery necessitated by this, or of the necessity of adjusting both to the conditions of the ground of the battlefield itself. "The results were disastrous," and dissonance-increasing information was continuously provided in the form of machine-gun-fire-shredded and artillery-torn corpses.[95] Yet, the hold of the prewar system remained firm and, with but minor adjustments, emphasis continued to be placed on vigorous assaults to seize ground defended in depth, supported by massive artillery bombardments which, spectacular though they might have been, often had little to do with tactical realities.

Lessons were learned and innovations provided, but these were fed into a well-established system immune to the dissonant challenges provided by an enemy more willing to learn from experience. French's and Haig's post–Neuve-Chapelle behavior can be seen as indicative of immense struggles with dissonant situations and information. First of all, while the role of "impulse" in BEF decision making cannot be known with certainty, it should be obvious from the previous discussion that decisions were made (particularly in the case of the 1916 and 1917 operations) after the consideration of alternatives. Once those decisions had been made, commitment to such was manifested in tenacious adherence both to official optimism and fixed goals. This had to result in overlooking, or at least minimizing, difficulties that previously had been viewed as important.

As we noted earlier several times, Douglas Haig showed an interest in machine guns before World War I. However, once the war began and this weapon posed challenges to overall assumptions and plans, he almost perversely chose to undervalue it—and would continue to do so for some time. Neuve-Chapelle was hardly a victory and Loos was definitely a defeat, but, in the mind of Sir John French, these had to have been victories and he bitterly resented those who chose not to view them as such. Before the Somme campaign, and during its early stages as well, there was a mass of dissonance-producing information concerning the effectiveness of the bombardment, the losses sustained, and the significance of what gains there were. This was suppressed or ignored at all levels. During the last few months of the Somme operation, the enemy was continuously perceived as being on his last legs; just one more assault, delivered with vigor, would suffice to bring him to ruin. Perhaps of greater importance was the fact that certain vital lessons about what was entailed in attacking defenses in depth were either ignored or suppressed.

While it is wrong, as we observed earlier, to say that the British military never attempted anything new and deprecated innovation, fundamental assumptions remained basically unchanged and an almost obscene form of repetition compulsion prevailed. This was responsible for Haig's changing of goals after his Somme and Flanders offensives failed to achieve previously anticipated breakthroughs. Yet, those who knew Haig (with the exception of Lloyd George, who had his own fish to fry) described him as basically honest. His goal changing thus can be seen as an effort that was consonant with the need to preserve intact widely held assumptions.

Naturally, there are military leaders and decision makers in all countries who have responded to dissonant situations and information in the same way as those in England. However, the British military seems to have been unique in its persistent tendency to adhere to a "system" or "plan" in the face of overwhelmingly dissonant information. A variety of its representatives can be compared to the true believer described in *When Prophecy Fails*, Leon Festinger's earliest (1956) work. This man, with a coterie of friends, was expecting to be contacted by flying-saucer-borne aliens. Time and time again they were disappointed. After a particularly distressing disappointment he remarked: "Well, all right. Suppose they [the aliens] gave us the wrong date . . . I don't know. All I know is that the plan has never gone astray. We have never had a plan changed. . . . I'm not sorry a bit. I won't be sorry no matter what happens."[96]

WHY ENGLAND?

All of this brings up the inevitable—and necessary—question: Why England? Why did its military leaders and planners demonstrate a persistent inclination to deal with dissonant information and situations in the manner of our continuously frustrated flying saucer buff? Again, in dealing with this question, one cannot lose sight of the fact that cognitive dissonance is no respecter of national boundaries. In World War I, examples of its influence can no doubt be found with military decision makers of all the nations involved. In this regard, the previously considered case of Robert Nivelle comes immediately to mind, and cognitive dissonance theory has proved useful in examining pre-twentieth century (and non-British) military and political fiascos.[97] What must concern us is why cognitive dissonance assumed the, as we see it, peculiarly singular role that it did in British military planning. Adherence to established prewar doctrine has been mentioned. Yet, pressing beyond this, can one offer a suggestion as to why adherence to established military dicta was so prominent among British military men? Recognizing the extremely hypothetical nature of any answer that might be offered, we will explore one possibility.

One of the most prominent values of pre–World War I (Victorian/Edwardian) England, itself a recrudescence of accumulated cultural residues, was a fundamental respect for the proper way of doing things, a fundamental belief in form. Individuals such as Jack the Ripper may have posed disquieting challenges to this, but this attitude prevailed up to the time of the First World War. The hold that it had on at least bourgeois society was amply revealed by the *Titanic* disaster. Immediately after the tragedy, Sen. William Alden Smith of Michigan put together an investigation committee. A substantial number of the victims were Americans, and Smith—and probably the overwhelming majority of Americans conversant about the disaster—did not think it untoward that surviving members of the British crew be questioned about it.

Despite various gaffes on Senator Smith's part, there can be little doubt that much useful information—a good part of it later confirmed by the British Board of Trade investigation—was obtained. The British press, for the most part, exhibited considerable hostility toward Smith in particular and the investigation in general. It was considered bad taste to point out that half-filled lifeboats did not return to rescue hundreds of people crying out as they froze to death in ice-chilled waters.[98] Outside of criticisms of Senator Smith's admitted lack of expertise in maritime matters, the primary objection seemed to be that such an investigation was unseemly as it cast doubt upon certain presumed Anglo-Saxon virtues: sense of duty, order, dignity under pressure, chivalry, adherence to form. Certain principles—virtues, perhaps—were taken as given, at least among Anglo-Saxons. To point out that these principles had been tried and found wanting constituted a transgression against the belief in propriety and form which, in turn, was one of the most singular of these assumed virtues.

For the Britons who found Senator Smith's *Titanic* hearings untoward and who either planned or lent guileless support to the disastrous undertakings of 1916 and 1917, there were proper ways of doing things, proper virtues that required unquestioning respect. "I am," Gen. Sir Hubert Gough declared, "for one thing, a firm supporter of the Old School Tie. To love—and to feel strongly the pull of all these lesser loves [of school, university, or regiment] and loyalties does not prevent or minimize the greater one—one's love of one's country."[99] Furthermore, on reflecting nostalgically upon the era that produced those responsible for World War I's horrors, Gough stated (in considering his father's service in India): "The young men of Great Britain of those days did not suffer from nerves. War was then a very simple affair. Courage and a steady nerve were probably the most important qualities."[100] Again, the existence of certain qualities and values, at least among Anglo-Saxons, was assumed. The assault was the form in which such qualities attained articulation.

World War I battles were planned and fought by individuals who were imbued with belief in these values. The Boer War, increasing class conflict, the mass armies and battles of World War I, the Irish question, the campaign for women's suffrage—all posed massive challenges to British political and social forms. Indeed, political and social turmoil had reached such levels that Lloyd George's usually mild-mannered predecessor, Herbert H. Asquith, reflecting in early 1915 upon the status of World War I, declared it to have been a stroke of "*luck*" that had enabled the government to sweep domestic issues under the rug.[101] Would it not be too much to suggest that, under the circumstances, when "such forms are pressed by unusual situations or unusual intentions" they tend "to operate in unusual ways"?[102] A stolid unwillingness to change "tried-and-true" methods—oft-"tried" but seldom proved "true"—certainly must strike the observer as being unusual.

In any society, the military tends to view itself as the protector and sustainer of generally accepted social and cultural norms. For the personality types who, like Haig, French, or subordinates, were "professional" military men, challenges to established plans quite probably were not viewed as mere questioning of particular military decisions, but rather as attacks upon an accepted commitment to form and proper behavior that called into question the value system with which they were imbued, a system already under severe strain. Eventually, it challenged their raison d'être. As Festinger points out: "This source of resistance to change lies in the fact that an element is in relationship with a number of other elements. To the extent that the element is consonant with a large number of other elements and to the extent that changing it would replace these consonances by dissonances, the element will be resistant to change."[103] Resistance to change, an almost quite literally tragic inflexibility, was the factor responsible for a phenomenon that we have noted previously, particularly with regard to Frederick the Great and Napoleon—namely, a tendency to act as if very basic military realities either did not exist, or did not apply to those in leadership positions. With regard to British military behavior in World War I, the theory of cognitive dissonance poses an answer.

It also raises an extremely disquieting consideration. F. Scott Fitzgerald, speaking through the main protagonist in *Tender Is the Night*, Dick Divers, described the Great War as a conflict fired by "middle class love," the "last love battle." This battle—and Fitzgerald is describing the fighting on the western front—was one that would not be repeated for some time, if ever. Among other things, it was made possible by consciousness of "the exact relations that existed between the classes."[104] Soldiers did as they were expected to do and, except in rare cases or at the very end of the war, there was little breach of discipline. As we have noted earlier, the British army was the only major one in the west that *never broke*. Whether or not, as at least one author has claimed, the average British soldier retained faith in the always distant Haig, there can be no doubt that this soldier stuck things out to a degree which, to the present generation, must seem unimaginable. Sir Douglas Haig and other commanders, aloof as they were from the men they commanded, certainly must have had some sense that "their" soldiers could be called upon to stick to the tasks assigned them, if not cheerfully, then at least with a stolid determination. Haig and his colleagues certainly overestimated the ability of their armies to overcome defenses in depth, appalling weather conditions, and various deficiencies in tactics and ordnance. They knew, or acted as if they knew, that the British soldier would do whatever was asked of him; that he could be called upon to advance through mud and rain, stumbling over the bodies of comrades and then, after a brief rest, be counted on to repeat the process all over again. Orders would be obeyed; "the exact relations that existed between the classes" had seen to that. Social values and customary usages might well be threatened in Great Britain as a whole, and disquieting challenges to even military patterns of behavior might well be perceived, if only in embryonic form. Yet, on the field of battle itself, the old values of obedience and persistence held sway. Even if one accepts widely held beliefs that loyalty to one's comrades, more than any other factor, keeps the soldier at his task in battle, British soldiers demonstrated a stolid adherence to "form" that strikes one as singular.

From our perspective, it is easy to see that—insofar as tactical considerations, loss ratios, and so forth were concerned—things were not as those who commanded the British army of World War I perceived them to have been. We can detect an almost willful concern to *see* things as they were not, something that can be explained, at least in our opinion, only by a variety of psychological dysfunctions. In the end, however, we must view World War I as an attritional conflict and Germany as having been defeated by overwhelming numbers and resources on the battlefield and by a blockade that, in point of fact, killed more civilians than all the air raids in World War II. Therefore, we must ask ourselves whether, if eventual "victory" (however hollow) is all that matters, cognitive dissonance played an almost positive role in the British war effort. After all, if Britain's military leaders had allowed themselves to have known about true circumstances and conditions and, having gained this knowledge, to have been affected by it to the point where they did not persist in the ghastly "wearing down" attacks of 1916 and 1917, would the decisive victory of 1918 have eluded them? Perhaps, even with the entry of the United States, there still might have been some unthinkable form of stalemate.

Here, we must consider a topic brought up in an excellent book by Robin Prior and Trevor Wilson, *Passchendaele: The Untold Story.* Focusing on the dismal 1917 campaign, the authors took issue with the notion that major Great War battles were informed by a sense of inevitability. Especially in situations in which a civilian government was in place, they could have been stopped at any time. The British army had demonstrated, in limited objective operations such as Arras and Messines, that it could be quite successful in "capturing some worthwhile ground and of inflicting severe losses on the enemy, without involving the martyrdom of British troops."[105]

Prior and Wilson make two good points: First, that a campaign such as Passchendaele, which developed in stages, could have been ended at any time should the government have wished to do so, and second, that the British army need not have committed itself to grandiose and costly schemes designed to conquer large amounts of territory while utterly destroying those armies with which it was confronted. Rather, successful and less costly limited-goals operations could have been accomplished.

It is plain that any operation undertaken by finite beings was, and is not, informed by "inevitability." Of course Passchendaele or, for that matter, the earlier Somme campaign *could* have been called off. Limited-goal operations *could* have been undertaken. Nevertheless, the political/psychological realities of that time really did not allow for major campaigns to be shut down, or for the pursuance of limited goals. As Prior and Wilson put it, "They [the British civilian leadership], along with Haig, yearned for a large undertaking accomplishing dramatic results."[106] Lloyd George might well have viewed Haig as a blundering nincompoop, and Haig might well have seen Lloyd George as a devious, self-serving politician, but both civilian and military leaders were committed to total victory. Thus, bearing in mind the technical and logistical realities of the times, while the continuation of ghastly campaigns to bitter ends need not literally have been "inevitable," from a practical point of view they might as well have been.

Thus, we must perhaps draw the extremely disturbing conclusion that pathologically inflexible adherence to a system grounded in seemingly archaic prewar concepts, a system responsible for mounded corpses in exchange for limited gains, was at least as important an ingredient in the ultimate victory as any other factor attaching to the conflict. Perhaps all modern wars are attritional. In all events, World War I was particularly so and thus, while emotionally absorbing, the question of "breakthrough" versus "wearing down" campaigns was not of real significance. Even with American involvement, after all, Germany was worn down rather than shattered on the battlefield. In the final analysis, we must perhaps come to the conclusion that the Somme and Flanders (if not earlier British military adventures) were successes in a variety of conflict in which remorseless adherence to inflexible plans was the key to victory. Inflexibility, something that had almost destroyed Frederick's army at Kunersdorf and had doomed Napoleon's army in Russia, had proved to be a vital ingredient for those who could afford it in an age of mass warfare sustained by mass nationalism and the wonders generated by a technology run amok.

There is one last important question with which we must deal. Granted, British soldiers displayed a remarkable willingness to persist in seemingly mindless assaults ordered by generals who, in turn, showed a maddening (and inflexible) loyalty to prewar conceptions. Were not Dominion troops (that is, those from Canada, Australia, and New Zealand)—soldiers who were not representative of societies and supportive doctrines under stress—equally persistent in assault and obdurate on defense? Of course they were. Moreover, it is of more than passing interest to note that Haig and his colleagues were certainly aware of this; that, in point of fact, Dominion soldiers were often called upon to spearhead assaults in the most difficult of circumstances. While there was much bitter talk of this by many Canadian and Australian officers and men, it is certainly not true that British generals were indifferent to losses sustained by "non-British" troops. Denis Winter, a recent critic of Haig, suggests there is another reason why Dominion soldiers were often called upon to accomplish next-to-impossible tasks.

In *Haig's Command: A Reassessment*, Winter displays such great hostility toward his subject that he at times makes some rather hyperbolic assertions. Probably the most questionable of these is that "the German Army had not been defeated in the field."[107] In fact, he paints so rosy a picture of its state in the last weeks of the war that one is compelled to wonder why its high command thought it necessary to call for an armistice. Yet Winter, besides suggesting that Haig essentially rewrote important parts of his diaries after the war, offers the persuasive argument that Sir Douglas made "use of Dominion men as storm troops" because he was aware that they were better soldiers than their British comrades in arms, despite the dogged determination shown by the latter.[108]

They were better for a reason Haig and his commanders could never bring themselves to admit: better training. British generals remained committed to prewar tactical doctrine that had called for a varied training program in which emphasis was placed on formalities such as close-order drill and wheeling into antiquated skirmish lines.[109] Once the war began, despite a number of fearsome lessons, rigid adherence to prewar tactical doctrine was reflected in equally rigid adherence to prewar training methods. New devices such as tanks might be introduced and used with increasing effectiveness, but they would be introduced into a system that, seemingly out of necessity, was wedded to attritional solutions. Dominion soldiers, while no braver than their British counterparts, were better prepared for what they had to do because those who trained them were *not* committed to pursuing antiquated methods of instruction. Hence, in the end, they were better soldiers and, for this reason, often used in extremely difficult situations. Of course, because Haig was in command of the BEF—of which they were a part—Canadians, Australians, and New Zealanders usually died uselessly anyway. Yet, they often accomplished tasks that British generals seemed to know were beyond the capabilities of most British soldiers.

While obviously aware that Dominion officers and men were better soldiers than their British counterparts, Haig and his friends were unwilling to see why this was the case. To do so would have necessitated abandoning tactical and training doctrines to which they were tied with umbilical cords made of piano wire. In the end, of course, the Germans *were* worn down by the Allied mass of which the mostly British BEF was an extremely important part. Dominion troops—even if, as Winter states, they were used in a "shock" capacity—were but a small portion of this army. In any case, through sheer, unreflective persistence, British soldiers managed to prevail even if at a cost that astounded many Dominion officers.[110] Thus, during and even after the war (at least for a while) sacrosanct doctrines could remain for the most part unchallenged. After all, they had "worked"—even if it seemed necessary from time to time to throw in Imperial soldiers from across the waters to provide a cutting edge for them. Sadly, it would seem that the very effectiveness of such soldiers, due almost entirely to better training methods, contributed to a situation in which ultimate success made it possible for dissonant information regarding British tactical and training doctrines to be suppressed.

Possessed of that languid confidence in the willingness of men to do as they were told no matter what was asked of them, a confidence characteristic of individuals aware of their social superiority, British generals were able to call upon their soldiers to endure the supposedly unendurable again and again. This was a "fact," certainly as much a one as the stopping power of machinegun fire or the ghastly obstacle offered by row upon row of barbed wire left uncut by days of bombardment. British military leaders, hardly sadistic (at least not consciously), but aware that their soldiers possessed a stolid devotion to duty seemingly unequaled by any others, could make use of this mass. They could be confident that, in the end, all would be justified by victory. What was "really going on"—above all the ghastly results attendant upon adherence to systems whose tactical deficiencies were being demonstrated for all to see— really did not concern them. In fact, it was, in view of the singular nature of, for soldiers, the most hideous of wars, perhaps best that it did not. Representatives of a society that from without and within was confronted with discomfiting challenges, British World War I military leaders could keep at their task, shielded from dissonant information by defenses strengthened by these very challenges.

Second Lieutenant John Glubb, the later trainer of Transjordan's Arab Legion, described what happened when sappers deepened a trench in which numerous bodies had been pressed into the floor. "They are pretty well decomposed," he remarked, "but a pickaxe brings up chips of bone and rags of clothing. The rest is putrid grey matter."[111] In the process of seeing such a war through to a "successful" conclusion, mental health might well have proven to be a hindrance.

CHAPTER SEVEN

WINSTON CHURCHILL, ARTHUR HARRIS, AND BRITISH STRATEGIC BOMBING

> It was as heroic, as self sacrificing, as Russia's decision
> to adopt her policy of "scorched earth."
>
> —J. M. Spaight, on Churchill's decision
> in May 1940 to undertake the bombing
> of Germany

THE AREA BOMBING approach of the British Bomber Command in World War II was, and remains, highly controversial. Culminating in the pointless bombing of Dresden in February 1945, it cost the lives of more than three hundred thousand German civilians and more than seventy thousand British airmen, while its strategic value was debatable. Winston Churchill, who as early as World War I questioned the value of mass aerial assault against urban populations, essentially gave the "go ahead" for area bombing in World War II. In a move that was unusual for him, a military leader known for taking great (and often unwanted) interest in strategic and tactical considerations of all kinds, he surrendered virtually all authority to Air Marshal Arthur Harris. While aware of the increasingly heavy toll area bombing was exacting upon Bomber Command, and of the serious questions concerning its effectiveness, Harris remained inflexibly committed to it. In considering the problems presented by persistent adherence to area bombing doctrine, we will use two approaches. With regard to Churchill, it appears that the cognitive/affective one utilized earlier with regard to Frederick the Great can be of value. In considering Arthur Harris's inflexible and costly adherence to an extremely questionable doctrine, the "trial-and-error" hypothesis seems to be most effective. We have already employed the first approach. The second will be explained in due course.

In the eyes of many, Great Britain led the way in determining that airpower could and would be utilized for strategic purposes. For Alexander P. De Seversky, whose eloquent and often overstated panegyrics to aerial bombardment contributed to an overly roseate evaluation of its potentials, everything from British bombing methods to the design of the bombers themselves pointed to an understanding of the strategic use of the airplane that had eluded both American and German military minds.[1] For Brig. Gen. Dale O. Smith, Britain's forming of the Royal Air Force (RAF) as an independent armed service in March 1918, just before the massive German spring offensive, was "courageous" and indicated an acceptance of Air Marshal Hugh Trenchard's pioneering concepts regarding the strategic uses of the airplane.[2] Even the commander of Germany's fighter command, Generalleutnant Adolf Galland, in many ways critical of the British approach to aerial warfare, readily conceded that it was England, not Germany, which succeeded in creating a "strategical air force," and that it was indeed this force which "eventually crushed Germany."[3] In point of fact, there can be no argument regarding the superior quality of British bomber aviation, especially when compared to that of Nazi Germany. One also has to appreciate the forward-looking nature of British aerial doctrine since the time Trenchard's reflections upon bombardment strategy first began to have a serious impact upon British military thinking in general.[4]

Furthermore, with Winston Churchill's assuming the post of prime minister in May 1940, Britain's war effort was apparently to be directed by an individual possessed of a keen military mind, one open to innovation, and with a far-reaching and imaginative strategic sense. Whatever criticisms one could bring to bear against Churchill—even those of today, in an age in which imperialistic pretense must appear to be both arrogant and ludicrous—there can be no gainsaying the fact that he was an excellent war leader, far better than Hitler in the long run.[5] To be sure, while serving as first lord of the Admiralty, Churchill seemed to have something of a blind spot with regard to the role of sea power vis-à-vis a powerful enemy air force. Thus, with the outbreak of a general European war in September 1939, he began to entertain truly fantastic notions about starting a naval offensive in order to break into the Baltic and, in so doing, disrupt German maritime activities. Even in the First World War, the Admiralty had considered such a move impossible. With the emergence of modern airpower, it most assuredly appeared to be chimerical.[6] Also, like many of those who had been brought up in the naval tradition, Churchill, again as first lord of the Admiralty, made the mistake of stating that Hitler's invasion of Norway on April 9, 1940, eventually had to fail because he would now "have to fight, if necessary, during the whole summer against powers possessing vastly superior naval forces and able to transport them to scenes of action more easily than he can."[7] Yet, in the final analysis, Churchill appeared to have learned his lesson, and learned it well. He fully appreciated that the Dunkirk evacuation had been made possible by British aerial cover that had caused the Germans to have "resigned all hope of air superiority at that point."[8] His moving tributes to the skill and courage of the RAF during the

Battle of Britain are well known. In his memoirs, Churchill pointed out the role Japanese command of the air played in the January 1942 victory in Malaya and bluntly stated that, without the gaining of air supremacy, the Allies "could not have won the war."[9]

Indeed, Churchill apparently became so impressed with the potentialities seemingly inherent in a strategic air offensive that, according to some observers, he seemed to think that bombing alone could bring Germany to its knees.[10] Furthermore, while Churchill's personal intimacy with the head of Bomber Command, Arthur Harris, was not strong, the latter's impact had been great indeed—so much so as to assure his command a considerable degree of autonomy.[11] Thus, it would appear that the "former naval person"—as he liked to refer to himself, most particularly in communications with Franklin D. Roosevelt, who also had a fondness for ships—had indeed come to terms with what has to be recognized as one of the most decisive elements of World War II: airpower. Yet, closer scrutiny of several areas of concern indicates that Churchill's attitude toward airpower was rather a complex one and something that has to raise questions regarding his posture toward strategic bombing in particular. In this regard, we will have to consider the prime minister's thoughts on the issue of airpower versus sea power before we consider the British strategic aerial offensive against Germany.

AIR- VERSUS SEA POWER

On the morning of April 10, 1940, a squadron of Skua bombers of the British Fleet Air Arm dive-bombed and sank the German cruiser *Koenigsberg* in Bergen harbor, where it had been sheltering after being damaged by Norwegian coastal batteries. It was the first major warship to be sunk by air attack in military history.[12] Eventually, the German invaders gained aerial supremacy, which proved to be the decisive event of the Norwegian campaign because Allied troops could not be supplied or assisted from the sea.[13] In April and May 1941, the German air force turned the British evacuations from Greece and Crete into bloody nightmares, while the victories gained by the Royal Navy against the Italian fleet were rendered nugatory by this same service. On May 27, 1941, the German battleship *Bismarck* was sunk after being first discovered and then fatally crippled by British naval aircraft. Certainly, events of 1940–41 had proved, once and for all, that warships without air cover were next to worthless.

It would appear that Churchill had learned a great deal from these experiences, and we have seen evidence of this reflected in his memoirs. Yet, there is ample evidence to suggest that, in a very real sense, he remained convinced of the possibility of sea power's operating in the face of substantive aerial opposition.

In October 1941, Russia was in a desperate, seemingly hopeless, position. Soviet armies were in full retreat and the convoys Great Britain and the United States had dispatched to Murmansk were under constant harassment from German air and naval units. Churchill's response to this was to call for a naval expedition to Norway and, in the face of superior German airpower, "a lodgment" of a substantial British force. Because such a lodgment would have to be made outside the range of British aircraft, it would have to be supported and sustained exclusively by sea power. The goals were both admirable and logical, namely, to draw German forces from Russia and to provide greater protection for the Murmansk convoys. However, the envisaged means were absurd, involving the use of things "only he [Churchill] believed possible." In the face of almost unanimous opposition from his military advisors, Churchill adhered to this extraordinary scheme with immense stubbornness. It was only with the greatest exertions that he could be, in Alanbrooke's words, "ridden off Trondheim."[14] Such may have been the case, but airpower considerations did not deter the prime minister from embarking upon even more daring schemes.

In an understandably jubilant letter to President Roosevelt dated May 28, 1941, Prime Minister Churchill reported on the sinking of the *Bismarck*. Among other things, he said: "The effect upon the Japanese will be highly beneficial. I expect that they are doing all their sums again." It is certainly possible that the Japanese did just that. The result of any sum redoing by the prime minister is not known. We do know that, at the end of October 1941, the battle cruiser *Repulse*, the battleship *Prince of Wales*, four destroyers, and the aircraft carrier *Indomitable* were ordered to Singapore. The *Indomitable*, of course, was to have supplied air cover. Unfortunately, an accident held up the carrier's departure, but the other ships were ordered to proceed as planned. The battle cruiser and battleship had been sent "to exercise that kind of vague menace which capital ships of the highest quality whose whereabouts is unknown can impose upon all hostile naval calculations."[15] By the fall of 1941— to say nothing of 1950, when Churchill's book was published—the kind of menace offered by capital ships to naval operations *supported by airpower* was quite vague indeed.

Admiral Tom Phillips, the newly appointed commander in chief of the Far Eastern Fleet, was captain of the *Prince of Wales* and, although he would have preferred to have had air cover (Air Vice Marshal C. W. B. Pulford could not promise him anything), was confident that the antiaircraft armament of his ship, plus the admittedly less adequate armament of the *Repulse*, would suffice to deal with any air attack. The disasters off Greece and Crete had been due to the "unsatisfactory handling of the high-angle guns." Indeed, in the spring of 1941 he had expressed opposition to "Churchill's plan to establish long-range fighter airfields along the North African coast to provide air cover for convoys of Royal Navy ships."[16] In this case there can be no question of Churchill's perspicacity. Nevertheless, the *Repulse/Prince of Wales* episode pointed to "an outdated, almost sentimental, confidence in sea power" that in the end caused him to ignore or suppress virtually all of the lessons learned during the opening years of World War II.[17]

When Japanese aircraft intercepted Phillips's "Force Z" in its search for a suspected Japanese landing force, they were able to sink both capital ships for a loss of four aircraft. Almost nine hundred sailors died. Admiral Phillips went down with his ship, devoted, brave, and—like those who sent him on his death cruise—utterly unappreciative of the inadequacies of a military doctrine that had been adhered to in the face of overwhelming evidence as to its uselessness.

In the final analysis, of course, Winston Churchill had been responsible for the death of Phillips and nine hundred or so other less-known folk. Intelligent, insightful, unusually sensitive for one who enjoys practicing the so-called "art of war," he could not surrender up dearly held values and beliefs in the face of military potentialities, the actualization of which had been in large measure responsible for his assuming the office of prime minister in the first place. The "former naval person" might well have been aware that the "battle of the life lines" that had become so central to the course of World War II was, to a very great degree, being waged in the air. Yet, when he declared that "The Battle of the Atlantic was the dominating factor all through the war," he was referring—and there can be little doubt about this—to a war of ships.[18] While he was in many respects a forward-looking thinker, most particularly in military affairs, Churchill was unable to divest himself of pro-naval sentiments. These, in turn, were responsible for a nexus of opinions some of which, if translated into action, had to spell disaster for the British military effort.[19] Aircraft were important, perhaps even *decisive*, but somehow, in an arcane yet historically concrete manner, naval gunfire and torpedoes were what *mattered*. There is no question but that the sinking of the battle cruiser *Scharnhorst*, which had harassed Allied shipping on the northern run to Russia, was of considerable importance. Churchill's description of the action, however, one which covered two pages in the fifth volume of his treatise on World War II, points to an unwillingness to accept that such actions had to have become increasingly peripheral to the major course of a war which, like it or not, was more and more characterized by singularly unromantic applications of technology plus the gray mass to tactical and strategic problems. Such a war was seemingly immune to those solutions stemming from traditional military values.[20]

CHURCHILL AND THE STRATEGIC AIR OFFENSIVE

As we have seen, several commentators on air warfare in World War II pointed out that Great Britain was the power that seemed, at least initially, to have the clearest conception of what constituted a strategic air arm. One of the most ardent admirers of the British approach to air bombardment was Alexander De Seversky, whose praises at times bordered on the fulsome. In *Victory through Air Power* he also considered various airpower "lessons." An important one of these, he thought (and something that had been demonstrated during the Battle of Britain), was the following: "*Destruction of enemy morale from the air can be accomplished only by precision bombing.*" The war thus far had demonstrated that "despite large casualties and impressive physical destruction, civilians can 'take it.'. . . Provided they have the necessary patriotism and the will to fight, they can adjust themselves to the threats and the sacrifices much more readily than had been foreseen."[21] With some passion, De Seversky lambasted "unplanned vandalism from the air," declaring that only attacks on strategically justifiable targets would serve any real purpose.

De Seversky's "pet," Bomber Command, after taking prohibitive losses in daytime raids directed against specific targets, turned to nighttime area bombing. There can be no question that, at least at first, Air Marshal Arthur Harris, who, it is true, had been bequeathed the area attack method, at first seemed to think that killing civilians would have a devastating effect on German morale and thus play a crucial role in ending the war.[22] Later on, at least in his *Bomber Offensive*, the Bomber Command chief declared that the notion that bombing could seriously affect the morale of enemy workers was the "counsel of despair," and that he had never taken it very seriously.[23] Perhaps in partial response to Harris, Churchill himself declared that he had been aware of the fact that, at least through 1942, night area bombing "did not lower Germany's production or civilian morale."[24] Industrialist Albert Speer went even further than Churchill, declaring that area bombing *as a whole* did not weaken morale, but rather served to toughen the German civilian population.[25] As Adolf Galland saw it, Harris's bombing campaign, at least originally, had been intended to have "a political and psychological effect." This had not occurred, though. There was no panic or even real disorganization in the cities, at least not "to the degree 'Bomber' Harris and others had forecast."[26]

As we have seen, by war's end Harris was claiming that he had never taken the morale argument very seriously. Nevertheless, he remained adamant in his conviction that area bombing had been extremely effective in damaging the German war effort. Initially, area bombing resulted from the inability of aircrews to find more specific targets in the dark. However, according to Harris, the Essen raid on May 5, 1943, demonstrated that so-called indirect effects of raids on working-class areas were extremely significant, and that incendiary attacks upon a "densely built up centre" could have a devastating impact upon "services, houses, and amenities." The damage created in such a fashion was just as important as that which would have resulted from direct hits on facto ries and railroads.[27] Bristling at postwar suggestions that the British bombing campaign against Germany was relatively ineffective (American assertions along these lines were particularly irritating for Harris), the air marshal declared that statements to this effect were "demonstrably inaccurate" and that the most effective attacks were indeed those which took in industrial cities as a whole.[28]

Yet, according to German sources (who admittedly might have had ideological axes of one sort or another to grind) saturation attacks were of less concern than the so-called daylight precision raids. As Speer saw it, the Allies could have won the war in 1943 if they had dropped all of their bombs upon "the centers of armament production" instead of utilizing most of them in "vast but pointless area bombing." From Speer's point of view, raids such as those on the ball-bearing plants at Schweinfurt, if continued at a very high level, could well have been fatal.[29] Galland described Speer's fears about the effects upon production of American precision bombing. Speer, on the other hand, tended to discount British night raids as spectacular but ineffective.[30] Eventually, as both Speer and Galland saw it, the successful Allied attack upon fuel lines and depots was the single most important factor in fatally crippling the German war effort.[31]

As we examine issues attaching to the British approach to strategic bombing, we must bear in mind the crucial fact that, at the time this was translated into action, some sort of at least provisionally effective bombing offensive was the only way in which Great Britain could have engaged Nazi Germany to any significant degree. Once the Soviet Union entered the war and began bearing the burden of being the only power directly engaged, on a massive scale, with the Germans, the need for a sustained approach to attacking this country increased markedly. It was with this in mind that J. M. Spaight wrote that Winston Churchill's May 1940 decision to bomb Germany was "splendid." "It was," he continued, "as heroic, as self sacrificing, as Russia's decision to adopt her policy of 'scorched earth.' It gave Coventry and Birmingham, Sheffield and Southampton, the right to look Kiev and Kharkov, Stalingrad and Sebastopol in the face."[32] What is of interest is why the British approach remained essentially unchallenged until D-Day and, in some respects, after that.

At this point, it is important to note that no observer, German or Allied, ever took Bomber Command lightly. Massive and, to a degree, militarily meaningless slaughters such as the burning of Hamburg were, from a tactical point of view, counterbalanced by the extraordinarily sophisticated attack on the rocket research and testing center at Peenemunde and by the attack on the Möhne Dam of May 17, 1943, which, while not as significant as initially suspected (by experts on both sides), nevertheless was at least as daring and precise as any raid carried out by the American Eighth Air Force. What was particularly striking to both German and Allied commentators was the British air arm's seeming unwillingness to apply the sophistication and tactical and strategic daring that had defeated the Luftwaffe, and its eagerness to embrace the military doctrine the latter had employed when it commenced its utterly pointless bombing attacks on London, Coventry, and other urban centers. Furthermore, while the British bombers had greater range than the Dorniers and Heinkels that had participated in the 1940 attacks on England, and could carry far greater payloads and possessed better defensive armament than their German counterparts, they were in many ways just as helpless in the face of a determined defense. In fact, no German raiding force ever met with a disaster comparable to that which Bomber Command did on the night of March 30–31, 1944, when, on a raid on Nürnberg, ninety-four of 795 planes were destroyed and seventy-one others sustained serious damage. While Bomber Command persisted in its area-bombing tactics, thus drawing the attention of German night fighters, the RAF failed to provide any sort of meaningful long-range fighter protection. Furthermore, British bombers continued to carry .303-caliber machine guns instead of the .50-caliber variety used by the American B-17 Flying Fortress and B-24 Liberator bombers. By 1943, German night fighters, which faced no effective opposition from their British counterparts, could be aircraft that were capable of dealing with American long-range fighters such as the P-47 Thunderbolt and P-51 Mustang. Furthermore, they were often impervious to .303-caliber ammunition.[33]

Yet Harris, almost always supported by Churchill, persevered in his aerial bombing campaign, even as the cost became increasingly apparent. While a variety of sophisticated navigational aids were utilized to guide the bombers to their area targets, there was little substantial improvement in the equipment itself. Harris was inflexibly committed to his plans "as they were," while Churchill, who had to deal with operational problems in all areas, voiced few real concerns.

Since it is clear Churchill appreciated the fact that air supremacy was a crucial element in assuring victory over Nazi Germany, this strikes one as curious. This is especially so since he had been rather forward-looking in his reflections upon the role of airpower in modern warfare. In 1917, Britain, which earlier had endured periodic visits from Zeppelins, was being subjected to more frequent bombing raids by twin-engine German Gotha aircraft. The use of aircraft to terrorize an enemy civilian population was under serious consideration and Churchill, at that time the minister of munitions, stated:

> It is improbable that any terrorization of the civil population which could be achieved by air attack would compel . . . surrender . . . we have seen the combative spirit of the people roused, and not quelled, by the German air raids. Nothing that we have learned of the capacity of the German population to endure suffering justifies us in assuming that they could be cowed into submission by such methods or . . . not be rendered more desperately resolved by them.[34]

Thus, *as early as 1917*, the future prime minister was not only taking aircraft seriously as an offensive weapon, he also was anticipating a major drawback to its indiscriminate use against civilians. We also mentioned Churchill's concern in 1934 that London was open to aerial assault. Once the war began, he showed an impressive interest in expanding Britain's strategic bombing fleet. At the same time, as he had in 1917, Churchill seemed to be aware of some of the problems confronting the use of bombers in mass raids. In cooperation with his scientific advisor, F. A. Lindemann (later Lord Cherwell), the prime minister concerned himself with the problems that early bomber types and strategies had in finding their targets, much less ensuring that significant damage was inflicted.[35] In August 1941, a member of the War Cabinet secretariat put together a report on the effectiveness of British strategic bombing. The so-called Butt Report was a devastating critique and outraged Churchill. He declared that he doubted "whether bombing by itself will be a decisive factor in the present war. On the contrary, all that we have learnt since the war began shows that its effects, both physical and moral, are greatly exaggerated."[36]

It was plain that the prime minister, who at one time thought that strategic bombing was just about the only way that Germany could be brought to its knees, had become bitterly disappointed with the dismal performance of Bomber Command, which at the time was still carrying out a significant number of its missions during daylight hours and often attempting to hit specific targets. It was because of increasing doubts at all levels regarding Bomber Command's effectiveness that the aggressive and self-assured Arthur Harris became its commander in February 1942. This, plus the development of improved bomber aircraft and navigational aids, restored much of Churchill's faith in strategic bombing. He was never quite as optimistic as he had been earlier. Nevertheless, not until very late in the war did he seriously question the effectiveness of area bombing, an approach to which Harris, after some vacillation, became fanatically committed.

There was, of course, a degree of realism informing Churchill's support of Harris. Daytime attacks had proven to be costly failures, and, as mentioned earlier, the British never developed a truly effective long-range fighter to serve in an escort capacity. Churchill had come to the logical conclusion that unescorted bombers could not fight their way through to targets and then back to home base, at least not in the daytime, something American air planners learned only after several aerial disasters.[37] Even if we bear in mind that memoirs such as Churchill's (the overall nature of which compelled one critic to suggest it ought to have been entitled "My war and how I won it") were perhaps more than a trifle self-serving, there is little doubt that he possessed a first-rate military mind. Nonetheless, as in the case of his attitude regarding confrontations between air- and sea power, Churchill's approach to strategic bombing presents us with some problems.

Harris pointed out that Churchill, while upset over the casualties sustained by Bomber Command, nevertheless sought to wage all-out war against Germany. He did not wish "to destroy cities for revenge," but he did understand the "vast strategic consequences" of raids such as the first thousand-plane attack, the May 30, 1942, raid on Cologne.[38] Although he later accused Churchill, no doubt quite justifiably, of being a "bad listener," Harris was adamant in declaring that the prime minister gave him an enormous degree of freedom of action, and, in fact, never pressed him to do anything Churchill wanted to do—or, for that matter, to refrain from things Harris thought were necessary.[39] In point of fact, it would appear that Churchill who—judging not only from his memoirs, but also from the comments of wartime friends and colleagues—took an at times almost morbidly paternalistic interest in all aspects of the war, abandoned the development of air strategy to an officer whose forceful arguments and apparent total commitment to the most simplistic of all approaches—that is, the continuous bombing of urban centers— had made an impression on him.[40] An early advocate of area bombing, Air Chief Marshal Sir Charles Portal, the chief of the air staff and Harris's superior, might, like the Americans, have become an advocate of at least occasional selective bombing. Air Marshal Sir Arthur Tedder, Gen. Dwight D. Eisenhower's deputy, might also have pressed for more attacks on Germany's transportation system. However, it was Harris who ultimately carried the day with Churchill. In fact, appreciating Churchill's support of Harris, Air Chief Marshal Portal rarely overruled his subordinate.[41] Indeed, even after Allied commanders brought immense pressure upon him in 1944, Harris allowed his bombers to participate in precision nighttime raids on Germany's oil centers and transportation system (in which the British proved to be quite effective), but he always placed major emphasis on area bombing. Portal had objections, but he could do little about them.

There is a crucial problem here. As Anthony Verrier, quoting Noble Frankland, has pointed out, Churchill devotes "surprisingly little" attention in his memoirs to the air offensive other than to attempt to justify certain sporadic decisions and controversies surrounding its implementation. Eloquent descriptions, such as the one mentioned above about the sinking of the *Scharnhorst*, are utterly lacking with regard to the bomber offensive, an operation the prime minister himself recognized as absolutely crucial. Neither Churchill nor Roosevelt, for that matter, "really understood the scientific and technical aspects of air power, nor appreciated that the strategic air offensive was also subject to the same laws of war as that governing naval, amphibious, and ground operations."[42] In Roosevelt's case, this was perhaps understandable. After all, he was not a military man in any sense of the term, seemed to appreciate this, and, as in the case of domestic politics, relied on his well-known "charm" and apparent general commitment to certain basic principles to see him through in areas of general strategy.[43] Churchill, however (and with some reason), thought himself possessed of a first-rate military mind. What his ancestor had accomplished at Blenheim, he could and would accomplish—and on a much larger scale—in the twentieth century. Thus, his abandoning to Harris an arena that he himself saw as one of great importance cannot be viewed in the same way that we view Roosevelt's lack of *interest*. Why did Churchill—who was involved in everything from tank construction to the creation of the artificial harbors code-named "Mulberries" that would prove to be of such enormous value in June 1944—express little if any interest in the weak defensive armament of the British bombers and, more important, in the lack of an adequate long-range fighter escort? Why was this man—who had been so repelled by the straightforward frontal assaults of World War I and, as we have seen, had early on appreciated the senselessness of attempting to break the morale of an enemy population through simple terror raids—so willing to acquiesce in a strategy that in its own way was analogous to Field Marshal Haig's?

Indeed, Churchill was unusually truculent and at times downright defensive in this regard. In considering Maj. Gen. Ira Eaker's utilization of the Casablanca Conference in January 1943 as a forum for pressing for greater daylight B-17 raids on Europe, Churchill—even with the retrospective knowledge that precision raids had been, at the very least, of immense significance in crippling the German war effort—declared that "if at the beginning they [the Americans] had put their money on night bombing we should have reached our climax much sooner." Indeed, the prime minister continued to doubt whether or not the American bombing campaign could be (and, in retrospect had been) truly effective. Even with regard to Germany's air defenses, it was the German night-fighter force that was given the "cream of their pilots." It was this force that remained formidable even as the standards of the day force, the one that confronted the Americans, declined—a decline Churchill attributed mainly to the increasingly successful British nighttime area raids.[44] To say that simple nationalism, or for that matter, even egotism, was involved here probably would miss the point. Rather, what is important was Churchill's unwillingness to confront issues raised by a form of warfare he found distasteful.

As we have seen, Churchill seemed to appreciate the fact that sea power had been overtaken by airpower. Yet, when it came to certain crucial decisions, the presumably "*former* naval person" acted as if he were the American naval officer who had offered to stand bareheaded on the bridge of the target ship *Ostfriesland* when Brig. Gen. Billy Mitchell had a go at sinking it. Also, even with the knowledge of what had been proven during the Second World War close at hand, Churchill spent a great deal of time describing naval actions in much the same manner that Napoleonic engagements might have been depicted. *In fact*, airpower might have become predominant. Yet, in some strange way, the battleship still constituted a "vague menace" and lodgments in Norway could be affected in the face of superior enemy airpower. Churchill, in his own eyes and those of Air Marshal Harris, certainly seemed to have an understanding of strategic bombing's potential. In fact, he appears to have gained this understanding quite early in the history of air warfare. In his memoirs, however, he spent relatively little time on the strategic bombing campaign. Crucial technical issues were of no interest to him and he avoided serious strategic reflection. We thus are confronted with the same issue that surfaced with regard to sea versus airpower: namely, a willingness to accept, in a purely intellectual fashion, certain critical technological developments and the tactical and strategic changes that flowed from them, while refusing, in certain critical situations, to pursue them through to logical conclusions. With regard to the naval issue, Churchill, with reason (whether or not we agree with his conclusions), thought—or, perhaps in this case, to employ an overused term, "felt"—that he had a firm grasp of things. His extraordinary intellectual perspicacity caused him to have an *intellectual appreciation* for strategic bombing. However, that self-same romanticism that caused Churchill to view himself as a defender of *imperium* necessitated that he not really concern himself with the issues raised by this phenomenon which, unlike naval warfare, really was "beyond" him. To be sure, the Battle of Britain was crucial. In fact, he himself coined the phrase. This was, however, a knightly sort of affair, a duel in the skies. How one went about reducing an enemy's war potential through sustained strategic air bombardment was quite another matter. As long as air warfare was a problematic sort of thing, one could reflect upon it in a putatively serious manner. After 1941, however, strategic aerial bombardment had become a reality—as palpable as a destroyer, cruiser, tank, or Bren gun. Whether one attacked industries, communications, or entire cities had become pressing issues. An individual who had participated in cavalry action at Omdurman was not in a position to decide how a method of warfare for which he had no affective, as opposed to cognitive, appreciation was to be applied.

The upshot of all this is that it was better *not* to reflect upon the issues involved. The ethical concerns raised might call into question the validity and purpose of war itself. It is only *apparently* paradoxical that, under the circumstances, Churchill was willing, even eager, to turn the matter over to one who seemed to be quite able, and in some ways eager, to disengage himself from concerns that might fall more within the purview of the theologian rather than that of the military commander. Warfare had always been ugly. The Allies' strategic air offensive was, with regard to the *number* of casualties inflicted and the *manner* in which they were inflicted, not much uglier than the slaughters perpetrated in earlier times with more primitive weapons. Now, though human beings were the same as ever, military valor—that part of them which seemed to make them human, in the noblest sense of the word—was about to be overshadowed, if not eroded, by technological realities. Under the circum-

stances, it was of almost existential necessity that someone like Winston
Churchill, an embodiment of all that was both far- and shortsighted in the
nineteenth century, leave certain crucial decisions in the hands of others. In
the end, the justification of those policies pursued by individuals such as Air
Marshal Harris had to be justifications of themselves—and of the fact that a
person having essentially nineteenth-century sensibilities was leading his nation into a war in which the modes associated with those sensibilities were being ruthlessly extirpated.

On a strictly cognitive level, Churchill could recognize the necessity of strategic bombing. Emotionally, however—and quite understandably—he was
unable to do so. In his persistent devotion to sea power, Churchill revealed an
inflexible commitment to an idealized approach to war that his intellectual
half recognized as obsolete. Under the circumstances, it was best that he abandon a field for which he had little affective appreciation to one who seemed
to possess it in abundance.

AIR MARSHAL HARRIS:
A PSYCHOLOGICAL PERSPECTIVE

Bomber Command has in many ways been equated with the remarkable leadership of Air Marshal Sir Arthur Harris. From beginning to end he (with, as we
have seen, Churchill's blessings) dominated British air strategy. Persistence is
often admirable, but in this instance it was costly; strategies and tactics were
defined by operational capabilities linked to a single principle.[45]

Solutions were constrained by an overriding commitment to a doctrinally
defined problem (area bombing), and were characterized by what can be aptly
described as trial-and-error learning. American psychologist Edward Lee Thorndike was the first to describe this type of learning process. In an initial series of
experiments, hungry animals were placed in boxes from which they could escape to obtain food. The escape mechanisms varied from strings to thumb
latches.[46]

Initially, an animal (for example, a cat) placed in the box would try nonfunctional responses such as biting and clawing. Sooner or later, the animal
would pull the string or press the latch and escape. Eventually the animals
succeeded in getting out of the box in successively shorter times, but the learning curves were so irregular as to cause Thorndike to speculate that learning
consisted of stamping in correct responses, and stamping out incorrect.[47] Reasoning could not be inferred. He theorized that learning was accomplished by
forming an association between the situation (the box) and any response that
allowed the animal to escape. His ideas subsequently became an integral part
of behaviorism.

Thorndike, like most animal psychologists, began to make invidious comparisons with human behavior. Human thought was conceived as a body of associations categorized as ideas and habits. The origin and strengthening of these connections followed the same mechanistic principles derived from animal behavior. Anticipating Skinner, he argued that the consequences of the responses determined whether the connection was strengthened or weakened.[48]

Although learning was conceived along mechanical-deterministic lines, Thorndike was certainly not unaware of the complexities associated with human learning. For example, in a subsidiary law (the Law of Prepotency) he suggested that a response in a given situation was likely to be more strongly influenced by certain elements of the situation than others.[49] Bomber Command (that is, Harris) never really looked outside the situational elements connected directly with area bombing. Like the cat, he never believed there was life beyond the box.

The distinction between trial and error and problem solving is important. Problem solving involves the exploration of hypotheses, which in turn involves a careful delineation or even reconceptualization of the task. Starting with an initial definition of the situation, problem solving involves the generation of proposed solutions, testing, and evaluation. In some instances, the end result is that the problem situation is reconceptualized, and the process repeats itself.[50]

Most problem-solving models assume that rational cognitive processes underlie attempts at solution. Objectivity is crucial. In reality, decision making involves strong components of individual motivation and affect, which subvert the logical model.[51] Hence, the number of alternatives psychologically available to the individual can be remarkably constrained. In the case of Bomber Command, where doctrine dominated solutions, responding was so limited as to approximate Thorndike's trial-and-error model. There was often little evidence suggesting higher-order conceptual activity.[52] That is, while scientific products were gratefully accepted, their usage was limited to a fixed problem definition.

Basically, in most trial-and-error situations some response produces a solution that results in immediate satisfaction. The cat gets out of the box, but is not likely to "understand" the relationship between the escape response and the escape mechanism. In any problem-solving situation one may accidentally stumble on a solution. This is not, however, a solution in the classical sense. Without some insight, the behavior pattern reverts to a trial-and-error pattern. The solver simply does not know *why* the solution worked; one cannot replicate the appropriate behavior. It is obvious that if the cat is always placed in the same box, the animal becomes more efficient at getting out. However, if the escape mechanism is modified, the animal has a problem (pun intended). Moreover, even if the problem is solved, without an understanding of the relationships (that is, insight) between the solution and the nature of the problem, transfer (that is, the utilization of old knowledge in a new situation) becomes very difficult if not impossible. In a trial-and-error pattern, the subject can best be described as trying "something."

This is a far cry from having insight. It can be argued that when a person has "solved" a problem, behavior should move from something approaching randomization toward purposefulness based on the newly acquired knowledge.[53] Behavior thus should demonstrate that some understanding has taken place. In modern warfare, where the nature of problems may change dramatically, insight can be assessed by determining if the proposed solutions take into account potential enemy responses. That is, to what extent are the decision's ramifications explored? Failing to do this adequately results in a tendency to adopt the trial-and-error model, where immediacy of effect takes precedence.

Harris thought that crippling industry was of primary importance in winning the war. Using such indices as acreage destroyed or German workers "dehoused," he could argue that area bombing was producing the desired results.[54] But Harris was using self-serving (and generally nonvalidated) criteria to defend an established policy, the inflexibility of which was determined by adherence to a doctrine. While the measures and countermeasures Harris utilized were clearly instances of learning from one's mistakes, the major assumptions concerning overall strategies and tactics were never really questioned. By restricting options, depth and breadth of conceptualization were also severely limited. To the cat, the box was the problem; for Harris, it was area bombing.

Harris's inflexibility in maintaining his beliefs may have been in part a reaction to the Luftwaffe's failures during the Battle of Britain. If anything could be said to characterize the German air offensive in that campaign, trial and error would be most fitting. The Luftwaffe's initial aims simply were not commensurate with resources, nor even prioritized.[55] As a result, Luftwaffe tactics vacillated between such diverse approaches to gaining aerial supremacy as attrition of the RAF and bombing radar sites and eventually airfields. In fact, the final switch to area bombing saved the RAF. Fortunately for the British, Goering and Hitler had no real idea what would accomplish their initially defined goal.[56] Harris also had a goal: the destruction of German industrial potential by disrupting, if not eliminating, urban life. Area bombing was the means to this end. Harris intended to succeed where the Luftwaffe had failed. He would persevere in his approach and he had a far more effective instrument at his disposal. In so doing, "trial and error" would prevail at the strategic rather than the tactical level.

When Bomber Command switched to night bombing, the critical factor was that daylight attacks were proving too costly. In all fairness, however, the decision to go from precision to area attacks was made before Harris took command.[57] Nevertheless, the guiding assumptions about how Bomber Command could be used most effectively were never really challenged. Night area bombing continued, even though by 1943 Bomber Command could point to only a

60 percent gain in accuracy within a three-mile radius.[58] It would continue even in the face of losses that eventually bordered on the prohibitive. The whole menagerie of navigational aids—Oboe, Gee, H2s, master bomber, 100 Group, and visual flares—grew out of trial-and-error responses to specific enemy actions. It was not that the devices were primitive; indeed, the later ones were quite sophisticated. But there never seemed to be any thinking beyond a sacrosanct definition of the problem. The British development of the concentrated bomber stream to overcome a new German defensive system called the Kammhuber Line is a classic example. Eventually these formations proved useless under other circumstances. From these misfortunes rose the development of 100 Group.[59] It is true, as Galland pointed out, that there was often no time to experiment,[60] but much of Bomber Command's thinking supports the belief among devotees of programmed instruction that humans are incapable of seeking information beyond the next single proposition. Indeed, the all-out assaults on transportation and communication preceding D-Day,[61] as well as the subsequent oil industry blitz,[62] were comparatively isolated examples of a clearly defined strategy derived from a rational problem analysis. As a rule, Harris condemned focusing upon what he called "panacea targets."[63]

In summary, Harris's inflexible insistence on area bombing stemmed from his doctrinally determined solution to a problem. In retrospect, perhaps trial and error was the only solution method available. Certainly the daily tactical demands encouraged quick-and-dirty solutions, but there was no significant encouragement given to redefining the problem, much less extrapolating the impact of proposed solutions.

There is, of course, the inevitable question of whether the dogmatism created trial and error, or vice versa. While the relationship is hardly unilateral, the evidence nevertheless suggests that the thrust lay in the direction of the overriding influence of doctrine. While it is true that many critical problem areas were resolved by initially satisfying solutions (that is, quality and quantity of equipment and personnel), it is equally true that the types of solutions employed did not basically change. Generally, no solutions were permitted that proposed abandoning the problem as initially defined. It thus was inevitable that responses reflecting immediacy and supportive of the established solution to the problem were encouraged. The air strategy decision-making process might well be considered as tinkering rather than thinking.

Winston Churchill had a far-reaching military imagination. In the end, however, with regard to strategic bombing, he was either unwilling or unable to concern himself with the messy details involved in its application. He was inflexibly rooted in affectively informed notions of what war ideally was about. Necessarily, then, he surrendered most authority with regard to decision making to an individual who was eager to assume full responsibility. Arthur Harris, inflexibly committed to a doctrine whose uselessness had been demonstrated during the German aerial assaults on Great Britain, was responsible for a bombing campaign which, while raising serious moral issues, was both terribly costly to Bomber Command and of doubtful strategic worth. In a very real sense, Churchill's dysfunctional response, a splitting of cognitive and affective elements, to the terrible challenges posed by strategic bombing was responsible for determining that the British effort would be directed by a man who was inflexibly committed to what came to be seen by many as a campaign of aerial terror. Ironically, Harris was the only major British military leader not honored for his role in achieving victory in World War II.

Yet, in an age of mass warfare that necessarily has involved mass terror and mass destruction, we must again pose a question raised in the previous chapter: If we see that destruction of German cities was at least a *contribution* to victory, then was not Harris's inflexibility—and Churchill's seeming acceptance of it—an important, if not necessary element?

Here we should bear in mind the *very* strong probability that Richard Overy's assessment is valid. He has agreed with those who have maintained that *direct* effects upon civilian morale and the production of goods related to the war effort were not nearly as great as the champions of area strategic bombing thought they would be. Nevertheless, "secondary" effects played a vital role in the Allied victory. In a word, Bomber Command's somewhat simplistic approach—that is, leveling cities over time—managed to produce, at the very least, worry and discouragement. Problems with regard to quality of production, absenteeism due to physical exhaustion, and understandable desires to look out for family needs and concerns—overall, the increasing possibility of physical annihilation—all played a crucial role in sapping Germany's wartime strength. Also, of course, much of the nation's military production had to go into the manufacturing of varieties of antiaircraft weapons and tracking devices. Finally, the necessity of keeping large numbers of aircraft "at home" to defend Germany against strategic bombing, much of it by the British, weakened German airpower on all fronts, perhaps, most significantly, on the eastern one. So, no matter what forms of psychological dysfunctionalism Churchill and Harris displayed, what resulted from a campaign that was hideously costly for airmen and civilians alike was "worth it."[64]

Thus, we again are confronted with the unpalatable possibility that under certain circumstances, most particularly attritional ones, psychological dysfunctionalism may play a crucial "positive" role in determining that victory will go to the side most able to endure heavy losses over time. The question is a disturbingly ambiguous one. In a perhaps perversely satisfying way, we will not have to deal with such ambiguities in the next chapter.

CHAPTER EIGHT

STALINGRAD: A GHASTLY COLLABORATION BETWEEN HITLER AND HIS GENERALS

I won't go back from the Volga.
—Adolf Hitler, on being informed that
the German Sixth Army was surrounded

IN VIEW OF THE complex nature of the Stalingrad campaign, it is useful to bear the following in mind:

The invading German Army, and attached allied units, were divided into:

Army Group North
Army Group Middle
Army Group South

For the ill-fated 1942 offensive, Group South was divided into Groups A and B, the former attacking in the Caucasus, the latter north, toward Stalingrad.

The high command of the German armed forces was the Oberkommando der Wehrmacht (OKW).

The army high command was the Oberkommando der Heeres (OKH).

Supposedly, the OKH was subordinate to the OKW, which consisted of the triumvirate Feldmarschall Wilhelm Keitel, Generalleutnant Alfred Jodl, and Hitler. After Kurt Zeitzler became chief of staff of the OKH in late September 1942, however, he became Hitler's sole confidant. The result was that strategic and tactical decision-making authority was, for all intents and purposes, removed from the OKW.

Perhaps, as distinguished military historian Walter Görlitz has suggested, the Battle of Stalingrad was not the military, but rather the psychological turning point of World War II; the former being the Kursk-Orel salient battle of July 1943.[1] However, if history is indeed made in men's minds, then a "psychological" turning point is of crucial importance.

In considering the role of psychological processes and dysfunction in the Stalingrad disaster, we must first of all acknowledge that the actions—or, at times, lack of them—of some of the participants can be explained fairly well in "conventional" terms, unless one were to have recourse to extremely sophisticated forms of depth psychology, which the lack of supportive evidence would render inappropriate. Individuals such as Wilhelm Keitel and Alfred Jodl, who with Hitler comprised the increasingly marginal OKW, can be seen as marginal sycophants whose roles were influenced by an overriding desire to please their führer. Kurt Zeitzler, the OKH chief of staff during most of the Battle of Stalingrad, was at least retrospectively aware of the problems and dangers confronting the German military in general and the doomed Sixth Army in particular. Yet, although he at times confronted Hitler with his views on the matter, he did not dare to take action on his own. Reichsmarschall Hermann Göring, the very intelligent and self-promoting chief of the Luftwaffe, had seen his career slip into the shadows after various failures, the Battle of Britain being the most notable of them. Now, a bloated, self-absorbed ruin, he was in desperate need of regaining Hitler's favor and would say or do just about anything he thought Hitler wanted.

The behaviors of others, as we will consider in due course, are more baffling and cannot be explained through enlightened common sense. Due to the extremely complex nature of the Stalingrad battle—more correctly viewed as a campaign—with the panoply of individuals, organizations, and motives involved, it will be necessary to apply several approaches to varieties of problems not collectively present (at least to the same degree) in earlier battles or campaigns. Again, the outcome will be inflexibility. This behavior, however, will be the product of interacting processes, each of which will require a different approach to explicate.

Adolf Hitler, commander in chief of the Wehrmacht, has been the subject of a variety of well-known psychohistorical studies.[2] They are not in total agreement with one another, although each is grounded in acceptance of certain basic Freudian assumptions. Furthermore, some of the conclusions drawn about the rather shadowy aspects of Hitler's life—for example, when he became anti-Semitic, his dietary and sexual preferences, and so forth—have been seen as dubious.[3] Nonetheless, certain general conclusions seem to offer convincing explanations of his behavior while at the same time being congruent with widely accepted interpretations rooted in conventional varieties of historical understanding. What follows is a general description of Hitler's personality that represents a précis of these generally acceptable conclusions.

Adolf Hitler was brought up in a rather typical patriarchal central European

household. He was subjected to a perhaps greater degree of abuse than average from his father, but that is a matter of debate.[4] At the same time, his
mother, who had endured the loss of three other children plus another after
Adolf's birth, pampered young Adolf without meeting all of his needs—and,
of course, without being able to protect him from the occasionally vented fury
of his father. What resulted, first of all, was an individual who dreaded being
the helpless victim of others, one who developed an extreme form of aggression in order to assure that this situation could not arise. Here, there is a
marked resemblance between young Adolf and the young Frederick the
Great. Yet, there was a crucial difference: The adult Adolf Hitler has been described as a "narcissistic personality," that is, an individual morbidly preoccupied in dealing with underlying feelings of shame and worthlessness through
continuous efforts at bolstering his self-esteem. Such an individual can never
permit himself to be perceived as wrong; is outwardly grandiose in talk, and
often in action; demands constant affirmation of his importance from ac-
quaintances (and thus usually has few, if any, real friends); tends, more than
most of us, to project all that he detests in himself onto others; and, again more
than most, will practice the arts of avoidance and denial when confronted
with displeasing circumstances.[5] Inwardly uncertain of his own worth, he will
"want it all," while being unwilling, at times hysterically so, to accept any sort
of responsibility for failures along the way.

Hitler's father, who brutalized him (once again, the degree of this brutaliza-
tion is a matter of opinion), has been deemed responsible for inflicting severe
injuries to young Adolf's self-esteem and, as suggested above, helping to shape an
aggressive personality unwilling to passively endure assaults, real or fantasized.
In this regard, one can talk of response to "narcissistic injury."[6] Here, one can see
a marked resemblance between young Adolf and the young Frederick. It would
appear, though, that it was Hitler's mother who, by almost always treating him as
someone very special, was responsible for his full-blown narcissism.[7] Mistreated
by his father, doted over by his mother, a "survivor" while siblings died before and
after him, Hitler came to view himself as destiny's darling. His will would be
done, if not in heaven, then most assuredly on earth. At the same time, underlying uncertainties about his real worth made it impossible for Hitler to deal realistically with those uncertainties and challenges that had to arise in the wake of
his monomaniacal drive for self-affirmation. Mood swings and rages masked a
personality that was, at heart, fearful of change and, in the end, inflexible.[8]

We must still deal with the question of how such a personality dealt with
the problems present at Stalingrad, and with his generals in particular. Here,
the initial work of John Dollard and his colleagues at Yale, described earlier in
the chapter on Hood, provides an interesting explanation for Hitler's actions.[9]
Because of the complexities of the Stalingrad campaign, we think it useful to
recapitulate this hypothesis.

Basically, starting in 1934, they embedded Freud's death instinct (that is, the aggression drive) within a stimulus-response framework, leading to the famous frustration-aggression hypothesis. This hypothesis assumes that when some sequence of behaviors is prevented (that is, frustrated) from terminating in a predicted goal response, the result is an aggressive response. In fact, frustration is always defined in terms of interference. Aggression, in turn, is presumed to be a set of behaviors in which physiological or psychological injury to the frustrating agent is the major objective. Furthermore, it was suggested that where aggression against the source of frustration leads to a reduction in the aggressive drive, per se, there is no parallel diminution of the originally frustrated behaviors.[10] Hence, whatever Hitler's original motives, they were not reduced by attacks on the frustrating agents.

As mentioned earlier in our consideration of Hood, the researchers went on to derive a set of basic theoretical postulates. First, the strongest aggressive action will be taken against those perceived as most directly responsible for the frustration, with weaker actions toward those seen as less responsible. Second, the more inhibitions there are to direct acts of aggression, the more likely it is the individual will engage in indirect aggressive acts. That is, if one cannot get mad at the boss, one can always kick the cat. The equivalent Freudian construct is displacement. In some cases, the aggression may be directed at one's self, if one is prone to self-blame.[11] However, following Saul Rosenzweig's categorization of aggressive behaviors, Hitler could best be described as extrapunitive, that is, tending to place the blame on others.[12] At no time during the Stalingrad campaign did Hitler fail to berate his staff.

The basic outline of the frustration-aggression hypothesis has remained essentially unchanged over the years, although Leonard Berkowitz's work resulted in a number of modifications. First of all, Berkowitz argued that anger is the driving force behind aggression, but whether or not any aggressive behaviors are observed is dependent on a great many situational deterrents. For example, the strength of the aggressive drive is proportional to the anger released as well as the presence of appropriate cues for expression of hostility.[13]

Psychologists have long been aware of a phenomenon called pain aggression. If two animals, such as rats, are penned in close proximity on an electric grid, and a charge is passed through the surface, the animals will begin to fight.[14] Among humans, the presence of noxious stimuli will also induce aggression. Such cues as foul odors, high room temperatures, or even frightening information will serve to increase aggression both in terms of gastronomical responses or punishment meted out to another person. Moreover, stimuli previously associated with aversive events can trigger aggression.[15]

Second, Berkowitz recognized the existence of instrumental aggression, in which the behavioral emphasis is on the attainment of some goal rather than doing injury. For example, the crews of planes engaged in a bombing raid, as we saw in a preceding chapter, did not necessarily have any significant feelings of anger about the populace.[16] This is important, because we must distinguish between Hitler's anger toward the Russians in the fighting around Stalingrad and his feelings regarding the German general staff. After all, as Hood must have felt about his Yankee opponents, one expects the Russians to create trouble.

Third, frustration that is perceived as unexpected or arbitrary is more likely to produce stronger aggressive drives. Fourth, aggression does not necessarily lead to catharsis. Rather, an opportunity to express hostility may lessen the initial anger, but also evoke or strengthen habitual hostile tendencies.[17] Naturally, no single psychological hypothesis can explain all of Hitler's decisions, or the lack of them, at Stalingrad—or, for that matter, in other contexts. Nonetheless, we believe that Hitler *can* be described as a narcissistic personality whose fear of being the target of aggression or abuse, combined with a constant need for self-affirmation that led to a sense of grandiosity, caused him to react to stress in ways best covered by the frustration-aggression hypothesis.

Yet, while Hitler certainly bore the primary responsibility for the destruction of the Sixth Army at Stalingrad, he did not act in a vacuum. His generals all played important roles, even if they saw—or chose to see—themselves as being limited in this regard by their oaths of allegiance to the führer. Although some involved in the Stalingrad disaster—for example, Generaloberst Friedrich Paulus, the Sixth Army commander and the single general upon whom we will focus most of our attention—might be candidates for more in-depth analysis, we do not think that such an approach would be as fruitful as one that could be used to offer an explanation for the actions (or lack of them) of Hitler's generals as a group called upon to respond to profound challenges. Most assuredly, *within* the group, there were singular responses to problems posed by the Soviets and, on the other side, the commander in chief of the German armed forces. These will be considered. We do think, however, that those German generals of consequence in the Stalingrad campaign displayed actions, or failed to act, in ways that can best be described by an approach that examines group behavior. This approach, formulated by Irving L. Janis, is called "groupthink." Grounded in the earlier work of Kurt Lewin and Leon Festinger, among others, it analyzes efforts to arrive at consensus through suppressing dissent, doubts, or searches for alternatives once certain decisions grounded in overriding attitudes have been made.[18]

The groupthink hypothesis does not rule out the possibility that individual members of a group can have inner doubts or even that they might at times pose challenges to generally held attitudes or the decisions that result from them. In the end, however, group members, for the sake of consensus—or perhaps of greater importance, out of a need for acceptance by the group as a whole—will quash inner doubts and "go along" with given decisions no matter how disastrous the perceived consequences. At times, groupthink necessitates a willful ignoring or suppression of evidence, or even distortion of reality, in order that the integrity of certain widely held views and the decisions informed by them be preserved.[19]

Groupthink provided an excellent complement for Hitler's responses, informed by an underlying pattern of frustration-aggression that necessitated the suppression of evidence and distortion of facts. During interpersonal dyadic interaction these dysfunctional approaches to the awesome challenges posed by Stalingrad at times were responsible for something that has been described as *"folie à deux,"* or, less poetically, "induced psychosis." This is a situation in which an individual is able to influence one or more others in such a manner that his or her altogether unrealistic or even fantasized view of reality becomes shared.[20] As we will see, there were several crucial encounters between Hitler and his generals and between the leaders at Stalingrad itself where this condition appears to have prevailed.

The use of the groupthink hypothesis in analyzing the Stalingrad campaign can be seen as problematic. After all, its formulator, Irving Janis, has maintained that it can be applied only in situations in which decisions are arrived at in a relatively free atmosphere. Indeed, he has specifically ruled out its application in situations where decisions were made in a totalitarian environment, such as Hitler's original decision to invade the Soviet Union. One must readily concede that Hitler's generals knew they were ultimately answerable to an individual who did not appreciate opposition. Yet, while their views of the Soviets were generally not as colored by ideological considerations as those of their chief, they had arrived at overconfident views of a stereotyped enemy characteristic of individuals who have fallen victim to groupthink.[21] The results will be particularly apparent when we consider the immediate pre-Stalingrad situation and the Sixth Army's early responses to encirclement.

Instances of avoidance and denial at all levels added further dimensions to the general patterns of psychological dysfunctionalism that prevailed during the Stalingrad disaster. Taken together, they added up to an extraordinary inflexibility of adaptation to reality responsible for the greatest disaster up to that point in German military history.

PRE-STALINGRAD PROBLEMS

Most observers agree that Hitler had an intuitive grasp of military concerns, at least at the tactical level. As is generally known, it was Hitler who encouraged the daring approach to the 1940 western campaign proposed by Generalfeldmarschall Erich von Manstein, an approach that emphasized placing the main weight (or "Schwerpunkt") of the attack in the thinly defended area of the supposedly impenetrable Ardennes Forest.[22] Hitler could appreciate what was daring and innovative. Moreover, he had an almost encyclopedic memory with regard to matters of detail, such as the ranges of various artillery pieces, tank tonnage and armament, aircraft characteristics, and so forth.[23] As a result, he could indeed be formidable in a debate over tactical considerations.

Yet, observers noted that Hitler could also be extremely nervous and indecisive once an operation began. Once the armored breakthrough occurred in the west, in large measure rendered possible by Hitler's acceptance of Manstein's plan, he became overly concerned about possible Allied counterattacks along the extended flanks of the armored column as it raced toward the Channel coast. Then there was the, for some, baffling "stop order" given to armored units about to close on Dunkirk as the famed evacuation of the BEF, some French troops, and remnants of the Belgian army got under way.[24]

Once the Russian campaign began, the German armed forces and various allied formations initially enjoyed victory after victory and German radio listeners became accustomed to hearing these announced, accompanied by appropriate fanfares based on Franz Liszt's stirring *Preludes*. From August on, however, Hitler revealed a quality that would have very serious consequences for the Russian campaign in general, and the Stalingrad campaign in particular: an inflexible concern to have everything all at once, to feel himself to be "secure" everywhere—something that would translate into a rigid unwillingness to concentrate men and resources on one operation that might well have proven decisive.[25] Most of his generals wanted to concentrate on a thrust toward Moscow, leaving large Soviet units in areas in the southwest portions of the Soviet Union that had been, or were about to be, surrounded, to be dealt with later. Hitler refused to emphasize the assault on Moscow. Indeed, the advance was suspended while the surrounded units were destroyed. Hitler also ordered that Leningrad be besieged rather than directly attacked, even though many thought that it could have been taken at the time. There was indeed a massive and successful encirclement battle near Kiev that netted the Germans (according to their perhaps inflated accounts at the time) more than six hundred thousand prisoners. Hitler, after seeing his approach vindicated, was understandably elated. On October 3, 1941, he announced to the German people that the Russian enemy "was already broken and would never rise again." Some of his marshals were less impressed, however, and questioned the significance of the Kiev Kesselschlact.

Hitler's caution in 1940 and his unwillingness to concentrate on one possibly decisive tactical venture in 1941 pointed to a fixed concern with being secure everywhere. His fear of being surprised or assailed—or, for that matter, possibly being frustrated in assaults of his own, such as the one on Leningrad —was responsible for a situation in which German human and materiel resources were either scattered in disparate, albeit, usually successful, operations, or tied up in a frustrating, time-consuming siege. It was in large measure due to this fear on the part of one who never was able to transcend the residue of childhood humiliations that the Wehrmacht, for all of the hundreds of thousands of casualties it inflicted upon the Soviet armed forces, was unable to gain a strategic victory in 1941.

Once the advance on Moscow resumed, winter loomed, along with portions of an as yet uncommitted Soviet strategic reserve. The result, of course, was a massive Soviet counterattack on the Germans outside Moscow in December 1941. By the end of the month, the German army had lost more than a hundred thousand men. Yet, the disaster gave Hitler the opportunity to display aspects of his personality that existed in counterpoint to the timid qualities characteristic of a person fearful of being assailed. Overcome by feelings of narcissistic grandeur, he took the offensive against his own generals and ordered the beleaguered German troops before Moscow to stand firm. The inflexible unwillingness to take chances that had had extremely deleterious effects earlier in the campaign was now overridden (or at least counterbalanced) by an inflexible unwillingness to endure defeat, that is, to sustain substantive narcissistic injury. At the same time, Hitler, while overlooking his own role in the Moscow debacle, dealt with his frustrations (the "beaten" enemy had indeed "arisen again") by issuing an order that was "defensive" in nature with regard to the counterattacking Soviet armies but quite "aggressive" in relation to his own generals. They had let him down somehow, and Hitler was eager to punish them by assuming total control over the situation.

Most observers, particularly since the end of the war, have seen Hitler's "stand and fight order" as having been crucial. When the Soviets began to push the German armies back from Moscow in December 1941, most of Hitler's generals advised a retreat, even if it entailed some disorder. Hitler, except for the expected rubber-stamp approval of his two professional yes-men, Keitel and Jodl, stood alone in ordering his beleaguered forces to stand firm. Assuming "hedgehog" defensive positions, German troops were able to contain the Russian attacks. Hitler viewed himself as being vindicated and even generals usually critical of him, such as Günter von Blumentritt and Kurt von Tippelskirch, have gone on record as stating that the stand-fast order had served to prevent the sort of rout that had doomed Napoleon's Grand Armée more than a century earlier.[26] Respected military historians have lent their weight to this argument and, on balance, it would appear that Hitler's inflexible insistence upon "defense to the last man" had been correct under the circumstances.[27] In this regard, however, it is important to note an important qualification of the admittedly more conservative Generalfeldmarschall Gerd von Rundstedt. While agreeing that Hitler's order had averted possible disaster before Moscow, he stated that it had been "Hitler's decision for rigid resistance that caused the danger in the first place. It would not have arisen if he had permitted a timely withdrawal."[28] General and historian Rudolf Hofmann has been more critical. There was, he declared, "a very limited amount of truth in the contention" that Hitler's "stand fast" fanaticism had saved the German army from suffering the fate of Napoleon's. While a retreat no doubt would have entailed the loss of a great deal more equipment, there was no evidence of the general demoralization that could have led to panic. As it was, the order *not* to retreat led to severe losses that put a critical strain on German reserves. More certainly, the *apparent* success of Hitler's December 1941 decision was mainly responsible for his concluding that a "hold-on" policy was called for under all circumstances. This, of course, would have painful consequences in the future.[29] Overlooked at the time (except, of course, for those directly affected by it) was another, perhaps even more, inauspicious episode. The II Corps, holding on to perilously disposed hedgehog positions in the Valdai Hills between Moscow and Leningrad, had to be supplied largely by air. These operations proved to be difficult in the extreme, in fact, deadly for the Luftwaffe. As many as three hundred aircraft were required to supply the daily needs of this single corps and, even without the Red Air Force's consistent interdiction efforts, bad flying conditions had been responsible for very severe losses. At the same time, the supply effort proved to be inadequate.[30]

Of even greater importance with regard to future military decision making —or, at times, the lack of it—is that despite these difficulties, II Corps succeeded in holding out for three months against vastly superior Soviet forces. It would be this "lesson" that apparently would be remembered both by Hitler and his generals.[31] The former's overweening confidence in victory was bolstered by concepts of the subhuman enemy grounded in ideological concerns. From all accounts, however, it would appear that Hitler's generals, despite occasional warning voices, acted as if their problems in the winter of 1941–42 were due entirely to certain errors and oversights on their side. They seemed to be unwilling to own up to the fact that the enemy had a great deal to do with them.[32] As we have seen, shared underestimation of one's enemy, combined with an unwillingness to alter fixed views, are two of the most crucial characteristics of "groupthink." There can be little question that the generals, while more appreciative of some eastern front realities than their führer, were guided in their plans and actions by a persistent tendency to underrate their opponents. In a very real sense, this tendency had been reinforced by the successes the German army had enjoyed in overcoming crisis after crisis, such as the Russian counterattack in 1941 and II Corps's successful defensive actions. In the eyes of historian Walter Görlitz, the general perhaps most affected by these successes was Friedrich Paulus, the Sixth Army commander.[33]

In January 1942, sobered by winter failures, Hitler reversed a memorandum of July 15, 1941, which, written during the heady days of rapid successes, had envisaged the return to an almost peacetime economy. With the exception of tank production, the manufacture of military equipment was to have been cut back, in some areas drastically.[34] With the experiences of the Moscow debacle behind him, Hitler began planning for a spring offensive. More than ever before, it seemed obvious to him that two points had been borne out in past campaigns: first, the key to eliminating the Soviet Union was to be found in crippling war production and in destroying its armies, and second, that territories taken in pursuance of these aims had to be held with the utmost tenacity.

Yet, even more than in 1941, there was confusion as to goals. Hitler, as we have seen, was determined to accomplish what he failed to do the first time: smash the Soviet armies in battles having immense strategic and tactical significance. Furthermore, with an appreciation of economic and political realities lacking on the part of many of his generals, he recognized that eliminating Russian economic centers—something that would necessitate a swing to the north from *below* Moscow—was of primary significance. Further thrusts to the Urals and south to secure the Caucasian oil centers were envisioned. His generals, particularly those on the OKH general staff, certainly recognized the necessity of destroying the Soviet army, but goals informed by broader motives were not, at least originally, of as great importance as they had been for Hitler. In any event, between February and April 1942 conflicting sets of alternatives and goals emerged at various levels and, as was his wont—in order to strengthen his role as ultimate arbiter—Hitler did little to reconcile them. First of all, there was Hitler's initial plan, which involved the destruction of the bulk of the Soviet armies and the seizing of areas crucial to the economy. Stalingrad played a role in this, as matters developed, but only as a pivot point for the swing north behind Moscow. Meanwhile, a drive toward the south into the Caucasus was recognized as a possibility. By April, the general staff had come up with a scheme of its own: taking the area between the Don and Volga Rivers, including the industrial and transportation center of Stalingrad. At the same time, a thrust would be made toward Voronezh, on the Don. While economic motives were not absent from this plan—Stalingrad was, of course, of immense significance in this regard—the *primary* goals were military, such as the destruction of the Red Army. At about the same time, Hitler announced that he had come up with a *second* plan: Stalingrad was seen as a transitory goal. Nor was there talk of advancing north, behind Moscow. Instead, the bulk of the German army was to head south to the Caucasus, with seizure of the area around Stalingrad merely a preliminary objective.[35] For the general staff, Stalingrad and Voronezh were a *primary objective*. For Hitler, Stalingrad was of importance, but mainly as a blocking and pivot point. Discrepancies between the two sets of plans continued to unfold until July, and had an impact upon the course of events.

Of no doubt far greater consequence insofar as German operations in 1942 were concerned was the existence of a massive Russian strategic reserve, numbering perhaps close to 1.2 million men. Stalin, ever distrustful of his Anglo-Saxon allies, told them nothing of it because German intelligence had failed to take note of it. In any event, the conditions necessary for turning a campaign of movement into an ill-starred Materialschlacht were present from the beginning.[36]

Initially, as they had in 1941, the German armies scored crushing victories against their opponents. Soviet efforts to recapture portions of the Crimea failed and Manstein seized Sevastopol. In May 1942, Soviet attacks near Kharkov, apparently efforts to smother the anticipated German offensive in that area, had been bloodily turned back after initial successes. Almost a quarter of a million Russians were captured. Friedrich Paulus's Sixth Army had played a crucial role in this great victory. On June 28, 1942, German Army Group South ("Group B") went over to the attack. Under the overall command of Generalfeldmarschall Fedor von Bock (successor to Generaloberst Walther von Reichenau, whom we will consider later), its initial goal was to take Voronezh on the Don. Soviet armies encountered along the way were to be eliminated and an advance from the Don to the Volga in the direction of Stalingrad undertaken as soon after reaching Voronezh as possible. Capturing Stalingrad was of secondary importance. While the northern sector entrusted to Bock's Army Group South was being secured, what was to have been the Schwerpunkt of the early summer offensive would unfold: an advance along the Sea of Azov, the capture of Rostov-on-Don, and a bold thrust into the Caucasus. Important to the overall success of this campaign was the destruction of all major Soviet forces west of the Don River.

After initial splendid starts, things began to go amiss. Bock was stalled in heavy fighting before Voronezh and it soon became obvious that the crucial goal of destroying all Soviet armies west of the Don could not be achieved. Hitler became increasingly incensed at delays and replaced Bock as commander in chief of Army Group South with Generaloberst Maximilian Freiherr von Weichs on July 13, 1942. From that point on, it appears that Hitler decided to pursue his Caucasian scheme with a vengeance. Generaloberst Hermann Hoth's Fourth Army (armored) originally was slated to have taken Stalingrad and, after doing so, to have turned the city over to Paulus's Sixth Army. The Sixth Army was then to have served as a reserve, available for service when and where needed. When Bock ran into unexpectedly heavy fighting before Voronezh, however, he had changed things a bit. Now, the Sixth Army was to assist in the attack near Voronezh, while Hoth was to take Stalingrad by himself. With Bock's dismissal, however, Hoth was ordered to the south, there to help force a crossing of the lower Don. The German army from northwest of Stalingrad to Voronezh was to go on the defensive and Paulus was ordered to take Stalingrad by himself. Maximum emphasis was thus to be placed on the southern thrust to the Caucasus, with Hoth's armor to be added to that of Generalfeldmarschall Ewald von Kleist, Generalfeldmarschall Siegmund List's subordinate. This was in keeping with a new operational directive sent on July 23, 1942. The order called for "Group A," now even on paper almost independent of Army Group South, to cut across the Don, while "Group B," under Weichs, was to take Stalingrad and secure the area between the Don and the Volga.[37]

Here, we are confronted with a seeming strategic contradiction. On one hand, Stalingrad was now playing a crucial role in Hitler's planning. Apparently, reports of Soviet troop buildups in that area had attracted his attention to it since the middle of July, and the term "bridgehead" was increasingly employed.[38] Yet, Hoth's army had been diverted south, into an area in which List's forces had been encountering diminishing resistance. Ironically, while Russian troop strength was growing in the area around Stalingrad, the city itself was thinly defended and Hoth quite probably could have taken it, particularly if operating in conjunction with Paulus. Instead, his army was added to List's to "assist" where it was not needed and where, according to armored commander Kleist, it blocked the roads and thus hindered his advance.[39] By the time Hitler became aware of the situation and was able to order the bulk of Hoth's force north to take Stalingrad, Russian strength had substantially increased in that area.

Throughout July it had become obvious that, in one area or another of that portion of the eastern front under consideration, maximum troop concentrations were necessary. Yet, Hitler, as several authors have pointed out, seemed equally concerned with conditions on the western "front." It was in keeping with this concern that, on July 9, he ordered one of the best panzer divisions in Russia, SS-Leibstandarte, withdrawn from its positions south of the Don front and sent to France despite strong protests from Generaloberst Franz Halder. On July 23, he ordered the Grossdeutschland Panzer Division to disengage itself in the midst of operations and head for France. This time, even Jodl joined Halder in protesting the order.[40] The SS-Leibstandarte Division eventually arrived in France, but played no role in the German army's repelling, with heavy losses, the Allied raid on Dieppe on August 19. Russian operations against Army Group Center resulted in the Grossdeutschland Division's departure being canceled and its assignment to that sector.

In analyzing what happened, we must bear in mind that Hitler was a gambler who nonetheless wished to avoid taking chances and did not dare to put maximum effort behind one strategic, not to mention tactical, venture. He could not risk not "covering himself" everywhere—the chance of error was too much to bear for one whose fabled "will" covered up deep-seated fears of humiliation. To be sure, he had by this time decided that, with regard to the eastern front at least, the oil regions of the Caucasus were of primary importance. Hence, the original shift of Hoth to the south. Yet, according to the operational directive of July 23, 1942, informed by Hitler's optimism due to the capture of Rostov, it was vital that a strong *bridgehead* be secured to the north in order to effectively seal off the southern thrust. Moreover, Stalingrad now *had* to be taken, and as soon as possible. What resulted from Hitler's desire that the advance into the Caucasus proceed with maximum possible dispatch was, for the first time, the placement of Stalingrad *at the very center* of tactical considerations! Commentators are in full agreement on this point: by directing the German army toward two goals separated by a three-hundred-kilometer gap that could be covered only by mobile formations, the commander in chief had created a tactically impossible situation.

Of crucial importance was Hitler's tendency—something he shared with his idol Frederick the Great—to underestimate his enemy. Here, one should bear in mind an observation of his soon-to-be-replaced army chief of staff, Franz Halder, recorded in his diary the day Hitler issued his Directive 45, calling for offensive operations to be pressed both in Stalingrad and in the Caucasus: "This chronic tendency to underrate enemy capabilities is gradually assuming grotesque proportions and develops into a positive danger. The situation is getting more and more intolerable. There is no room for any serious work."[41] The situation was made even more ominous by yet another factor. In yet another far-reaching example of his inflexible desire to be secure everywhere, Hitler had ordered a buildup of troop concentrations in France. To be sure, *on paper* —and the führer, sharing this inclination with one of his opposite numbers, Churchill, tended to be most impressed with paper figures—there were twenty-nine more divisions on the eastern front by July 1942 than had been there in June 1941.[42] In the other theaters of operation, a net loss of six divisions had been recorded during the same period. However, the German armies in the east were actually down in combat strength, and this pointed to the fact that, while operations in that theater had been *expanded* to a truly extraordinary degree, severe manpower shortages had greatly decreased reserve potential.[43] Thus, during what would prove to be a fateful time for the National Socialist war effort in Russia, increasing reliance would have to be placed upon the formations of the so-called Allied Armies—the poorly motivated and ill-equipped units from Romania, Italy, and Hungary.

To be sure, the prowess of the Hungarian troops had yet to be tested to any significant degree in this new war. Italian troops, on the other hand, had seen combat in large numbers by the spring of 1942—and almost everywhere had been found wanting. Romanian troops, whose World War I performance had not been spectacular, did well enough in the capture of Odessa and in the nearby Nikolayev area. Mostly, however, they were noted for hating their Hungarian "allies" (a feeling that was fully reciprocated), and for excesses against the Jews. The latter probably turned the stomachs of some of the regular German army personnel familiar with them.[44] The Romanian formations, which constituted the largest single bloc of "allied" troops in Russia, were badly equipped and ill trained. The German command, and most assuredly Hitler himself, had been aware of various substantial deficiencies in the Romanian army for some time. As early as February 16, 1942, one Colonel Metz, a liaison officer between German and Romanian forces, had complained of these in a letter to Paulus. He declared that his efforts to improve matters had been exhausting, and that he "scarcely saw one success. A mountain of false notions, judgements and spiritual confusion must be cleared away."[45] Sensitive to the dangers posed by these deficiencies, the German command had assumed some responsibility for training Romanian officers and, to the degree possible, reequipping Romanian units.[46] However, even before being exposed to the Stalingrad purgatory, morale was low at all levels in the Romanian army, and the state of its equipment, despite German efforts to improve it, remained poor. Here it must be noted that much of the Romanian army was equipped with French weapons captured by the Germans in 1940, and that each Romanian division had at its disposal but one antitank company equipped with 37-mm antitank guns whose shells had a disquieting tendency to bounce off the formidable armor of Soviet T-34 and KV model tanks. Not until October 1942, after repeated pleading by Gen. Petre Dumitrescu, commander of the Romanian Third Army, were German 75-mm antitank guns made available, and at the not impressive allotment of six per division. Romanian armor consisted overwhelmingly of Czech model 38 tanks equipped with 37-mm guns. Indeed, considering the parlous state of Romanian armament in the fall of 1942, it is difficult to imagine how Romanian soldiers could have been effective even if well trained and well motivated.[47] The situation was not improved by Hitler's bringing together the Romanian and German units on the Volga-Don front into a unified "Army Group Don" under the command of the Romanian chief of state, Marshal Ion Antonescu, a man whose military prowess was nowhere near the equal of his supposed ideological enthusiasm.[48]

As for the Italian Eighth Army, it was a matter of concern for all German commanders. Hitler had his own particular worries, for the operations staff's logbook records that, as early as August 16, he had expressed concern that Stalin might counterattack in the same general area in which he had defeated General Wrangel's White Army in 1920.[49] The Italian Eighth Army was on the Don River, covering Rostov, and this was the area under consideration. Consequently, Hitler ordered the 22nd Panzer Division detached from the Sixth Army and placed behind the Italians to bolster them in the face of an anticipated attack. Because this division was engaged in heavy fighting, it would be some time before the order could be carried out, and this caused the führer no small degree of grief.[50] On August 20, a Russian battalion attacking the Eighth Army's positions on the Don succeeded in routing an entire Italian division.[51] "Once and for all," the 22nd Panzer was ordered to move to the area of concern. Tactical considerations made this impossible, and the 22nd Panzer, plus one other division, would not be removed from the Sixth Army and put in place behind the Italian Eighth until one month after Hitler had first expressed his concern over the possibility of Stalin's repeating his 1920 venture on the Don. Hitler had reason to be concerned and, as we have seen, he certainly was not entirely insensitive to problems concerning the allied troops. Yet, he seemed unable to appreciate that the battles that were now raging, due, of course, almost entirely to his strategic decision, did not allow troops to be whisked from one portion of the front to another with effortless asperity. Moreover, his obvious concern for events in the Don-Volga area did not inhibit him from issuing an order on August 23 calling for a sustained attack on Leningrad to take place on September 14 (a maneuver dubbed Operation Northern Lights). This decision caused no small degree of rancor, but Hitler held to it for the time being—indeed, perhaps even being *encouraged* to do so by rancor on the part of generals he was increasingly coming to despise.[52]

At this time, the Sixth and Fourth Armies, attacking under Paulus's overall command from north and south of the city, were making the first concerted effort to take Stalingrad. The defenders resisted violently and, although some progress was made, losses were high. The attacking Germans were deficient in infantry and artillery strength and lacked training for city fighting. As one historian observed, the high losses that were sustained from the time of Paulus's initial attack "were attributable to this last deficiency, above all." Hoping to shatter the Russians' will to resist, the Luftwaffe's Fourth Air Fleet undertook a massive bombing raid on the night of August 23–24. More than forty thousand civilians were killed in the inferno that followed. The Russian lines held, nonetheless, and Hitler had his worries. However, as Stalingrad became more and more a focal point for both the German and Russian leadership, it became increasingly obvious that at least the Romanians were serving the purpose of *freeing* what German troops were available for operations in the immediate Stalingrad area.[53]

Yet, while recognizing Hitler's primary role in the developing Stalingrad catastrophe, we must also bear in mind that his subordinates served him poorly in some ways. For example, in the report delivered to Reichsmarschall Göring by General der Flieger Wolfram Freiherr von Richthofen, commander of the Fourth Air Fleet, on August 28, the airman declared that he had made a personal reconnaissance over the Stalingrad area and had seen no substantial enemy forces in the region. Moreover, he had obtained the impression that the Russians lacked even a unified command. By this time, Paulus's Sixth Army was encountering bitter resistance and, in fact, had been stopped cold at some points.[54] Furthermore, it is important to point out that, as the Romanians saw it—at least when they made their feelings known after the Stalingrad campaign ended—their pleas for assistance and warnings about imminent and massive Soviet counterattacks on their forlorn front had been virtually ignored at *all* levels of command in the German army. One would, of course, suppose this included the Sixth Army.[55] In any case, while appreciating that General-oberst Paulus had made certain concerns known to Hitler, one can at least question how forcefully he presented them. The overconfidence characteristic of groupthink was responsible for almost ignoring the warnings of an ally for whom the German generals had little respect.

A BRIEF HISTORY OF THE SIXTH ARMY

If the massive Soviet counterattack feared by the Romanians were to take place, Sixth Army would be the German unit most threatened. At this point, it is necessary to give brief consideration to the history of this army and to its commander, Friedrich Paulus. Until December 1941, the Sixth Army had been under the command of Walther von Reichenau. Under the leadership of this dynamic—and pro-Nazi—general, it had gone from victory to victory, its most spectacular performance being turned in during the 1940 western campaign. After the invasion of the Soviet Union, Reichenau saw to it that Hitler's decrees about the ideological and racial nature of the new campaign were translated into terrible reality. On October 10, 1941, he issued one of his own instructing soldiers of the Sixth Army to treat Communists and/or Jews who fell into their hands as subhumans.[56] His apparent ideological enthusiasm, along with his tactical prowess and overall vigor, greatly impressed Hitler. In December 1941, after an argument with the commander of Army Group South, Generalfeldmarschall Gerd von Rundstedt, Hitler replaced him with Reichenau, who was by then suffering from a heart condition. On December 3, the day on which he officially took command of Group South, Hitler met with him and others at Poltava. There it was decided that Paulus, who had once served on Reichenau's staff and was a man who had no field experience, would take over leadership of the Sixth Army. It is unknown if, when later besieged at Stalingrad, he had an opportunity to reflect upon the delicious irony of Poltava—the site of Charles XII of Sweden's decisive defeat at the hands of Peter the Great's army in 1709—being the place where it was decided that he be given command. In all events, Friedrich Paulus assumed formal command of the Sixth Army on January 5, 1942. Reichenau died twelve days later, either in the crash of a plane taking him to a hospital in Leipzig or in the hospital itself, and Fedor von Bock assumed command of Group South.

In any event, certain problems with regard to Paulus's performance as a field commander surfaced in due course. On August 29, Hoth's Fourth Panzer Army launched a furious attack on the Russian positions near Abganerova, about seventy-five miles due south of Stalingrad as the crow flies. The attack, while not exactly catching the Russian command (Stavka) by surprise, precipitated a confused retreat, one which, to the astonishment of Hoth—and more unpleasantly, to the Russians—rapidly degenerated into a rout. By the following day, thousands of prisoners had been taken during the course of an incredible twenty-mile advance that saw Hoth's army establish a bridgehead on the banks of the Volga at Gavrilovka. Smelling victory, Hoth sent an urgent message to Paulus urging him to move south as soon as possible and thus forge an iron ring around Stalingrad, one in which upwards of twenty thousand Soviet troops would be trapped. Paulus, whose troops had sustained heavy losses, did not move. Another urgent message was sent. Still, Paulus did not budge. Precious time passed, and the Soviet commander in chief on the Stalingrad front, Gen. Andrei Yeremenko, was able to pull the twenty thousand threatened troops back toward the city. This was a crucial turn of events in the eyes of some historians.[57] However one chooses to interpret this episode, it was the last chance the Germans had to use their advantage in mobile warfare in a decisive manner in the Stalingrad area.

Paulus, despite some successes, had never been very certain of himself as a field commander. Although willing to assume full responsibility for actions taken, he appears to have been determined to take as few of these as possible. People above him seemed always to know what was best, even if those on the scene presumably had a more immediate view of what was going on in the area concerned. While this usually proved not to have been the case, Paulus apparently latched on to any event that seemed to validate this assumption.[58]

Hitler appears not to have taken Paulus's lack of initiative very seriously. Perhaps he even approved of it. On September 12 he met with Paulus and Weichs, the most recent commander of Army Group South ("B"), at his headquarters at Vinnitsa. The "final" attack on Stalingrad was to take place on the day following this conference, and he was determined to give his seemingly apprehensive subordinates his version of a pep talk. Again, Paulus expressed nervousness over his left flank. Hitler who, as we have seen, had been largely responsible for the paradoxical situation in which emphasis on the Caucasus had brought on an increased focus upon Stalingrad, now seemed to be primarily absorbed with List's operations. To be sure, success at Stalingrad was important. That was why the conference was taking place. Nonetheless, the führer made light of Paulus's concern. Hitler apparently had reverted back to an earlier, almost Pollyannaish attitude revealed in an April conversation with Kleist. At that time he had declared that the "flank along the Don from Voronezh to its southerly bend, and beyond Stalingrad to the Caspian . . . [were] the easiest sectors to hold" and hence could be entrusted to the care of allied troops.[59] Only this can serve to explain his declaring that neither Paulus nor Weichs had anything to worry about since the left flank was now being secured—precisely, of course, by the allied troops whose assumed unreliability had been the primary source of concern in the first place.[60] Both Paulus and Weichs appear to have been sufficiently reassured, this despite their shared awareness of the miserable state of the allied armies. Hitler exuded confidence, and this apparently was decisive. Hitler's ability to persuade two of his generals—who were very much aware of the dangers posed on their front by the miserable state of the Romanian troops—that there *was* no real danger approximates the psychological phenomenon known as *"folie à deux."* Throughout the war he dealt with the qualms of nervous subordinates by utilizing a seemingly *omniscient* will upon individuals who desperately needed to be told that things were not as they seemed. Thus, Hitler's ability in political situations to cause others to see things as they would not see them on their own had military applications. By allowing Hitler to essentially co-opt their critical abilities, his generals saw themselves "as fighting unconsciously for what appeared to be their own psychological integrity."[61] Paulus (if not perhaps Weichs)—modest, insecure, an individual of a "sensitive nature," as Görlitz put it—could easily have been encouraged by a man who, on an earlier occasion, had once declared that "This little matter of operational command is something that anyone can do."[62] The "little matter"—which had to have been somewhat discomfiting to Paulus, whose Sixth Army was now engaged, *per* the order of September 12, in an all-out fight for Stalingrad—was the long-sought-after detaching of the 22nd Panzer and 113th Infantry Divisions and their dispatch to the area of the Don occupied by the Italian Eighth Army.[63] Paulus's concern for the reliability of the troops on his left flank was indeed being addressed, but in a fashion unhappily unanticipated by this increasingly forlorn general.

As we have seen, Hitler was primarily concerned with events in the Caucasus, where, after initial successes, things were not going so well. Now, List's advance was encountering increasingly heavy resistance and Hitler's interference had been responsible for creating the situation we considered earlier, namely, confusion as to goals. This had not helped matters and, while not choosing to ponder his role in an increasingly difficult situation, Hitler sent Jodl to visit List and convey his sense of impatience. On September 6, 1942, Jodl did just this, only to be persuaded by the harried List that he had indeed acted in keeping with the führer's orders. Hence, responsibility for any failures should not devolve upon *him.* Jodl, taking his courage in hand, flew back to present his master with the unwelcome news that not only was List, for the moment at least, hopelessly bogged down, but he had apparently gotten himself into this situation in large measure from following Hitler's instructions. Hitler exploded, showering Jodl with abuse. Keitel, who had made an unwonted, albeit feeble, effort to defend Jodl, was also given a severe dressing-down. On September 9, List was removed from command and Hitler himself took over the direction of Army Group A. In late November, faced with crises in Stalingrad and North Africa, he turned the post over to Kleist, List's most prominent subordinate.[64] Hitler's fury at his generals was responsible for the rumor that earthshaking changes were to take place. There was indeed one change with far-reaching consequences: On September 24, 1942, Franz Halder, who frequently questioned Hitler's tactical decisions, was replaced by Kurt Zeitzler as chief of the OKH general staff. According to Zeitzler himself, writing somewhat after the fact: "[T]hat was his [Hitler's] usual method. Whenever he made a mistake he placed the blame upon someone else, who was then dismissed and a new man appointed in his place."[65] Zeitzler became Hitler's sole confidant, and Jodl's role as OKW chief was greatly reduced. With Zeitzler in charge, the OKH fell directly under Hitler's control, and a dangerous gap was thus created between it and the now greatly enfeebled overall "High Command."[66] Nevertheless, the now favored Zeitzler, like his predecessor, believed in calling off the Stalingrad campaign and apparently voiced this view to Hitler. Although Paulus was becoming increasingly convinced of the wisdom in curtailing the push to Stalingrad, he asked Zeitzler to give him three fresh infantry divisions.[67] One can, of course, suggest that Paulus's request showed a complete lack of understanding of Hitler's psychology. After all, a call for reinforcements would be indicative of a desire to press on with offensive operations. Why, in view of the fact that Paulus was increasingly concerned about the dangers posed by the Stalingrad struggle, would he have made such a request? Paulus's call for reinforcements revealed that his tactical concerns were informed by a strong desire to be assured of the continued approval of one whose will had, in some ways, become inseparable from Paulus's own. Unlike the conference of September 12, he was no longer in Hitler's presence. However, the *folie à deux* state, or at least something approximating it, prevailed.

Probably one of the most obvious examples of Paulus's desire to demonstrate his determination was his order directing the Sixth Army headquarters to design an armband commemorating the fall of a fanatically defended Russian grain elevator on September 20, 1942.[68] The existence of this state revealed something else: an unwillingness to appear out of line, much less weak, by going against the course of group actions, even if Paulus, and not a few others as well, were having grave inner reservations. A fear of appearing weak in the eyes of associates is an important characteristic of groupthink.[69] Hitler would not hear of giving up the offensive, but gave Paulus only five engineer battalions, possibly useful in house-to-house fighting, but hardly enough under the circumstances. Paulus, however, did receive something that he had not requested: through the new head of the personnel office, faithful Nazi Rudolf Schmundt, he learned that he was in line to assume Jodl's post at OKW as soon as Stalingrad was taken. Whether or not Hitler was seriously contemplating that move, or whether this was merely a means of keeping Paulus's nose to an increasingly abrasive grindstone, is uncertain to this day.[70]

By this point, Hitler had become almost totally disgusted with his generals. The Soviets still held Stalingrad; the goals on the Caucasus had not been achieved, and everywhere he turned he heard calls for reinforcements and excuses for lack of success. From now on, he was determined to have as little as possible to do with the chicken-hearted and ideologically ill-schooled representatives of the increasingly detested professional army. Moreover, he began eating his famed vegetarian meals alone and no longer deigned even to shake hands with members of his staff.[71]

Hitler's fury, while in part understandable in very ordinary terms—he was angered by the seeming incompetence of his generals—must also be understood as that of an individual who had to be secure and successful everywhere and saw his generals as the means to that end. Out of the grandiose narcissism that prevailed in tandem with these fears, he responded to repeated frustrations by massively aggressive behavior against his senior subordinates. His taking over personal command of Army Group A was indicative of this, as was his self-imposed isolation from his staff. As for the generals themselves, several of whom (Paulus in particular) he had been able to engage in a reality-denying *folie à deux* relationship, uncertainties did exist. Yet, their appreciation of the very real dangers that prevailed in the Stalingrad area was dulled not only by a faith in their commander in chief that at least some of them held, but, more importantly, by that tendency to underestimate their opponents crucial to "groupthink." This tendency, as well as the one to undervalue crucial information supplied by their Romanian allies, was grounded in experience to some degree. Nonetheless, appreciation of past experiences was selective, to say the least, and awareness that the future could hold surprises, while probably not altogether absent, was not allowed to play a strong role in the hypotheses and actions of individuals who, though to a much lesser degree than Hitler, were severely handicapped by collectively held illusions of their own.

Such was the state of affairs by the end of September 1942. Ominous reports were accumulating on all sides, reinforcements were virtually nonexistent, and relations between Hitler and his subordinates, even previously trusted ones, had never been worse. Yet, perhaps because there appeared to be no other choice, everyone went about his appointed task. The situation can be compared to that which prevailed on the *Titanic* where, fifteen minutes after an iceberg had slashed a three-hundred-foot wound in her side, a downward pitch had become noticeable. Quite a few people perceived this, "but it seemed tactless to mention the matter."[72]

ATTACK AND ENCIRCLEMENT

Perhaps in part buoyed by his success against an enemy that, up until the fall of 1942, had offered little in the way of effective aerial opposition, the commander of the Fourth Air Fleet, General der Flieger Richthofen, had been critical of what he perceived to be the Sixth Army command's timidity in exploiting the opportunities his fliers had presumably made possible.[73] Recall that a reconnaissance flight he personally undertook convinced him that there were no major Russian troop formations in the area. By the end of October 1942, however, there was no doubt in his mind that the Russians were planning a massive operation against the Romanians on the left of Paulus's embattled army. Warnings to this effect were sent to all levels of the army command and to the OKW. Hitler took the reports seriously enough to order that the Romanian Third Army be strengthened. Yet, his previous dispositions of what reserves there were had served to make any meaningful bolstering of the Romanians impossible.

Hitler, in fact, never really made any serious inquiries as to what *was* possible along these lines. It was as if he was attempting, by issuing largely paper orders, to absolve his conscience of what was about to occur.[74] In any case, his continuous demands that Stalingrad be taken, whatever the cost—and here he was attacking his generals as well as the Russians—required his almost total absorption. Furthermore, what evidence we have available would suggest that even the Sixth Army's command, for all of its apparent fears and uncertainties, never really appreciated the dangers that could be posed by a massive Russian attack.[75] The impossibility of simultaneously taking Stalingrad *and* covering the left flank never fully struck home. Individuals whose reality-defying submergence in groupthink complemented Hitler's reality-defying narcissistic grandiosities could not have allowed it to happen. As for the fighting in Stalingrad itself, there appeared to be no sign of a letup. Paulus, however—in a crucial letter to Schmundt, an individual whose office and ideological enthusiasm allowed him to have immediate access to Hitler—declared on October 7: "The struggle over Stalingrad continues to be bitter. It's going very slowly; but, each day, a little bit forward. The whole thing is a question of men and time. But, we will be finished with the Russians in due course."[76] Uncertainties were being quashed by the desperate efforts of an individual concerned that he be perceived not only as part of a group, but also as an individual over whom Hitler had scored a major emotional victory.

As far as the German public knew, there was little to fear. In an October speech in the Berlin Sportspalast at a mass demonstration in honor of Germany's rural population, Hermann Göring declared that, so far as the coming winter was concerned, there was little to fear. "'This time,' he almost boasted, 'we are immune. We already know what a Russian winter is like.'"[77] Hitler, after making various arrangements—again, largely on paper—took his special train to Munich to address a gathering of the party faithful on the evening of November 8, the anniversary of the ill-fated *putsch* he attempted in 1923. Meanwhile, British and American troops were coming ashore in North Africa. This, in conjunction with Gen. Bernard Law Montgomery's earlier victory at El Alamein, put the Axis forces there in a truly dangerous situation. Although the situation in the east seemed to be as bleak as usual, Hitler assured the party faithful that Stalingrad would soon fall. "I wanted to take it—and you know we are modest—we really have it. There are only a very few small places left there. Now, the others say: 'Why don't you make faster progress?' Because I don't want to create a second Verdun . . . but prefer to do the job with small shock troop units."[78]

First of all, we must see that this and various other pronouncements served to rob Hitler of needed flexibility. Especially in the November 8 address, in which he really was speaking more as führer of a movement supposedly informed by divine mission than as commander in chief of the armed forces, "the political demagogue Hitler robbed the Generalismo Hitler of all room to maneuver."[79] As Görlitz put it elsewhere with great perceptivity, "An evacuation of Stalingrad in keeping with flexible combat leadership had been precluded by Hitler himself, because the 'Führer' always had to be right!"[80] For one attempting to analyze decisions taken or not taken during the Stalingrad battle, this statement is apposite in many ways. Then there is Hitler's conjuring up of the image of Verdun. Despite his encouragement of experimentation in all tactical areas, Hitler's own military experience was rooted in World War I. His 1942 decisions concerning the eastern front in general, and Stalingrad in particular, had been largely responsible for creating what Alan Clark called a "Verdun on the Volga." Furthermore, despite his questionable assertion that "in 1916, Falkenhayn's mincing machine had been turned off when another month would have destroyed the whole French Army," Clark makes the, to this writer, incontrovertible point that for Hitler, and possibly others in a decision-making capacity, Stalingrad *probably had assumed this role*.[81]

First of all, there is the obvious point that, like Verdun, Stalingrad represented an opportunity to kill large numbers of enemy soldiers. Such, of course, had been the original plan of the architect of Verdun, Erich von Falkenhayn.[82] Also, at least for Hitler, Stalingrad had come to have extremely important symbolic significance. Such had been the case with both the German and French armies in 1916, although, to be sure, it was probably more so for the French. *Unlike* Verdun, Stalingrad was, in itself, of considerable strategic importance, situated as it was along the Volga, one of the Soviet Union's "lifelines," and being, before the battle anyway, a major industrial and transportation center. Also, it is well to recall that although both Verdun and Stalingrad were battles of attrition (in the case of the latter, one could say that this would end in November 1942), the *type* of fighting was different—Verdun being a battle focused upon taking and retaking fortified positions, whereas Stalingrad was characterized by street-by-street, house-to-house fighting.

However, for Hitler, who wanted to avoid "another Verdun," the taking of Stalingrad was of crucial importance for a reason attaching to the narcissistic aspects of his personality: He, the founder of the "Thousand-Year Reich," would succeed where Falkenhayn, at one point the commander in chief of the army in which Hitler had served as a humble soldier, had failed. He would take Stalingrad, if necessary, *in spite* of his generals, who, failed professionals like Falkenhayn, seemed determined to let him down. Thus, frustration in the enterprise had to have been especially difficult to bear and was responsible for a situation in which Hitler probably hated his generals and staff more than he did the enemy. His monomaniacal aggression against them was grounded in a mélange of fears and ambitions that blinded Hitler to both tactical and strategic realities. Here, some considerations are important. A war of attrition obviously favors the side, which, in the end, can bring to bear the greatest human and materiel resources. The *Allies*, if not the French alone, enjoyed this advantage in 1916. Ultimately, in the *strategic* sense, so did the Russians in 1942, and their efforts were conducted by a more ruthless leadership. Furthermore, success at Stalingrad in large measure depended upon at least *satisfactory* performances by unreliable non-German troops, units whose shakiness had been at least in part ensured by indifferent treatment on the part of the German military establishment. Falkenhayn at least had an all-German army at his disposal (in every sense of the word).

From the Germans' point of view, what transpired at Stalingrad was the inexorable chewing up of an army, as a whole untrained for the shock tactics described by Hitler with such enthusiasm. What shock units there were for the most part, other than in the increasingly warped perceptions of the commander in chief, existed on paper. Hitler *had* his Verdun, despite assurances to his "Old Fighter" cronies. In an increasingly frustrating war stripped of those tactical and logistical certainties necessary for one who, in the final analysis, could leave nothing to chance, it was best to fall back upon something with which Hitler could identify, an experience that was, in its deepest meaning, his own writ large. Yet, unlike Falkenhayn, he would not fail. Hitler, however—like Falkenhayn, only with more disastrous consequences—made decisions that in the end had to assure stalemate against a foe of relative parity, defeat against one that could up the ante to the point where no answer was forthcoming. He made them because of the demands of a personality that needed to be secure at all points while being certain that it would prevail in a world filled with those who would frustrate him.

On November 12, Richthofen, sensing disaster, recorded in his journal that a massive Russian attack against the Romanians was certain. He only hoped that they "don't succeed in making too bad of a break-through."[83] On November 17, Hitler spoke with Paulus. One last effort was necessary. Hitler admitted that his forces had been weakened. The Russians, however, were far weaker. Paulus replied: "I am convinced that this command will provide a new impulse for our gallant troops." Hitler had his own concerns. Nervous about the situation on the Romanian Third Army's front, he ordered the 22nd Panzer Division, which, as we have seen, had been used to bolster the Italians, to back up the Romanians. The measure failed. It seems that mice—in this case true "heroes of the Soviet Union"—had nibbled through wires on virtually all of the division's tanks. Almost the entire unit was immobilized.[84]

At dawn on November 19, three thousand Russian artillery pieces opened up along the front of Dumitrescu's Third Army. Richthofen was certain that all of the forward positions had been shattered. By evening, Army Group B's command knew that more than the forward positions were gone. By day two of a Russian assault that almost everybody, to one degree or another, knew had to take place, both OKH and OKW saw the seriousness of the situation. Nonetheless, the staffs of each acted in a most lapidary manner, apparently not recognizing the "compelling necessity for those decisions which could have made allowances for the actual situation between Don and Volga."[85]

In a word, during the first twenty-four hours, the commands of those units that already were being or were soon to be attacked with devastating force received no precise instructions of any kind. Zeitzler did notify the command of Army Group B that he had *requested* Hitler's permission to release the only meaningful reserve unit in the area of the threatened front, Panzer Group H, but Group B itself received no concrete orders. As for the armored unit concerned—released after much procrastination—it was itself attacked before it could assume a suitable tactical position. Zeitzler then asked that Hitler order an immediate withdrawal from Stalingrad. The führer refused to issue the order. Eventually, however, he sent word through Jodl advising Zeitzler that OKH command "should consider [!] whether it would not be possible to bring up one armored division from Army Group A, in the Caucasus."[86] Zeitzler understandably expressed astonishment at this modest proposal. Although obviously upset, he took no action of his own, issued no orders. The interpretation usually offered is that Zeitzler knew that Hitler had summoned Manstein, his best overall strategist, to depart Vitebsk, the headquarters of Group Center of which Manstein's Eleventh Army was a part, and proceed to that of Army Group B, there to rectify the situation. This being the case, the chief of the army general staff did not want to prejudice any measures that Manstein might conceivably propose by offering any of his own.[87]

By November 21, Hitler was planning aerial relief measures for the Sixth Army and, in the interim, had gone so far as to allow for the bringing up of *two* divisions from the Caucasus. In reality, Zeitzler already knew what Hitler ultimately had in mind. His first face-to-face meeting with him had ended with his leader shouting: "I won't leave the Volga! I won't go back from the Volga." What Ronald Lewin has described as the "mystical significance" of Stalingrad, *the* city of the man Hitler most respected, had become all too apparent. The commander in chief would not surrender the "possibility" of a crushing ideological victory. Hitler's temper tantrum also pointed to a personality for whom withdrawal was a testimony to vulnerability; a person for whom withdrawal would not allow him to succeed where Falkenhayn had failed. His generals could not be allowed to have the last word and thus humiliate him. On November 21, the day on which Hitler began planning the foredoomed aerial relief effort, OKH issued the order that eventually had the effect of ensuring that most of the Sixth Army would indeed never leave the Volga. Paulus was told to hold fast.[88]

Meanwhile, on November 20, the Russians shattered the Romanian Fourth Army on Paulus's right. Again the attack was not unexpected. Again it was completely successful. Despite the obvious dangers involved with these successful Soviet assaults and despite the up to then lack of direction from above, the Sixth Army command itself gave the impression of being fairly confident. Emphasizing isolated local successes, its report dispatched to Army Group B's headquarters at 7:40 A.M. was "not unfavorable."[89] Such an evaluation appears to reflect an unreal, almost abstract view of the situation, consonant with denial of a high order. This is evident in the answer given by Paulus's chief of staff, Generalleutnant Arthur Schmidt, a much more pro-Nazi and hard-headed sort than his commander, to a query posed by Generalleutnant Martin Fiebig, commander of the VIII Flying Corps and thus subordinate to Richthofen, regarding the state of affairs at the Kalach Don bridges to the rear of the Sixth Army. Schmidt declared that he saw "no immediate danger for the bridges. There is sufficient security for the bridges on the heights near Kalach." This reply, given on the evening of November 21, was, as Görlitz pointed out, "completely correct in the abstract [an sich]." Unfortunately, by this time both Schmidt and Paulus knew that the bridges were about to fall to the Russians. Schmidt, with Paulus apparently listening in on the conversation (and again, it is important to remember that both of them apparently already knew of the crisis at Kalach) went on to declare that his chief was "entertaining the thought of going into a 'hedge-hog position' [zu igeln]." While the precise situation at the Kalach bridges themselves was apparently unknown to Fiebig and Richthofen, they were aware that the nearby airfield had been overrun. Thus, it would appear that Fiebig might have known that the situation at the bridges was untenable. He might also have known that Paulus and Schmidt knew this even if they did not care to comment upon it. Whatever the case, Paulus and Schmidt did know of the situation, and that the bridges' inevitable fall would mean that Sixth Army's major supply lines had been cut. How, queried Fiebig, did Schmidt think the Sixth Army could now be supplied? "By air," Schmidt replied. Fiebig's response was immediate and unequivocal: "It is impossible to supply an entire army by air. The Luftwaffe does not have enough transport aircraft at its disposal."[90] Richthofen went on to note in his November 21 journal entry that all efforts were being made to convince the Sixth Army command that supplying them in their proposed hedge-hog position through aerial means was impossible.

This conversation is of critical importance and demonstrates the validity of Kehrig's assertion that *even the command of the now critically threatened Sixth Army was itself* not willing to recognize the dangers posed by the immediate situation and the pressing need for drastic decisions.[91] Indeed, Sixth Army's leaders seemed almost eager to deceive others, and possibly themselves, as to the real state of affairs. They knew that the Kalach bridges were about to fall. At the very least, they knew the air force was aware the nearby airfield had been overrun. Nonetheless, they could not bring themselves to formally confirm this, or at least to grasp what the exigencies of the situation entailed. Moreover, as everyone realized, the only way by which Sixth Army, now cut off from overland supply and attempting to assume a hedgehog position, could be supplied was by air. This, though, was in the eyes of those who would be immediately involved in such an operation—which was clearly out of the question—and Paulus and his subordinate Schmidt were aware of this view. As far as a hedgehog defense was concerned, Hitler himself was most enthused about the idea. Zeitzler, like Hitler, was also miles removed from the front, but he knew that turning Stalingrad into a fortress was impossible. Geographical and climatic conditions could not be surmounted.[92] These conditions were certainly known to Paulus and Schmidt, who were both on the scene. Yet, the Sixth Army command was "entertaining" the idea of turning Stalingrad into a fortress that could be supplied by air even though the airmen had said it could not be done. Hitler's delusions about turning Stalingrad into a fortress and supplying it by air were, perhaps, understandable if not excusable. Those of the people on the scene and in direct contact with Fiebig and Richthofen were neither. Indeed, they seemed to reflect an almost desperate need to see things as they were not.

Sixth Army's leaders were united in their massive denial of the gravity of the situation. Schmidt, Paulus's chief of staff, seemed to function as Hitler's representative (in fact, he was far more of a "true believer" during and after Stalingrad than Hitler gave him credit for being).[93] While in his presence, Paulus would neither raise objections to nor even pose queries about views and schemes that flew in the face of reality. Perhaps the successful resolution of the Valdai Hills crisis in the early spring of the year was something that came to mind. Yet even as illusions were crumbling at Army Group B headquarters, those in command of Sixth Army, the unit in immediate danger, clung to them—Schmidt, perhaps out of ideological principle, Paulus perhaps out of unwillingness to be viewed as weak. Whatever their motives, a sort of bland variant of groupthink prevailed.

While Sixth Army's senior leaders seemed unwilling to see things as they were, Fiebig and his superior, Richthofen—who, it is important to remember, were as much onlookers as participants—did. After the astonishing conversation with Schmidt (and in spirit, it would seem, with Paulus) the Fourth Air

Fleet commander put in a frantic call to Generaloberst Albert Jeschonnek, Göring's chief of staff. It was simply impossible, he almost screamed, to undertake air operations sufficient to sustain 250,000 men. It would be a useless sacrifice and the whole business had to be called off. Göring himself had to see to it.[94] Göring already had told Hitler something he desperately wanted to hear, namely that relief from the air could be accomplished to a satisfactory degree. As a result, the air chief's general decline in prestige in military circles was forgotten. The virtual rejection of evidence and the conclusions to be drawn from it, something far too profound to be called "cavalier," is illustrated in a conversation on November 22 involving Generaloberst Hoth, Generalleutnant Schmidt, and General der FlugabwehrartillerieWolfgang Pickert, commander of the 9th Antiaircraft Division and entrusted by Richthofen with attending to the details of organizing the effort to supply the Sixth Army. Schmidt asked Pickert what should be done. "Immediate breakout to the southwest," he said without hesitation. Schmidt replied, "That won't work because of shortages in fuel, and would lead to a catastrophe such as Napoleon's." Pickert said his antiaircraft crews could be utilized to remove much of the Sixth Army's artillery, with ammunition being hand carried. Schmidt rejected the offer. Sixth Army was now in duty bound to defend Stalingrad and would go into the prescribed hedgehog defense. As had Generalleutnant Fiebig earlier, Pickert declared that, particularly under the prevailing winter conditions, it was impossible to supply an entire army by air. "*It must be done anyway!*" replied Schmidt, referring of course, to the proposed defense. If necessary, there were many horses available to be eaten.[95]

By November 22, however, Paulus knew that it was necessary to evacuate Stalingrad immediately. He informed Weichs of this and he in turn sent the recommendation on to OKW at Rastenburg.[96] The picture Paulus presented was a rather confused one at this point, however, because he refused to face up to the fact that Sixth Army could not be supplied by air and was unwilling to overrule the strident declaration, presumably presented on his behalf, that his subordinate Schmidt had made to the Luftwaffe personnel immediately involved in the relief effort.[97] As adherence to group norms previously had been responsible for his participation in a *folie à deux* charade with Hitler, a perhaps attenuated form of it prevailed in Paulus's relationship with his strong-willed chief of staff. Meanwhile, at Rastenburg itself, Zeitzler on November 23 argued for withdrawal. His anxiety was compounded by a message from Weichs stating that the Luftwaffe could supply barely a tenth of Sixth Army's needs and that Paulus thus should be given orders to break out immediately.[98] Hitler at first seemed to give reluctant permission to do so. Then, however, he decided—once and for all—against it. A new tank model, the Tiger, was coming off the assembly lines. If these were to be thrown into the battle, the tide would be turned. To be sure, Zeitzler agreed, this weapon promised marvelously well—and, incidentally, the 88-mm armed monster proved its effectiveness in battles on the Donetz later in February. There were, however, hardly enough of them available at this time to be of significant importance.[99] Hitler was adamant. "Sixth Army will stay where it is," said the führer. "It is the garrison of a fortress, and the duty of fortress troops is to withstand sieges. If necessary, they will hold out all winter, and I shall relieve them by a spring offensive." Hitler rejected Zeitzler's contention that Stalingrad was not really a fortress and that Göring was wrong in claiming that he could supply the encircled troops by air. "I am *not leaving the Volga!*" Hitler declared. He then called for Keitel and Jodl. Keitel, his "eyes flashing," thundered, "My Führer! Do not leave the Volga!"[100] Jodl presented a somewhat less histrionic appraisal in which he nevertheless ended up agreeing with Keitel. Göring, against every bit of information and advice supplied him by Richthofen, once again declared that he could guarantee the Sixth Army adequate supplies. He made this assertion despite the fact that several high-ranking Luftwaffe officers had told him that, at the very most, only 350 tons of supplies could be brought in per day. Göring, who had himself said that at least five hundred tons were required, still exuded confidence.[101] Zeitzler's arguments were rejected. Hitler once again issued the command to hold at all costs. Fighting would continue for more than two months, but there can be no doubt that Albert Seaton is basically correct in stating that, from November 23, "Paulus's Sixth Army was doomed."[102]

The Russians, of course, had a great deal to say about this situation. It is equally obvious, or should be so, that a fundamental unwillingness—indeed, at times even more than that, an inability to recognize things as they were or to act on such knowledge—operated at all levels. As we have seen, even Schmidt, someone immediately involved with the disaster, was almost petulantly unwilling to fathom its dimensions and consequences. At the same time, his commander, Paulus, with perhaps less of a *positive* emotional involvement in this, played almost a double role. He knew that evacuation was the only recourse, yet he acquiesced in his subordinate's unwillingness to act upon this necessity. The call from above to hold fast seemed to fulfill a certain need. Hitler's role, on the surface at least, seems to have been all too obvious. Moreover, the curious mixture of strong will and spiritual confusion—which had always characterized him as a leader in whom fear and efforts to avoid narcissistic injury acted in tandem with narcissistic rage—was exaggerated by the situation at Stalingrad. Zeitzler certainly saw things for what they were, but he seems to have assumed the role of a person witnessing a natural disaster. He was revolted, made suggestions, but he could do nothing himself. Göring played the role of sanguine yea-sayer, although this most intelligent individual knew what had to be done and that he, in fact, could not do it. Keitel and Jodl, the latter perhaps chastened for having once told Hitler what was actually happening in the Caucasus, said little and did nothing. Meanwhile, Manstein remained to be heard from. Before we consider his efforts to deal with the Stalingrad crisis and with its eventual denouement we must first focus upon two episodes that provide their own poignant commentaries upon the general course of events.

As we have seen, the Romanians, who had been assigned such crucial positions, were badly equipped. This, plus their general lack of good leadership, bad training, and poor motivation made them easy marks for the successful Soviet attacks on November 19 and 20. As a rule, these attacks met little effective resistance. One of the few places where such was encountered was where the attacking Russians ran up against the remnants of four Romanian divisions commanded by Gen. Mikhail Lascar. For several days, Lascar conducted an energetic defense with his thirty-nine thousand men (the equivalent of about two and one-third 1940 regular German infantry divisions). Wedged into an ever-shrinking pocket between the Chir River and the city of Kletskaya on the Don, it was obvious that sooner or later the group would have to surrender or be totally destroyed. In a November 23 telegram, Hitler informed Antonescu that he was confident Lascar's group would fight its way out and join the XXXVIII Panzer Corps. He expected the Sixth Army to hold and—with new divisions from the west operating in conjunction with the Romanian I Corps—launch a successful flank attack on the enemy. "I am of the firm conviction," he went on to say, and here we can easily see ideology intruding into tactical considerations, "that, as so often before in the struggle against the Soviet Union, better leadership and better troops will prevail over the initial success of the enemy."[103] In recognition of the spirit displayed by Lascar and in anticipation of his continued struggle, Hitler awarded him the oak leaves of the Knight's Cross to the Iron Cross, the highest award that could be granted to an allied soldier. Lascar might well have been gratified by the news. On November 24, however, he saw an opportunity for at least a remnant of his troops to escape and released four thousand of them to seek out the XXXVIII Panzer Corps on their own. There was no way out for the rest. More than thirty-four thousand Romanians died or were captured, Lascar among them. The order to fight until the last bullet, until all had died, was in the end disobeyed. In recognizing the need to capitulate, General Lascar and his commander, Gen. Ilie Steflea, showed that they "valued responsibility for their soldiers higher than obedience to an order that had become unfulfillable and senseless due to the development of events."[104] Willingness to perceive reality made Generals Lascar and Steflea exceptional figures in the whole pathetic situation. Hitler's effort to fend off an unwanted conclusion with words and tokens, which amounted to a highly maladaptive denial and avoidance of humiliating reality characteristic of the narcissistic personality, would be repeated on a grander scale in due course.

General der Artillerie Walther Seydlitz-Kurzbach, commander of the LI Corps, was descended from a long line of military men prominent in German military history. Since the massive Soviet attacks beginning on November 19, he had become convinced that a general withdrawal of the Sixth Army was absolutely necessary. Orders from higher authorities, particularly those emanating from Rastenburg, left him unmoved, except to arouse his disgust. To hold on meant annihilation. On November 23, acting on his own, he ordered his corps to evacuate its position, a highly exposed one in the northeast corner of the Stalingrad pocket. In so doing, he sought to create a situation in which Paulus would be compelled to order a general withdrawal. By acting on his own, he hoped to make it easier for Paulus to disobey Hitler. The result of this unilateral action was catastrophic. Seydlitz-Kurzbach's move, which was not complemented by similar ones by adjoining units, left one of his divisions, the 94th, completely exposed. Overwhelmed by masses of Soviet infantry and armor, it was virtually annihilated.[105] To put it mildly, this action was controversial and has been called mistaken, wrong-headed, even mutinous. Ironically, Hitler, who at first knew nothing of Seydlitz-Kurzbach's role in the November 21 disaster, issued an order on November 25 making the general directly responsible *to him* (presumably he still was to Paulus as well) for defending the entire crucial northern sector of the Stalingrad pocket.[106] Paulus at first knew nothing of Seydlitz-Kurzbach's action. In fact, details of it did not reach him until *after* Hitler became aware at least of its consequences. Even after he had learned of it and of the führer making the corps commander directly responsible for defending the northern sector, Paulus made no protest, no objections. As controversial, perhaps even "mutinous," as Görlitz put it, as Seydlitz-Kurzbach had been, it was as if he were functioning as Paulus's reality-observing and executive ego, carrying out, albeit in a single-handed, even frenetic fashion, that which the Sixth Army commander knew had to be done, even if rigid adherence to norms consonant with what he perceived to be the group ethic prevented him from doing it.[107]

MANSTEIN AND THE END

In a revealing postwar interview, General der Artillerie Walter Warlimont declared that, in his opinion, Hitler knew that the war was lost by the end of September 1942.[108] This certainly could have been true. Some have even suggested that Hitler had been driven by a death wish all along. In any case, his actual role in day-to-day Stalingrad decision making fell off sharply during the crisis period of November 1942–January 1943, which was indicative of a form of withdrawal or denial.[109] Having proclaimed a general policy of "no withdrawal," Hitler played a relatively limited role in tactical planning. What was involved was an unwillingness to involve himself in actions that might fail, that is, putting himself in such a position that his generals, to say nothing of the German people as a whole, could see that he was wrong. Most assuredly, there were ideological reasons for this. The self-proclaimed führer of the Thousand-Year Reich could not be viewed as a failure. As we have seen, however, avoidance and denial are leading characteristics of the narcissistic personality.

There can be little doubt, however, that when catastrophe loomed in November 1942, he took one action that, at least on paper, indicates he was interested in saving things. On November 21, Hitler instructed Erich von Manstein to leave his Eleventh Army headquarters at Vitebsk and head south to Novocherkask, just east of Rostov. There he was to assume command of a newly formed Army Group Don and at the same time take over direction of operations from Weichs. If anyone could turn things around, it was Manstein, a man, who, as we have seen, had great military talent and was of a seemingly independent cast of mind.

To be sure, on paper at least, the new Army Group Don consisted of almost nothing. Sixth Army supposedly was part of it, but it was hardly in a position to be a real component. Hoth's Fourth Army was subordinated to Manstein, but by itself could not provide the needed punch to allow for meaningful offensive operations. The few Romanian units available were virtually in a state of shock. A fresh armored division, the 6th, had just arrived from France, and the 17th Panzer and 16th Motorized Divisions were on their way. Yet, even with these additions (plus the forlorn twenty-five tanks of the 23rd Panzer Division), Army Group Don was hardly a "Group" in any sense of the word.[110] In fact, Manstein, in *Verlorene Siege* (*Lost Victories*), went so far as to label it "a fiction." Such would appear to have been the case, particularly if one bears in mind that Paulus presumably owed direct allegiance to Hitler, something assured by the presence of a liaison officer at Stalingrad.[111] On the other hand, there can be little doubt that Manstein's tactical skills were highly respected and that Paulus expected great things from him. Also, knowledge that the architect of the western victories and the significant victory at Sevastopol was on the way was a tonic to Sixth Army's morale in general. These factors, plus the strong beliefs of Paulus and Schmidt in Hitler's ability to perform military miracles, were of immense psychological significance.[112] At the very least, Paulus, who believed that Hitler had allowed him no freedom of action, certainly thought that Manstein could intercede or perhaps offer solutions of his own.

When Manstein was ordered south, one of the first things he did was send telegrams to Army Group B headquarters stating that Sixth Army was to be instructed to immediately pull out all of its defensive strength in order to anchor its front at the Kalach Don crossing. As we have seen, this occurred at about the same time as the fall of the bridges there. Whether Manstein could have known of this is uncertain, as is the precise situation at Kalach when his message was sent. Furthermore, Manstein was never "able to ascertain if these instructions were given over to the 6th Army."[113] Even as Manstein's train was heading south, Paulus, with Seydlitz-Kurzbach and the latter's chief of staff, Colonel Clausius, had reached the conclusion that an immediate breakout was absolutely necessary and that a guarantee of maximum freedom of action from Hitler was required. As we have seen, Seydlitz-Kurzbach had lost almost all of his confidence in Hitler and later would undertake a disastrous withdrawal on his own. Yet, when it came to sending a message to Rastenburg that presented the grim facts in all of their totality, to say nothing of asking for total freedom of action, they hesitated. Finally, on November 23, a precious day after the three had conferred, they sent a somewhat watered-down radio communication requesting permission to break out but failing to describe the truly desperate state of affairs. Not only were Paulus and his subordinates unwilling to take concerted action on their own—something that Schmidt later condemned as "mutinous"—they were even reluctant to *inform* Hitler of just how serious matters had become.[114] It would perhaps be pushing things a bit to say that formal groupthink still held sway at Sixth Army headquarters. Rather, Paulus, faced with crumbling illusions, seems to have surrendered his will to Schmidt, a man for whom adherence to principle necessitated denial.

On November 24, two days before formally assuming command of Army Group Don, Manstein sent a wire to OKH presenting his formal evaluation of the situation. He thought it was still possible for Sixth Army to break out to the southwest. He added that the supply situation was such that leaving it at Stalingrad constituted *"an extreme risk."* However, Manstein had come to the conclusion that the optimal time for a breakout already had passed. Hence, from an operational point of view, it would be best for Sixth Army to hold out until a relief operation could be undertaken. Of decisive importance in all of this was the assurance that needed supplies could be provided by air. Manstein possessed a copy of Paulus's November 23 telegram to Hitler when he sent this message. As we have seen, no one had taken the initiative to describe how truly desperate the situation had become. Furthermore, according to Manstein, the command of Army Group B had told him that the conditions necessary to support a breakout—that is, an operation to shorten the front in the area to be affected—could not be met before November 28. Perhaps this knowledge had influenced him in his recommendation that Sixth Army should try to hold out in anticipation of relief. At any rate, in his memoirs, Manstein declares that the optimal time for a breakout had already passed and that probably the best Paulus could have done was to have broken out earlier, without waiting for Hitler's permission, and thus confront him with a *fait accompli*. Paulus, not out of fear, but out of his sense of loyalty to Hitler, could not bring himself to do this and had instead sought permission, something that of course was denied. Whether Manstein at this point (he had not yet assumed formal command of the "fictive" Army of the Don) was in a position to do more than he did at the time, that is, other than advise Sixth Army to hold, is unclear. According to his memoirs, two of his subordinates who had just returned from a visit to the encircled army informed him that the situation was not all that bad, that supplies were adequate for the moment. Manstein emphasized Göring's role in convincing Hitler that he could provide what was necessary. It was not until later that Manstein became aware the Luftwaffe chief had been giving his leader false information since at least November 23.[115]

Throughout his memoirs, Manstein was consistent about two points: first, if Paulus were to have broken out, it would have to have been done early, and, second, failing that, holding out until relieved would require that adequate supplies be brought in by air. While Manstein might not have had access to the same information as Richthofen and Fiebig, his memoirs suggest a certain degree of uncertainty in this crucial area. Yet, despite this, and despite messages from the Stalingrad Kessel clearly conveying Paulus's increasing desperation for an order allowing him greater freedom of action, Manstein never took the seemingly logical step of flying into Stalingrad to see for himself what was going on there. Instead, as described above, he relied on staff personnel to perform this function. Manstein declared that, after a particularly desperate freedom-of-action request from Paulus on November 26 and after being provided information (from General der Flugabwehrartillerie Pickert) that the Sixth Army did not have enough ammunition and fuel to accomplish a successful fighting breakout, he did indeed contemplate flying in to personally evaluate the situation. His staff, however, pointed out that weather conditions could not be counted on to allow him more than the briefest of visits. Furthermore, since not only the Sixth Army's fate but that of the entire front was at issue, he could not afford to be away from his headquarters.[116]

Somehow, this does not ring true. Most assuredly, the Sixth Army occupied but a portion of the front and Manstein did have other concerns to consider. Yet, the fate of 250,000 men was, one would think, of at least some importance. Also, even if weather conditions allowed for only the briefest of visits, Manstein seemed satisfied with information obtained by subordinates during *their* brief visits, as well as by General der Flugabwehrartillerie Pickert, who left for Stalingrad for the same purpose. Surely someone as tactically gifted as Manstein —and modesty was never one of his most prominent qualities—might have been able to obtain a clearer view of things had he bothered to look for himself. Manstein, in pointing out that Hitler could never be persuaded to visit critical sectors of the eastern front, seemed to suggest that he really did not want to know what was happening. Manstein was receiving conflicting views regarding the supply situation. Furthermore, at least in his memoirs, he placed a great deal of emphasis on the fact that Hitler had a liaison officer with Paulus, and that officer might have been a strong inhibiting influence.[117] If these factors weighed heavily on his mind (and there is ample evidence to suggest that they did) one is entitled to ask why Manstein did not decide on making the briefest of visits. The feeble nature of his justification for remaining at his headquarters suggests that, perhaps like his commander in chief, he really wanted to avoid knowing what was happening at Stalingrad. Manstein, who on one level of reality testing had just about written off the Sixth Army, was, on another level, also practicing that denial, with the constriction of reality testing and limitation of affective reaction so often consonant with the guiding principles of the "Nur Soldat" ("soldier only"). He was, in other words, functioning in a dissociated or self-contradictory manner that resonated with Hitler's own style.

After November 24, and the dismal failure of Seydlitz-Kurzbach's effort, Paulus and his subordinates came up with no concrete plans for a breakout.[118] Obviously, from this point on, they were counting on some sort of positive lead, if not from Rastenburg—Schmidt's presence probably served to prevent such from even being requested—then at least from Manstein. Manstein's unwillingness to visit Stalingrad is made all the more mystifying precisely because he was involved in organizing a major relief operation. In a November 24 cable he told Paulus of this, and of the necessity of Sixth Army being in position to "if necessary . . . clear a supply channel toward the southwest."[119]

Again, despite the fact that a relief operation necessitated as precise knowledge as possible regarding conditions within the Stalingrad pocket itself, Manstein never paid it a visit. The relief operation was to be undertaken by the unit most readily available, Hoth's Fourth Army. On November 28, Manstein sent Hitler a communication in which he emphasized the necessity of an immediate, strongly reinforced relief operation. Even if a corridor could be cut to the Sixth Army over which supplies could be sent, it still had to be evacuated. Holding out for long over so narrow a front was impossible, especially when the enemy had his hands free to maneuver over a far wider area.[120] What Manstein was asking for was a greater commitment of reinforcements for his relief effort—not of the so-called Army Group Don, which at that point was really no group at all, but rather of Hoth's already severely tried Fourth Army. He was also stating that the relief operation had to be crowned by pulling back from Stalingrad, something absolutely necessary if the front was to be shortened in an effort to achieve greater tactical flexibility.

Hitler did not reply to this critical message until December 3, five days after his receipt of Manstein's evaluation. In his reply, he stated that he clearly recognized that the situation was critical and that the Russians had a considerable superiority in committed formations. At the same time, though, he did not want the front shortened north of Stalingrad. In a word, he did not want Stalingrad to be abandoned. Furthermore, he thought that the Russian formations had themselves been seriously weakened by the bitter fighting and that, precisely because of their "surprising successes," they also were confronting problems of supply and leadership.[121] Although he was quite willing for a relief operation to take place, he could not, or at least would not, commit substantially more forces to such an operation. While carving out a supply corridor was necessary, Stalingrad could not be abandoned. He seemed to know that, as things stood, the Sixth Army was at that point in the position of having to be supplied by air. Yet everyone, Hitler included, knew that a necessarily much greater aerial effort was impossible. Be that as it may, no more forces were available for a relief operation, and tactical flexibility could not be purchased at the now emotionally unacceptable price of shortening the front. Such a maneuver required withdrawing forces, and withdrawal, for Hitler, was an unacceptable sign of weakness. The conventional "sortie in relief" had to be just that, and it would have to be at a time and place in which more than convention was called for. Manstein recognized that Hitler did not then have, nor had he ever had, any intention of pulling Sixth Army out of Stalingrad. It was to remain where it was while an almost foredoomed effort to "relieve" it was undertaken. It was under these cruelly inauspicious conditions that Operation Winter Tempest (Wintergewitter) was undertaken.

The offensive, which was supposed to at the very least open up a supply corridor to the Sixth Army, began on December 12, 1942, and made some progress, initially against light but increasingly severe opposition. As Manstein, in his November 28 message to Hitler, had anticipated, the Soviets enjoyed the strategic advantages of an enemy able to maneuver over a front of several hundred kilometers instead of having to focus efforts in a limited area. Between Hoth's advancing columns and the forlorn Stalingrad pocket there were deployed the following Soviet forces: Fifty-first Army, Second Guards Army, one armored corps, one mechanized corps, three motorized corps, one cavalry corps (perhaps hypothetically superannuated, but always dangerous in winter conditions), two almost full-strength infantry divisions (Soviet divisions consisted of a rough bayonet strength of 10,000), and an independent armored brigade.[122] German tank crews were, as a rule, superior to their Russian counterparts. However, the rugged, mechanically reliable ("peasant-proof") T-34 tank was more maneuverable than any German variant, and its 76-mm gun had superior weight of shot. Also, there were many more of them. The Soviets thus could afford to give ground, perhaps even to suffer occasional tactical defeats.

Throughout the operation, Manstein gave the impression of one who recognized that the enterprise was doomed from the beginning. The relief operation should have been more strongly supported, but all he could do was try and persuade OKH and Hitler of this. Indeed, in this regard he seemed to have abandoned Sixth Army's fate to Zeitzler.[123] Perhaps some sort of impression would have been made if, in protest, he had offered to step down from leadership of Army Group Don (that "fictive" organization); but he did not. Only after the relief operation clearly had failed was such an offer made, but by that point it was meaningless. For Winter Tempest to have had any chance of success, some sort of action had to have been undertaken by Sixth Army itself. To do that, Manstein would have had to persuade Hitler that, if it were to break out, it could not at the same time continue to hold Stalingrad.[124] On the other hand, Paulus had to be persuaded to make an attempt. It would, to be sure, be a desperate one. Generalleutnant Hans Hube's XIV Panzer Corps, the one relatively intact armored corps within the pocket, could muster only between fifty and eighty tanks, some of them in a poor state of repair, and only about 10 percent of what was left of the Sixth Army could function as effective infantry.[125] About 40 percent of those inside could be labeled "Trossknechten," that is, supply personnel. Under the circumstances, they were indeed "camp followers."[126] Yet, *some* sort of offensive move from the pocket had to be made. Paulus previously had made urgent requests for freedom of action. Now, however, with the Hoth relief operation under way, he seemed indecisive, hesitant. It was obvious that Manstein had a crucial role to play in this.

Indeed, Manstein had planned an attack out of the pocket, to be called "Thunderclap" ("Donnerschlag"). In his memoirs, Manstein has pictured himself as one who, against Hitler's wishes and in the face of Zeitzler's lack of resolve, desperately attempted to urge Paulus to undertake some sort of action. While not accusing Paulus of cowardice, Manstein depicted him as an officer who took his loyalty oath to Hitler too seriously. He was unwilling to respond to Manstein's clear hints that he should undertake Thunderclap.[127] At any rate, Paulus, no doubt aware of the slim chance such an operation had of succeeding, did not act with boldness. Furthermore, Winter Tempest, after initial successes, was soon in trouble. Russian resistance had stiffened, losses were heavy and, on December 19, the Italian Eighth Army, on the Don to the north, had had its front shattered by a strong Soviet attack. It was entirely possible—and, in fact, such eventually did occur—that units from Hoth's Fourth Army would have to be detached to help bolster the sagging front in that area. At this point, Paulus finally bestirred himself. He sent a wire to Manstein asking specifically whether he should begin psychological preparations for an attempted breakout. It cannot be overemphasized that Manstein's permission was crucial here. Of course, as we saw earlier, there was also a liaison officer from Hitler in the pocket. Yet Paulus never received a *specific, direct* order from Hitler (the rather vague, general ones to "hold out" cannot be counted) through this officer, to say nothing of one from Hitler himself. Manstein, meanwhile, had steadily maintained that his own army was a "fiction." There is no doubt, however, that Paulus saw himself as being under Manstein's immediate command and that he was waiting to receive direct orders from one whose judgment he trusted, indeed, *had* to have trusted.[128] Such orders were never given, either on December 19 or later. Manstein's unwillingness to provide these, or even really

substantive moral support, was made easier for him by his never visiting the
Sixth Army, thus avoiding troubling perceptions of reality.

On the evening of December 18, Manstein sent an intelligence officer, Major Eismann, into the Stalingrad pocket to find out whether Paulus was willing
to undertake Thunderclap. He was not unequivocally *ordered* to do so, even
though he was told that this was really his only chance. He was asked, though,
his opinion as to whether such an operation could succeed. Paulus was reluctant to commit himself, despite statements from his operations chief and quartermaster general that a breakout was still possible at that point. Schmidt, at
this point probably the only Nazi *sans phrases* among those trapped at Stalingrad, had the last word. He declared that a breakout was clearly impossible. It
would be "an acknowledgement of disaster. Sixth Army will still be in position
at Easter. All you people have to do is to supply it better."[129] Paulus did not
contradict Schmidt. He was still willing to participate in a sort of negative *folie
à deux*. Manstein, now worried about the collapse of the Italian Eighth Army,
sought OKH's permission for Sixth Army to break out while at the same time
asking its commander if he thought such an operation could succeed. Paulus,
who was looking not only for specific instructions from Manstein, but also his
assurance that he could do so without Hitler's approval, simply emphasized
the difficulties involved in undertaking Thunderclap.[130] Manstein urged Paulus to break out, but shied away from declaring that he should do so without
Hitler's permission. Hitler stated that Sixth Army could indeed try to reach
Hoth, but that it would have to continue to hold Stalingrad as well. Zeitzler,
meanwhile, increased his efforts to persuade Hitler that the army had to be ordered to break out. Such was the only choice, especially since Hoth's attack
had finally ground to a halt thirty miles from Paulus's beleaguered force.

Manstein continued to try to convince Hitler that Sixth Army had to move,
but the weight of his arguments, even when combined with Zeitzler's, accomplished nothing. Furthermore, Hitler sought to use one of Paulus's own statements against the idea of the breakout. In an exchange with Manstein, he
pointed out that Paulus had himself stated that he had fuel enough to sustain
a fighting breakout for only about twenty miles. Thus, any effort along these
lines would be doomed to failure.[131] Zeitzler had been confronted with a similar argument. To this he responded that Hitler *already* had given Paulus permission to break out, only if he retained his hold on Stalingrad as well. Thus,
the fuel shortage argument was invalid.[132] According to Zeitzler, Hitler "went
pale with anger, and did not reply." In all of this, one can certainly detect immense confusion of motives on Paulus's part. He could not break out unless he
received orders to do so. Yet, when asked if such a breakout could be accomplished, he offered technical arguments that lent support to Hitler's decision
not to allow him to do so.[133] Manstein, in his memoirs, declared that if Paulus
had wanted to undertake Donnerschlag, he probably could have found

enough previously hidden ("*schwarz*") fuel for such an operation. The decision not to take advantage of the last opportunity to evacuate Stalingrad was Paulus's alone, at least according to Manstein. Indeed, during the crucial period between December 19 and the dismal Christmas, he had provided him every opportunity to do so, even going so far as to relieve Paulus of the onus of responsibility for ordering it.[134] Yet, as mentioned before, Manstein never gave Paulus what this psychologically crushed man desperately needed to hear: *a clear order to break out*—that is, to commence Thunderbolt—even without Hitler's permission to do so. Also, and this is most instructive, he never offered the possibility that, lacking permission from OKH or Hitler to receive permission to issue such an order, he would resign.[135]

At 5:40 in the afternoon on December 23, 1942, there began an anguished conversation between Manstein and Paulus. Manstein inquired about the possibility of Paulus's making a breakout effort if he were assured of added supplies. Paulus replied that there were immense difficulties but that, if there were to be such an effort, the sooner it commenced, the better. He then posed the crucial question: "May I regard this conversation as authority to start Operation Thunderclap?" To this, Manstein offered what turned out to be the final, meaningful answer: "I am not yet in a position to give you such authority."[136] As an apparent afterthought, he asked, "But what I want to know is whether you think that you can force your way through to Hoth." Paulus replied: "There is nothing else to do."[137] No breakout order was given.

On December 29, 1942, Oberst Hans-Gunther van Hooven met General Paulus at Gumrak Airfield at Stalingrad. He arrived with greetings from two of Paulus's old friends, Generalleutnant Erich Fellgiebel and his chief of staff, Oberst Hahn. Once and for all he declared that Sixth Army's only hope was to break out in a last effort to link up with Hoth's Fourth Army. Such a breakout could, everyone knew, have political implications and consequences. It would, after all, constitute an act of disobedience against the führer. In his conversation with Paulus, however, van Hooven saw no sign whatsoever that he attached any sort of *political* significance to such an act. He was, Paulus declared, just a soldier. He did not have a picture of the total situation. His own was almost hopeless. He knew that. However, he had no choice but to obey, although he attached no political significance to either obeying or disobeying.[138] Manstein who, of course, did have this "total picture," saw Sixth Army's fate in perspective: involved was the fate of the eastern front as a whole and that of the German armies in the Caucasus in particular—a conclusion with which his führer could only agree.[139] In a very real sense, Manstein's massive denial and avoidance, which prohibited him from visiting Stalingrad personally, was probably important in preserving his adaptation to what he perceived to be a totality of both political and military "realities."

On January, 22, 1943, after, on order of Hitler, rebuffing a Soviet surrender demand made two weeks earlier, Paulus responded to his commander in chief's order to hold all along the line: "My *Führer*. Your command will be followed! Long live Germany! Heil, mein *Führer!*"[140] On January 30, Hitler promoted Paulus to the rank of field marshal hoping that he would be inspired by the fact no German officer of that rank had ever surrendered. It did not have the desired effect; Paulus surrendered the following day. On February 2, the last remnants of the Sixth Army did the same. More than ninety thousand frozen and half-starved survivors began the trek to Soviet prison camps, from which only about five thousand returned.

CONCLUSIONS

Walter Görlitz maintained that the ultimate source of the Stalingrad disaster lay in the fact that the July 1942 summer offensive had been such a "bungled" operation from the beginning and that once Group A was threatened with possibly being cut off in the Caucasus "Sixth Army had no alternative but to hang on in a situation which now had become desperate." That also was Manstein's view, at least as he articulated it in his memoirs. Whatever the case, both the bungled operations that led to Stalingrad and the reactions of German leaders once the disaster unfolded were in large measure due to varieties of psychological dysfunctionalism. On December 16, 1942, one day before Hoth's ill-fated relief operation was to begin, General der Flieger Richthofen, after a conversation with Manstein, recorded in his diary that "We both feel the same—that we're like a couple of attendants in a lunatic asylum!"[141] As indicated earlier, if the asylum metaphor is to be used, Manstein would have to be seen in the dual role of attendant and inmate. In any case, some general conclusions regarding the roles of German leaders in the disaster, and the varieties of dysfunctionalism that informed them, are now in order.

As he both set the stage for and reacted to the Battle of Stalingrad, Adolf Hitler displayed characteristics that have been brought together under the frustration-aggression hypothesis described at the beginning of this chapter. The source of these characteristics was an extremely narcissistic personality which, dreading assault or humiliation, exhibited limitless grandiosity. His desire to "have it all" was responsible for a two-pronged offensive that posed tactical and strategic problems that proved impossible to surmount. The failures of his generals were interpreted as attacks on him and he at times seemed more concerned with punishing them than the Soviet enemy. Aware of the possibility of a Soviet counterattack in the Stalingrad region, he was nonetheless determined to have the city at all costs, at the same time doing his generals one better by avoiding "another Verdun." Increasing frustration led to increasing rage, and inflexible plans and perceptions remained intact. Once the counterattack occurred, he was satisfied with giving only one real order: that Sixth

Army was to hold on while being supplied by an airlift that only sycophant in chief Göring thought could succeed. Unpleasant situations such as those posed by the collapse of resistance by General Lascar's Romanian troops or the eventual capitulation of what was left of the Sixth Army could be obviated through symbolic acts of compensatory significance only to a personality awash in grandeur and able to call upon patterns of avoidance and denial to assist in its preservation. Toward the end, he probably wrote off the Sixth Army. Even if it was annihilated and his generals killed, captured, or humiliated, he would not be defeated. In a curious sort of way, his continued rigid commitment to National Socialist ideals would allow him to emerge victorious in his own mind. Indeed, particularly after learning that Paulus had surrendered rather than kill himself, Hitler no doubt viewed *himself* as the only true idealist around, the only real Mensch.[142] In the end, Germany's anguish would be his glory, while the rage that had sustained him all along remained intact.

Hitler was the ultimate architect (an especially appropriate word in his case) of the Stalingrad disaster. His generals, however, had a crucial role in this. Even after the sobering winter campaign of 1941–42, German generals grossly underrated their enemy. The possibility that they could respond to German attacks in significant ways of their own—a possibility that Hitler himself had recognized—seems never to have occurred to them. To be sure, the German army, after a tough winter, seemed to have overcome all of its difficulties by the spring of 1942. Sevastopol had fallen, Soviet attacks had been bloodily repulsed, and the Wehrmacht was on the move again. Through the summer and fall of 1942, German military leaders at all levels were possessed of a quiet confidence. Warnings of possible problems, particularly those provided by the Romanians, were virtually ignored. Confident of their own abilities and those of their soldiers, grandiosely and persistently underrating their enemies while despising their allies, German military leadership was caught up in groupthink, which, as in the resonating case of Hitler, produced inflexibility. Individuals might have had doubts or even fears, but these were quashed. One individual in particular who had bouts of uneasiness was the Sixth Army commander, Friedrich Paulus.

Perhaps because he had little real field experience, perhaps because the flanks of his army were covered by Romanian troops whose miserable equipment and poor leadership were well known to him, Paulus evidenced more uncertainty than other German military leaders. At one point this uneasiness was publicly shared by his immediate superior, Generaloberst Maximilian von Weichs, commander of Group B of Army Group South. Nevertheless, a conference with Hitler seems to have assuaged their fears. In a striking example of *folie à deux*, the führer was able to persuade them that matters were not as they perceived them to have been even though they had greater familiarity with local conditions. Once the Russian counterattacks began, Weichs was able to perceive and comprehend the reality of the situation. Paulus, however, who throughout October had persistently told Hitler what he wanted to hear, at first seemed not to recognize just how dangerous the conditions had become. At least at first, he seems to have been concerned not to displease Hitler by telling him just how grave matters were. While illusions central to groupthink were crumbling at intermediary levels, Paulus and his colleagues seem to have clung to them for the first crucial days of the Soviet offensive. Paulus, uncertain of himself as a field commander, knowing that in ways both positive and negative he was no Reichenau, was not going to disturb matters unduly by giving voice to suppressed fears. His chief of staff, Arthur Schmidt, a committed National Socialist to the end, seemed to represent Hitler for Paulus, indeed, probably *was* Hitler at Stalingrad. Aggressively ideological, his aggression would translate into the passive kind as he functioned as his chief's alter ego. The incident concerning the Kalach bridges, another, perhaps more attenuated form of *folie à deux*, showed the two of them acting in pitiful harmony as they denied the obvious. As late as mid-December, Paulus, even as illusions had all but vanished, would still not contradict Schmidt when he presented his tragically absurd hypotheses to visitors to the besieged and starving Sixth Army.

Erich von Manstein, upon whom Paulus came to depend, did disagree with Hitler from time to time, knowing, however, that he, as much a Nur Soldat as Paulus, could never defy him. Shielding himself from the realities of Stalingrad almost as much as Hitler was doing, he could be critical both of his chief and of Paulus, blaming each of them for their respective roles in the disaster while never assuming responsibility for not ordering a breakout attempt whether or not Hitler gave permission to do so. Probably he was relieved by not thinking himself able to do this. After all, in the broader scheme of things, at least insofar as Manstein saw it in his memoirs, the Sixth Army's fate, while important, was secondary to overall eastern front concerns. Here, Manstein's unwillingness to visit Paulus and see for himself just what the conditions were like for the besieged troops—something that may have caused him to alter his own fixed concerns—might well have served him in a strangely "positive" sense. Whether or not this was the case, Manstein showed patterns of denial and avoidance that complemented the psychological dysfunctionalism of others involved in the Stalingrad affair. Taken all together, and in turn complemented by actions and failures to act on the parts of others, these pathologic processes functioned in a bizarrely synergistic group interaction to assure that the army which once had played so crucial a role in serving the interests of the Thousand-Year Reich would disappear in its name.

In the end, Hitler was provided with an ideal entourage that functioned to assure that his fabled but grossly inflated "will" would prevail. Hitler would triumph over his generals, indeed, over the Sixth Army, even if he could not triumph over the Soviets. Interacting patterns of psychological dysfunctionalism had produced what amounted to a ghastly collaboration that doomed all but a remnant of the Sixth Army to extinction even as the ideology that sent it on the road to disaster retained, at least for one, its spiritual value. In the eyes of Hitler, Joachim Fest's "unperson," these values were those of the "new man."[143] In the eyes of history they were a kind of necrophilia. Hitler and his generals had been sullen partners in an immense dance of death.

CONCLUSION

L ET US ASSUME THAT we can leave behind the hoary Social Darwinian assertion that war is necessary to preserve the biological health of nations. However, arguments as to whether such deadly aggression is an innate trait or the consequence of external influences have been going on for centuries without a universal resolution. Still, it is quite apparent that humans are perhaps unique among all species in harboring beliefs that seem capable of initiating conflict on a scale that we call "war." While war itself can be validly construed as "dysfunctional," it nevertheless has been an integral part of our human experience, cursed as well as exalted. Ironically, heroes and villains have been accorded equal attention.

Unfortunately, when conflict attains the level at which members of the same species kill each other in large numbers we are then confronted with a seemingly paradoxical situation. In a word, a form of behavior that can be broadly viewed as dysfunctional can also come to be perceived as inevitable, if not acceptable within the context of our existential situation. Sherman may have described war as "hell," but it is also true that few in the North, much less the troops under his command, were shedding tears over the plight of Georgia and South Carolina.

Hence, when we critically analyze various forms of military behavior or decision making, categorizing some as militarily dysfunctional and attempting to determine the underlying sources for such phenomena, we essentially beg an important issue. We have assumed that within the context of war there are forms of planning and action that somehow are better than others. This, of course, suggests that we have decided that behavior critical to operations within a basically dysfunctional system can itself be characterized as either functional or nonfunctional.

Perhaps a way out of this dilemma, one that is to some extent informed by ethical considerations, is to accept the inevitability of war much as we view diseases. After all, at least in our present lifetime, a killer such as cancer is most assuredly an ever-present, albeit dysfunctional, phenomenon in terms of human existence. We may wish for the disappearance of cancer, but it is still there in spite of our fervent efforts to find a cure.

Continuing this frame of thought, by its nature cancer must necessarily generate at times extremely difficult and painful challenges for those involved in decisions and actions relating to it. Moreover, one can anticipate that under such trying circumstances decisions are made which would never even be considered under less stressful circumstances. For example, a family may decide to "pull the plug" on a terminally ill member of the family, but look on in horror at the behavior of a Kevorkian. Pulling the plug to avoid further suffering may seem humane for loved ones, but perhaps less so when an individual's career is devoted to such an activity.

In a similar manner, individuals in positions of military leadership are always concerned with seeing matters through to a successful conclusion. It is part of their training and an integral part of their belief system. Yet, as Napoleon so bluntly put it, that may require acceptance of the truism that making an omelet requires breaking the eggs. The result is that, in the stress of combat command, circumstances can create the potential for decisions that not only result in heavy casualties, but also can subsequently be viewed from a military point of view as not "good" decisions. Nevertheless, it must be remembered that within the context of that particular situation the objective was, of course, to succeed.

Indeed, commanders do have options. Depending on the circumstances of time and place, success can be achieved in a variety of ways. At times, boldly seizing the initiative will be necessary. On other occasions, a cautious approach will be best—perhaps even going on the defensive and making the enemy come to you. With the emergence of modern long-term campaigns, success can perhaps be gained through simple attrition. In any event, military leaders must be able to decide on courses of action or reaction the consequences of which can often be grasped only retrospectively.

As in most of life's activities, success in war has strong subjective factors attached to it. One hopes for success, or at least to avoid failure, not only in the interest of one's country or military establishment, but also for personal reasons. Matters of pride and reputation are often of as much or greater importance for a general or national military leader. This is also true for those engaged in less spectacularly articulated avocations.

Indeed, there is quite a difference between the pursuit of success in fields such as science, the humanities, art, business, and so on, and success in war. Most of us engaged in one of these other enterprises may operate at times in a dysfunctional manner due to a particular mental state, unusual circumstances, or some combination of factors. Generally we can recognize that such behavior is quite often likely to lead to unacceptable outcomes in our profession. Usually, if we are honest with ourselves, we acknowledge the errors and hope to do better. Most likely, relatively few other people have been negatively affected, although this is not always true—as, for example, in the case of a large corporation.

Consider, however, the military commander who executes his command duties by visiting mass death upon an enemy, or at times accepts the slaughter of those under his command in order to wear down the enemy or take territory not already under his control. Unless such an individual has divorced himself completely from humanity, these actions have to create at some time in one's career incredible intrapersonal conflicts. There is a difference between death and dismemberment as a consequence, as opposed to unemployment lines or bored students.

Worse yet, every military leader is aware of the fact that decisions made in the psychological furnace of combat may well be viewed with abhorrence decades later in a war college, or criticized by some armchair strategist with all the wisdom of hindsight. Thus, for the military leader, questions regarding the goodness of military judgment may come from both military peers as well as nonmilitary sources. Moreover, while a lost battle or even a campaign can in the end be made good, the consequences are far greater for all concerned. The casualties resulting from the Somme offensive will forever exceed by far the consequences of faulty medical diagnoses. This may be of small comfort to the patients involved, but expectations for a long life were considerably less for the advancing British troops.

Still, while a military commander is, in the final analysis, a human performing in a less than socially justifiable series of circumstances, he may also see war as the one time he is apt to be considered of value. Rudyard Kipling put his finger on it when he pointed out that in times of peace the Tommy was serving in a less-than-desired profession, but that "when the troopship was on the tide" things changed. For the military commander, the desire to succeed in wartime is likely to be accompanied by a prior set of experiences in which he was not particularly esteemed by the society he was obligated to defend. It is small wonder, perhaps, that military men tend to see their world in more isolated and provincial terms.

The overarching theme in this book has been to consider the causes and consequences of human decision making in war, where stress can reach unbearable heights. We have attempted to show that a large number of different psychological factors can lead to actions constrained by intra-individual psychological turmoil not exhibited before, or where previously this conflict did not have such far-reaching consequences. Nor is this particular fault limited to the military. After all, the research was generally conducted with civilian populations, usually college students.

Indeed, even in more pacific enterprises, a common response to heavy stress or to unexpected challenges is to cling to established beliefs or patterns of behavior. In confronting the unknown, that which is familiar, things to which we have become accustomed, can be of enormous, albeit temporary, comfort — even if these are of little use or even detrimental to dealing with new conditions or situations. The physician in the emergency room may not have the luxury to deliberately and systematically speculate on available options, as does his colleague who is preparing for surgery the following week. How much more is this the case in conditions or situations informed by the stresses and uncertainties of war? Consider, for example, the contributions of technology to the dilemmas facing the military.

Technological developments in the military, as in other areas, have exploded. Many of the senior commanders in World War II who had fought in World War I took a long time to integrate the changed technology developed between the wars into their operations. One has to wonder how such individuals would cope with the massive changes engendered by new weaponry, complex high-speed computers, or, for that matter, the motivation of the forces they would lead. The military academies are attempting to prepare their students for this ever-changing scene, but how much of the future can they anticipate? The one inescapable fact is that regardless of advances in equipment, there remains that human element which can subvert the contributions of any technology.

In analyzing the contributions of the human element, we have tried repeatedly to demonstrate that there is no single parsimonious explanation. Thus, for military leaders, we cannot simply lump all instances of inflexibility in thought and action as something only associated, for example, with the ever-popular authoritarian personality, that is, with that "type" of individual who is perceived (often correctly) as being most likely to choose a military career. Such a personality might well be more prone to falling into the trap of psychological rigidity. Yet, the pressures generated by war itself have been and continue to be of such a nature as to render everyone in decision-making positions, whether held by authoritarian personality types or not, open to the enticement and consequences of inflexibility.

As we have shown, particularly with reference to Frederick the Great, inflexibility can be traced back to deep-seated concerns and problems. For others, however, this trait can be seen as a response to some set of current circumstances that engender inflexibility by virtue of their unprecedented or unanticipated challenges. This may result in the unwillingness of a Lee to see that he is being confronted with something that is unprecedented, resulting in decisions or actions guided by personal schema impenetrable to choice. Throughout this work, we have recognized that whatever the sources or precipitating causes for inflexibility in wartime decisions, it is probably a very common form of dysfunctionalism. Moreover, as we have seen, it is not something that can be associated only with leaders who have gone into the history books as failures or as high-level mediocrities.

We believe we can buttress our rationale by briefly reviewing the eight case studies presented in this work. We shall then attempt to put a "gloss" over what we have found and present some general conclusions.

FREDERICK THE GREAT AT KUNERSDORF

Frederick II of Prussia, generally recognized as a true "military genius," maintained as his guiding principle that "the Prussian Army always attacks." He did this, we believe, for several reasons. First of all, as a child he had been subjected to the furious, often physical, assaults of his father, Frederick William. This, we believe, left him with a lifelong dread in which defeat inevitably was the result of being the helpless victim of an assault, or even being perceived of as such. Rather than being the passively waiting target, he operated almost axiomatically on the principle of seizing the initiative. While attacking is a legitimate tactical response, it is not necessarily applicable in all situations—unless forces outside of military logic are driving the decision.

Thus, in both of his major wars (the minor, comically stalemated "War of the Bavarian Succession," 1778–79, has not been considered), he saw to it that, whenever possible—and even at times when it proved to be impossible—the Prussian army advanced. Often, especially against second-rate opponents, this inflexible approach was crowned with success, although the toll was usually high for all concerned.

We have also hypothesized that high losses did not concern Frederick to any major extent due to the fact that the Prussian army, *the* major creation of his father, *was*, in fact, a deeply internalized symbol of Frederick William. Thus, battering it, even while achieving victories that were Frederick's alone, may well have proved to be psychologically satisfying. The disaster at Kunersdorf, a battle in which Frederick's inflexible adherence to the assault produced staggering casualties in a lost cause can, to a great extent, be seen as an outcome of Frederick's general approach to war, which in turn was a consequence of his paternal fear and hatred.

On the other hand, in assigning Kunersdorf to our speculations regarding Frederick, we have had to consider the problem of why the Russians seem to have brought out his worst generalship. Here, it has been suggested that Frederick, who viewed the Russians as savages and had little respect for them, additionally identified this foe with his father, further contributing to a figure whose savage behavior could elicit feelings of fear on Frederick's part, but for whom he had little respect. It has been hypothesized therefore, that when confronted with the Russians, powerfully affective aspects of Frederick's personality took over. The result was that he battered his father's instrument, the army, in frantic efforts to destroy an enemy that was itself an embodiment of the feared old patriarch.

NAPOLEON AND THE RUSSIAN CAMPAIGN

Napoleon's behavior in Russia must strike the attentive observer as odd. For a fact, it is the antithesis of his earlier campaigns. Once one penetrates beneath the layers of bellicose bombast and strained hyperbole, we find a general who possibly from the very beginning of the campaign, but certainly at least very early in its course, showed signs of *not* wanting to face the Russians, at least not directly.

Rather, he concerned himself with occupying and administrating territory. What resulted from this strategy was an inflexible commitment to a rapid advance in which Murat's cavalry was forced to set a literally killing pace. Moreover, even as Murat moved forward, the emperor himself often lagged behind, concerned with relatively trivial administrative issues. When, during the course of the advance to Moscow, Napoleon did encounter the Russians, a foe for which he seemed to have had mixed views, he really seemed uneager to fight them. As a consequence, his battlefield performance was extremely sloppy.

Until Waterloo, a little less than three years later, the Battle of Borodino was probably the worst fought of his career. Indeed, from what we know of it, Napoleon played little direct role in the engagement once it began. As we have seen, however, the emperor's indecisiveness and uncertainty resulted from an inflexible insistence on conquering and occupying territory at the cost of destroying enemy forces in the field. The Russian campaign became one in which he robbed himself of the flexibility that had played such a crucial role in his earlier successes.

Applying elements of field theory to explain his preoccupation with territorial gain, we have argued that this concern was counterbalanced by, or stemmed from, personal anxieties about confronting a foe that in many ways was a mystery to him. As was the case with Frederick, Napoleon perceived the Russians as both mysterious and savage. This eventually brought out Napoleon's worst generalship—albeit for somewhat different reasons—from one often also declared to be a "military genius." This, of course, would not be the last time.

McCLELLAN'S FLAWED CAMPAIGN

As has often been noted, George B. McClellan's campaign to seize Richmond in 1862 was a strategically sound plan—albeit largely on paper. It would allow him, in theory at least, to even the odds by limiting the geographical area in which his well-trained but, as he saw it, outnumbered forces would meet the enemy. McClellan, however, was himself an almost textbook case of someone who, while outwardly concerned with success, was in reality a hollow shell more concerned with avoiding any personal responsibility for failure.

As a consequence, once the campaign was under way, he hesitated at every critical moment. To justify his fears, he clung to a set of self-justifying beliefs that included wildly inflated estimates regarding the strength of Lee's heavily outnumbered forces. That being the case, he had to proceed with caution. On occasion, however, this otherwise most cautious of generals placed his army in tactically dangerous situations. At such times it appeared he was inviting a military disaster for which he could blame the distant and increasingly unsympathetic civilian leaders in Washington. He seemed to revel equally in the roles of martyr and general.

Ironically, the general who acquired the sobriquet of the "Young Napoleon" was, beneath the surface, an individual paralyzed by fears of failure. The result was that in situations where he could indeed act in a Napoleonic manner, if glory was on a par with failure, his personal conflicts undid him. Concerns for his army never went beyond concerns for himself, which he managed to equate to ease his mind. Yet, one can only wonder how the course of American history, and most certainly presidential politics, would have changed if McClellan had struck directly and swiftly at Richmond or ordered up his reserves at Antietam through the gap formed at the Bloody Lane.

LEE AT GETTYSBURG

Robert E. Lee's behavior on the third day of the Battle of Gettysburg was certainly in contrast to that of the timorous McClellan. For the unhappy soldiers of Pickett's and Pettigrew's divisions, condemned to the killing ground before Cemetery Ridge, this was most unfortunate. They went bravely to their fate, but one might suppose that not a few of the survivors thought Lee might have made a mistake this time. However, one did not openly criticize the godhead of the Confederacy. Besides, who else was there? Still, even at the very end of the war, Brig. Gen. Henry Wise told Lee that he had become the sole cause for continuing the fight. That kind of loyalty engendered an almost mystical belief that losing was simply not an option.

Lee, an offensively minded leader in the generally accepted Napoleonic tradition of that era, was for the most part forced to assume the tactical and strategic defensive by a foe that outnumbered him in manpower and resources. Still, he had been successful against an army commanded by a mind-boggling succession of mediocrities. Their contributions not unexpectedly led Lee down a path on which he became simply unwilling or unable to believe that at Gettysburg he was at last confronting a foe that, properly led, could stop him dead in his tracks. Major General George Meade, while not tactically gifted, was at least adequately competent, especially in a defensive situation. Adequacy was all that was needed to emerge victorious when, against all common sense, an outnumbered opponent led by a victory-gorged leader attacked him at precisely the expected point. His inflexible adherence to a plan based on previous Northern timidity and ineptitude savaged his army, even as Meade's hesitancy in following up a decisive victory allowed the war to drag on for another twenty-one months.

HOOD AND THE TENNESSEE CAMPAIGN

John Bell Hood was also an ardent devotee of the bold assault. Unlike Lee, however, he was rarely successful at it. His disastrous setbacks in the defense of Atlanta, as well as the failure of the Tennessee campaign, provide sufficient evidence for this assertion. In November 1864, sensing that his subordinates had deprived him of a possible overwhelming victory at Spring Hill, Tennessee, he was determined, once and for all, to purge his army of what he perceived to be timidity at all levels. The best way to accomplish this, of course, was to adhere all the more to the assault doctrine.

Our argument is that the attack was meant to accomplish two objectives: to defeat the Union army and to restore his own army's valor. These somewhat conflicting desires caused Hood to persist in an inflexible adherence to an approach that, at Franklin, insured both a tactical and strategic defeat.

In dealing with Hood's rigid mind-set at Franklin, we utilized as an explanatory model the frustration-aggression hypothesis. Less than a century later this model again proved useful when considering Adolf Hitler's performance at Stalingrad. Both strove to succeed not only in the more traditional military sense, but also to resolve personal issues. Both also discovered that the two objectives are not necessarily compatible—with disastrous consequences for their commands.

HAIG AND THE BRITISH MILITARY LEADERSHIP

In focusing upon British military leadership in World War I, we have devoted most of our attention to Sir Douglas Haig, as representative of the British high command. We noted earlier that Norman Dixon suggested that Haig's concern for success, and the career advancement attaching to it, might well be traced back to an authoritarian upbringing.[1] Success was seen as indicative of something approaching divine favor.

Although his behavior in World War I was consonant with the leading characteristics of such a personality, we chose to analyze Haig's performance as representative of problems presented by British military leadership as a whole. It is certainly plausible to suggest that Haig's colleagues were the products of similar upbringings. Dixon sees patterns of British military incompetence from the Crimean War on as indicative of this common background. However, we think that this sort of "cohort" approach—an approach that has been utilized brilliantly by Peter Loewenberg, among others—would go beyond the evidence available to the authors. Even assuming that Haig can be seen as an authoritarian personality, we chose instead to utilize the cognitive dissonance approach to deal with problems presented by World War I British military leadership as a whole.

This leadership, from the spring of 1915 up to and including the Flanders offensive in 1917, revealed an almost petulant unwillingness to break from prewar concepts. The most important of these was the emphasis upon the attack, properly supported by increasingly heavy concentrations of artillery, seizing ground from the enemy and holding it.

To be sure, as we pointed out, the military establishments of all the great powers involved in World War I emphasized what indeed came to be known as "the cult of the offensive." On the western front, however, its most persistent hold was upon British military thinking. The consequences of applying the prewar "system" to the realities posed by World War I were always the same, that is, minimal advances in exchange for staggeringly high casualties.

While attempting to preserve the integrity of a "system" in which the British military believed with the fervor of a religious principle, it was necessary that realities be ignored, overlooked, or in some cases reshaped. The cognitive dissonance model was one that appeared to offer the greatest potential for explanatory promise. Thus, no matter how badly things were going, everything was perceived of as going "according to plan." Breakthroughs were always "just around the corner," but even if none occurred, one could find solace in the knowledge that the enemy was being worn down in great, appropriately named, "wearing-down battles."

World War I—a war that even in a century in which wars can be seen as being unusually attritional in nature—involved a very pernicious form of psychological dysfunctionalism that paradoxically led to the belief that such tactics were indeed the correct solution. On one hand, dissonance prevented any rational balancing of losses against possible outcomes. On the other, if British military leaders had actually allowed themselves to know of the terrible toll attritional warfare was taking, and if they were not willing to continue to pursue the will-o'-the-wisp breakthrough (and instead accept wearing-down battles when this was seen as no longer possible), then perhaps they would not have had the stomach to persist in offensives that ultimately succeeded in wearing down an enemy poorer in men and resources.

CHURCHILL, HARRIS, AND STRATEGIC BOMBING

The problems posed by the conduct of British strategic bombing in World War II point to several varieties of inflexibility. First of all, there is Winston Churchill, who had shown an appreciation for the potential use of airpower as early as 1917 and was a strong supporter of the strategic bombing of Germany in World War II. Yet, in spite of this intense personal commitment, he seemed to have been unwilling to concern himself with operational planning, much less execution, to any significant degree.

In chapter 1 we focused on a cognitive-affective splitting with regard to Frederick the Great. The same problem seems to have afflicted Churchill. Recognizing that airpower had rendered traditional naval roles obsolete, and seeing that it had a crucial role in defeating Nazi Germany, he was nonetheless unable to rid himself of affective ties to almost romantic conceptions of warfare. In the end, Churchill was inflexibly bound to essentially nineteenth-century forms of warfare, resulting perhaps from his participation in one of the last formal charges made by British cavalry. Consequently, Churchill virtually surrendered operational planning and direction of the World War II British strategic bombing offensive to Air Marshal Arthur Harris.

Having become rigidly wedded to the doctrine of area bombing, Harris persisted in increasingly costly operations whose strategic value was, and remains, controversial. This inflexibility was articulated in an extremely simplistic trial-and-error approach that effectively precluded any significant challenge to established doctrine. Moreover, it might well be argued that changes being developed as improvements in tactics from this "hit-or-miss" system helped sustain the mass bombing strategy. In effect, the changes in tactics and technology never questioned the strategy itself.

Here, however, we confront an uncomfortable question raised by the British military in World War I. Even if one assumes that the destruction of German urban life was perhaps not as crucial as Harris and his supporters maintained, it might also be argued that it at least played a meaningful role in the Allied victory in World War II. Ultimately, as had been the case with regard to the British approach in World War I, Britain's World War II aerial offensive ended up being attritional in nature.

Perhaps in sustaining this terribly costly approach, rigidity—albeit not in a form covered by the cognitive dissonance hypothesis—had as important a role to play for Bomber Command in World War II as it had for French, Haig, and a variety of others in World War I. The question becomes: Did the rigid doctrine of area bombing held by Harris and, for that matter, by Churchill, have at least some value in contributing to victory? Whatever the answer, the very fact that the question can legitimately be posed is disquieting and offers if not a poignant commentary upon war in general, then at least on that variety of it engaged in by industrial societies.

HITLER AND STALINGRAD

The Battle of Stalingrad can and has been analyzed in terms reserved for more or less "conventional" engagements. It can and must be seen, however, as something that also resulted from attitudinal considerations in addition to military concerns. We have argued that when they became conflated, it necessitated a somewhat more multifaceted approach than demanded by more traditional considerations. This is particularly important when we bear in mind that Nazi ideology, at least as embodied by its most important and strident representative, Adolf Hitler, was to no small degree informed by individual pathology.

The parallels to Hood at Franklin are startling. Hood had his own particular ideology, namely, the doctrine of attack. The ghost of Verdun supplied Hitler with a rationale similar to that which Spring Hill provided for Hood. While Hood sought to purge his army of a certain weakness of ardor, Hitler was intent on punishing his generals. Finally, at the end, neither of them did or could recognize what they had done.

In our analysis of Stalingrad and Hitler's persistence in continuing the campaign, we found that some depth psychology was necessary to explain in part Hitler's motives. Hitler, like Frederick the Great—although probably not to the same degree—had been brutalized as a child. However, unlike that Prussian king for whom he had so much admiration, Hitler was doted on by a mother who, having lost three other children, treated him as someone special. The result was that he became an individual who, like Frederick, dreaded being an object of attack. In all circumstances, he felt that he had to be safe everywhere; he had to be able to seize the initiative, or at least be able to respond to any threat, real or imaginary.

Unlike Frederick, though, his mother's favor resulted in Hitler having a narcissistic personality. He thus could never own up to having made a mistake. Moreover, his fabled "will"—a cover for multiple insecurities—had always to prevail. At Stalingrad he became the National Socialist ideology incarnate, particularly when having to deal with, as he saw it, chicken-hearted generals who seemed determined to frustrate him.

Thus, he at times gave the distinct impression that he was as much at war with his own generals as he was with the Russians. This was particularly true in his dealings with the commander of the doomed Sixth Army, Friedrich Paulus, a man uncertain of his own role or abilities. Hitler was able to maintain a relationship that can be best described as *folie à deux*. Paulus could see for himself what conditions really were like and what was really happening. Hitler, at times through a sort of ideological surrogate, Arthur Schmidt, was able to convince Paulus that matters either could be set aright or at least were different than he, in some part of his mind, knew differently.

Of equal importance, however, was the fact that Paulus was part of an organization in which an especially pernicious form of groupthink prevailed at all levels. Thus, an uncertain Paulus, besides being under immense pressure from his führer, was also forced to conform to a widely held belief system, at the heart of which was a stereotyped view of the enemy, to say nothing of a downright contemptuous view of Germany's Romanian ally. Groupthink crumbled fairly rapidly after the massive Soviet counterattacks of mid-November 1942. By that time, however, it was too late, and vestiges of it were still perceivable in the command of the now critically endangered Sixth Army.

The would-be rescuer of this army was Erich von Manstein, who soon came to believe that the Sixth Army was doomed. Manstein, who never once visited the city, kept telling Paulus to fight his way out and link up with Hermann Hoth's Fourth Army. Of course, Manstein first needed to get Hitler's express approval for Paulus to start. Unfortunately for both, Hitler had declared that the city could never be abandoned, due largely to inflexible personal concerns that had found ideological expression. Indeed, Paulus on at least one occasion provided Hitler with arguments that the führer could and did use as objections against Paulus fighting his way out from the city.

When combined with motives and rationalizations that do not require psychological investigation, a variety of dysfunctional patterns of thought and behavior joined together to produce the inflexibility that doomed the Sixth Army to annihilation. The surviving pitiful remnant at last surrendered, but Paulus, who had been promoted to field marshal in the hope that he would kill himself, failed to do so. Hitler's victory over his generals, a group he perceived of as the source of his aggression-producing frustrations, was complete. As the half-starved survivors of the worst German military disaster up to that time trudged off to Soviet prison camps, Hitler's rage could in part be transformed into a sense of moral superiority.

A GLOSS AND CONCLUDING REMARKS

As indicated earlier in this chapter, dysfunctional thoughts, perceptions, and behavior influence all people, and thus can have untoward, or at least unexpected results in a variety of avocational situations. The basic argument is that the military leader is a psychological product of his life's experiences, and there is no exception to this fact of our existence. Both internal and external sets of factors contribute to any military decision, with the caveat being that what works in one situation may prove disastrous in another. In any event, we have considered cases in which demands posed on leaders under stress were responsible for strategy and tactics (or at times a lack of action) that flew in the face of military realities. Of course, any reader interested in military history can no doubt think of other, even more blatant, examples of inflexibility. The ones provided in this book come out of the authors' own interests and readings.

Again, it must be emphasized that inappropriate behavior is not solely confined to the military. In war, however, the consequences are usually fatal to a lot of people. As we noted previously, a physician may unexpectedly botch a diagnosis and the patient (singular) dies. This is not quite the same as the twenty-one thousand Englishmen killed on the first day of the Somme offensive in 1916. Furthermore, while the Somme offensive proceeded unabated, usually there is an investigation after a failed routine operation, with the physician asked to explain the causes. In fact, he may be asked to cease his surgical practice until the matter is resolved. Haig, on the other hand, answered to no one after that first day and continued blithely on until things became quite impossible to ignore.

Our arguments concerning both personal and environmental factors should not be construed as one dominating the other. For example, in discussing Haig's failings we acknowledge the contributions of his authoritarian personality. However, it is equally true that cultural attitudes may prove to be a major contributor to command failures, even overriding personality constructs.

This was particularly noticeable with regard to attitudes toward the Russians, which created some unusual and additional problems for Frederick the Great, Napoleon, and Hitler. For good historical reasons, Russia has often been viewed as a rather primitive place, a sort of antediluvian shambles that, thanks to social and economic backwardness, would crumble with appropriate military pressure. Frederick the Great, Napoleon, and Hitler and their supporting minions all thought so and planned and acted accordingly. In any event, stereotyping supported by accompanying ideological superstitions often becomes, in large measure, a sort of quasi-religious rationalization for the stereotypes. This can infuse inflexibility with a sense of purpose that borders on the ethical: That is, how can one not defeat these people?

Nor is this denigration confined to the Russians. When the Japanese military command started to war-game the Midway invasion, the staff would not accept a situation in which the Americans might spot the Japanese fleet first. The Battle of the Coral Sea might have provided some evidence for that new scenario, but the Japanese admirals did not even remotely consider the possibility. They believed the submarine cordon would provide early warning (it arrived too late), the *Yorktown* could not possibly be ready (it was), and the American admirals were not ready or capable of defeating the Japanese fleet (a rather serious error in judgment). Yamamoto was more realistic about the Americans, but he was racing against time.

Even today, the cultural influences encompassing armed combat still remain, although the scope of battle has diminished considerably. There is simply no comparison, in terms of the numbers of troops involved, between Operation Desert Storm or the U.S. invasion of Afghanistan and the Battle of Stalingrad. Moreover, although the area of conflict has been reduced, modern weaponry has produced significantly greater casualties than might be predicted for the size of the forces engaged. Moreover, if one reads the accusations hurled at each other's foe or foes, and the accompanying rationale for assuming a Just Cause, nothing has really changed. The need, therefore, for belief systems of one sort or another remains. Since the revolutionary age, which produced Napoleon, such systems, as well as the military establishments that have functioned as their expression, have been facts of life. A fact of life, as the negotiators would tell anyone, is that Serbs and Croats simply do not like each other.

Thus, in arguing about the relative strength of the factors impinging upon military decisions, we recognize that at a given point in time no universal psychological model suffices. Moreover, both people and circumstances change. American psychologist Edwin Guthrie has noted that the single best predictor of what a person will do in a given situation is what he did in the past, but the axiom is based on group data. You simply cannot bet with absolute certainty that the truism will hold for a particular individual—hence, the unexpected can happen. Who would have guessed that Ulysses S. Grant, a failed entrepreneur and sometimes drunk, would be the one to finally organize the might of the North into a crushing force?

In writing this work we have revealed a fair amount about ourselves. Among other things, it is perhaps painfully obvious that our motives were informed by a certain degree of morbid curiosity. It is in this context that we bear in mind the words of Russell F. Weigley:

> The grand-scale battle, with tens of thousands of soldiers fighting, cursing, trembling, falling, screaming in agony, dying, all in a spectacle covering an amphitheater-like field—this dramatic epitome of war is the chief source of the enduring fascination of military history. The thirst to experience vicariously the intense emotions of battle goes far to explain why books of military history are written and read, however much their authors and readers may profess higher concerns about removing or at least palliating the scourge of war.[2]

Of greater importance, however, is the fact that, while critical of both war and the nation state, they seem to have accepted them as givens, as part of the human condition. To be sure, Weigley, without question one of the most honest of those who have chosen to confront the issue of why people—particularly males, one supposes—are fascinated by military history, declared that, in analyzing major battles between the Thirty Years' War and the age of Napoleon, warfare was almost never decisive in determining political issues of real importance. Turning Carl von Clausewitz on his head, he ended his truly extraordinary work with the following observation: "war was not the extension of policy but the bankruptcy of policy."[3] Yet, according to Martin van Creveld, another justifiably respected military historian, even if the nation-state "idea" becomes increasingly represented by bands of international thugs and terrorists (and, one should recall, he wrote this work ten years before the atrocities of September 2001), the fascination of particularly men with war will never end. In the end, many will prefer to abandon families, or even singular sensual relationships with women, than to give up the visceral excitement of combat. I think that even those fascinated by the hideousness of the military experience sincerely hope that this man is wrong in his dystopian vision.[4] Again, although we have accepted war and the nation state as "kind of giveaways," they have shown no small degree of inflexibility of their own. Perhaps historians of a better future will chide us for our narrowness. Better that than having no one at all left to condemn us for being unable to extricate ourselves from a parochialism that, in however minuscule fashion, contributed to the destruction of our planet.

Ultimately, of course, war, by its very nature, is itself a testimony to life-denying inflexibility. Seeking out patterns of inflexibility within it leads one down the path of infinite regress. In the end, efforts to rationalize the irrational by somehow suggesting that it can be made more acceptable if only its planners and participants were just a bit more flexible in how they went about doing their jobs could well lead to that ultimate absurdity best captured by the poet Archibald MacLeish:

The End of the World

Quite unexpectedly, as Vasserot
The armless ambidextrian was lighting
A match between his great and second toe,
And Ralph the lion was engaged in biting
The neck of Madame Sossman while the drum
Pointed, and Teeny was about to cough
In waltz-time swinging Jocko by the thumb—

Quite unexpectedly the top blew off:
And there, there overhead, there, there hung over
Those thousands of white faces, those dazed eyes,
There in the starless dark the poise, the hover,
There with vast wings across the cancelled skies,
There in the sudden blackness the black pall
Of nothing, nothing, nothing—nothing at all.[5]

NOTES

Preface

1. Gordon W. Prange, with Donald M. Goldstein and Katherine V. Dillon, *Miracle at Midway*, pp. 370–71.

Introduction

1. Norman Dixon, *On the Psychology of Military Incompetence*.
2. See Dixon's efforts to deal with Montgomery's botched effort at Arnhem, ibid., pp. 145–48.
3. This is a paraphrase of "from private neurosis to public policy" in Robert G. L. Waite's *The Psychopathic God: Adolf Hitler*, where it is the title of his chapter 5.

1. Frederick the Great at Kunersdorf, August 12, 1759

1. Gerhard Ritter, *Frederick the Great: A Historical Profile*, p. 133.
2. Ibid.
3. According to legend, Frederick, recognizing that Hohenfriedberg had been a true "soldier's battle," wrote the "Hohenfriedberg March," dedicating it to the Prussian army. Recent scholarship, however, has called into question the notion that Frederick actually wrote this stirring piece of music.
4. Statistical data has been taken from Sidney B. Fay and Klaus Epstein, *The Rise of Brandenburg-Prussia to 1786*, p. 126. A *taler* (also spelled *thaler*), from which the term *dollar* is derived, was a silver coin worth approximately three marks, or about $1.20. It was first coined in Bohemia in 1518, at the town of Joachimsthaler, hence the title was an abbreviation.
5. The oblique battle order itself was hardly original. The first use of it of which we are certain was by Epaminondas of Thebes, who employed it to defeat the Spartans at the Battle of Leuctra in 371 B.C. What it involved was the holding back ("refusing") of one flank or "wing" and concentrating upon the other flank. Thus, a numerically inferior army could "go up" its opponent.
6. Even when the mercenary element in Frederick's army waxed large, the "native" contingents were often relied upon in especially desperate situations.

7. While most psychology courses carefully distinguish between operant conditioning (voluntary cognitive behavior) and classical conditioning (involuntary, including emotional behaviors), the fact is that both are functional in all endeavors. Examples of purely operant-type behaviors generally do not exceed in complexity certain kinds of licking responses in rats.

8. Anna Freud, *The Ego and Mechanisms of Defense.*

9. Frederick the Great, *Frederick the Great on the Art of War*, pp. 178–82.

10. Ibid., pp. 142–43, and 172–76.

11. Ibid., p. 143.

12. Ibid., p. 176.

13. Ibid., p. 172.

14. At Kolin, Frederick's fanaticism for the offense was responsible for an altercation between him and some of his soldiers, about forty all told. Furious at his impending defeat, he wanted to lead this handful of men against a well-emplaced Austrian battery. For once, the commonsensical aspect of the Prussian peasant prevailed: An adjutant responded to Frederick's tirades by inquiring, "Will your majesty take the battery alone?" William Fiddian Reddaway, *Frederick the Great and the Rise of Prussia*, p. 224.

15. Ritter, *Frederick the Great*, p. 135.

16. Frederick, *On the Art of War*, p. 266.

17. Ibid., p. 265.

18. Ibid., p. 266.

19. The phrase "The Prussian army must always attack the enemy" is one that appeared in his writing as late as 1770. This can be seen as demonstrating an extraordinary inflexibility on Frederick's part and an unwillingness to assimilate painfully taught lessons. It probably also can be seen as pointing to the tenacious hold that powerful psychological needs exercised upon his thoughts and actions.

20. Ibid., p. 359.

21. Jay Luvaas, Introduction to Frederick, *On the Art of War*, p. 25. In this regard, one could compare the general eighteenth-century approach to that of George B. McClellan whose tactics during the peninsular campaign and at the Battle of Antietam pointed to an almost perverse unwillingness—for a general at least—to assume risk. McClellan, however, apparently was motivated in part by a desire to avoid heavy losses, i.e., by a benign concern for his men. At the same time, however, as will be pointed out in a later chapter, McClellan's "limited risk" approach often served to put his troops in great danger. Eighteenth-century generals tended to view losses in fiscal and resource terms. Frederick in particular never expressed inordinate concern for the welfare of his troops, except where it might have benefited him politically.

22. For a fine discussion of such problems, see Ritter, *Frederick the Great*, pp. 133–38.

23. It was rigid adherence to Frederican tactics—or what at least were perceived as such—that contributed to Prussia's downfall in 1806. The looser Napoleonic formations, and the Corsican's use of skirmishers and snipers, confronted his dim-witted opponents with a deadly bafflement. Parenthetically, while it is true that Frederick had several Jäger units in his army, there never were enough of them to make much of a difference.

24. For examples of such bombast, see Friedrich von Bernhardi, *How Germany Makes War*, pp. 178, 218.

25. Delbrück was particularly critical of Frederick's unwillingness to concentrate his forces, something upon which Napoleon placed a great deal of emphasis both hypothetically and in practice. For Frederick it would appear that his concerns in this regard were mostly hypothetical. See Hans Delbrück, *Geschichte des Kriegskunst, im Rahmen der politische Geschichte, vierten Teil*, p. 428.

26. A most interesting, if somewhat naïve account of Frederick's behavior at Hochkirch has been provided by Ernst Friedrich Rudolf von Barewisch in his memoirs, *Meine Kriegserlebnisse in den Jahren 1757–1763*. Most of the appropriate portions concerning Hochkirch are in Peter Paret, comp., *Frederick the Great: A Profile*, pp. 121–28. From the description provided here, it would appear that Frederick did not recognize the necessity of retreating until the last possible moment.

27. Christopher Duffy, *The Military Life of Frederick the Great*, p. 177.

28. Quoted in ibid., p. 178.

29. In a letter for his father dated September 11, 1728, Frederick wrote that his conscience was clear with respect to his father and that he no longer thought his father was a kind man (see Louis L. Snyder, *Frederick the Great*, pp. 41–42). His father's reply indicates that he recognized Frederick's stubbornness as aggressive behavior: "You care for nothing but having your own way."

30. Persons characterized as having adopted learned helplessness assume that events are independent of one's efforts. They do not cope with the environment, believing that their actions do not count. See Martin E. P. Seligman, *Helplessness: On Depression, Development, and Death*.

31. A very good treatment of this is in Edith Simon, *The Making of Frederick the Great*, pp. 57–58. This story, which Simon herself said was possibly "just an extra" (p. 4), has been challenged by many historians, among them a recent biographer. See Robert B. Asprey, *Frederick the Great: The Magnificent Enigma*, p. 40.

32. With regard to flute playing as subliminal exercise, see Simon, *Making of Frederick the Great*, p. 258.

33. This phrase appeared in a 1744 "instruction" for the young duke, Karl Eugen von Württemberg. See "Fürstenspiegel oder Unterwiesung des Königs für der jungen Herzog Karl Eugen von Württemberg (1744)," in *Ausgewählte Werke Friedrich des Grosses, zweiter Band, Politische und Philosophisches Schriften, Gedichte und Briefe*, ed. Gustav Berthold Volz, p. 39.

34. Erik H. Erikson, "Identity and the Life Cycle," p. 92.

35. Which is not to say that major Enlightenment figures were not themselves prejudiced. Voltaire's anti-Semitism is well known.

36. Rollo May, *Power and Innocence*, p. 40.

37. For a good sketch of Frederick William's diplomatic bumbling, see H. W. Koch, *A History of Prussia*.

38. According to one military historian, "The army of Frederick the Great, properly speaking, came into existence only from 1763, and it was to be inferior in almost every respect to its predecessor." See Duffy, *Military Life*, p. 245.

39. See Simon, *Making of Frederick the Great*, pp. 152–83, 264–65, 268.

40. As quoted in ibid., p. 272.

41. Ibid., pp. 272–73. Simon shows considerable insight in this. In Frederick's eyes, his boorish and cruel father was a figure to be feared but not respected. Thus, he could, in the end, be "the better man."

42. On Frederick's lack of identification with what was in truth his father's army, see Ritter, *Frederick the Great*, pp. 118–19.

43. On Kolin and Torgau, respectively, see Duffy, *Military Life*, pp. 130–31 and 218.

44. On his contempt for the Russians, see Ritter, *Frederick the Great*, pp. 96, 107. Also, Ludwig Reiners, *Frederick the Great: A Biography*, p. 196. At times, particularly when comparing his own troubles with those of his generals, he would comment on Russian toughness, but this seemed to be more of a device to excuse himself for disasters such as Kunersdorf. See Asprey, p. 514.

45. Reddaway, *Frederick the Great*, pp. 271–72.

46. Carl von Clausewitz, *On War*, p. 298. Sources often differ widely with regard to casualties. This is particularly the case in eighteenth-century battles. Depending on whom one reads, Frederick lost anywhere from 19,000 to 25,000 men at Kunersdorf, and between 13,000 and 17,000 at Torgau (November, 1759). On Kunersdorf, please see Russell F. Weigley, *The Age of Battles: The Quest for Decisive Warfare from Breitenfeld to Waterloo*, pp. 190–91, and Giles MacDonogh, *Frederick the Great: A Life in Deed and Letters*, pp. 286–87. For Torgau, see Weigley, *Age of Battles*, pp. 192–93; Mac-Donogh, *Frederick the Great*, pp. 300–301.

47. Quoted in Asprey, *Frederick the Great*, p. 520.

48. This demonstrated the eighteenth-century concern with secure territory and supply lines rather than with the outright destruction of the enemy's army. However, as we have seen, Frederick, too, was consistently concerned with holding on to Silesia and with covering Berlin, which was temporarily occupied anyhow by the Russians in 1760. See Delbrück, *Geschichte des Kriegskunst*, pp. 428–29.

49. Reddaway, *Frederick the Great*, p. 275.

50. Quoted in Snyder, *Frederick the Great*, p. 21.

51. In one way, at least, Frederick *did* anticipate Napoleon: His ego seemed to be involved only with those troops under his immediate command. It was Napoleon's apparent indifference to Wellington's consistent shattering of French armies in Portugal and Spain that was responsible for his declaration, before the Battle of Waterloo, that Wellington was a "bad general," that the British were "bad troops," and that what was about to occur would be a "picnic."

52. Delbrück, *Geschichte des Kriegskunst*, p. 430.

53. In a battle of encounter, swiftness of initial action might be suitable. In this instance, however, Frederick was moving upon a foe who was entrenched and waiting.

54. Duffy, *Military Life*, p. 313.

55. William F. Battig, "Parsimony or Psychology?"

56. Fred I. Greenstein, *Personality and Politics: Problems of Evidence, Inference, and Conceptualization*, p. 54. Emphasis in original.

57. MacDonogh, *Frederick the Great*, p. 75.

58. Ritter, *Frederick the Great*, p. 133.

2. *Napoleon in Russia*, 1812

1. Morton Deutsch, "Field Theory in Social Psychology," p. 182.

2. Kurt Lewin, A *Dynamic Theory of Personality*.

3. Robert W. Leeper, *Lewin's Topological and Vector Psychology: A Digest and a Critique*.

4. Kurt Lewin, *Principles of Topological Psychology*, p. 181.

5. Deutsch, "Field Theory," p. 191.

6. Leeper, *Lewin's Topological and Vector Psychology*, pp. 92–95.

7. Ibid., p. 205. We will ignore such other characteristics as permeability-fluidity-rigidity and reality-irreality since they do not contribute to the main thrust of this analysis.

8. Lewin, cited in Deutsch, "Field Theory," p. 204.

9. Owen Connelly, *Blundering to Glory: Napoleon's Military Campaigns*, pp. 1–2, 221–22.

10. The taking of territory and destruction of enemy forces were tied together in the early Italian campaigns.

11. Connelly, *Blundering to Glory*, p. 222.

12. Alan Palmer, *Napoleon in Russia*, p. 108.

13. Connelly, *Blundering to Glory*, pp. 87–90.

14. Ibid., pp. 105–107.

15. Ibid., pp. 108–10.

16. Ibid., pp. 112–16.

17. Curtis Cate, *The War of the Two Emperors: The Duel Between Napoleon and Alexander—Russia, 1812*, pp. 87–88; Connelly, *Blundering to Glory*, pp. 158–59.

18. General Carl von Clausewitz put the number of combat troops at 489,000 plus about 150,000 noncombat troops. R. F. Delderfield, in *The Retreat from Moscow*, put the number of combat troops at 350,000. To this he added 150,000 noncombat troops. Due to the fact that von Clausewitz was a highly skilled military observer, particularly so with regard to logistical matters, we tend to favor his estimate. So do most general sources.

19. Gen. Armand de Caulaincourt, *With Napoleon in Russia: The Memoirs of General de Caulaincourt, Duke of Vicenza*, p. 5.

20. Count Philippe-Paul de Ségur, *Napoleon's Russian Campaign*, from the editor's preface, p. xiii.

21. Caulaincourt, *With Napoleon in Russia*, p. 28.

22. Ibid., p. 32. Emphasis in original.

23. Connelly, *Blundering to Glory*, pp. 157–58.

24. As quoted in ibid., p. 160.

25. Anthony Brett-Jones, *1812: Eyewitness Accounts of Napoleon's Defeat in Russia*, from the Introduction, pp. 6–7.

26. Cate, *War of the Two Emperors*, p. 77; Palmer, *Napoleon in Russia*, p. 20.

27. L. Henry La Chouque, *Napoléon: 20 ans de Campagnes*, pp. 241–42.

28. Brett-Jones, *1812*, from the Introduction, pp. 6–7.

29. La Chouque, *Napoléon*, p. 233.

30. Palmer, *Napoleon in Russia*, p. 65; Cate, *War of the Two Emperors*, pp. 153–55.

31. Cate, *War of the Two Emperors*, p. 155.

32. Ibid., p. 161.

33. Ségur, *Napoleon's Russian Campaign*, p. 31.

34. Brett-Jones, *1812*, quotation from Maj. Marie-Joseph Rossetti, p. 58.

35. As quoted in ibid., p. 93.

36. Ségur, *Napoleon's Russian Campaign*, p. 34.

37. As quoted in Delderfield, *Retreat from Moscow*, p. 54. Emphasis in original.

38. As quoted in Palmer, *Napoleon in Russia*, p. 81.

39. Several authors vary between 155,000 and 165,000 men. General von Clausewitz offered the highest estimate: 182,000 men.

40. Of particular interest is Carl von Clausewitz, *The Campaign of 1812 in Russia*, p. 57. According to Clausewitz, such a thinning out of resources affected mostly Davout (whose name he spells "Davoust").

41. Connelly, *Blundering to Glory*, p. 164.

42. Curtis Cate is a particularly severe critic.

43. As an example of this, see Cate's discussion in *War of the Two Emperors*, pp. 206–10.

44. Ibid., pp. 217–18.

45. Ségur, *Napoleon's Russian Campaign*, p. 59.

46. Palmer, *Napoleon in Russia*, p. 108.

47. Ségur, *Napoleon's Russian Campaign*, p. 63. See Arno Karten, *Napoleon's Glands: And Other Ventures in Biohistory*, p. 10. While cautioning against efforts to tie Napoleon's behavior to physical or psychological disorders, Karten suggests that, at Borodino and elsewhere, the emperor suffered primarily from bilharzia, probably con-

tracted when he was in Egypt in 1798–99. See *Napoleon's Glands*, pp. 18–19. With regard to the role Napoleon's health played in his military decision making, see also Weigley, *Age of Battles*, p. 449.

48. Brett-Jones, *1812*, quotation from Gen. Jean Rapp, p. 120.

49. Ibid., quotation from Colonel Lejeine, p. 132.

50. As quoted in Caulaincourt, *With Napoleon in Russia*, p. 99.

51. Ségur, *Napoleon's Russian Campaign*, p. 67.

52. Brett-Jones, *1812*, quotation from Rapp, p. 130.

53. As quoted in Ségur, *Napoleon's Russian Campaign*, p. 69.

54. Ibid.

55. von Clausewitz, *Campaign of 1812*, p. 115.

56. Ségur, *Napoleon's Russian Campaign*, p. 71. Emphasis in original.

57. As quoted in ibid.

58. As quoted in ibid., p. 74.

59. As quoted in Caulaincourt, *With Napoleon in Russia*, p. 103.

60. Charles Fair, *From the Jaws of Victory: A Study of Military Stupidity from Crassus to Westmoreland*, p. 182. A "fugue" state is one in which a person seems to suffer from amnesia, acts as if he or she were another person, and has no memory of what has occurred afterward.

61. Napoleon's behavior at Borodino can be compared to that of Maj. Gen. Ambrose Burnside at the Battle of Fredericksburg, December 13, 1882. As Burnside, for the most part quaking in his tent, heard of the slaughter of his men on the other side of the Rappahannock, he continuously cried out: "Oh those men, those men over there! I cannot get them out of my mind." As Fair put it, "It was almost as if they had been overtaken by some great natural disaster, at which Burnside, like everyone else present, had simply been a stunned spectator" (Fair, *From the Jaws of Victory*, p. 253).

62. Ségur, *Napoleon's Russian Campaign*, p. 80.

63. Georges Blond, *La Grande Armée, 1804–1815*, p. 345. Cate suggests that Napoleon's losses at Borodino were quite a bit higher. See Cate, *War of the Two Emperors*, p. 255.

64. Ségur, *Napoleon's Russian Campaign*, pp. 80–81.

65. As quoted in Palmer, *Napoleon in Russia*, pp. 129–30.

66. As quoted in ibid.

67. As quoted in ibid.

68. Napoleon Bonaparte, *Correspondance de Napoleon I*, p. 24:207.

69. Ségur, *Napoleon's Russian Campaign*, p. 82.

70. Caulaincourt, *With Napoleon in Russia*, p. 135.

71. Ibid., p. 139.

72. Ségur, *Napoleon's Russian Campaign*, p. 128.

73. Ibid., p. 129.

74. As quoted in Caulaincourt, p. 155.

75. Napoleon Bonaparte, *Memoirs of Napoleon Bonaparte, the Court of the First Empire*, p. 3:868.

76. Caulaincourt, *With Napoleon in Russia*, p. 155.

77. Ibid., p. 209.

78. Cate, *War of the Two Emperors*, p. 161.

79. Lewin, cited in Deutsch, "Field Theory," p. 200.

80. Deutsch, "Field Theory," p. 205.

81. D. Cartwright, "Decision-time in Relation to the Differentiation of the Phenomenal Field," *Psychological Review* 48 (1941).

82. To some extent, the reality-irreality dimension for regions applies here — Napoleon could not continue to ignore the skirmishing around the city, as well as the ruined condition of Moscow. He may have tried to convince himself earlier that all was well, but selectivity of perception and judgment can only go so far.

83. Bonaparte, *Correspondance*, p. 24:190.

84. We have already considered the criticism of Curtis Cate. One of Kutuzov's most severe contemporary critics was von Clausewitz. See his discussion of Kutuzov, in von Clausewitz, *Campaign of 1812*, p. 141, where he launches a furious attack upon the former's conduct at the Battle of Borodino.

85. General Wilson was a critic of Kutuzov, but even he was forced to admit the Russian general's somewhat Fabian tactics had managed to preserve the Russian army as an intact striking force. See Palmer, *Napoleon in Russia*, p. 224.

86. Caulaincourt, *With Napoleon in Russia*, p. 237.

87. Ségur, *Napoleon's Russian Campaign*, p. 184.

88. Bonaparte, *Memoirs*, pp. 884–85.

89. Brett-Jones, *1812*, quotation from Capt. Louis Begos, p. 257.

90. La Chouque, *Napoléon*, p. 267; Palmer, *Napoleon in Russia*, p. 240.

91. As an example of this, see La Chouque, *Napoléon*, p. 275.

92. Bonaparte, *Correspondance*, p. 24:277.

93. Ibid., p. 329.

94. As quoted in Caulaincourt, *With Napoleon in Russia*, p. 277.

95. As quoted in Blond, *La Grande Armée*, p. 397.

96. A very fine, and pithy, analysis of Napoleon's masterful conduct of post-1812 disaster campaigns is found in Weigley, *Age of Battles*, chaps. 17 and 18.

97. As quoted in Delderfield, *Retreat from Moscow*, p. 226.

98. As quoted in Brett-Jones, *1812*, p. 263.

99. As quoted in Felix Markham, *Napoleon*, p. 194.

100. As quoted in von Clausewitz, *Campaign of 1812*, pp. 69–70.

3. McClellan's Flawed Campaign

1. Philip Langer, "Malvern Hill (July 1, 1862): A Behavioral Analysis" (paper presented at the annual meeting of the Rocky Mountain Psychological Association, Denver, Colo., May 1981).

2. James M. McPherson, *Crossroads of Freedom: Antietam*, p. 13.

3. Ibid., p. 14.

4. T. Harry Williams, *McClellan, Sherman, and Grant*, p. 31.

5. Stephen W. Sears, *George B. McClellan: The Young Napoleon*, pp. 130–31.

6. Ibid., pp. 149–50.

7. McPherson, *Crossroads of Freedom*, p. 28.

8. Capt. Robert E. Lee, *Recollections and Letters of General Robert E. Lee*, p. 416.

9. James Longstreet, *From Manassas to Appomattox*, p. 66.

10. Ibid., p. 220.

11. James Longstreet, "The Seven Days, Including Frayser's Farm," in *Battles and Leaders of the Civil War: Being for the Most Part Contributions by Union and Confederate Officers*, p. 2:405.

12. Warren W. Hassler Jr., *George B. McClellan: Shield of the Union*, pp. xv–xvi.

13. See, e.g., George B. McClellan, *McClellan's Own Story: The War for the Union, The Soldiers Who Fought It, the Civilians Who Directed It and His Relations to It and to Them*, p. 343. This work was published two years after McClellan died. In describing

the benefits of a move to the James and subsequent operations, McClellan appears to assume that once he decides what he wants to do, the enemy would oblige his moves. Thus, in explaining why he did not concentrate north of the Chickahominy, he argued in effect that the strategy would not work because the enemy would not meet McClellan's needs (ibid., pp. 422–23).

14. Williams, *McClellan, Sherman, and Grant*, pp. 23–25.

15. Sears, *McClellan*, p. 104.

16. William S. Myers, *A Study in Personality: General George Brinton McClellan*, pp. 21–22.

17. McClellan, *McClellan's Own Story*, p. 408. In a letter dated June 22, 1862, McClellan wrote: "Every poor fellow that is killed or wounded almost haunts me."

18. William S. McFeely, *Grant: A Biography*. See, e.g., comments on pp. 37 and 110. While neither McFeely nor Myers would argue that this was the whole story, it seems certain in McClellan's case that the shock of battle was at best a rationalization for his failures.

19. Myers, *Study in Personality*, p. 21.

20. McPherson, *Crossroads of Freedom*, p. 14.

21. Thomas Rowland, *George B. McClellan and Civil War History: In the Shadow of Grant and Sherman*, pp. 45–46.

22. Ibid., p. 11.

23. Ibid., pp. 16–20.

24. Henry Alexander Murray, *Explorations in Personality: A Clinical and Experimental Study of Fifty Men of College Age*, p. 80.

25. Ibid., pp. 81–82.

26. Ibid., pp. 76–77.

27. Ibid., pp. 39–43.

28. Ibid., p. 118.

29. Ibid., p. 120.

30. Sears, *McClellan*, p. 106. McClellan could never accept the fact he had blundered, although in the West Virginia campaign there was evidence of indecision and a willingness to blame others under his command (ibid., pp. 90–92).

31. Elizabeth G. French and Francis H. Thomas, "The Relationship of Scientific Motivation and Problem-Solving Effectiveness," *Journal of Abnormal and Social Psychology* 56 (1958): 45–49.

32. Richard De Charms and George H. Moeller, "Values Expressed in American Children's Readers," *Journal of Abnormal and Social Psychology* 62 (1964): pp. 136–42.

33. Myers, *Study in Personality*, pp. 3–5.

34. John W. Atkinson, "The Mainsprings of Achievement-Oriented Activity," in *Motivation and Achievement*, ed. John W. Atkinson and Joel O. Raynor, p. 20.

35. Ibid., pp. 30–33.

36. Ibid., p. 18.

37. Sears, *McClellan*, pp. 89–90.

38. Ibid., p. 295.

39. Ibid., pp. 311–15.

40. A good layman's analysis of McClellan's fears was undertaken by James V. Murfin in chapter 1 of *The Gleam of Bayonets: The Battle of Antietam and the Maryland Campaign of 1862*. Many of his peers (e.g., Meade) were aware of his problems and actually saw him as afraid of failure.

41. McClellan, *McClellan's Own Story*, pp. 227–28. The Confederate withdrawal actually forced a change to the Fort Monroe landing, although McClellan states that it was an administrative decision.

42. Hassler, *McClellan*, p. 60. The Confederates saw this as a good move, too.

43. Ibid., p. 33.

44. McClellan, *McClellan's Own Story*, pp. 229–30. A letter to Secretary of War Edwin Stanton is most revealing. McClellan takes justifiable pride in his organization of the Army of the Potomac, but insists it was not prepared to attack.

45. Sears, *McClellan*, pp. 132, 138–46.

46. Ibid., p. 134.

47. Fair, *From the Jaws of Victory*, p. 206. McClellan advances the same ideas in *McClellan's Own Story*, p. 121.

48. Shelby Foote, *The Civil War: A Narrative*, p. 1:410.

49. Williams, *McClellan, Sherman, and Grant*, p. 21.

50. Myers, *Study in Personality*, p. 234.

51. Hassler, *McClellan*, pp. 51–52.

52. Ibid., p. 63. See also Foote, *Civil War*, p. 1:405.

53. Sears, *McClellan*, pp. 106–107. Sears refers to a "messianic complex."

54. McClellan, *McClellan's Own Story*. Writing some twenty years later, McClellan was still convinced he had been a victim of plots by others, especially Stanton. However, the purpose of the argument seems more to support his devoutly held belief that he had been hamstrung militarily; pp. 281–83.

55. McClellan, *McClellan's Own Story*, p. 254. The first troops left in mid-March (Hassler, *McClellan*, p. 72).

56. McClellan, *McClellan's Own Story*, p. 235.

57. Foote, *Civil War*, pp. 399–407.

58. Sears, *McClellan*, pp. 170–71.

59. Ibid., pp. 170–71.

60. Ibid., p. 179.

61. Ibid., pp. 172, 179. They believed that the Confederates had an army of 150,000 troops assembled for a raid on Washington.

62. Ibid., p. 175.

63. McClellan, *McClellan's Own Story*, pp. 267–70. He cited numerous other individuals to support his contention, but the purpose was always the same: to justify his attempt at a siege, the safest course of action.

64. Bruce Catton, *This Hallowed Ground: The Story of the Union Side of the Civil War*, p. 129. McClellan had at least fifty thousand troops to Magruder's fifteen thousand.

65. Hassler, *McClellan*, p. 88.

66. Ibid., p. 87.

67. McClellan, *McClellan's Own Story*, p. 264.

68. Catton, *Terrible Swift Sword*, p. 320. Franklin was released April 10, and would arrive April 20.

69. Ibid., pp. 289–90.

70. Hassler, *McClellan*, pp. 110–11.

71. Richard De Charms, *Personal Causation: The Internal Affective Determinants of Behavior*, pp. 273–74.

72. Sears, *McClellan*, p. 189. He was forever the eternal victim.

73. Myers, *Study in Personality*, p. 210. As early as the fall of 1861, McClellan vastly overestimated Confederate resources. Pinkerton, to be sure, was generally inept in this matter (as were others), but more important, his exaggerations served to strengthen McClellan's evident desire to delay. Hassler also points out this theme in McClellan's thinking, but he never comes to grip with the significance of this belief (*McClellan*, pp. 29–30).

74. Antietam is another example of this tragic flaw in McClellan's personality. Even when given Lee's plans, he hesitated, suggested he was outnumbered, and attacked in a piecemeal manner. The delay was tactically fatal, but McClellan thought he was lessening the possibility of failure, which he considered to be more critical than fighting at some risk, which might lead to victory.

75. McClellan, *McClellan's Own Story*, p. 265.

76. Ibid., p. 265.

77. Sears, *McClellan*, p. 191.

78. See Smith's report in *The War of the Rebellion: A Compilation of the Official Records of the Union and Confederate Armies*, ser. 1, vol. 11, pt. 1, pp. 365–66. Hereafter referred to as OR. Unless otherwise stated, material is from series 1.

79. McClellan, *McClellan's Own Story*, p. 289.

80. Sears, *McClellan*, p. 182. To McClellan, proper warfare was a script in which he organized the actions for both sides.

81. Catton, *Terrible Swift Sword*, pp. 294–95.

82. Foote, *Civil War*, pp. 1:410–11.

83. Hassler, *McClellan*, p. 107. Hassler as well as others have noted how early in the campaign McClellan began contemplating this major shift in strategy.

84. McClellan, *McClellan's Own Story*, p. 343.

85. Sears, *McClellan*, pp. 191–92. See also Hassler, *McClellan*, pp. 111–12.

86. McClellan, *McClellan's Own Story*, p. 364.

87. Ibid., pp. 345–46. McClellan assigns the land move to McDowell as the major reason for the failure of his campaign (p. 346). He wanted McDowell to come by water to enhance the James River strategy.

88. Ibid., p. 364.

89. Sears, *McClellan*, p. 190.

90. Ibid., p. 351. Lincoln really had no choice. If McClellan had been moving aggressively against Johnston, it is likely that Jackson's northern movements would have been curtailed. Although his operations against Jackson failed, Lincoln displayed considerably more aggressiveness than McClellan ever did (Catton, *Terrible Swift Sword*, pp. 296–305). See also Hassler, *McClellan*, pp. 112–13. What McClellan failed to accept was that by moving swiftly on Richmond, Jackson had to be recalled. Jackson could not take Washington, but McClellan could take Richmond.

91. Catton, *Terrible Swift Sword*, p. 305.

92. McClellan, *McClellan's Own Story*, pp. 375–76.

93. Catton, *Terrible Swift Sword*, pp. 312–14.

94. Sears, *McClellan*, p. 207.

95. Hassler, *McClellan*, p. 130.

96. Seven Pines is quite instructive. Even after the fight he could not change his plan, which called for a siege of Richmond. In a sense, it was a portent of Malvern Hill.

97. McClellan, *McClellan's Own Story*, p. 391.

98. Catton, *Terrible Swift Sword*, p. 320.

99. Ibid., pp. 317–18. See also Hassler, *McClellan*, p. 135. He describes McClellan as being "uneasy."

100. McClellan, *McClellan's Own Story*, pp. 391–92.

101. Ibid., p. 391.

102. Ibid., p. 392.

103. Ibid., p. 411.

104. Catton, *Terrible Swift Sword*, p. 323.

105. Ibid., pp. 312–15.

106. Ibid., pp. 318–19.

107. Ibid., pp. 326–28.

108. Ibid., p. 327.

109. Foote, *Civil War*, pp. 1:482–83. It was a risky attack, but Lee had the measure of the man. See Catton, *Terrible Swift Sword*, p. 319.

110. The research cited earlier in Atkinson, "Mainsprings," p. 33, is applicable. One tactical move would have been to fall back upon White House. But considering how he had led himself into this dilemma, a retreat would smack more of personal failure. McClellan also could have shifted north of the Chickahominy to concentrate his forces, or gone swiftly along the river toward Richmond to force Jackson to conform to his movements. These maneuvers involved risks, of course, but also chances for success. They were more moderate compared to the James option, which he himself had labeled as very risky, and so were precluded by McClellan's fear of failure. At this point he had to demonstrate that he had been doomed by others, that only the riskiest (or safest) decisions forced upon him were left.

111. Hassler, *McClellan*, p. 150.

112. Foote, *Civil War*, p. 1:484.

113. Catton, *Terrible Swift Sword*, p. 329.

114. Foote, *Civil War*, p. 1:484.

115. McClellan, *McClellan's Own Story*, p. 415. Longstreet declared that McClellan could very well have reinforced the Beaver Dam position and held off Jackson. He considered the withdrawal to be McClellan's most serious mistake. See Longstreet, "Seven Days," p. 2:398.

116. Foote, *Civil War*, pp. 1:481–84. If McClellan had held his position at Beaver Creek it could well have been a different story, but not McClellan's.

117. One is left to ponder what the outcome of the Richmond campaign might have been if Porter had commanded in the field and McClellan had stayed behind to train troops.

118. McClellan clearly supports the hypothesis that he knew he was accepting a high-risk venture: "Such a change of base, in the presence of a powerful enemy, is one of the most difficult undertakings in war" (McClellan, *McClellan's Own Story*, p. 412). Hassler even goes so far as to credit McClellan for saving the Union army (*McClellan*, p. 149). The logic, of course, is upside down.

119. McClellan, *McClellan's Own Story*, p. 415.

120. Longstreet, *From Manassas to Appomattox*, pp. 125–29. Longstreet cites a message from Lee asserting that if the Boatswain's Dam position was not taken "the day was lost" (p. 127). There is every reason to believe that if McClellan had made an effort to hold, Lee would have had to seriously reconsider his strategy. McClellan did send some reinforcements, but he cited his own commanders' concerns as evidence that they could not divert many troops (McClellan, *McClellan's Own Story*, pp. 420–21). McClellan definitely needed to believe his commanders in order to support his own rationalizing and support the James move. Moreover, he had been telling them all along how badly they were outnumbered. Some were utterly convinced.

121. McClellan, *McClellan's Own Story*, p. 422. There is some evidence he contemplated moving north. The tenor of his dispatches to Porter displays at various times evidence of both assuming the offense and retreating (Catton, *Terrible Swift Sword*, p. 332). In the end, the James strategy won out. After all, what if he had held off Lee and

Jackson and been forced to recant his letter of June 25 to Stanton, which had *a priori* accepted defeat?

122. McClellan, *McClellan's Own Story*, p. 417. In fact, McClellan even argued it was impossible to tell which side of the river represented the main thrust of the Confederate army (p. 419).

123. McClellan, *McClellan's Own Story*, pp. 425–26. Even Hassler had trouble swallowing this act of insubordination (*McClellan*, pp. 138–39). In those less complex times he most certainly would have been dismissed, if not hanged (Catton, *Terrible Swift Sword*, p. 334).

124. Lee, in a letter to Magruder on June 28, 1862, did consider the possibility of McClellan utilizing the James strategy (Clifford Dowdey and Louis H. Manarin, eds., *The Wartime Papers of Robert E. Lee*, p. 204). However, in another letter to Jefferson Davis on June 29, he clearly acknowledged that the possibility of McClellan going south occurred only after he discovered McClellan had not fallen back on the line of the York, which he felt would have been a more prudent move (ibid., pp. 205–206).

125. Sears, *McClellan*, pp. 217–18.

126. Ibid., pp. 218–20.

127. E. P. Alexander, *Military Memoirs of a Confederate*, pp. 153–55. One could always wonder what might have happened if McClellan had gone down (*as had* Johnston) and someone more aggressive had taken over. The new general might very well have had the Richmond siege and more, with a defeated Confederate army pinned in the city.

128. Sears, *McClellan*, p. 225.

129. Ibid., p. 221.

130. Douglas Southall Freeman, *Lee's Lieutenants: A Study in Command*, p. 1:583.

131. Sears, *McClellan*, pp. 221–22. McClellan put himself on the extreme right. The Union army needed a few breaks.

132. Foote, *Civil War*, pp. 1:509–10.

133. Alexander, *Military Memoirs*, pp. 158–59. Freeman makes the same comments in *Lee's Lieutenants*, p. 1:584. Brigadier General William Pendleton demonstrated the same ineptness he would again show at Gettysburg.

134. Foote, *Civil War*, pp. 1:512–14.

135. Ibid., p. 1:514.

136. D. H. Hill, "McClellan's Change of Base and Malvern Hill," in *Battles and Leaders*, p. 2:394.

137. Freeman, *Lee's Lieutenants*, p. 1:602; D. H. Hill, OR, vol. 11, pt. 2, pp. 628–29. Although his is a badly garbled account, Hill declares that Union infantry was also heavily engaged. Porter makes a similar claim (Fitz-John Porter, "The Battle of Malvern Hill," in *Battles and Leaders*, p. 2:405). McClellan also concurs in the infantry action (*McClellan's Own Story*, pp. 436–37). It is possible that Freeman could not believe that Lee's perception of a demoralized Union infantry was in error.

138. Catton, *Terrible Swift Sword*, p. 339.

139. McClellan, *McClellan's Own Story*, p. 490. He suggests that the army could have moved after a few days.

140. Porter, "Battle of Malvern Hill," p. 423. He argued that they should at least hold the ground and then advance. He was overruled.

141. McClellan, *McClellan's Own Story*, pp. 484–85.

142. Ibid., p. 485.

143. Ibid., p. 482.

4. Lee at Gettysburg

1. Although Vicksburg surrendered the day after Gettysburg, one must assume even then the greater influence of the Eastern establishment.

2. George R. Stewart, *Pickett's Charge: A Microhistory of the Final Attack at Gettysburg, July 3, 1863*, p. 199.

3. Foote, *Civil War*, pp. 500–14.

4. Bruce Catton, *Never Call Retreat*, pp. 12–24.

5. Glenn Tucker, *Lee and Longstreet at Gettysburg*, pp. 2–3, 9–11.

6. Michael A. Palmer, *Lee Moves North: Robert E. Lee on the Offensive*, p. 63.

7. Tucker, *Lee and Longstreet*, p. 96.

8. Ibid., chapter 1.

9. Douglas Southall Freeman, *Robert E. Lee: A Biography*, pp. 148–50; Clifford Dowdey, *Lee*, pp. 369–89. Freeman is much less critical of Longstreet in his later work, *Lee's Lieutenants: A Study in Command*. However, his initially harsh judgment of Ewell remains (see vol. 3, chap. 9). In fact, Freeman points out that if Longstreet had struck earlier on the second day, the inadequate reconnaissance by Johnston would have resulted in a disaster (ibid., pp. 174–76). Tucker makes the same point (*Lee and Longstreet*, p. 261). Dowdey is simply constitutionally incapable of admitting that Lee had a major share of the responsibility (see esp. *Lee*, p. 385).

10. Longstreet, *From Manassas to Appomattox*, pp. 398–410. Longstreet was not that articulate, and his two harshest critics, Ewell and Pendleton, were not about to stick too close to the truth, especially in light of their own errors.

11. Dowdey, *Lee*, p. 389.

12. Grady McWhiney and Perry D. Jamieson, *Attack and Die: Civil War Tactics and the Southern Heritage*, p. 180. This appeal to national character mars an otherwise rational assessment of Lee's behavior.

13. Ibid., pp. 184–91. There is even an attempt to link the rebel yell with Celtic war cries.

14. Ibid., pp. 27–48. The authors cite DeVoto and Eckenrode, who claimed that the Confederacy died in Mexico. There is something to be made of that point from a behavioral view.

15. Freeman, *Lee's Lieutenants*, pp. 3:169–70. Stewart suggests that the contagion infected the army at all levels (*Pickett's Charge*, p. 10).

16. John Millenson and Julian C. Leslie, *Principles of Behavioral Analysis*, pp. 371–75.

17. B. F. Skinner, *Science and Human Behavior*, chapter 2.

18. Palmer, *Lee Moves North*, p. 65.

19. Millenson and Leslie, *Principles of Behavioral Analysis*, pp. 26–61. In addition, there is a fourth process: *extinction*. In this instance there are no discernible consequences and the behavior is suppressed. A common example is a parent ignoring a child's temper tantrum.

20. Foote, *Civil War*, pp. 2:445–46. There is no mistaking Lee's absolute confidence in his ability to deal with the Union army.

21. Palmer, *Lee Moves North*, p. 63.

22. As quoted in Stewart, *Pickett's Charge*, p. 273.

23. Lee to Hood, May 21, 1863, in Dowdey and Manarin, eds., *Wartime Papers*, p. 490.

24. Stewart, *Pickett's Charge*, p. 10. Edwin B. Coddington makes essentially the same point: Lee's overconfidence "perhaps was the fatal defect" (*The Gettysburg Campaign: A Study in Command*, p. 25).

25. The fighting at Gettysburg clearly demonstrated that the leadership ability was there at all ranks. Hancock, Warren, and others did what was necessary and the Union successes were not fortuitous. See Freeman, *Lee's Lieutenants*, p. 3:170.

26. Compte de Paris, *The Battle of Gettysburg: From the History of the Civil War in America*, p. 5.

27. Freeman, *Lee's Lieutenants*, p. 3:269. While speaking of subsequent Union successes along the Rappahannock, Freeman points out that the Confederates would not admit to themselves that the Union forces at Gettysburg had beaten them. He earlier attributed the Union success at Gettysburg, at least in part, to competent leadership and tough veteran troops (ibid., p. 3:170).

28. Catton, *Never Call Retreat*, p. 178.

29. Ibid., pp. 179–84.

30. Coddington, *Gettysburg Campaign*, pp. 318–20.

31. Naisawald points out that there were forty-one Union guns waiting atop Cemetery Hill. It would have been no piece of cake under any circumstances, much less after the first day of fighting. See L. Van Loan Naisawald, *Grape and Canister: The Story of the Field Artillery of the Army of the Potomac, 1861–1865*, p. 362.

32. Coddington, *Gettysburg Campaign*, pp. 330–32.

33. Ibid., pp. 341–51, 445–46. Some historians have argued that Sickles's move was tactically sound (e.g., Comte de Paris, *Battle of Gettysburg*, pp. 152–57). However, the good count also thought McClellan's change of base during the Peninsular campaign was justified, which makes him rather suspect. Most military historians have generally criticized the move as a mistake (e.g., Coddington, *Gettysburg Campaign*, pp. 445–47).

34. See esp. the reports of Brig. Gen. William Harrow, *OR*, vol. 27, pt. 1, p. 420; Doubleday, *OR*, vol. 27, pt. 1, p. 258; Brig. Gen. George Stannard, *OR*, vol. 26, pt. 1, p. 349; Maj. Gen. Winfield Scott Hancock, *OR*, vol. 27, pt. 1, p. 371; and Brig. Gen. Alexander Webb, *OR*, vol. 27, pt. 1, p. 427. It is interesting to note that Freeman in his earlier work is rather vague about the successes of the Union counterattacks (*Robert E. Lee*, pp. 103–106).

35. Foote, *Civil War*, pp. 2:502–12.

36. Wright is quoted in Freeman's *Lee's Lieutenants*, p. 3:126. Brigadier General John Gibbon, commanding a Union II Corps division, wrote that by the time Wright reached his lines, his men were pretty well spent as an attacking force (Trudeau, *Gettysburg*, p. 402). Still, it is part of the mythology that pervades Southern analyses of the battle. Actually, Coddington is correct in pointing out that the Confederates had not achieved a single major objective in the day's fighting (*Gettysburg Campaign*, p. 443). Much of the ground in front of II Corps had been retaken, although the Peach Orchard, the Devil's Den, and the wheat field remained in Confederate hands.

37. Coddington, *Gettysburg Campaign*, pp. 438–41. Confederate claims of a "near thing" apply to this fight, too—and with equally dubious validity.

38. Ibid., pp. 424–26.

39. Lee, *OR*, vol. 27, pt. 2, p. 308.

40. Trudeau, *Gettysburg*, pp. 388–90.

41. Stewart, *Pickett's Charge*, p. 9. He probably overestimated the damage done to the Union forces.

42. Trudeau, *Gettysburg*, p. 421; Jeffry D. Wert, *Gettysburg: Day Three*, pp. 29–30.

43. Freeman, *Lee's Lieutenants*, p. 3:170.

44. Coddington. *Gettysburg Campaign*, pp. 442–43.

45. Lee, *OR*, vol. 27, pt. 2, p. 305. Lee clearly was not interested in an extended campaign, but after Fredericksburg and Chancellorsville he felt confident about his ability to handle whatever combination of Union forces opposed him.

46. Herman Hattaway and Archer Jones, *How the North Won: A Military History of the Civil War*, p. 83.

47. Lee to Jefferson Davis, June 10, 1863, in Dowdey and Manarin, eds., *Wartime Papers*, pp. 507–509.

48. Trudeau, *Gettysburg*, pp. 6–7.

49. Wert, *Gettysburg*, pp. 43–44.

50. Palmer, *Lee Moves North*, pp. 45–49.

51. Wert, *Gettysburg*, p. 43.

52. Alan T. Nolan, *Lee Considered: General Robert E. Lee and Civil War History*, pp. 69–72.

53. Ibid., pp. 62, 72–74.

54. Lee to Jefferson Davis, July 31, 1863, in Dowdey and Manarin, eds., *Wartime Papers*, p. 565. However, in a letter to Margaret Stuart dated July 26, he recognized that he had failed to deter the Union forces, which after all had been his objective (ibid., p. 561). Hattaway and Jones also consider the campaign a success (*How the North Won*, p. 421). However, most writers regard Gettysburg as a serious Confederate defeat (e.g., Coddington, *Gettysburg Campaign*, pp. 535–36).

55. Nolan, *Lee Considered*, pp. 95–96, 98.

56. *OR*, vol. 27, pt. 2, p. 320. Lee is very terse in his commentary. See also *OR*, vol. 27, pt. 2, p. 359, and Longstreet, *From Manassas to Appomattox*, p. 385. Actually, Lee restrained himself in his report when he said Longstreet was not ready; Longstreet was preparing for a flanking move (*OR*, vol. 27, pt. 2, p. 359.)

57. Trudeau, *Gettysburg*, p. 436.

58. *OR*, vol. 27, pt. 2, pp. 358–59. In his account, Longstreet leaves a very definite impression that the Union forces were far from finished.

59. Foote, *Civil War*, pp. 2:531–39.

60. Longstreet, *From Manassas to Appomattox*, p. 393; *OR*, vol. 26, pt. 2, p. 359. Longstreet felt the troops would have too far to go under artillery fire.

61. Trudeau, *Gettysburg*, p. 436.

62. Hattaway and Jones, among others, argue that the Union army had withstood just as bad or worse, and they offer all the military options available, including a retreat to fortified cities, the recall of McClellan and Grant, and reinforcement from other parts of the country (*How the North Won*, pp. 419–20). They do not take into account the political fallout, particularly foreign recognition, which might well have followed a Confederate victory.

63. *OR*, vol. 27, pt. 2, p. 320.

64. Coddington, *Gettysburg Campaign*, p. 443.

65. Foote, *Civil War*, p. 2:525. Meade flat out told Gibbons that Lee would attack the center.

66. McWhiney and Jamieson, *Attack and Die*, pp. 19–23. Lieutenant General John C. Pemberton's losses included the surrender of the army at Vicksburg.

67. Tucker, *Lee and Longstreet*, p. 223.

68. *OR*, vol. 27, pt. 2, p. 308.

69. Coddington, *Gettysburg Campaign*, p. 461.

70. Ibid., pp. 461–62. Staff work was not a strong point in Lee's command. Freeman quotes Col. Charles S. Venable as telling Heth that the choice of his division was a poor one (*Lee's Lieutenants*, p. 3:181). The key here is that they had indeed made good on previous mistakes in leadership.

71. Trudeau, *Gettysburg*, pp. 440–43.

72. As quoted in Freeman, *Robert E. Lee*, p. 110.

73. Stewart, *Pickett's Charge*, pp. 5–7. See also Coddington, *Gettysburg Campaign*, pp. 465–76, for a description of the Union defense of Culp's Hill.

74. Alexander, *Military Memoirs*, pp. 414–24.

75. Ibid., p. 423. The number of guns involved on both sides is still being debated. Fairfax Downey gives the ratio as 220 Union to 172 Confederate (*The Guns of Gettysburg*, p. 139). Hunt estimated the Union batteries at 80 effective and the Confederates between 100 and 120 (*OR*, vol. 27, pt. 1, p. 239). He did not include batteries on Cemetery Hill, which brought the number of Union guns to over 100. Pendleton estimated the Confederate numbers at about 150 guns (*OR*, vol. 27, pt. 2, p. 352), while Alexander estimated the Confederates had 172 guns (Alexander, *Military Memoirs*, p. 419).

76. Wert, *Gettysburg*, p. 121.

77. Alexander, *Military Memoirs*, pp. 421–24. The note to Pickett is on p. 423. Longstreet's first note clearly states that it would be up to Alexander to advise Pickett when to launch his assault (p. 421). A subsequent note seems to remove much of the responsibility from Alexander (p. 421). Nevertheless, Longstreet's delays indicate that he did not want to attack. In the end, his appraisal of the situation was more accurate than Lee's.

78. Wert, *Gettysburg*, p. 183.

79. Alexander, *Military Memoirs*, pp. 424–25.

80. *OR*, vol. 27, pt. 1, p. 373. To his dying day, Hunt swore that if Hancock had conserved his ammunition he would have broken the Confederate attack before it ever reached the Union lines.

81. Foote, *Civil War*, p. 2:552. See also Alexander, *Military Memoirs*, p. 420.

82. Trudeau, *Gettysburg*, p. 452.

83. Coddington, *Gettysburg Campaign*, pp. 493–97.

84. John Gibbon, *Personal Recollections of the Civil War*, pp. 147–50. Naisawald, *Grape and Canister*, p. 420, makes the same comment.

85. Stewart, *Pickett's Charge*, p. 88.

86. Ibid., pp. 172–73; Trudeau, *Gettysburg*, p. 477; Wert, *Gettysburg*, p. 106.

87. Wert, *Gettysburg*, p. 146.

88. Longstreet, *From Manassas to Appomattox*, pp. 386–87.

89. Stewart, *Pickett's Charge*, p. 207. There was only a low stone wall at Ziegler's Grove. The idea of a fortified position helps maintain the Southern tradition that Union infantry could not stand up to the Confederates without help.

90. Coddington, *Gettysburg Campaign*, p. 252.

91. Naisawald, *Grape and Canister*, pp. 34–39.

92. Ibid., p. 201.

93. *OR*, vol. 27, pt. 2, p. 321. Also see Fairfax, *Guns of Gettysburg*, p. 161.

94. The whole issue of whether or not Lee should have assumed the tactical defense has been thoroughly debated (e.g., Tucker, *Lee and Longstreet*) but is not really relevant. Lee was aware of the critical factor; in a letter to Jefferson dated June 10, 1863, he stated that the superiority of resources in the North would eventually prevail (Dowdey and Manarin, eds., *Wartime Papers*, pp. 507–509). Lee believed that one more major victory coming after Chancellorsville and Fredericksburg might well force the North to sue for peace. In this regard, he was not engaging in fantasy. His problem was that with competent Union command he might not be able to find that one more victory.

95. Naisawald, *Grape and Canister*, p. 179.

96. Trudeau, *Gettysburg*, p. 461.

97. Stewart, *Pickett's Charge*, pp. 179–80.

98. *OR*, vol. 27, pt. 1, p. 750; *OR*, vol. 27, pt. 2, p. 386.

99. Wert, *Gettysburg*, pp. 192–93.

100. Ibid., p. 216.

101. A cardinal principle of behaviorism is that in a given situation the individual's most likely response is the one requiring the least effort. In Lee's case, continuing the advance was his first choice.

102. *OR*, vol. 27, pt. 1, pp. 461–62; Stewart, *Pickett's Charge*, pp. 193–94.

103. Wert, *Gettysburg*, p. 204.

104. Ibid., p. 205.

105. Coddington, *Gettysburg Campaign*, p. 513.

106. Stewart, *Pickett's Charge*, pp. 14, 204–206.

107. Wert, *Gettysburg*, p. 220.

108. *OR*, vol. 27, pt. 1, pp. 349–50.

109. Freeman, *Robert E. Lee*, pp. 125–28. Freeman erroneously argued that the Confederates had maintained their formations (p. 125), when in fact his own description indicated the final Confederate assault at the Angle consisted of a disorganized mob of men. See also Stewart, *Pickett's Charge*, p. 221.

110. Stewart, *Pickett's Charge*, pp. 220–21. Stewart even suggests that the Confederates reaching the Angle had a chance, although this appears to be wishful thinking.

111. Ibid., pp. 263–67. Given the incomplete, inaccurate, and missing Confederate returns, which has plagued Civil War historians continuously, this analysis appears most reasonable in the light of all the evidence.

112. Dowdey, *Lee*, p. 389.

113. Ibid., p. 390. This was the same man who, after Hill's disaster at Bristoe Station (October 14, 1863) remarked, "Well, General, bury the poor men and let us say no more about it" (Freeman, *Lee's Lieutenants*, p. 3:247).

114. Freeman, *Lee's Lieutenants*, pp. 3:169–70.

115. Ibid., p. 169.

116. Dowdey, *Lee*, chapter 15. Lee had his problems accepting the harsh realities of the Gettysburg campaign. It is only in a letter to Jefferson Davis dated July 31 that he recognizes he was defeated both tactically and strategically (Dowdey and Manarin, eds., *Wartime Papers*, pp. 564–65). Understandably, he was loathe to recognize how grievously he had underestimated the Union army. In a letter dated August 8 he offered to resign (ibid., pp. 589–90). Of course nothing came of it. Davis simply had no one else.

117. Foote, *Civil War*, p. 2:578. Freeman cites the OR figures of 20,451 Confederate casualties (*OR*, vol. 27, pt. 2, p. 346), but even he admits these figures are likely too low (Freeman, *Lee's Lieutenants*, p. 3:190).

118. Trudeau, *Gettysburg*, p. 529.

119. Dowdey, *Lee*, esp. pp. 381, 385.

120. Tucker, *Lee and Longstreet*, pp. 93–94.

5. Franklin, Tennessee

1. Richard O'Connor, *Hood: Cavalier General*, p. 240.

2. Stanley F. Horn, *The Army of Tennessee: A Military History*, p. 399.

3. Foote, *Civil War*, p. 3:672.

4. Jacob Cox, *The March to the Sea: From Franklin to Nashville*, p. 94. Cox generally supported Schofield's perceptions of the campaign.

5. Horn, *Army of Tennessee*, p. 404.

6. James L. McDonough and Thomas Lawrence Connelly, *Five Tragic Hours: The Battle of Franklin*, pp. 157–61. These figures are somewhat higher than the more traditional fifty-five hundred (cf. Horn, *Army of Tennessee*, p. 404).

7. Stanley F. Horn, "The Spring Hill Legend," *Civil War Times Illustrated*, April 1969, pp. 20–32. While Horn is certainly free to change his mind, he does not attempt to modify his perceptions of Hood. In fact, the article is not intended to exonerate Hood, but to further damage his reputation for destroying Horn's beloved army. See also Thomas Lawrence Connelly, *Autumn of Glory: The Army of Tennessee, 1862–1865*, pp. 501–502, and McDonough and Connelly, *Five Tragic Hours*, p. 56.

8. Richard M. McMurry, *John Bell Hood and the War for Southern Independence*, p. 190. Connelly makes the same point (*Autumn of Glory*, p. 470). What it amounted to was that Hood was in over his head. As a division commander he was in his element.

9. O'Connor, *Hood*, p. 234. Cheatham was an especial target of Hood's wrath.

10. Joseph E. Johnston, *Narrative of Military Operations Directed during the Late War between the States*, chapter 11. His letter to Davis dated January 2, 1864, is most revealing. He generally questions the validity of Davis's perceptions of the situation, pp. 272–76.

11. Richard M. McMurry, *Atlanta 1864: Last Chance for the Confederacy*, p. 140.

12. Ibid., p. 5.

13. Dowdey and Manarin, eds., *Wartime Papers*, p. 821.

14. McMurry, *Atlanta 1864*, p. 96.

15. Ibid., pp. 78–79, 117.

16. Ibid., p. 138.

17. Ibid., p. 187.

18. O'Connor, *Hood*, p. 208.

19. Connelly, *Autumn of Glory*, pp. 40–44.

20. Horn, *Army of Tennessee*, p. 354. Horn characterized the Peachtree attack as "brilliant."

21. Ibid., pp. 355–56. Hardee subsequently was reassigned. Horn cites Gen. Francis Blair, who also described this assault as "brilliant" (*Army of Tennessee*, p. 357).

22. Hood, *Advance and Retreat*, pp. 179–80. Hood continuously associated valor with casualty figures. See also Connelly, *Autumn of Glory*, p. 431.

23. Connelly, *Autumn of Glory*, p. 478.

24. Hood, *Advance and Retreat*, p. 259.

25. McDonough and Connelly, *Five Tragic Hours*, pp. 12–14. The dream of reaching the Ohio River was possibly encouraged by Davis's injudicious references to this plan (Connelly, *Autumn of Glory*, p. 479). Davis was probably trying to boost morale for a dying cause, but unfortunately it struck a resonant chord in Hood.

26. Connelly, *Autumn of Glory*, p. 490.

27. Hood, *Advance and Retreat*, p. 267.

28. Thomas B. Van Horne, *The Life of Major-General George H. Thomas*, pp. 260–61.

29. Ibid., p. 266.

30. Hood, *Advance and Retreat*, p. 272. To compound matters, logistics would forever remain a mystery to Hood.

31. Schofield had eighteen thousand infantry plus four brigades of cavalry at Pulaski (*OR*, vol. 45, pt. 1, p. 341).

32. O'Connor, *Hood*, p. ix. Wilson, for one, thought the campaign held promise, even though Hood may not have possessed the necessary manpower.

33. Craig A. Anderson and Jrad J. Bushman, "Aggression," *Annual Review of Psychology* 53 (2002): pp. 27–39.

34. John Dollard, Leonard W. Doob, Neal E. Miller, O. H. Mowrer, and Robert Sears, *Frustration and Aggression*, pp. 1–3.

35. Ibid., p. 9.

36. Ibid., p. 11.

37. Ibid., p. 39.

38. Saul Rosenzweig, "Types of Reaction to Frustration: An Heuristic Classification," *Journal of Abnormal and Social Psychology* 29 (1934): pp. 298–300.

39. Hood, *Advance and Retreat*; see especially p. xi.

40. Leonard Berkowitz, *Aggression: A Social Psychological Analysis*, pp. 28–29. Hood's undiminished rage after Spring Hill was obvious.

41. Ibid., pp. 32–33.

42. Ibid., pp. 30–32.

43. As quoted in Freeman, *Lee's Lieutenants*, p. 3:544.

44. Berkowitz, *Aggression*, pp. 40–41.

45. Ibid., chapter 8.

46. John M. Schofield, *Forty-six Years in the Army*, p. 168.

47. Hood, *Advance and Retreat*, pp. 282–83.

48. Connelly, *Autumn of Glory*, p. 492.

49. Horn, "Spring Hill Legend," pp. 20, 31–32.

50. James H. Wilson, *Under the Old Flag: Recollections of Military Operations in the War for the Union, the Spanish War, the Boxer Rebellion, etc.*, p. 41. There was no love lost between Schofield and Wilson, and Wilson is critical of Schofield throughout. He insisted, and rightly so, that Schofield's duty was to stay between Hood and Thomas (ibid., pp. 39–40). Actually, the Confederate infantry had moved across at dawn (Hood, *Advance and Retreat*, p. 283).

51. Schofield, *Forty-six Years*, pp. 171, 185.

52. Wilson, *Under the Old Flag*, p. 43.

53. Schofield, *Forty-six Years*, pp. 183–84.

54. Maj. Gen. David F. Stanley, *OR*, vol. 45, pt. 1, p. 113. The 1st Division under Kimball had dropped off to protect the crossing at Rutherford's Creek.

55. Stanley, *OR*, vol. 45, pt. 1, pp. 113–14. Van Horne argues that by holding at Columbia, Schofield was clearly disobeying Thomas's intentions. In fact, Thomas wired Schofield at 3 A.M. on November 29 to withdraw across the Harpeth at Franklin (*Thomas*, pp. 278–79).

56. Horn, "Spring Hill Legend," p. 25.

57. Connelly, *Autumn of Glory*, p. 495.

58. McDonough and Connelly, *Five Tragic Hours*, p. 46.

59. Ibid., p. 48.

60. Ibid., p. 49.

61. Connelly, *Autumn of Glory*, p. 499.

62. O'Connor, *Hood*, pp. 231–32.

63. Ibid., p. 232.

64. Ibid., p. 231. Considering other accounts, Cheatham's statements do not ring true. Schofield arrived at about 7 P.M. with Roger's division, but Cox did not come in until about 11 P.M. (Stanley, *OR*, vol. 45, pt. 1, p. 114). Mason, Hood's assistant adjutant general, says he did not send the note, but Cheatham insists he got it (Horn, *Army of Tennessee*, pp. 390–91). Considering Cheatham's behavior that day, one is inclined to believe Mason. Cheatham's statement implies that there was nothing he could do, that the plan was already compromised.

65. Horn, *Army of Tennessee*, p. 392. The other side of the coin was that Cheatham was paying attention to some ladies that night (O'Connor, *Hood*, p. 232).

66. Connelly, *Autumn of Glory*, p. 501.

67. Col. Emerson Opdycke, *OR*, vol. 45, pt. 1, p. 239. Opdycke was no weakhearted individual: his contributions at Franklin would show that.

68. James L. McDonough, *Schofield: Union General in the Civil War and Reconstruction*, p. 112.

69. Horn, "Spring Hill Legend," p. 32.

70. Col. Henry Stone, "Repelling Hood's Invasion of Tennessee," in *Battles and Leaders*, p. 4:446.

71. James M. McPherson, *Battle Cry of Freedom: The Civil War Era*, p. 812.

72. Thomas Robson Hay, *Hood's Tennessee Campaign*, pp. 91–93.

73. Ibid., p. 102. Even the common private saw Hood's physical condition as disqualifying him for command (Sam R. Watkins, *"Co. Aytch," Maurys Grays, First Tennessee Regiment; or, A Side Show of the Big Show*, p. 226).

74. Berkowitz, *Aggression*, pp. 86–90.

75. Hood, *Advance and Retreat*, p. 290.

76. Hay, *Hood's Tennessee Campaign*, p. 120.

77. Col. Ellison Capers, *OR*, vol. 45, pt. 1, p. 736.

78. Hood, *OR*, vol. 45, pt. 1, pp. 653–54. Hood himself acknowledges he had only one battery per corps available. See also Horn, *Army of Tennessee*, p. 398.

79. Maj. Gen. George D. Wagner, *OR*, vol. 45, pt. 1, pp. 231–32.

80. Maj. Gen. Jacob D. Cox, *OR*, vol. 45, pt. 1, p. 352. Schofield also berates Wagner (*Forty-six Years*, pp. 181–83). Hays cites Gist, who suggests that Wagner was not entirely to blame (*Hood's Tennessee Campaign*, pp. 248–49).

81. Cox, *March to the Sea*, p. 353.

82. Opdycke, *OR*, vol. 45, pt. 1, p. 240. The smoke was so heavy that Opdycke never realized that the Confederates held the outer works (Cox, *March to the Sea*, p. 354). The Confederate forces just west of the pike were generally Brown's men, while Cleburne's troops were mainly to the east (McDonough and Connelly, *Five Tragic Hours*, p. 119).

83. McDonough and Connelly, *Five Tragic Hours*, pp. 132–33. Stewart and Bates were also repulsed, although they persisted in their attacks (ibid., pp. 142–45).

84. Ibid., pp. 132–33.

85. Ibid., pp. 149–50.

86. Hay, *Hood's Tennessee Campaign*, p. 123. Stone reports thirteen separate attacks, which probably also suggests persistence. The difference lies in the fact that Stone probably recorded even attempts by relatively small groups ("Repelling Hood's Invasion," p. 4:453).

87. Maj. Gen. Edward C. Walthall, *OR*, vol. 45, pt. 1, pp. 720–21. He describes the Union fire as the most deadly he had ever seen. Included in the Union forces were troops armed with repeating rifles.

88. Watkins, *"Co. Aytch,"* pp. 218–21.

89. Horn, *Army of Tennessee*, p. 405. O'Connor lists the same three choices (*Hood*, p. 243).

90. Hood, *OR*, vol. 45, pt. 2, p. 628. See also Hood, *Advance and Retreat*, pp. 295–96. His rhetoric betrays the underlying motives. The argument is not one of sadness, but restored glory. However, in a letter to Sedon on December 8, he blamed Cheatham for the failure at Franklin (Hood, *Advance and Retreat*, p. 290). A reappraisal had set in and the casualties were real now, so he began castigating others—just as he did throughout his military career.

91. Connelly, *Autumn of Glory*, p. 513.

92. O'Connor, *Hood*, p. 242.

93. Connelly, *Autumn of Glory*, pp. 506–507.

94. Wilson, *Under the Old Flag*, pp. 49–50. On the other hand, Forrest perceived that he had held off Wilson (Forrest, *OR*, vol. 45, pt. 1, p. 754). At any rate, there was no help for Hood in that direction.

95. Horn, *Army of Tennessee*, pp. 405–406. He describes the step as a compromise between the offensive and the defensive.

96. McDonough and Connelly, *Five Tragic Hours*, p. 169.

97. Hood, *OR*, vol. 45, p. 654. Hood makes a similar point in his memoirs (*Advance and Retreat*, pp. 299–300).

98. Hood, *Advance and Retreat*, p. 304. To the bitter end, Hood never would admit he had botched the campaign—or even had a part in the failure.

6. Beyond Conventional Historical Explanations

1. Leon Festinger, *A Theory of Cognitive Dissonance*, p. 3. See also Lance Kirkpatrick Canon, "Self-confidence and Selective Exposure to Information," pp. 83–96.

2. Festinger, *A Theory of Cognitive Dissonance*, pp. 44, 176.

3. Leon Festinger et al., *Conflict, Decision, and Dissonance*, pp. 154–55. At the same time, though, Festinger and his colleagues state that a decision can be made in an impulsive manner. The difference between pre- and post-impulsive behavior is thus often a quantitative one.

4. Vernon Allen, "Uncertainty of Outcome and Post-Decision Difference Reduction," pp. 43–44. See also the conclusion of Festinger et al., *Conflict, Decision, and Dissonance*, pp. 155–56, and Jack Williams Brehm and Arthur Robert Cohen, *Explorations in Cognitive Dissonance*, p. 300.

5. On tactical changes, see Brian Bond, *War and Society in Europe, 1870–1970*, p. 102.

6. Basil H. Liddell Hart, *The Real War 1914–1918*, p. 42. Alan Clark, *The Donkeys*, p. 126. We will have more to say about prewar British military doctrine later in the chapter.

7. John Terraine, *Ordeal of Victory*, p. 19; Sir James Marshall-Cornwall, *Haig as Military Commander*, p. 18.

8. As quoted in Clark, *Donkeys*, p. 163.

9. Ibid., pp. 102 (first quote), 126 (second quote).

10. Marshall-Cornwall, *Haig as Military Commander*, p. 148.

11. Eric Keir Gilbourne Sixsmith, *Douglas Haig*, pp. 90–91.

12. David French, "Allies, Rivals, and Enemies: British Strategy and War Aims During the First World War," p. 28.

13. French's mishandling of the reserves played a large role in his being replaced by Haig. See George H. Cassar, *The Tragedy of Sir John French*, pp. 263–66, 279–80; Clark, *Donkeys*, 163–67.

14. Clark, *Donkeys*, p. 173.

15. Ibid., p. 271.

16. Sir Llewellyn Woodward, *Great Britain and the War of 1914–1918*, p. 138.

17. Sir Hubert Gough, *The Fifth Army*, p. 104.

18. Woodward, *Great Britain*, pp. 138–39.

19. Ibid., p. 139.

20. Norman Dixon, *On the Psychology of Military Incompetence*, p. 249.

21. Ibid., p. 250; Leon Wolff, *In Flanders Fields: The 1917 Campaign*, p. 41.

22. Dixon, *On the Psychology of Military Incompetence*, pp. 280, 283, 371–72.

23. Ibid., pp. 250–51.

24. Ibid., pp. 251–53. See also Wolff, *In Flanders Fields*, pp. 40–41.

25. On Haig's attitude toward cavalry, see Philip Warner, *Passchendaele: The Tragic Victory of 1917*, pp. 41–42. On Haig's interest in innovations see Terraine, *Ordeal of Victory*, pp. 95–96.

26. According to Dixon, Haig's "conventional views" were responsible for his rapid advance.

27. As quoted in Sir Douglas Haig, *The Private Papers of Douglas Haig, 1914–1919*, pp. 15–16 (first quote), 29 (second quote).

28. Haig, *Private Papers*, p. 125.

29. On the slowness shown at all levels with regard to supplying the British army with appropriate weapons, shells, and even helmets, see Woodward, *Great Britain*, pp. 39–43.

30. On Haig's firm belief in divine guidance and mission, see Lyn MacDonald, *Somme*, pp. 39–40, and Marshall-Cornwall, *Haig as Military Commander*, p. 183.

31. Terraine, *Ordeal of Victory*, pp. 203, 212.

32. Marshall-Cornwall, *Haig as Military Commander*.

33. As quoted in ibid., p. 189.

34. Terraine, *Ordeal of Victory*, p. 178. At least on this occasion, British commanders evidenced the sort of group process described as "groupthink." See Irving L. Janis, *Victims of Groupthink: A Psychological Study of Foreign-Policy Decisions and Fiascoes*.

35. Liddell Hart, *Real War*, pp. 126–27.

36. Haig, *Private Papers*, p. 154.

37. MacDonald, *Somme*, p. 178.

38. To this day, there is still a great deal of controversy over who suffered the greatest losses on the Somme. Marshall-Cornwall, a defender of Haig, claims that the Allies eventually suffered 623,907 casualties; the Germans, 680,000 (*Haig as Military Commander*, 207). Terraine, also one of Haig's defenders, thinks that German casualties probably were somewhat higher, but even if they were about the same, the German losses were proportionally greater because they had fewer men to lose. Critics such as Churchill and Lloyd George insisted that Allied losses were much higher than those of their opponents (Terraine, *Ordeal of Victory*, pp. 231, 235–36).

39. On German concern over Somme losses and awareness of Allied superiority in men and material see Marshall-Cornwall, *Haig as Military Commander*, p. 208, and Terraine, *Ordeal of Victory*, pp. 230–31.

40. As quoted in Woodward, *Great Britain*, p. 149.

41. MacDonald, *Somme*, p. 267. Emphasis in original.

42. Ibid., pp. 245–46.

43. Ibid., p. 245 n.

44. Ibid., p. 337.

45. Lt. Col. John H. Boraston, ed., *Sir Douglas Haig's Despatches, December 1915–April 1919*, p. 27.

46. Ibid., pp. 51–54.

47. More recently, John Terraine has insisted that Haig, in coming close to wrecking the German army, won a substantial victory (*Ordeal of Victory*, p. 230). A useful corrective to Terraine's "Haigiography" is Tim Travers's *The Killing Ground: The British Army, the Western Front, and the Emergence of Modern Warfare, 1900–1918*.

48. Woodward, *Great Britain*, p. 151.

49. MacDonald, *Somme*, p. 318.

50. Wolff, *In Flanders Fields*, p. 76.

51. Terraine, *Ordeal of Victory*, pp. 282–83, 286–87, 307.

52. Lloyd George, *War Memoirs of David Lloyd George*, p. 4:356.

53. S. L. A. Marshall, *The American Heritage History of World War I*, p. 208. For an excellent treatment of the mutinies that occurred as a result of the Nivelle disaster, see Richard M. Watt, *Dare Call It Treason*. Robert Nivelle's behavior is itself worthy of extensive consideration. From all accounts it is obvious that his publicly expressed confidence in the success of his anticipated attack grew in direct proportion to his awareness of the enemy's knowledge of his plans.

54. Wolff, *In Flanders Fields*, p. 128.

55. Ibid., pp. 138–39.

56. Ibid., pp. 173, 178 (Chateris quote), 183. See also Marshall-Cornwall, *Haig as Military Commander*, p. 246.

57. Wolff, *In Flanders Fields*, p. 183; Woodward, *Great Britain*, p. 291.

58. Wolff, *In Flanders Fields*, p. 187.

59. Warner, *Passchendaele*, p. 132. Emphasis in original.

60. Ibid., p. 142.

61. Boraston, ed., *Despatches*, p. 115.

62. Ibid., p. 133. Again, we can see Haig's tendency to persistently declare that enemy losses were higher than his own. The report issued in 1922 by the British War Office corrected this. Interestingly enough, however, the British *Official History*, published in 1948, gave the British casualty total as 244,897 as opposed to a German loss of "about 400,000"—a palpable absurdity. See Wolff, *In Flanders Fields*, p. 234. General Sir Hubert Gough also believed that the Somme battle had seen the British inflicting greater casualties than they sustained (although he provided no figures with regard to German losses), and that the battle had worn down the enemy, lowering his morale, and leaving him severely shaken (*Fifth Army*, pp. 144, 160–61). In any case, British losses were such that an initially successful, tank-led attack at Cambrai, on November 20, 1917, could not be sustained.

63. Boraston, ed., *Despatches*, p. 135.

64. Gough, *Fifth Army*, p. 175. Later in this same work, the author became even more impassioned about the value of Haig's 1917 Flanders campaign. It could well, he said, have saved the French army from "an overwhelming disaster" (*Fifth Army*, p. 308). Gough expressed the same opinion in his memoirs, which were written after World War II. See Sir Hubert Gough, *Soldiering On: Being the Memoirs of General Sir Hubert Gough*, p. 142.

65. Lloyd George, *War Memoirs*, p. 4:417. Lloyd George, a man not noted for assiduous adherence to principle, had a multitude of axes to grind with Haig and the British military establishment in general. Nothing has appeared, however, that invalidates his opinions of Haig's operations, if not those of Haig as a person.

66. Marshall-Cornwall, *Haig as Military Commander*, p. 260.

67. See Tim Travers, "The Allied Victories, 1918"; idem, *How the War Was Won: Command and Technology in the British Army on the Western Front, 1917–1918*; Paddy Griffith, *Battle Tactics of the Western Front: The British Army's Art of Attack, 1916–18*.

68. Niall Ferguson, *The Pity of War: Exposing World War I*, pp. 297, 300–303, 314, 386–87.

69. Lloyd George, *War Memoirs*, p. 4:269. Emphasis in original. Here we can see another example of Haig's unwillingness to accept reality. In 1918, the Allies—Haig included, of course—were succeeding, whereas Haig, *on his own*, had not in 1916 and 1917. Therefore, there could not have been any successes. A very laudatory treatment of Haig's role in the 1918 victory is provided by John Terraine in *To Win a War: 1918, the Year of Victory*. In our opinion, nothing brought forth by Terraine invalidates the notion that Haig often was oblivious to reality.

70. Boraston, ed., *Despatches*, pp. 300, 327–28. Upon reflection, Gough seemed willing, indeed eager (for then all failures could be blamed upon the weather) to point out the role mud played in frustrating Haig's offensive: "General Winter of Russia could not offer more problems to Napoleon than did General Mud, of Flanders, to the British Command" (Gough, *Soldiering On*, p. 92). Gough further observed: "Wounded men falling headlong into the shell holes were in danger of drowning. . . . No battle in history was ever fought under such conditions as that of Passchendaele" (ibid., p. 215).

71. Clark, *Donkeys*, p. 175.

72. Haig, *Private Papers*, p. 77.

73. Wolff, *In Flanders Fields*, p. 149.

74. Ibid., p. 228. According to a more recent writer, this story may have been apocryphal. See Paul Fussell, *The Great War and Modern Memory*, p. 84.

75. George H. Cassar offers this as part of a most inauspicious introduction to his work on Sir John French: "At the outset, as a student of the First World War, my attitude towards French was unfavorable, but, I was determined to be objective. However I regret to say that before long I had, if anything, formed an even lower opinion of my subject" (*The Tragedy of Sir John French*, from the preface).

76. Cassar, *Tragedy of Sir John French*, pp. 136, 292.

77. Terraine, *To Win a War*, p. 487.

78. Ibid., pp. 478–79, Sixsmith, *Douglas Haig*, pp. 162–63.

79. Sixsmith, *Douglas Haig*, pp. 226–27. In recognizing the need for specially designed amphibious craft, Haig sought to provide for the landing of both tanks and infantry. No doubt he also had in mind the Gallipoli disaster of 1915.

80. Wolff, *In Flanders Fields*, p. 239.

81. Major General Sir John Kennedy made this point in defense of Haig, in whose army he served as a young officer. See Marshall-Cornwall, *Haig as Military Commander*, p. 293.

82. Terraine, *To Win a War*, p. 482; Marshall-Cornwall, *Haig as Military Commander*, pp. 294–95. Shelford Bidwell has stated that, with respect to World War I, "There were only two courses open, to stop the war, or settle it by attrition" (*Modern Warfare: A Study of Men, Weapons, and Theory*, p. 59).

83. Terraine, *To Win a War*, p. 481.

84. Eric Keir Gilbourne Sixsmith, *British Generalship in the Twentieth Century*, pp. 158–59.

85. Ibid., pp. 149, 159.

86. Sixsmith, *Douglas Haig*, p. 164.

87. Sixsmith, *British Generalship*, p. 161.

88. Wolff, *In Flanders Fields*, p. 140. Terraine, Marshall-Cornwall, and just about everybody else have come down hard on Charteris.

89. As quoted in ibid., p. 145.

90. Shelford Bidwell and Dominick Graham, *Fire Power: British Army Weapons and Theories of War, 1904–1945*, pp. 26–27.

91. Ibid., pp. 56–58. Sixsmith, *British Generalship*, pp. 38–39.

92. For the biting remarks of one Captain Wetherell (remarks that were largely ignored) on the "madness" of sending soldiers out to attack defenders armed with modern rifles and machine guns, see Bidwell and Graham, *Fire Power*, p. 31.

93. Interestingly enough, Sir Hubert Gough and Sir John French both showed a prewar interest in increased and more sophisticated use of firepower (ibid., p. 55).

94. See Jack Snyder, "Civil-Military Relations and the Cult of the Offensive, 1914 and 1984," *International Security* 9 (1984).

95. Bidwell and Graham, *Fire Power*, p. 27.

96. Leon Festinger, Henry W. Riecken, and Stanley Schachter, *When Prophecy Fails: A Social and Psychological Study of a Modern Group That Predicted the Destruction of the World*, p. 166.

97. As an example of this, see Richard C. Raack, "When Plans Fail: Small Group Behavior and Decision-Making in the Conspiracy of 1808 in Germany," *Journal of Conflict Resolution* 14 (1970): pp. 3–20.

98. Wyn Craig Wade, *The Titanic: End of a Dream*, p. 323.

99. Gough, *Soldiering On*, p. 15.

100. John Turner, "British Politics and the Great War," p. 118. Probably the most useful general overview of the domestic troubles afflicting Great Britain in the years immediately preceding World War I remains George Dangerfield's classic, *The Strange Death of Liberal England*.

101. Gough, *Soldiering On*, p. 16.

102. Clifford Geertz, *The Interpretation of Cultures: Selected Essays*, p. 28.

103. Festinger, *A Theory of Cognitive Dissonance*, p. 27. See also Milton Rokeach, *The Open and Closed Mind: Investigations into the Nature of Belief Systems and Personality Systems*, pt. 3.

104. F. Scott Fitzgerald, *Tender Is the Night*, p. 57.

105. Robin Prior and Trevor Wilson, *Passchendaele: The Untold Story*, pp. 196–97.

106. Ibid., p. 198.

107. Denis Winter, *Haig's Command: A Reassessment*, p. 239.

108. Ibid., p. 144.

109. Ibid., pp. 145–47.

110. Ibid., p. 145.

111. As quoted in Richard Holmes, *Acts of War: The Behavior of Men in Battle*, p. 179. According to Dixon, the dogmatically inflexible Haig was "the perfect figurehead for such a fight" (*On the Psychology of Military Incompetence*, p. 391).

7. Winston Churchill, Arthur Harris, and British Strategic Bombing

1. Alexander P. De Seversky, *Victory Through Air Power*, pp. 193–194, 244.

2. Dale O. Smith, *U.S. Military Doctrine: A Study and Appraisal*, p. 134.

3. Adolf Galland, *The First and the Last: The Rise and Fall of the German Fighter Forces*, p. 64.

4. In one aspect at least, Trenchard's influence was perhaps *too* great. It was one of his cardinal beliefs that heavily armed bombers would always "get through" to their targets. Thus, the question of escort fighters of any kind, much less long-range ones, became a secondary one for RAF tacticians and strategists. On this subject, see Noble Frankland, "Bombing: The RAF Case," p. 142. Frankland's essay was drawn from materials presented in his four-volume *Strategic Air Offensive Against Germany*, which he coauthored with Charles Webster. On the role of the Trenchard doctrine, see also Anthony Verrier, *The Bomber Offensive*, p. 10.

5. As the war, particularly the air war, began to turn against Germany, Hitler increasingly removed himself from the picture, refusing to visit bomb-ravaged areas (in this respect, of course, he differed greatly from Churchill). On this refusal and Goebbel's frustration at being unable to reap propaganda rewards from some such display of concern on Hitler's part, see Albert Speer, *Inside the Third Reich Memoirs*, pp. 299–300.

6. See Arthur Bryant, *The Turn of the Tide: A History of the War Years Based on the Diaries of Field Marshal Lord Alanbrooke, Chief of the Imperial General Staff*, p. 55.

Bryant also described the very important prewar buildup of the RAF, most particularly, Fighter Command. See his discussions of this on pp. 31 and 162.

7. De Seversky, *Victory Through Air Power*, p. 34.

8. As quoted in ibid., p. 42.

9. On the role of Japanese air superiority in the Malayan campaign, see Winston S. Churchill, *The Second World War: The Hinge of Fate*, pp. 4:38, 42. The quoted statement comes from *The Second World War: Closing the Ring*, p. 5:519.

10. See Verrier, *Bomber Offensive*, p. 29. See also Peter Calvocoressi and Guy Wint, *Total War: Causes and Courses of the Second World War*, p. 337. Understandably, this was particularly the case in the summer of 1940, after the British army had been driven from the continent. What relatively few heavy bombers Britain then possessed represented the only means by which the beleaguered country could fight back. As Churchill put it in a missive dated August 8 (before the "Battle of Britain" officially began), what was necessary was "an absolutely devastating, exterminating attack by very heavy bombers from this country on the Nazi homeland. We must be able to overwhelm them by this means, without which I do not see a way through." A month or so later, he declared, "The Navy can lose us this war, but only the Air Force can win it" (as quoted in Alan J. Levine, *The Strategic Bombing of Germany, 1940–1945*, p. 25). As we shall see, Churchill's views on the effectiveness of strategic bombing will vary depending on time and circumstances.

11. See Verrier, *Bomber Offensive*, p. 88.

12. Telford Taylor, *The March of Conquest: The German Victories in Western Europe, 1940*, p. 122.

13. Later, as chief of the Imperial General Staff, Alanbrooke recognized that sea power had been overtaken by airpower. See Bryant, *Turn of the Tide*, p. 66.

14. Ibid., pp. 205, 209.

15. Winston S. Churchill, *The Second World War: The Grand Alliance*, pp. 3:320 (Churchill quote), 615–16.

16. Richard Hough, *Death of the Battleship: The Tragic Close of the Era of Sea Power*, pp. 141, 142.

17. Stanley L. Falk, *Seventy Days to Singapore: The Malayan Campaign, 1941–1942*, p. 116.

18. Churchill, *Second World War*, p. 5:6.

19. As an example of just how perspicacious Churchill could be with regard to airpower, one can consider his comments during a July 23, 1934, debate in the House of Commons. He used this occasion to call attention to London's vulnerability to air attack, referring to the city as a "fat cow, a valuable cow tied up to attract the beast of prey." See Verrier, *Bomber Offensive*, p. 42.

20. Churchill, *Second World War*, pp. 5:275–76.

21. De Seversky, *Victory Through Air Power*, p. 245. Emphasis added.

22. On Harris's attitude (something which the air marshal himself chose not to discuss in his postwar memoirs), see Verrier, *Bomber Offensive*, p. 4. On Harris's being presented with an already well-established doctrine, see Arthur Harris, *Bomber Offensive*, pp. 73, 77. According to some, Harris became converted to the night bombing approach only after the failure of several attempts at daylight precision bombing. See Levine, *Strategic Bombing of Germany*, pp. 37, 190.

23. Harris, *Bomber Offensive*, p. 76. Levine has declared that "Unlike other advocates of area bombing, he [Harris] had no great faith in smashing morale, although he occasionally stressed this for tactical purposes" (*Strategic Bombing of Germany*, pp. 37–38).

24. Churchill, *Second World War*, pp. 5:518–19.

25. Speer, *Inside the Third Reich*, p. 277.

26. Galland, *First and the Last*, pp. 179, 308.

27. Harris, *Bomber Offensive*, p. 73.

28. Ibid., p. 259.

29. Speer, *Inside the Third Reich*, pp. 280, 285–86.

30. Galland, *First and the Last*, p. 192.

31. On this issue, see Speer, *Inside the Third Reich*, p. 406, and Galland, *First and the Last*, p. 307. Galland does state that British night raids were sometimes more effective in damaging oil production. As a rule, though, Bomber Command persisted with area bombings.

32. As quoted in Sven Lindqvist, *A History of Bombing*, p. 82. Of course, at this point the intensity of the fighting in Russia had yet to be appreciated; nor were the problems involved in the British approach to strategic bombing widely acknowledged. Lindqvist, in his most originally organized and thought-provoking work, offers a pithy history of strategic bombing from 1911 to the present.

33. In *Bomber Offensive*, Air Marshal Harris expressed bitterness over the failure of British wartime planners to provide long-range escort fighters for Bomber Command. He also was greatly disturbed over the unwillingness of such people to replace the .303-caliber machine guns on British bombers with the .50-caliber variety. See Harris, *Bomber Offensive*, pp. 163–64. On the lack of long-range escort protection, see also Verrier, *Bomber Offensive*, p. 3. The RAF did have one officially designated night fighter at its disposal: the heavily armed Bristol Beaufighter. However, this twin-engined aircraft, while quite effective in so-called intruder attacks on German airfields, was too slow and suffered from a lack of maneuverability possessed by the German Me-110 and American P-38 Lightning. Hence, it was not terribly effective in an escort capacity. Yet, despite all of Harris's at least after-the-fact concerns, they were never great enough to make him consider an approach other than nighttime area bombing.

34. As quoted in Calvocoressi and Wint, *Total War*, p. 491.

35. Churchill, *Second World War*, pp. 5:517, 4:279.

36. As quoted in Alan F. Wilt, *War from the Top: German and British Decision Making during World War II*, pp. 227–28; Levine, *Strategic Bombing of Germany*, pp. 30–31.

37. Churchill, *Second World War*, p. 5:518. It is interesting to note that the prime minister, who ordinarily showed little interest in the technical aspects of air warfare, was persistent in urging the development of the American P-51 fighter, a machine which, when powered by a superior two-thousand-horsepower Rolls-Royce engine, proved to be an excellent long-range fighter. The Mustang saw extensive service escorting American bombers on daylight raids. See Levine, *Strategic Bombing of Germany*, p. 113.

38. Harris, *Bomber Offensive*, p. 113.

39. Ibid., pp. 109, 152. There was a terrible exception to this. Evidence points to Churchill being primarily responsible for the meaningless annihilation of Dresden on February 13–14, 1945. The primary motive apparently was to impress the Russians, something deemed to be of particular importance due to the recently concluded Yalta Conference. Levine, however, has suggested that Dresden had been on Harris's "hit list" for some time (*Strategic Bombing of Germany*, pp. 173, 177–78).

40. On this, see Verrier, *Bomber Offensive*, p. 16.

41. Levine, *Strategic Bombing of Germany*, pp. 142, 173.

42. Verrier, *Bomber Offensive*, pp. 315, 316.

43. For an interesting comparison of Roosevelt's and Churchill's respective approaches to military issues, see Bryant, *Turn of the Tide*, p. 335.

44. Churchill, *Second World War*, pp. 4:679–80 and 5:519, 524.

45. Verrier, *Bomber Offensive*, pp. 12–13.

46. Edward L. Thorndike, *Animal Intelligence: Experimental Studies*, pp. 29–34.

47. Ibid., pp. 74–75.

48. Edward L. Thorndike, *The Psychology of Learning: Educational Psychology*, pp. 2:2, 12–23. The eventual behavioral position was that the individual does not significantly transform the stimulus or modify the response except along clearly predictable dimensions, called gradients of change.

49. Ibid., pp. 2:13–14. Stimulus control may be viewed as either the stimulus forcing the response, as in a reflex, or setting the occasion as an operant learning. Thus, one is literally forced to blink by a puff of air to the eye, but we choose (or do not) to stop for a red light.

50. John R. Anderson, *Cognitive Psychology and Its Implications*, pp. 328–63.

51. Irving L. Janis and Leon Mann, *Decision Making: A Psychological Analysis of Conflict, Choice, and Commitment*, pp. 3–19. The economic or rational man is a great idea for computer simulations, but simple observation casts doubt on its real-world validity.

52. The Law of Belongingness implies an understanding of relationships approaching insight. Actually, it is trial-and-error learning explicated on a somewhat more elegant level. Thus, the bomber stream solution to the Kammhuber Line seemed viable in terms of overwhelming the box defenses (Verrier, *Bomber Offensive*, pp. 150, 293). However, there seemed to be no recognition of what might happen on deeper raids (when the Germans decided on attrition, rather than concentrating over the target). While one can recognize the pressures of daily actions, long-range planning seemed to be a simple additive series of daily actions. See Harris, *Bomber Offensive*, p. 126, for a pure example of an accidental solution involving the use of flares by the Stirling bombers.

53. The Somme campaign is a classic illustration of this principle. The British bombardment was essentially a massive extension of the preliminary shelling strategy. However, the mix of heavy and light shells was totally inadequate. Hence, the length of the bombardment, or even the total tonnage of shells, was not as critical as the proportion of high explosives which could exert a force downward to destroy the bunkers where the machine gunners were waiting. It was not as if no one knew that high explosives were needed. Nevertheless, the mystical belief that more of something would suffice almost ultimately prevailed (John Keegan, *The Face of Battle*, pp. 224–37).

54. Harris, *Bomber Offensive*, p. 88; Verrier, *Bomber Offensive*, p. 164.

55. Galland, *First and the Last*, pp. 12–13.

56. Although the Luftwaffe had clearly demonstrated the relative ineffectiveness of area bombing with respect to Harris's objectives, he always believed that more of the same (shades of the Somme!) would overcome logic.

57. Harris, *Bomber Offensive*, p. 77.

58. Verrier, *Bomber Offensive*, p. 195.

59. Ibid., p. 166.

60. Galland, *First and the Last*, p. 198.

61. Harris, *Bomber Offensive*, pp. 196–208. Harris was not happy about this, but he had no choice.

62. Verrier, *Bomber Offensive*, pp. 267–70.

63. Harris, *Bomber Offensive*, pp. 220–24. Harris never really believed that anyone besides himself was capable of maximally utilizing Bomber Command.

64. Richard Overy, *Why the Allies Won*, pp. 125–33.

8. Stalingrad

This chapter is, to a great extent, based upon Gil Kliman, M.D., and Robert Pois, "Adolf Hitler's Childhood: Tragic Synergy of Personal, Family, and National Processes in Germany" (presented at The Rise of Adolf Hitler and Other Genocidal Leaders: A Psychoanalytic and Historical Forum, San Francisco, Calif., April 21–22, 1989).

1. Walter Görlitz, "The Battle for Stalingrad: 1942–43," p. 251.

2. See Norbert Bromberg and Verna Volz Small, *Hitler's Psychopathology*; Helm Stierlin, *Adolf Hitler: A Family Perspective*; Rudolph Binion, *Hitler among the Germans*; and Waite, *Psychopathic God*.

3. Sexual preferences, always a matter of great interest, have been emphasized by Bromberg and Waite. Arguing largely by analogy and placing emphasis on sources whose reliability has been questioned, utilized by Walter C. Langer in a 1943 report for the Office of Strategic Services (OSS), they have come to the conclusion that Hitler was extremely masochistic with regard to sex and, so far as can be determined, probably never had "normal" sexual intercourse. For a summary of various points of view concerning when Hitler became an anti-Semite, see Waite, *Psychopathic God*, pp. 224–30. Ian Kershaw, in his excellent biography of Adolf Hitler, has been understandably dismissive of some of the wilder speculation regarding his subject's childhood and sex life, and how such putative problems influenced prejudices and decision making. See Ian Kershaw, *Hitler*, vol. 1, 1889–1936: *Hubris*, chapters 1 and 2, but esp. pp. 44–49. The authors of this work think that he has gone too far in this direction. For a balanced analysis of Hitler's physical and psychological states and the occasional interaction between the two, see Fritz Redlich, *Hitler: Diagnosis of a Destructive Prophet*, pp. 280–301, 332–39 in particular. Like Kershaw, Redlich is very suspicious of some of the more speculative hypotheses regarding Hitler's psychological state(s). As a psychiatrist with an obvious respect for Freud, he takes what he sees as well-grounded psychological and psychoanalytical hypotheses more seriously.

4. Most commentators have stated that Adolf's father, Alois Hitler, a customs officer, treated his son with considerable brutality. This view has been challenged, however, by those who have come to the conclusion that Alois was not much more brutal than the standard Central European parent of the late nineteenth century. See, for example, Franz Jetzinger, *Hitler's Youth*. Also see Bromberg and Small, *Hitler's Psychopathology*, pp. 33–34. In our opinion, even if Hitler's father was not inordinately brutal, he was stern and at times brutal enough to have had a lasting impact upon a young man who, at least at first, could be characterized as having delicate sensibilities.

5. For a succinct description of the narcissistic personality, see Bromberg and Small, *Hitler's Psychopathology*, pp. 9–14. Drawing upon the work of Otto Kernberg, Bromberg and Small as well as Waite have suggested that Hitler was also a "borderline personality," an individual who, while passing somewhat beyond what is usually described as being "neurotic," is not quite "psychotic," and hence able to function in the real world. While we think that there is ample evidence in favor of declaring Hitler to have been extremely narcissistic—and narcissism is an important feature of the borderline personality—we are not prepared to apply conclusions attaching to considerations of the borderline personality to the concerns of this chapter.

6. Alois Hitler—who was an illegitimate child and, from what we can tell, was brought up in a harsh family environment—probably suffered massive injuries to his self-esteem. As is often the case, he felt compelled to inflict the same variety of injuries upon his son. See Kliman and Pois, "Adolf Hitler's Childhood."

7. The most detailed discussions of Hitler's relationship to his mother are provided

by Stierlin, *Adolf Hitler*; Binion, *Hitler among the Germans*; and Bromberg and Small, *Hitler's Psychopathology*. While differing with regards to specifics, all agree that Hitler had an extremely intense relationship with his mother, one which, while often charged with ambivalence, provided him with the sense of being a very special person.

8. Rigidity is an important characteristic of the narcissistic personality. See Bromberg and Small, *Hitler's Psychopathology*, pp. 10–14, 181. John Keegan has maintained that the "ultimate cause" of Hitler's "inflexibility" was his "trench experience" in the Great War. There, the idea of "standing firm" and maintaining a rigid command was important. As we will see later, Hitler was at least implicitly very critical of one who thought along those lines: General der Infanterie Erich von Falkenhayn—the "architect" of the Verdun massacre. In any event, the authors believe that Hitler's inflexibility can be traced back to much earlier problems and issues. See John Keegan, *The Mask of Command*, pp. 303–304.

9. Dollard et al., *Frustration and Aggression*. For a more recent commentary on this subject, see Redlich, *Hitler*, pp. 276–79.

10. Dollard et al., *Frustration and Aggression*, pp. 1–2, 3–6, 7, 9, 11.

11. Ibid., pp. 39–40, 48.

12. Rosenzweig, "Types of Reaction to Frustration," pp. 298–300.

13. Berkowitz, *Aggression*, pp. 28–29, 32–33. See also James Averill, "Studies on Anger and Aggression: Implications for Theories of Emotion," *American Psychologist* 38 (1983): p. 1147.This also explains why crowds may get out of control at sporting events, particularly where the events observed include a lot of violence (e.g., football, boxing, etc.).

14. Kenneth E. Moyer, *The Psychobiology of Aggression*.

15. Leonard Berkowitz, "Aversively Stimulated Aggression: Some Parallels and Differences in Research with Animals and Humans," *American Psychologist* 38 (1983): p. 1139.

16. Berkowitz, *Aggression*, pp. 30–31.

17. Ibid., pp. 88–92, 196–228.

18. Janis, *Victims of Groupthink*.

19. Ibid., pp. 40–41, 198. With regard to the self-censorship a group can impose upon itself, the influence of Leon Festinger's cognitive dissonance hypothesis is obvious.

20. The *folie à deux* phenomenon has been an object of psychological interest since the late nineteenth century. Most case studies have involved families, but the term has been more widely employed over the years.

21. Janis, *Victims of Groupthink*, pp. 161–64, 165, 194, 198.

22. For a pithy discussion of Hitler's role in the development and implementation of blitzkrieg, see Arthur Bryant, *The Turn of the Tide: A History of the War Years Based on the Diaries of Field Marshal Lord Alanbrooke, Chief of the Imperial General Staff*, pp. 38–42.

23. For an interesting discussion of Hitler's mastery of detail, see Percy Schramm, *Hitler: The Man and the Military Leader*, pp. 103–106.

24. Erich von Manstein, *Verlorene Siege*, p. 127. Others have placed blame for the stop order on Gerd von Rundstedt, who issued it with Hitler's approval. As an example of this, see Taylor, *March of Conquest*, pp. 262–65.

25. On Hitler's unwillingness to take risks and to seize on opportunities as they arose, see Manstein, *Verlorene Siege*, pp. 303, 306. See also Generalleutnant Günter von Blumentritt's remarks in Seymour Freidin and William Richardson, eds., *The Fatal Decisions*, p. 51.

26. Basil Henry Liddell Hart, *The Other Side of the Hill: Germany's Generals, Their Rise and Fall, with Their Own Account of Military Events*, p. 288; Alan Clark, *Barbarossa: The German-Russian Conflict, 1941–45*, p. 182.

27. For overall comparisons, often too general, between Hitler and Napoleon, see Desmond Seward, *Napoleon and Hitler: A Comparative Biography*. On their Russian campaigns in particular, see chapter 7, "The Russian Fronts of 1812 and 1941."

28. As quoted in Liddell Hart, *Other Side of the Hill*, p. 289.

29. Rudolf Hofmann, "The Battle of Moscow," in *Decisive Battles of World War II: The German View*, ed. Hans Adolf Jacobsen and Jürgen Rohwer, trans. by Edmund Fitzgerald, pp. 177, 178; Liddell Hart, *Other Side of the Hill*, p. 288. Even Clark, who tended to be somewhat supportive of Hitler with regard to his command abilities, commented upon the unfortunate conclusions that Hitler drew from the Moscow experience (*Barbarossa*, p. 183).

30. Liddell Hart, *Other Side of the Hill*, pp. 291–92.

31. Walter Görlitz, *Paulus and Stalingrad: A Life of Field-Marshal Friedrich Paulus, with Notes, Correspondence, and Documents from His Papers*, p. 205.

32. Generaloberst Friedrich Paulus (considerably after the fact), as quoted in ibid., p. 146.

33. Ibid., p. 205.

34. Albert Seaton, *The German Army, 1933–45*, p. 187.

35. For the evolution of the several plans, see Clark, *Barbarossa*, pp. 188–92.

36. See Walter Kerr, *The Secret of Stalingrad*, pp. 29–30, 34–45.

37. In our opinion, the best detailed description of how this new plan came about is in Clark, *Barbarossa*, pp. 207–209.

38. Manfred Kehrig, *Stalingrad: Analyse und Dokumentation einer Schlacht*, p. 27. See also William Craig, *Enemy at the Gates: The Battle for Stalingrad*, p. 8.

39. Liddell Hart, *Other Side of the Hill*, p. 306; Clark, *Barbarossa*, pp. 210–11.

40. Walter Warlimont, *Inside Hitler's Headquarters, 1934–45*, p. 39.

41. Görlitz, "Battle for Stalingrad," p. 226; Manstein, *Verlorene Siege*, p. 323; Col. Gen. Kurt Zeitzler, "Stalingrad," in Freidin and Richardson, eds., *The Fatal Decision*, pp. 189–190; Halder, as quoted in Kershaw, *Hitler*, p. 2:529.

42. On Churchill's tendency in this direction, see Bryant, *Turn of the Tide*, pp. 539–0.

43. For a concise description of the manpower problems facing the German army in the summer of 1942, see Seaton, *German Army*, pp. 189–90.

44. Like many others, we assumed that the Wehrmacht played a greater role in the "Final Solution" and related enterprises that many folk somehow concerned with preserving this organization's integrity were willing to acknowledge. However, the full extent of the "regular army's" involvement revealed in recent publications absolutely astounded us. See, e.g., Omer Bartov, *Hitler's Army: Soldiers, Nazis, and War in the Third Reich*; and Hamburg Institute for Social Research, ed., *The German Army and Genocide: Crimes Against War Prisoners, Jews, and Other Civilians in the East, 1939–1944*. See also Kershaw, *Hitler*, pp. 2:464–69, and Anthony Beevor, *Stalingrad: The Fateful Siege, 1942–1943*, pp. 55–61.

45. As quoted in Görlitz, *Paulus and Stalingrad*, p. 165.

46. Kehrig, *Stalingrad*, p. 48.

47. On the state of Romanian armament, see ibid., pp. 65–66, and Clark, *Barbarossa*, p. 241.

48. Görlitz, "Battle for Stalingrad," p. 235.

49. According to Kehrig's account, Warlimont recorded that it was Halder who had called Stalin's 1920 tactics to Hitler's attention (*Stalingrad*, p. 90). Warlimont, as quoted in Liddell Hart, said that Hitler "came to know somehow"' about Wrangel's defeat. See Liddell Hart, *Other Side of the Hill*, p. 315. On the same issue, see Craig, *Enemy at the Gates*, p. 25, and Geoffrey Jukes, *Hitler's Stalingrad Decisions*, p. 53. This possibility remained an obsession of Hitler's for some time.

50. Jukes, *Hitler's Stalingrad Decisions*, p. 55.

51. Görlitz, "Battle for Stalingrad," p. 230. See also Kleist's remarks in Liddell Hart, *Other Side of the Hill*, p. 56.

52. Jukes, *Hitler's Stalingrad Decisions*, p. 56.

53. Kehrig, *Stalingrad*, pp. 29, 44.

54. Görlitz, "Battle for Stalingrad," p. 230.

55. Joachim Wieder, *Stalingrad und die Verantwortung des Soldaten*, p. 180.

56. Görlitz, *Paulus and Stalingrad*, p. 33. As Görlitz points out, Paulus canceled the order.

57. Craig, *Enemy at the Gates*, pp. 69–70. Clark has described the bitter resistance Paulus encountered during his advance to the north of Stalingrad, one that nevertheless had sufficed to bring the vital Soviet railroad bridge of Rynok within heavy mortar range. Clark has not placed as much emphasis upon Hoth's breakthrough at Abganerova, and perhaps in the overall scheme of things, it might not have been as important as Craig (and most certainly Hoth) thought. Nevertheless, what is notable in this case is Paulus's unwillingness to respond in a decisive manner to what appeared to have been an opportunity. See Clark, *Barbarossa*, pp. 216–18, and Beevor, *Stalingrad*, pp. 114–15.

58. During the May 1942 Russian attacks in the Kharkov area described earlier, Paulus, apparently nervous about their weight and ferocity, had recommended an immediate counterattack. Bock had supported him in this. Both were overruled by Halder and the OKH in general, who allowed the Soviets to commit virtually all of their forces, and then smashed their exposed flanks. Several commentators have attributed Paulus's later lack of decisiveness to this correct overruling by a field commander from above. See Görlitz, *Paulus and Stalingrad*, pp. 65–68, as well as his discussion in "Battle for Stalingrad," p. 222.

59. See Kleist's comments in Liddell Hart, *Other Side of the Hill*, p. 301.

60. Clark, *Barbarossa*, pp. 218–19; Görlitz, "Battle for Stalingrad," pp. 232–33.

61. John G. Stoessinger, *Why Nations Go to War*, p. 51.

62. As quoted in Clark, *Barbarossa*, p. 183.

63. Jukes, *Hitler's Stalingrad Decisions*, p. 66.

64. Ibid., p. 234; Seaton, *German Army*, pp. 192–93; Zeitzler, "Stalingrad," pp. 193–94. See also Warlimont's remarks in Liddell Clark, *Other Side of the Hill*, p. 314.

65. Zeitzler, "Stalingrad," pp. 133–34.

66. Warlimont, *Inside Hitler's Headquarters*, pp. 261–66.

67. Görlitz, "Battle for Stalingrad," p. 234.

68. Beevor, *Stalingrad*, p. 140.

69. Janis, *Victims of Groupthink*, pp. 33, 41.

70. Clark, *Barbarossa*, p. 237; Seaton, *German Army*, p. 193.

71. Zeitzler, "Stalingrad," p. 135; Clark, *Barbarossa*, p. 234; Kerr, *Secret of Stalingrad*, pp. 190–91.

72. Walter Lord, *A Night to Remember*, p. 15.

73. Craig, *Enemy at the Gates*, pp. 119–20, 135.

74. Görlitz, "Battle for Stalingrad," p. 78.

75. Kehrig, *Stalingrad*, p. 114.

76. Görlitz, *Paulus and Stalingrad*, p. 170.

77. Görlitz, "Battle for Stalingrad," p. 232. Probably Göring was picking up a hint from Hitler who told Goebbels (a well-known rival of the *Luftwaffe* chief) that German troops in Russia would be better off in winter there than most of them would have been in peacetime; Kershaw, *Hitler*, p. 2:537.

78. As quoted in Craig, *Enemy at the Gates*, p. 139. See also Zeitzler, "Stalingrad," p. 145, and Görlitz, *Paulus and Stalingrad*, p. 78. Earlier, when disavowing intentions to

take either Moscow or Leningrad by storm, Hitler had declared that he did not want "another Verdun."

79. Görlitz, "Battle for Stalingrad," p. 232. Cf. Beevor, *Stalingrad*, p. 214, "The political demagogue had manacled the warlord."

80. Görlitz, *Paulus and Stalingrad*, p. 79.

81. Clark, *Barbarossa*, p. 240. Clark makes no mention of Hitler's speech of November 8.

82. For a good summary of von Falkenhayn's initial plans, see Alistaire Horne, *The Price of Glory: Verdun, 1916*, p. 36. For a more recent account that in the end does nothing to invalidate Horne's conclusions, see Holger Afflerbach, *Falkenhayn: Politisches Denken und Handeln im Kaiserreich*, sec. 5, chapters 17 and 18.

83. Görlitz, *Paulus and Stalingrad*, p. 190.

84. Craig, *Enemy at the Gates*, p. 252 n.

85. Kehrig, *Stalingrad*, pp. 136, 150.

86. Zeitzler, "Stalingrad," pp. 147–49, 150.

87. Kehrig, *Stalingrad*, p. 151.

88. Zeitzler, "Stalingrad," p. 153 (Hitler quotation); Ronald Lewin, *Hitler's Mistakes: New Insights into What Made Hitler Tick*, p. 134; Görlitz, *Paulus and Stalingrad*, p. 209.

89. Kehrig, *Stalingrad*, p. 160.

90. Görlitz, *Paulus and Stalingrad*, p. 124. This exchange was recorded in Richthofen's journal. Richthofen himself did not know at the time that the vital bridge had been captured.

91. Kehrig, *Stalingrad*, pp. 162–63. Much of this lack of decisiveness was due to Paulus's realization, as he put it, that he was "not von Reichenau" (Görlitz, "Battle for Stalingrad," p. 227).

92. Zeitzler, "Stalingrad," p. 159.

93. For Hitler's conviction that Schmidt would betray the war effort after the surrender, see Clark, *Barbarossa*, p. 290.

94. Ibid., p. 177.

95. Görlitz, *Paulus and Stalingrad*, p. 225. Emphasis in original. Some of this conversation, without Schmidt's concluding remark, is in Craig, *Enemy at the Gates*, p. 180.

96. Craig, *Enemy at the Gates*, p. 175.

97. See Paulus's message of 6 P.M. Sunday, November 22, 1942, in Kerr, *Secret of Stalingrad*, pp. 231–32.

98. Seaton, *German Army*, p. 195.

99. Zeitzler, "Stalingrad," p. 162. On the early successes of the Tiger in Russia, see Clark, *Barbarossa*, p. 304.

100. Zeitzler, "Stalingrad," pp. 162, 163. Emphasis in original.

101. Kehrig, *Stalingrad*, p. 219. Another technical issue is important here: Besides the trimotored Junkers 52, only the Heinkel 111, an obsolete twin-engine bomber capable of carrying a very light payload, was available in large numbers for such an operation.

102. Seaton, *German Army*, p. 195.

103. As quoted in Görlitz, *Paulus and Stalingrad*, p. 230.

104. Kehrig, *Stalingrad*, p. 194. For another description of this, see Craig, *Enemy at the Gates*, p. 184. At the time of Paulus's surrender, Hitler *still* thought that Lascar had "fought to the death." See Warlimont, *Inside Hitler's Headquarters*, p. 304.

105. For descriptions of this action, see Kehrig, *Stalingrad*, pp. 206–211; Craig, *Enemy at the Gates*, pp. 187–88; Görlitz, *Paulus and Stalingrad*, p. 203; idem, "Battle for Stalingrad," p. 30ff.

106. For details of this appointment, see Craig, *Enemy at the Gates,* pp. 190–91; Kehrig, *Stalingrad,* p. 211.

107. For judgments of Seydlitz-Kurzbach's action, see Craig, *Enemy at the Gates,* 190–91; Görlitz, *Paulus and Stalingrad,* p. 241; and Wieder, *Stalingrad,* pp. 183, 185, 215–48, 291, 295. Seydlitz-Kurzbach's later role in the pro-Soviet League of German Officers, formed after Sixth Army's surrender, served in the eyes of many to compromise his position to no small degree.

108. Liddell Hart, *Other Side of the Hill,* p. 315.

109. Jukes, *Hitler's Stalingrad Decisions,* pp. 217–20. For Hitler's inability, or unwillingness, to make decisions, see also Kershaw, *Hitler,* p. 2:545. Keegan has stated that shifting his headquarters from Vinnitsa in the Ukraine, to the Berghof in Bavaria between November 11 and November 23, when matters really started to unravel, was symbolic of a kind of "psychological withdrawal" (*Mask of Command,* p. 289). Keegan also offers a good summary of some important data presented by Jukes (ibid., pp. 293–94).

110. For a description of it, see Craig, *Enemy at the Gates,* p. 196.

111. Manstein, *Verlorene Siege,* p. 331. For support of Manstein's contention, see Seaton, *German Army,* p. 196.

112. On their shared belief in Hitler's "fortune" ("*Gluck*"), see Wieder, *Stalingrad,* p. 192.

113. Manstein, *Verlorene Siege,* p. 327.

114. Kehrig, *Stalingrad,* p. 183.

115. Manstein, *Verlorene Siege,* pp. 332, 333–34, 337, 346–57.

116. Ibid., p. 345.

117. Ibid., pp. 331, 344.

118. Kehrig, *Stalingrad,* p. 226.

119. As quoted in Craig, *Enemy at the Gates,* p. 193.

120. Manstein, *Verlorene Siege,* p. 350.

121. Ibid., p. 351.

122. Figures on Soviet strength are from Görlitz, "Battle for Stalingrad," p. 246.

123. Wieder, *Stalingrad,* p. 155.

124. Manstein, *Verlorene Siege,* p. 369.

125. On armored strength, see Görlitz, "Battle for Stalingrad," p. 246, and Kehrig, *Stalingrad,* p. 451; on infantry strength, see Kehrig, *Stalingrad,* p. 451.

126. Kehrig, *Stalingrad,* p. 451.

127. Manstein, *Verlorene Siege,* pp. 369–71.

128. Wieder, *Stalingrad,* pp. 145–48.

129. Clark, *Barbarossa,* p. 271.

130. For a very unsympathetic treatment of Paulus, see Clark, *Barbarossa,* p. 272.

131. Kehrig, *Stalingrad,* p. 429; Clark, *Barbarossa,* p. 273.

132. Zeitzler, "Stalingrad," p. 172.

133. Clark, *Barbarossa.*

134. Manstein, *Verlorene Siege,* pp. 370–72.

135. Kehrig, *Stalingrad,* pp. 396–97.

136. As quoted in Görlitz, "Battle for Stalingrad," p. 248. See also Craig, *Enemy at the Gates,* p. 254; Kehrig, *Stalingrad,* p. 428.

137. As quoted in Görlitz, "Battle for Stalingrad," p. 248; Kehrig, *Stalingrad,* p. 428.

138. Görlitz, *Paulus and Stalingrad,* pp. 88–89.

139. Manstein, *Verlorene Siege,* p. 368; Kehrig, *Stalingrad,* pp. 168–69.

140. Kehrig, *Stalingrad,* p. 531.

141. Görlitz, "Battle for Stalingrad," pp. 258, 282 (Manstein quote).

142. Hitler's rage against Paulus for surrendering instead of killing himself was expressed to Zeitzler in a rather well-known diatribe. See Clark, *Barbarossa*, p. 290, and Keegan, *Mask of Command*, pp. 298–99.

143. Joachim C. Fest, *Hitler*, p. 511ff.

Conclusion

1. Such was the concern of Dixon's *On the Psychology of Military Incompetence*, to which we have referred at various points.

2. Weigley, *Age of Battles*, p. xi.

3. Ibid., p. 543.

4. Martin van Creveld, *The Transformation of War*, chapter 7, epilogue.

5. Archibald MacLeish, "The End of the World," p. 288. Copyright © by the Estate of Archibald MacLeish. Reprinted by permission of Houghton Mifflin Company. All rights reserved.

BIBLIOGRAPHY

Primary Sources

Alexander, Edward Porter. *Military Memoirs of a Confederate: A Critical Narrative.* New York: C. Scribner's Sons, 1907.

Bernhardi, Friedrich von. *How Germany Makes War.* Trans. Hugh Reese. New York: G. H. Doran, 1914.

Bonaparte, Napoleon. *Correspondance de Napoleon.* I Tome, 24. Paris: n.p., 1867.

——. *Memoirs of Napoleon Bonaparte, the Court of the First Empire.* Vol. 3. Ed. Baron C. F. de Méneval, his private secretary. New York: P. F. Collier, 1910.

Boraston, Lt. Col. John H., ed. *Sir Douglas Haig's Despatches, December 1915–April 1919.* London: J. N. Dent and sons, 1920.

Brett-Jones, Anthony. *1812: Eyewitness Accounts of Napoleon's Defeat in Russia.* New York: Macmillan, 1966.

Bryant, Arthur. *The Turn of the Tide: A History of the War Years Based on the Diaries of Field Marshal Lord Alanbrooke, Chief of the Imperial General Staff.* Garden City, N.Y.: Doubleday, 1957.

Caulaincourt, General Armand de. *With Napoleon in Russia: The Memoirs of General de Caulaincourt, Duke of Vicenza.* Ed. Jean Hanoteau, trans. Hamish Miles. London: Cassell, 1935–38.

Churchill, Sir Winston S. *The Second World War.* Vol. 3, *The Grand Alliance.* Boston: Houghton Mifflin, 1950.

——. *The Second World War.* Vol. 4, *The Hinge of Fate.* Boston: Houghton Mifflin, 1950.

——. *The Second World War.* Vol. 5, *Closing the Ring.* Boston: Houghton Mifflin, 1951.

Clausewitz, Carl von. *The Campaign of 1812 in Russia.* No translator named. 1843. Reprint, Hattiesburg, Miss.: Academic International, 1970.

——. *On War.* Ed. Anatol Rapoport. London: Penguin, 1978.

Dowdey, Clifford. *Lee.* Gettysburg, Pa.: Stan Clark Military Books, 1996.

——, and Louis H. Manarin, eds. *The Wartime Papers of Robert E. Lee.* New York: Da Capo Press, 1961.

Frederick the Great. *Frederick the Great on the Art of War.* Edited and translated by Jay
    Luvaas. New York: Free Press, 1966.
Galland, Adolf. *The First and the Last: The Rise and Fall of the German Fighter Forces.*
    Trans. Mervyn Savill. New York: Ballantine Books, 1957.
Gibbon, John. *Personal Recollections of the Civil War.* New York: G. P. Putnam's Sons,
    1928.
Gough, Sir Hubert. *The Fifth Army.* London: Hodder and Stoughton, 1931.
——— . *Soldiering On: Being the Memoirs of General Sir Hubert Gough.* New York: R.
    Speller, 1957.
Haig, Sir Douglas. *The Private Papers of Douglas Haig, 1914–1919.* Ed. Lord Robert
    Blake. London: Eyre and Spottiswoode, 1952.
Harris, Arthur. *Bomber Offensive.* London: Collins, 1947.
Hill, D. H. "McClellan's Change of Base and Malvern Hill." In *Battles and Leaders of
    the Civil War: Being for the Most Part Contributions by Union and Confederate
    Officers,* ed. Robert Underwood Johnson and Clarence Clough Buel. Vol. 2.
    New York: T. Yoseloff, 1956.
Hood, John Bell. *Advance and Retreat: Personal Experiences in the United and Confed-
    erate States Armies.* Bloomington: Indiana University Press, 1959.
Johnston, Joseph E. *Narrative of Military Operations Directed during the Late War be-
    tween the States.* Bloomington: Indiana University Press, 1959.
Klee, Ernst, Willi Dressen, and Voker Riess, eds. *"The Good Old Days": The Holocaust
    As Seen by Its Perpetrators and Bystanders.* Foreword by Hugh Trevor-Roper.
    Translated by Deborah Burnstone. New York: Free Press, 1991.
Lee, Capt. Robert E. *Recollections and Letters of General Robert E. Lee.* New York:
    Doubleday, Page, 1924.
Lloyd George, David. *War Memoirs of David Lloyd George.* Vol. 4: 1917. Boston: Little,
    Brown, 1939.
Longstreet, James. *From Manassas to Appomattox.* 1896. Reprint, Bloomington: Indi-
    ana University Press, 1960.
——— . "The Seven Days, Including Frayser's Farm." In *Battles and Leaders of the Civil
    War: Being for the Most Part Contributions by Union and Confederate Officers,*
    ed. Robert Underwood Johnson and Clarence Clough Buel. Vol. 2. New York:
    T. Yoseloff, 1956.
Manstein, Erich von. *Verlorene Siege.* Bonn: Athenäum Verlag, 1958.
McClellan, George B. *McClellan's Own Story: The War for the Union, The Soldiers
    Who Fought It, the Civilians Who Directed It and His Relations to It and to
    Them.* New York: C. L. Webster, 1887.
Porter, Fitz-John. "The Battle of Malvern Hill." In *Battles and Leaders of the Civil War:
    Being for the Most Part Contributions by Union and Confederate Officers,* ed.
    Robert Underwood Johnson and Clarence Clough Buel. Vol. 2. New York: T.
    Yoseloff, 1956.
Schofield, John M. *Forty-six Years in the Army.* 1897. Reprint, Harrisburg, Pa.: Archive
    Society, 1997.
Ségur, Count Philippe-Paul de. *Napoleon's Russian Campaign.* Trans. J. David
    Townsend, with a New Introduction by Peter Gay. New York: Time, 1965.
Snyder, Jack. "Civil-Military Relations and the Cult of the Offensive, 1914 and 1984."
    International Security 9 (1984): pp. 108–46.
Snyder, Louis L., ed. *Frederick the Great.* Englewood Cliffs, N.J.: Prentice-Hall, 1971.
Speer, Albert. *Inside the Third Reich Memoirs.* Trans. Richard and Clara Winston. New
    York: Macmillan, 1970.

Stone, Col. Henry. "Repelling Hood's Invasion of Tennessee." In *Battles and Leaders of the Civil War: Being for the Most Part Contributions by Union and Confederate Officers*, ed. Robert Underwood Johnson and Clarence Clough Buel. Vol. 4. New York: T. Yoseloff, 1956.

Volz, Gustav Berthold, ed. *Ausgewählte Werke Friedrich des Grosses, zweiter Band, Politische und Philosophisches Schriften, Gedichte und Briefe*. Berlin: n.p., 1918.

Warlimont, Walter. *Inside Hitler's Headquarters, 1934–45*. Trans. R. H. Barry. New York: F. A. Praeger, 1964.

The War of the Rebellion: A Compilation of the Official Records of the Union and Confederate Armies. 128 vols. Washington, D.C.: Government Printing Office, 1880–1901.

Watkins, Sam R. *"Co. Aytch," Maury Grays, First Tennessee Regiment; or, A Side Show of the Big Show*. Jackson, Tenn.: McCowat-Mercer Press, 1952.

Wilson, James H. *Under the Old Flag: Recollections of Military Operations in the War for the Union, the Spanish War, the Boxer Rebellion, etc*. New York: D. Appleton, 1912.

Zeitzler, Col. Gen. Kurt. "Stalingrad." In *The Fatal Decisions*, ed. Seymour Freidin and William Richardson, trans. Constantine Fitzgibbon. New York: W. Sloan Associates, 1956.

Secondary Sources

Afflerbach, Holger. *Falkenhayn: Politisches Denken und Handeln im Kaiserreich*. München: Oldenbourg, 1994.

Allen, Vernon. "Uncertainty of Outcome and Post-Decision Difference Reduction." In Leon Festinger et al., *Conflict Decision, and Dissonance*. Stanford, Calif.: Stanford University Press, 1964.

Anderson, Craig A., and Jrad J. Bushman. "Aggression." *American Review of Psychology* 53 (2002): pp. 27–51.

Anderson, John R. *Cognitive Psychology and Its Implications*. San Francisco: W. H. Freeman, 1980.

Asprey, Robert B. *Frederick the Great: The Magnificent Enigma*. New York: Ticknor and Fields, 1986.

Atkinson, John W. "The Mainsprings of Achievement-Oriented Activity." In *Motivation and Achievement*, ed. John W. Atkinson and Joel O. Raynor. Washington, D.C.: Winston, 1974.

Averill, James. "Studies on Anger and Aggression: Implications for Theories of Emotion." *American Psychologist* 38 (1983): pp. 1145–60.

Bartov, Omer. *Hitler's Army: Soldiers, Nazis, and War in the Third Reich*. New York: Oxford University Press, 1992.

Battig, William F. "Parsimony or Psychology?" Presidential address to the Rocky Mountain Psychological Association, Denver, Colorado, April 19, 1978.

Beevor, Anthony. *Stalingrad: The Fateful Siege, 1942–1943*. New York: Penguin, 1998.

Berkowitz, Leonard. *Aggression: A Social Psychological Analysis*. New York: McGraw-Hill, 1962.

——— . "Aversely Stimulated Aggression: Some Parallels and Differences in Research with Animals and Humans." *American Psychologist* 38 (1983): pp. 1135–44.

Bidwell, Shelford. *Modern Warfare: A Study of Men, Weapons, and Theory*. London: Allen Lane, 1973.

——— , and Dominick Graham. *Fire Power: British Army Weapons and Theories of War, 1904–1945*. London: Allen and Unwin, 1982.

Binion, Rudolph. *Hitler among the Germans*. New York: Elsevier, 1976.

Blond, Georges. *La Grande Armée, 1809–1815*. Paris: R. Laffont, 1979.

Bond, Brian. *War and Society in Europe, 1870–1970*. New York: Oxford University Press, 1986.

Brehm, Jack Williams, and Arthur Robert Cohen. *Explorations in Cognitive Dissonance*. New York: Wiley, 1962.

Bromberg, Norbert, and Verna Volz Small. *Hitler's Psychopathology*. New York: International Universities Press, 1983.

Calvocoressi, Peter, and Guy Wint. *Total War: Causes and Courses of the Second World War*. New York: Penguin Books, 1979.

Canon, Lance Kirkpatrick. "Self-confidence and Selective Exposure to Information." In Leon Festinger et al., *Conflict Decision, and Dissonance*. Stanford, Calif.: Stanford University Press, 1964.

Cartwright, D. "Decision-Time in Relation to the Differentiation of the Phenomenal Field." *Psychological Review* 48 (1941): 425–42.

Cassar, George H. *The Tragedy of Sir John French*. London: Associated University Presses, 1985.

Cate, Curtis. *The War of the Two Emperors: The Duel between Napoleon and Alexander — Russia, 1812*. New York: Random House, 1985.

Catton, Bruce. *Never Call Retreat*. Garden City, N.Y.: Doubleday, 1965.

———. *Terrible Swift Sword*. Garden City, N.Y.: Doubleday, 1963.

———. *This Hallowed Ground: The Story of the Union Side of the Civil War*. Garden City, N.Y.: Doubleday, 1956.

Clark, Alan. *Barbarossa: The German-Russian Conflict, 1941–45*. New York: William Morrow, 1965.

———. *The Donkeys*. London: Hutchinson, 1961.

Coddington, Edwin B. *The Gettysburg Campaign: A Study in Command*. New York: Scribner's, 1968.

Connelly, Thomas Lawrence. *Autumn of Glory: The Army of Tennessee, 1862–1865*. Baton Rouge: Louisiana State University Press, 1971.

Connelly, Owen. *Blundering to Glory: Napoleon's Military Campaigns*. Wilmington, Del.: Scholarly Resources, 1987.

Cox, Jacob. *The March to the Sea: From Franklin to Nashville*. Campaigns of the Civil War, vol. 10. New York: C. Scribner's Sons, 1882.

Craig, William. *Enemy at the Gates: The Battle for Stalingrad*. New York: Bantam Books, 1982.

Dangerfield, George. *The Strange Death of Liberal England*. New York: Capricorn Books, 1935.

De Charms, Richard. *Personal Causation: The Internal Affective Determinants of Behavior*. New York: Academic Press, 1968.

———, and George H. Moeller. "Values Expressed in American Children's Readers." *Journal of Abnormal and Social Psychology* 62 (1964): pp. 136–42.

Delbrück, Hans. *Geschichte des Kriegskunst, im Rahmen der politische Geschichte, vierten Teil*. Berlin: De Gruyter, 1962.

Delderfield, R. F. *The Retreat from Moscow*. 1st American ed. New York: Atheneum, 1967.

De Seversky, Alexander P. *Victory Through Air Power*. New York: Simon and Schuster, 1942.

Deutsch, Morton. "Field Theory in Social Psychology." In *Handbook of Social Psychology*, vol. 1, ed. Gardner Lindzey. Cambridge, Mass.: Addison Wesley, 1954.

Dixon, Norman. *On the Psychology of Military Incompetence*. New York: Basic Books, 1976.

Dollard, John, Leonard W. Doob, Neal E. Miller, O. H. Mowrer, and Robert Sears. *Frustration and Aggression.* New Haven, Conn.: Yale University Press, 1939.

Downey, Fairfax. *The Guns of Gettysburg.* New York: D. McKay, 1958.

Duffy, Christopher. *The Military Life of Frederick the Great.* New York: Atheneum, 1986.

Earle, Edward Mead. *Makers of Modern Strategy.* Princeton, N.J.: Princeton University Press, 1971.

Erikson, Erik H. "Identity and the Life Cycle." *Psychological Issues* 1, Monograph 1 (1959).

Fair, Charles. *From the Jaws of Victory: A Study of Military Stupidity from Crassus to Westmoreland.* New York: Simon and Schuster, 1971.

Falk, Stanley L. *Seventy Days to Singapore: The Malayan Campaign, 1941–1942.* New York: Putnam, 1975.

Fay, Sidney B., and Klaus Epstein. *The Rise of Brandenburg-Prussia to 1786.* New York: Holt, Rinehart, and Winston, 1964.

Ferguson, Niall. *The Pity of War: Exposing World War I.* New York: Basic Books, 1999.

Fest, Joachim C. *Hitler.* Trans. Richard and Clara Winston. New York: Harcourt Brace Jovanovich, 1974.

Festinger, Leon. *A Theory of Cognitive Dissonance.* Evanston, Ill.: Row, Peterson, 1957.

——— , et al. *Conflict, Decision, and Dissonance.* Stanford, Calif.: Stanford University Press, 1964.

——— , Henry W. Riecken, and Stanley Schachter. *When Prophecy Fails: A Social and Psychological Study of a Modern Group That Predicted the Destruction of the World.* New York: Harper and Row, 1964.

Fitzgerald, F. Scott. *Tender Is the Night.* New York: Scribner, 1934.

Foote, Shelby. *The Civil War: A Narrative.* 3 vols. New York: Random House, 1974.

Frankland, Noble. "Bombing: The RAF Case." In *Warplanes and Battles of World War II,* ed. Bernard Fitzsimons. New York: Beekman House, 1973.

Freeman, Douglas Southall. *Lee's Lieutenants: A Study in Command.* 3 vols. New York: C. Scribner's Sons, 1943–44.

——— *Robert E. Lee: A Biography.* New York: C. Scribner's Sons, 1935.

Freidin, Seymour, and William Richardson, eds. *The Fatal Decisions.* Trans. Constantine Fitzgibbon. New York: W. Sloan Associates, 1956.

French, David. "Allies, Rivals, and Enemies: British Strategy and War Aims During the First World War." In *Britain and the First World War,* ed. John Turner. London: Unwin Hyman, 1988.

French, Elizabeth G., and Francis H. Thomas. "The Relationship of Scientific Motivation and Problem-Solving Effectiveness." *Journal of Abnormal and Social Psychology* 56 (1958): pp. 45–49.

Freud, Anna. *The Ego and Mechanisms of Defense.* New York: International Universities Press, 1966.

Fussell, Paul. *The Great War and Modern Memory.* New York: Oxford University Press, 1975.

Geertz, Clifford. *The Interpretation of Cultures: Selected Essays.* New York: Basic Books, 1973.

Görlitz, Walter. *Paulus and Stalingrad: A Life of Field-Marshal Friedrich Paulus, with Notes, Correspondence, and Documents from His Papers.* With a Preface by Ernst Alexander Paulus. Trans. Col. R. H. Stevens. Westport, Conn.: Greenwood Press, 1974.

——— . "The Battle for Stalingrad: 1942–43." In *Decisive Battles of World War II: The German View,* ed. Hans Adolf Jacobsen and Jürgen Rohwehr, trans. Edmund Fitzgerald. New York: Putnam, 1965.

Greenstein, Fred I. *Personality and Politics: Problems of Evidence, Inference, and Con-ceptualization.* New York: Norton, 1975.

Griffith, Paddy. *Battle Tactics of the Western Front: The British Army's Art of Attack, 1916–18.* New Haven, Conn.: Yale University Press, 1994.

Hamburg Institute for Social Research, ed. *The German Army and Genocide: Crimes against War Prisoners, Jews, and Other Civilians in the East, 1939–1944.* Trans. Scott Abbot, with editorial oversight by Paula Bradish and the Hamburg Institute for Social Research. New York: New Press, 1999.

Hassler, William W., Jr. *George B. McClellan: Shield of the Union.* Baton Rouge: Louisiana State University Press, 1957.

Hattaway, Herman, and Archer Jones. *How the North Won: A Military History of the Civil War.* Urbana: University of Illinois Press, 1983.

Hay, Thomas Robson. *Hood's Tennessee Campaign.* New York: W. Neale, 1929.

Hofmann, Rudolf. "The Battle of Moscow." In *Decisive Battles of World War II: The German View,* ed. Hans Adolf Jacobsen and Jürgen Rohwer. Trans. Edmund Fitzgerald. New York: Putnam, 1965,

Holmes, Richard. *Acts of War: The Behavior of Men in Battle.* New York: Free Press, 1985.

Horn, Stanley F. *The Army of Tennessee: A Military History.* Indianapolis: Bobbs-Merrill, 1941.

——— . "The Spring Hill Legend." *Civil War Times Illustrated,* April 1969, pp. 20–32.

Horne, Alistaire. *The Price of Glory: Verdun, 1916.* New York: Penguin, 1978.

Hough, Richard. *Death of the Battleship: The Tragic Close of the Era of Sea Power.* New York: Macfadden-Bartell, 1963.

Jacobsen, Hans Adolf, and Jürgen Rohwer, eds. *Decisive Battles of World War II: The German View.* Trans. Edmund Fitzgerald. New York: Putnam, 1965.

Janis, Irving L. *Victims of Groupthink: A Psychological Study of Foreign-Policy Decisions and Fiascoes.* Boston: Houghton, Mifflin, 1972.

——— , and Leon Mann. *Decision Making: A Psychological Analysis of Conflict, Choice, and Commitment.* New York: Free Press, 1977.

Jetzinger, Franz. *Hitler's Youth.* London: Hutchinson, 1958.

Johnson, Robert Underwood, and Clarence Clough Buel, eds. *Battles and Leaders of the Civil War: Being for the Most Part Contributions by Union and Confederate Officers.* 4 vols. New introduction by Roy F. Nichols. New York: T. Yoseloff, 1956.

Jukes, Geoffrey. *Hitler's Stalingrad Decisions.* Berkeley: University of California Press, 1985.

Karten, Arno. *Napoleon's Glands: And Other Ventures in Biohistory.* Boston: Little, Brown, 1984.

Keegan, John. *The Face of Battle.* New York: Viking Press, 1976.

——— . *The Mask of Command.* New York: Viking, 1987.

Kerr, Walter. *The Secret of Stalingrad.* Chicago: Playboy Press, 1978.

Kehrig, Manfred. *Stalingrad: Analyse und Dokumentation einer Schlacht.* Stuttgart: Deutsche Verlags-Anstalt, 1974.

Kershaw, Ian. *Hitler.* Vol. 1, *1889–1936: Hubris.* New York: W. W. Norton, 1998.

——— . *Hitler.* Vol. 2, *1936–1945: Nemesis.* New York: W. W. Norton, 2000.

Koch, H. W. *A History of Prussia.* New York: Longman, 1978.

La Chouque, L. Henry. *Napoléon: 20 ans de Campagnes.* Paris: Arthaud, 1964.

Langer, Philip. "Malvern Hill (July 1, 1862): A Behavioral Analysis." Paper presented at the annual meeting of the Rocky Mountain Psychological Association, Denver, Colo., May 1981.

Leeper, Robert W. *Lewin's Topological and Vector Psychology: A Digest and a Critique.* Oregon University Monograph Studies in Psychology, no. 1. Eugene: University of Oregon, 1943.

Levine, Alan J. *The Strategic Bombing of Germany, 1940–1945.* New York: Praeger, 1992.

Lewin, Kurt. *A Dynamic Theory of Personality: Selected Papers.* New York: McGraw-Hill, 1935.

———. *Principles of Topological Psychology.* New York: McGraw-Hill, 1936.

Lewin, Ronald. *Hitler's Mistakes: New Insights into What Made Hitler Tick.* New York: William Morrow, 1984.

Liddell Hart, Basil Henry. *The Other Side of the Hill: Germany's Generals, Their Rise and Fall, with Their Own Account of Military Events, 1939–1945.* 2nd rev. ed. London: Cassell, 1973.

———. *The Real War, 1914–1918.* Boston: Little, Brown, 1930.

Lindqvist, Sven. *A History of Bombing.* Trans. Linda Haverty Rugg. New York: New Press, 2001.

Livermore, Thomas L. *Numbers & Losses in the Civil War in America, 1861–65.* Bloomington: Indiana University Press, 1957.

Lord, Walter. *A Night to Remember.* New York: Holt, Rinehart, and Winston, 1955.

MacDonald, Lyn. *Somme.* London: M. Joseph, 1983.

MacDonogh, Giles. *Frederick the Great: A Life in Deed and Letters.* New York: St. Martin's Press, 2000.

MacLeish, Archibald. "The End of the World." In *A Little Treasury of Modern Poetry: English and American,* ed. Oscar Williams. New York: Scribner, 1946.

Markham, Felix. *Napoleon.* New York: New American Library, 1963.

Marshall, S. L. A. *The American Heritage History of World War I.* New York: American Heritage, 1964.

Marshall-Cornwall, Sir James. *Haig as Military Commander.* New York: Crane, Russak, 1973.

May, Rollo. *Power and Innocence: A Search for the Sources of Violence.* New York: Norton, 1972.

McDonough, James L. *Schofield: Union General in the Civil War and Reconstruction.* Tallahassee: Florida State University Press, 1972.

———, and Thomas Lawrence Connelly. *Five Tragic Hours: The Battle of Franklin.* Knoxville: University of Tennessee Press, 1983.

McFeely, William S. *Grant: A Biography.* New York: Norton, 1981.

McMurry, Richard M. *Atlanta 1864: Last Chance for the Confederacy.* Lincoln: University of Nebraska Press, 2000.

———. *John Bell Hood and the War for Southern Independence.* Lexington: University Press of Kentucky, 1982.

McPherson, James M. *Battle Cry of Freedom: The Civil War Era.* New York: Oxford University Press, 1988.

———. *Crossroads of Freedom: Antietam.* New York: Oxford University Press, 2002.

McWhiney, Grady, and Perry D. Jamieson. *Attack and Die: Civil War Tactics and the Southern Heritage.* Tuscaloosa: University of Alabama Press, 1982.

Millenson, John, and Julian C. Leslie. *Principles of Behavioral Analysis.* 2nd ed. New York: Routledge, 1979.

Moyer, Kenneth E. *The Psychobiology of Aggression.* New York: Harper and Row, 1976.

Murfin, James V. *The Gleam of Bayonets: The Battle of Antietam and the Maryland Campaign of 1862.* Baton Rouge: Louisiana State University Press, 1965.

Murray, Henry Alexander. *Explorations in Personality: A Clinical and Experimental Study of Fifty Men of College Age*. New York: Oxford University Press, 1938.

Myers, William S. *A Study in Personality: General George Brinton McClellan*. New York: D. Appleton-Century, 1934.

Naisawald, L. Van Loan. *Grape and Canister: The Story of the Field Artillery of the Army of the Potomac, 1861–1865*. New York: Oxford University Press, 1960.

Nolan, Alan T. *Lee Considered: General Robert E. Lee and Civil War History*. Chapel Hill: University of North Carolina Press, 1991.

O'Connor, Richard. *Hood, Cavalier General*. New York: Prentice-Hall, 1949.

Overy, Richard. *Why the Allies Won*. New York: W. W. Norton, 1995.

Palmer, Alan. *Napoleon in Russia*. New York: Simon and Schuster, 1967.

Palmer, Michael A. *Lee Moves North: Robert E. Lee on the Offensive*. New York: John Wiley, 1998.

Paret, Peter, comp. *Frederick the Great: A Profile*. New York: Hill and Wang, 1972.

Paris, Comte de. *The Battle of Gettysburg: From the History of the Civil War in America*. New, rev. ed. Philadelphia: J. C. Winston, 1907.

Prange, Gordon W., Donald M. Goldstein, and Katherine V. Dillon. *Miracle at Midway*. New York: McGraw-Hill, 1982.

Prior, Robin, and Trevor Wilson. *Passchendaele: The Untold Story*. New York: Oxford University Press, 1996.

Raack, Richard C. "When Plans Fail: Small Group Behavior and Decision-making in the Conspiracy of 1808 in Germany." *Journal of Conflict Resolution* 14 (1970): pp. 3–20.

Reddaway, William Fiddian. *Frederick the Great and the Rise of Prussia*. London: G. P. Putnam's Sons, 1904.

Redlich, Fritz. *Hitler: Diagnosis of a Destructive Prophet*. New York: Oxford University Press, 1998.

Reiners, Ludwig. *Frederick the Great: A Biography*. Translated and adapted from the German by Lawrence F. P. Wilson. New York: Putnam, 1960.

Ritter, Gerhard. *Frederick the Great: A Historical Profile*. Translated and introduced by Peter Paret. Berkeley and Los Angeles: University of California Press, 1974.

Rokeach, Milton. *The Open and Closed Mind: Investigations into the Nature of Belief Systems and Personality Systems*. New York: Basic Books, 1960.

Rosenzweig, Saul. "Types of Reaction to Frustration: An Heuristic Classification." *Journal of Abnormal and Social Psychology* 29 (1934): pp. 298–300.

Rowland, Thomas. *George B. McClellan and Civil War History: In the Shadow of Grant and Sherman*. Kent, Ohio: Kent State University Press, 1998.

Schramm, Percy. *Hitler: The Man and the Military Leader*. With an Introduction and trans. Donald S. Ditwiler. Chicago: Quadrangle Books, 1971.

Sears, Stephen W. *George B. McClellan: The Young Napoleon*. New York: Ticknor and Fields, 1988.

Seaton, Albert. *The German Army, 1933–45*. New York: St. Martin's Press, 1982.

Seligman, Martin E. P. *Helplessness: On Depression, Development, and Death*. San Francisco: Freeman, 1975.

Seward, Desmond. *Napoleon and Hitler: A Comparative Biography*. New York: Viking, 1989.

Simon, Edith. *The Making of Frederick the Great*. Boston: Little, Brown, 1963.

Sixsmith, Eric Keir Gilbourne. *Douglas Haig*. London: Weidenfeld and Nicolson, 1976.

———— . *British Generalship in the Twentieth Century*. London: Arms and Armour, 1970.

Skinner, Burrhus Frederic. *Science and Human Behavior*. New York: Macmillan, 1953.

Smith, Dale O. *U.S. Military Doctrine: A Study and Appraisal*. New York: Duell, Sloan and Pearce, 1955.

Stewart, George R. *Pickett's Charge: A Microhistory of the Final Attack at Gettysburg, July 3, 1863*. Boston: Houghton Mifflin, 1959.

Stierlin, Helm. *Adolf Hitler: A Family Perspective*. New York: Psychohistory Press, 1976.

Strachan, Hew, ed. *World War I: A History*. New York: Oxford University Press, 1998.

Stoessinger, John G. *Why Nations Go to War*. 5th ed. New York: St. Martin's Press, 1990.

Taylor, Telford. *The March of Conquest: The German Victories in Western Europe, 1940*. New York: Simon and Schuster, 1958.

Terraine, John. *Douglas Haig: The Educated Soldier*. London: Hutchinson, 1963.

———— . *Ordeal of Victory*. Philadelphia: Lippincott, 1963.

———— . *To Win a War: 1918, the Year of Victory*. Garden City, N.Y.: Doubleday, 1978.

Thorndike, Edward L. *Animal Intelligence: Experimental Studies*. New York: Macmillan, 1911.

———— . *The Psychology of Learning*. Vol. 2, *Educational Psychology*. New York: Teachers College, Columbia University, 1913.

Travers, Tim. *How the War Was Won: Command and Technology in the British Army on the Western Front, 1917–1918*. New York: Routledge, 1992.

———— . *The Killing Ground: The British Army, the Western Front, and the Emergence of Modern Warfare, 1900–1918*. Boston: Allen and Unwin, 1987.

———— . "The Allied Victories, 1918." In *World War I: A History*, ed. Hew Strachen. New York: Oxford University Press, 1998.

Trudeau, Noah Andre. *Gettysburg: A Testing of Courage*. New York: Harper Collins, 2002.

Tucker, Glenn. *Lee and Longstreet at Gettysburg*. Indianapolis: Bobbs-Merrill, 1968.

Turner, John, ed. *Britain and the First World War*. Boston: Unwin Hyman, 1988.

———— . "British Politics and the Great War." In *Britain and the First World War*, ed. John Turner. Boston: Unwin Hymin, 1988.

Van Creveld, Martin. *The Transformation of War*. New York: Free Press, 1991.

Van Horne, Thomas B. *The Life of Major-General George H. Thomas*. New York: C. Scribner's Sons, 1882.

Verrier, Anthony. *The Bomber Offensive*. New York: Macmillan, 1968.

Wade, Wyn Craig. *The Titanic: End of a Dream*. New York: Penguin, 1980.

Waite, Robert G. L. *The Psychopathic God: Adolf Hitler*. New York: Basic Books, 1977.

Warner, Philip. *Passchendaele: The Tragic Victory of 1917*. New York: Atheneum, 1988.

Watt, Richard M. *Dare Call It Treason*. New York: Simon and Schuster, 1963.

Webster, Charles, and Noble Frankland. *The Strategic Air Offensive against Germany*. 4 vols. London: HMSO, 1961.

Weigley, Russell F. *The Age of Battles: The Quest for Decisive Warfare from Breitenfeld to Waterloo*. Bloomington and Indianapolis: Indiana University Press, 1991.

Wert, Jeffry D. *Gettysburg: Day Three*. New York: Simon and Schuster, 2001.

Wieder, Joachim. *Stalingrad und die Verantwortung des Soldaten*. Munich: Nymphenburger Verlagshandlung, 1962.

Williams, Oscar, ed. *A Little Treasury of Modern Poetry, English and American*. New York: C. Scribner's Sons, 1946.

Williams, T. Harry. *McClellan, Sherman, and Grant*. New Brunswick, N.J.: Rutgers University Press, 1962.

Winter, Denis. *Haig's Command: A Reassessment.* London and New York: Viking, 1991.

Wilt, Alan F. *War from the Top: German and British Decision Making during World War II.* Bloomington: Indiana University Press, 1990.

Wolff, Leon. *In Flanders Fields: The 1917 Campaign.* New York: Viking, 1958.

Woodward, David R. *Lloyd George and the Generals.* Newark: University of Delaware Press, 1983.

Woodward, Sir Llewellyn. *Great Britain and the War of 1914–1918.* New York: Beacon Press, 1967.

INDEX

Achievement, need for, 53–54
Advance and Retreat (Hood), 108
Aggression and human behavior, 106–110, 176–178, 211–212, 225–226
Alexander, Edward Porter, 69, 86–87, 90–91, 93, 246n77
Alexander I, Tsar, 28
Anderson, Richard, 83, 89
Anger and human behavior, 106–110
Anglo-Saxon culture, 149–155
Antietam, Battle of, 53, 54, 55, 71, 78, 85, 240n74
Antonescu, Ion, 186
Apraksin, Fedor Matveeich, 10
Armistead, Lewis, 70
Artillery: British, 147–148; Civil War, 92–96, 246n94; German, 205
Asquith, Herbert H., 150
Atkinson, John, 53
Atlanta, Ga., 103–104
Augustus the Strong, 12

Bagration, Peter Ivanovitch, 37
Baker-Carr, C. D., 143
Bate, William B., 113
Battle strategies: Adolf Hitler's, 178–188, 192–211, 193; Douglas Haig's, 124–126, 131–135; Frederick the Great's, 6, 10–11, 15–16, 17–18, 232n19; George McClellan's, 50–51, 57–68, 237–238n13, 241nn110,120, 241–242n121; John Bell Hood's, 104–106, 110–116; Napoleon's, 27–31, 34–35, 48; Robert E. Lee's, 92–96, 246n94; Winston Churchill's, 158–168, 171, 185
Beatty, John, 55

Beauregard, Pierre, 102
Belliard, Augustin Daniel, 38
Bennigsen, Theophil von, 29, 36
Berkowitz, Leonard, 108, 176
Bernhardi, Friedrich von, 9
Berthier, Louis Alexandre, 38
Bessières, Jean-Baptiste, 38
Blond, Georges, 39
Blumentritt, Günter von, 180
Blundering to Glory (Connelly), 27
Bock, Fedor von, 183, 188, 262n58
Boer War, 123, 127, 150
Borodino, Battle of, 37, 40, 43, 220
British military: artillery of, 147–148; bombing of Germany during World War II, 160–168; casualties during World War I, 140–141, 252n38, 253n62; and the decision to begin bombing Germany, 156–158, 224–225, 256n10; delusions of the, 130–131; early success in World War I, 123–124; Flanders offensive, 135–142; at Neuve-Chapelle, 124–127; resistance to change by, 145–146, 149–155, 222–224; sea power of, 158–160; Somme campaign by, 129–135, 138, 217, 252n39, 258n53; use of Dominion soldiers by, 153–155
Bromberg, Norbert, 259nn4–5
Brown, John, 113–114, 116, 119
Brusilov, Aleksey, 132
Buford, John, 82
Burnside, Ambrose, 60, 74, 75, 236n61

Carlyle, Thomas, 9
Catt, H. A., 10, 20
Caulaincourt, Armand de, 30, 33, 37–38, 40–41, 47

ABOUT THE AUTHORS

Robert Pois (1940–2004) was Professor of History at the University of Colorado–Boulder. Among his books are *The Great War; National Socialism and the Religion of Nature;* and *Friedrich Meinecke and German Politics in the Twentieth Century.*

Philip Langer is Professor of Educational Psychology and Faculty Fellow at the University of Colorado–Boulder Institute of Cognitive Science. Although his previously published research was focused on issues relevant to psychology and education, a lifelong interest in military history has culminated in this book.